YOU MUST KNOW YOUR CONSTITUTION

By the Same Author

India's Legal System: Can It Be Saved? (2006)

Before Memory Fades: An Autobiography (2010)

The State of the Nation (2013)

God Save the Hon'ble Supreme Court (2018)

Harmony amidst Disharmony: The Indian Framework
(The Arbitration Series—Volume 1) (2020)

Harmony amidst Disharmony: The International Framework
(The Arbitration Series—Volume 2) (2020)

Beyond the Courtroom (2025)

Legally Speaking (2025)

YOU MUST KNOW YOUR CONSTITUTION

FALI S. NARIMAN

HAY HOUSE

HAY HOUSE INDIA
New Delhi • London • Sydney
Carlsbad, California • New York City

Hay House Publishers (India) Pvt Ltd
Muskaan Complex, Plot No. 3, B-2, Vasant Kunj, New Delhi – 110070, India

Hay House LLC, P.O. Box 5100, Carlsbad, CA 92018-5100, USA
Hay House UK Ltd, 1st Floor, Crawford Corner, 91-93 Baker Street, London W1U 6QQ, UK
Hay House Australia Publishing Pty Ltd, 18/36 Ralph St., Alexandria NSW 2015, Australia

Email: contact@hayhouse.co.in
Website: www.hayhouse.co.in

First published by Hay House India, 2023
Reprint, 2026
15 14 13 12 11 10 9 8 7 6

ISBN 978-81-959917-2-3
ISBN 978-81-959917-3-0 (ebook)

Printed at Replika Press Pvt Ltd

FSC www.fsc.org
MIX
Paper | Supporting responsible forestry
FSC™ C016779

To
The little Indian
in whom rests
the future of the nation

The "Little Indian" has been reproduced (with permission) from Dr. Dharmendra Bhandari's book *R.K. Laxman – The Uncommon Man*

NOTE FOR THE READER

In this book, decisions of the Supreme Court of India (SC) are mentioned with citations either from SCALE—a weekly almanac (Law Report), and/or from the Regular Law Reports—AIR (All India Reporter) and SCC (Supreme Court Cases).

Abbreviations:

C.A.D: Constituent Assembly Debates

(Vol.) U.S. (page): This is how decisions of the Supreme Court of the United States of America are reported.

EWHC: England and Wales High Court

Wikipedia: a website that allows any user to change the information it contains.

Queen's Bench and King's Bench: When England's monarch was female/male, the reported cases of the High Court of Justice before October 2009 used to be cited as (Vol.) Q.B. (page) or (Vol.) K.B. (page).

A.C.: Appeal Cases—This is how decisions of the Judicial Committee of the House of Lords were cited before the establishment (in October 2009) of the Supreme Court of the United Kingdom (whose decisions are now reported as UKSC: United Kingdom Supreme Court).

***Rajpramukh*:** Title of the head of a State in India: it existed only from 1947 until 1956 (now obsolete).

***Sadar-i-Risayat*:** Title that had been given to the executive head of Jammu & Kashmir State under the Constitution: after the Constitution was enacted (now obsolete).

Contents

Introduction

Why You Must Know Your Constitution

'Like old clocks, our judicial institutions need to be oiled, wound up, and set to true time.'
—Lord Harry Woolf[1]

John Milton's *Paradise Lost* is one of the great epic poems in English literature, and it is also one of the longest. Dr Samuel Johnson[2] had written that none wished it *longer than it is.* The same is often said about India's written Constitution. As enacted in 1950, it contained 395 Articles (with a glorious chapter on fundamental rights) together with an Appendix of Eight Schedules, occupying in the Official Edition 251 printed pages (As now amended, it has been recently described as "a 146,385 – word tome"!).

By October 1947, Constitutional Advisor, B. N. Rau, had prepared the first draft of INDIA's Constitution, and during two-and-a-half years of intense debate and discussion in the Constituent Assembly, the Constitution of India was ultimately finalised on 26 November 1949. But leading Commonwealth historian of the time was not impressed! Delivering a lecture on India's Constitution at the University of Madras, in 1951, Sir Ivor Jennings[3] described it as: '*Too long, too rigid, too prolix*', and said that the dominance in the Constituent Assembly of lawyer-politicians had contributed to its complexity! In fact, he characterised India's Constitution as *'a truly oriental display of occidental constitutional devices.'* Harsh words!

But harsh words, like chickens, sometimes come home to roost. Long ago, when I mentioned this to my friend, Desmond Fernando (then president of the International Bar Association), he told me that the same Ivor Jennings had been entrusted with the task of drafting the Constitution of Ceylon[4] (now, Sri Lanka); and he took great care to see that it endured, *but it lasted only fourteen years:* which only goes to show that a finely-worded document is no guarantee of its success. It is only a spirit of constitutionalism (amongst the representatives of the people) that helps to keep it alive and functioning.

Besides, written constitutions do not function on their own; they have to be worked. It is under this 'lawyer's Constitution' (as Jennings had sneeringly characterised it) that—since 1952—periodic elections have been held under its provisions once every five years, on the basis of adult franchise. And whenever governments have been voted out of office, whether at the centre or in the states, the transfer of power has been in accordance with its provisions: *even if occasionally, not in conformity with its true spirit.*

I recall James Callaghan's tribute when Mrs Gandhi was defeated at the polls in March 1977. The former British prime minister had said that the ultimate mark of a true democracy was the willingness of a government defeated at the ballot box to surrender power peacefully to its opponents. This is what happened when the Janata Party swept the polls in March 1977, after the end of the oppressive Internal Emergency of June 1975. And this is what happened again when those who held power since then were, in turn, defeated at the general elections of 1980, when the same Mrs Gandhi was swept back to power.

Truly then, this Constitution of ours—activated by the earthquake of partition—was not just a compulsion of geography; it was also a compelling accident of history. In 1947, the British hurriedly left us somewhat in pique, leaving Indians to fend for themselves as best as they could. And only recently, we got to know the reason why.

On a visit to Calcutta (now Kolkata) in 1956, the former Labour Prime Minister, Clement Attlee, had told the Chief Justice of Calcutta—then acting as governor of West Bengal—that it was the mutiny in Bombay (in February 1946) by a section of the Royal Navy that led to Britain's hastly departure. 'It made us realise,' Attlee said, 'that Indian armed forces could no longer be trusted to protect the British in India[5]'

Whatever may have been the true reason for the hurried exit of the British in 1947, members of India's Constituent Assembly took it in their stride; charged with the task of preserving the political and cultural unity of India, they proceeded to put together a written constitution for the people of India—a constitution that has now lasted more than seventy odd years.

However, no one has any idea of how long a written Constitution *would* last (or for that matter, *should* last). Thomas Jefferson—American statesman, Founding Father, and third president of the United States (from 1801 to 1809)—thought that 19 years was about right! Around the world, many written constitutions have lasted, on an average, only 17 years before being scrapped.[6] But not the US Constitution: with less than 8000 words, it has—so far—lasted (with only 27 amendments) for more than 200 years! India's Constitution has endured for over seven decades, with more than a hundred amendments (the last being in 2021).

The life of a written Constitution—like the life of the law—is not logic (or draftsmanship), but experience. Seventy-odd years of experience on this subcontinent has shown that it is easier to *frame* a Constitution than to *work* it. In the same subcontinent, Pakistan and Bangladesh had crafted written constitutions at different times, but they were interspersed with periods of martial law, and civil and military dictatorships. We will never be able to piece together a new Constitution in the present day and age simply because innovative ideas however brilliant and howsoever encouragingly expressed in consultation papers and reports of commissions, can never give us an *ideal* Constitution. In constitution-making, there are hidden forces that must not be ignored, viz., *the spirit of persuasion, of accommodation, and of tolerance.* In India—as in the rest of the world—all three are at a very low ebb today[7]. According to the World Bank, Chile is one of the fastest growing economies in South America. In October 2020, 78 per cent of all Chileans approved of a proposal to have a new constitution for the country, but when it was put together and presented in a referendum in the year 2022, it was unhesitatingly rejected by the people! Commenting on this in the *New York Times* in September 2022, Benjamin Appelbaum (on the Editorial Board of *Time* magazine) observed:

> Writing a new Constitution strikes many Americans as a transgressive idea. The US Court is the oldest in the world and it has come to seem immutable. The last really substantive change was a 1971 amendment lowering the voting age to 18. *Instead of updating a text written more than 200 years ago, Americans have come to rely on the imagination of its Nine Justices who decide what they think it should say.*

The Constitution of India (1950) opens with the words: 'WE THE PEOPLE OF INDIA . . . DO HEREBY ADOPT, ENACT AND GIVE TO OURSELVES THIS CONSTITUTION. If this means the people of India who were born before 1950 (as were the Constitution's Founding Fathers), then it must surely be out of tune with the vast majority of the people of India, who have been born since then. But there is some magic in the words 'WE THE PEOPLE'. The same three words were also the opening words of the world's oldest Constitution—that of the United States of America. And the answer to the conundrum as to what relevance a written Constitution has for the overwhelming majority of its people—who were not born before its promulgation and therefore, not included in the phrase 'We the People'—was offered by Congresswoman Barbara Jordan. On July 24, 1974 (referring to the US Constitution) she said:

> '*We the people*' a very eloquent beginning. But, when that document was completed on 17 September 1787, I was not included in that 'We the People'. I felt somehow for many years that George Washington and Alexander Hamilton just left me out by mistake.
>
> *But I realise that it is through the process of interpretation and Court decision that I have been finally included in 'We the People'.*

Well put. In a nutshell it describes the role of India's Supreme Court. By interpretation in court decisions it has broadened the reach of the provisions of our Constitution. It has included within the range of its beneficent provisions those who were not born when India got independence. Judges—past and present—have interpreted and helped sustain a Constitution that had been framed for only 350 million people, most of whom are not even alive today. This is one of the ways in which a written Constitution is made to grow into a dynamic living document.

But why have a written constitution? Perhaps the answer is: because it fosters respect for 'The Law': a sentiment captured in a heart-warming passage in the play—*A Man for All Seasons*—which is about the life of Sir Thomas More (1478-1535)[8], scholar and saint, who was also Lord Chancellor of England in the reign of King Henry VIII (1509-1547)[9], a monarch known for his radical changes to England's unwritten constitution. In the play (written by Robert Bolt), one of the King's spies, Richard Rich, approaches Thomas More to extract an admission from him that he regards his church even higher than his own sovereign (only in order to carry the treasonable tale back to the king), at which, More's son-in-law, Roper, asks him to arrest Rich forthwith, since he is the very devil, adding: 'As Lord Chancellor, you have the power to do so.' But Thomas More demurs, *only because the man has not broken any law*. And then there follows a fascinating piece of prose:

> Roper: So now you'd give the Devil the benefit of law!
>
> More: Yes. What would you do? Cut a great road through the law to get after the Devil?
>
> Roper: I'd cut down every law in England to do that!
>
> More: (roused and excited): Oh? (advances on Roper) And when the last law was down and the Devil turned round on you—where would you hide, Roper, the laws all being flat? This country is planted thick with laws from coast to coast . . . do you really think you could stand upright in the winds that would blow them?
>
> (quietly) *Yes, I'd give the devil the benefit of law, for my own safety's sake.*
>
> Roper: (weakly responds): I have long suspected this—*the law's your God.*

But in the end—ideally—how should a written Constitution be framed?

Justice Louis Brandeis, who served on the Supreme Court of the United States from 1916 right through until his retirement in 1939, believed that an ideal Constitution was one that expressed the will of the people, to be ascertained *by living with the people.* He illustrated this with a story about Montenegro (one of the smaller countries in the continent of Europe). After it had secured its independence, in the 19th century, its ruling prince wanted his country to have a code of laws like other civilised nations. So, the prince requested the Czar of Russia to lend him the services of a scholarly professor of law at the University of Odessa to prepare a Code for Montenegro. The professor was duly authorised and undertook the task, but instead of relying on law books or his own knowledge of the law, he went to Montenegro, lived with its people for two years, studying their customs and practises (to familiarise himself with their 'roots'), and only then did he draft a Constitution from all that he had learned from the people; and (as Brandeis always used to say) *'they respected it because it expressed the will of the people'.*[10]

Incidentally, this is how Gandhiji wanted India's constitution to be written. And in 1946, before the first meeting of India's Constituent Assembly, economist Shriman Narayan had already written a book which he proudly called: *The Gandhian Constitution for Free India.* It introduced for the first time the complete draft of an *indigenous 'Indian Constitution'* with decentralised legislative, executive, and judicial bodies based on village panchayats. It also laid down a set of fundamental duties to go along with fundamental rights. Gandhiji endorsed Shriman Narayan's proposal by contributing a foreword to the book.

But, I am afraid, this was *not* the way India's Constitution was written—neither the Brandeis way, nor the Gandhian way. *You will simply have to read the book to know how India's document of governance had been framed, and how it has evolved.*

15 August, 2023 — **Fali S. Nariman**

Notes and References: *fn**

1. Quote from an inaugural speech by England's 'Master of the Rolls' (President of England's Court of Appeal) at the 12th Commonwealth Law Conference (12-15 September 1999) in Kuala Lumpur, Malaysia. Lord Woolf was Lord Justice of England & Wales from June 2000 till October 2005, and thereafter Lord Chief Justice.

---

*fn** You will find notes and references at the end of each Chapter. Why footnotes? Footnotes are necessary—they help assure the reader that the passages in the text are not fake-news!

Judges in America often embellish their judgments with foot-notes. And the most famous footnote in American constitutional law is FOOTNOTE 4: the footnote in Justice Harlan Stone's judgment in *U.S. v. Carolene Products Co: 304 US 144 (1938):* it raises the question whether courts may use a higher degree of scrutiny to review legislation when prejudice against "discrete and insular minorities" may hamper the democratic safeguards that would ordinarily protect those minorities.

2. In the 'Life of Milton', Dr Samuel Johnson recalled that *Paradise Lost* 'is one of the books which the reader admires and lays down and forgets to take up again': '... *none ever wished it longer than it is.*'

3. Sir Ivor Jennings (1903-1965), British lawyer and academic who served as Vice-Chancellor of the University of Ceylon (1942-1955) and Vice-Chancellor of the University of Cambridge (1961-1963). Jennings was an authority on constitutional law, and author of a definitive book on the workings of the unwritten British Constitution. He had advised in the drafting of the Constitution of Ceylon to form the Dominion of Ceylon.

4. Playwright George Bernard Shaw (1856-1950) visited Ceylon in 1948 – and he was ecstatic about its people. This is what he wrote to Jawaharlal Nehru: "I was convinced that Ceylon is the cradle of the human race because everybody there looks an original. All other nations are obviously mass produced."! (Typically Shavian)

5. Mentioned by former Chief Justice P.V. Chuckraborty in a letter dated 30 March 1976: Quoted by Dhananjay Bhat in an article entitled 'RIN Mutiny Gave a Jolt to the British', *The Tribune*, Chandigarh, Sunday, 12 February 2006 (Spectrum Supplement).

6. In their 2009 book *The Endurance of National Constitutions*, American scholars Zachary Elkins, Tom Ginsburg and James Melton show that on an average, Constitutions have lasted only 17 years since 1789! And among the 12 Asian countries that gained independence after World War II and had drafted Constitutions, only three Constitutions have survived – India's, Taiwan's and South Korea's!

7. In the Opinion Page of the *Hindustan Times*, July 22, 2023, Gopalkrishna Gandhi has written: "*Concord is under strain in our life in India. Manipur is the most searing example. I can imagine the flag, downcast, wanting to lower itself to half-mast in Manipur in agony and shame and grief. But then, listening to what our Chief Justice DY Chandrachud has said about constitutional democracy and wanting to see remedial action taken swiftly, I can see the flag fluttering in new self-confidence.*"

8. Sir Thomas More (7 February 1478-6 July 1535) is venerated in the Catholic Church as Saint Thomas. A lawyer, judge, social philosopher, author, statesman, and noted Renaissance humanist, he served Henry VIII as Lord High Chancellor of England from October 1529 to May 1532. More opposed the Protestant Reformation and also Henry VIII's separation from the Catholic Church, refusing to

acknowledge Henry as supreme head of the Church of England and the annulment of his marriage to Catherine of Aragon. After refusing to take the Oath of Supremacy, he was convicted of treason and executed. On his execution, he was reported to have said: 'I die the King's good servant, and God's first.'

9. Henry VIII is known for his radical changes to the English Constitution, ushering in the theory of the divine right of kings in opposition to papal supremacy. He also greatly expanded royal power during his reign. He achieved many of his political aims through the work of his chief ministers (Lord Chancellors), some of whom were banished or executed when they fell out of his favour; amongst them were Thomas Wolsey, Thomas More, Thomas Cromwell, Richard Rich, and Thomas Cranmer.

10. See Melvin I. Urofsky: *Louis D. Brandeis: A Life,* pages 432-433.

Chapter One[1]

From Undivided British India, through Partition, to the Dominion of India, and finally, to the Republic of India[2]

I. India's diversity begins with its geography

The Indian subcontinent—that now includes the independent nations of Pakistan (since 1947) and Bangladesh (since 1971)—was once a self-contained geographical entity bounded by high mountains in the north, and great seas to the west, south, and east. The ancient Persians called it Hindu-stan—the prefix (Hindu) being a reference to the Sindhu or the Indus river, indicating persons who lived on-its-other-side.

Within the subcontinent, in a vast triangle narrowing down from the everlasting snows in the north to the perennial sultry heat of Cape Comorin (Kanyakumari) in the south, there are (as there always have been) separate geographical regions:

- In the far north, north-east and north-west, are the mountain ranges of the Himalayas[3]—where stand the world's highest peaks—revered as holy by most of the inhabitants of Hindustan.[4]
- Immediately below the Himalayas, a vast alluvial plain stretches in an unbroken surface for some 1690 miles (2720 kilometres) across northern India and was formed by the three great rivers of the north: the Indus, the Ganges (or the Ganga), and the Brahmaputra. Scorching

hot in summer and bitterly cold in winter, the Indo-Gangetic plain is one of the more densely populated regions in the world.

- In the far west, lie the desolate salty marshlands of the Great Rann of Kutch[5]—home to the world's dwindling population of the *onager* (the Asian wild ass), and the breeding ground for that gregarious bird, the flamingo.
- Nearer, but still in the west, are 38610 square miles (a hundred thousand square kilometres) of dune-covered deserts of (what is now) Rajasthan.
- On the far side, in the east, at the mouth of the Ganges, are the Sunderbans—the world's largest single block of tidal mangrove forest and home to the Bengal tiger.
- A range of hills in central India (the Central Highlands) separates the southern two-thirds of the subcontinent, whose main geographical feature is a massive tableland (the Deccan Plateau) that protrudes down into the Indian Ocean. Hugging its western side (along the Arabian Sea) are located some of the world's most ancient mountain ranges known as the Western Ghats, whilst running parallel to the Bay of Bengal, along the eastern coast are the Eastern Ghats.
- The Deccan Plateau occupies a major portion of the southern part of the country. It consists of a gigantic triangular block, a hundred metres high in the north and almost a kilometre tall in the south, containing much of India's mineral wealth.

["There is a sharpening North South divide in terms of culture, "the politics of language", economic development and social transformation," according to Prof. Kalaiyarasan, and Prof. Christophe Jaffrelot (Professor of Indian Politics and Sociology at King's India Institute, London) "economic inequality has deepened between the North and the South: the South has been a pioneer in promoting a culture of reading by instituting public libraries; three-fourths of over 27,000 public libraries in India are located in the Southern States; economic inequality has deepened between the North and the South partly because investors are attracted to places with good infrastructure and well-trained manpower. ....The exercise to delimit parliamentary constituencies could deepen the north-south divide. The south has controlled population growth by following central government policies. The continued emphasis on women's education in the south has contributed to a fall in the total fertility rates in the region much before several other states in the country and now is in the zone of less than replacement rate. As a result, the population of these states is growing far more slowly compared to states in the north...."]

Up until the 19th century, the Indian subcontinent could be approached and was accessible either only by sea-fearing vessels, or by land through narrow passes in the north-west—a cul-de-sac to successive migratory waves of invaders, who intermingled with indigenous inhabitants to such an extent that radically distinct categories of people became hard to identify. Language and religion, rather than ethnic origin, became the primary distinguishing features of the people of Hindustan.

In this great land mass of nearly 17 lakh square miles (approximately 44 lakh square kilometres) of undivided India, there dwelt—in the mid-20th century—over 294 million (over 29 crores) inhabitants[6], distributed throughout the provinces of British India, which was then more than one-fifth of humanity. The figure did not include persons living in *the native states* (then called the 'princely states')[7]. They were scattered in bits and pieces throughout an aggregate area of about two-fifths of the Indian subcontinent, their rulers or chieftains having entered into treaties or arrangements with the British[8].

With the passage of the Government of India Act, 1858 by Britain's Parliament, each of the princely states came under the direct protection and suzerainty of the British Crown, enjoying internal autonomy, but with the British Government exercising exclusive control of their external affairs.

The geographical location of the princely states did not correspond to any ethnic, religious, or linguistic pattern, but the people residing in the provinces in British India and the people living in the princely states had close ties of cultural affinity as well as of blood and sentiment; each group having suffered alike—over time—from successive waves of foreign invaders, and of foreign domination.

What distinguished the princely states from the provinces in pre-partition India was that they were not annexed as a part of British India. None of them had any independent international status, because the Government of India's Official Gazette Notification of August 1891 had pontifically declared, that '*the principles of international law have no bearing upon the relations between the Government of India as representing the Queen-Empress on the one hand, and the Native states on the other. The paramount supremacy of the former presupposes and implies the subordination of the latter.*' Pledging loyalty to the British Crown, the chieftain or ruler of each Indian state was its monarch and all local laws emanated from his edicts, and, in turn, the British Government granted the chieftain or ruler safety from external attack and internal revolt.[9]

II. The people of India were (and still are) as diverse and disparate as India's geography

After his retirement as a member of the Governor-General's Council, John Strachey (1823–1907), an English civil servant, placed on record his experiences in the subcontinent in a book titled, *India* (first published in 1888). To Strachey, the thought that the men and women of the Punjab, of Bengal, of North-West Provinces, and of Madras should ever feel that they belonged to *one nation* was '*impossible*'. 'You might with as much reason and probability,' he wrote, 'look forward to a time when a single nation will have taken the place of the various nations of Europe.'[10] But John Strachey was English; he did not *belong* to India and was not enthused with the *idea of India*. On the other hand, India's future first prime minister, Jawaharlal Nehru, was obsessed with it.

In 1944, in the confines of a prison (during his ninth term of imprisonment for revolting against the British), Jawaharlal Nehru wrote about the diversity of India and in his 700-page book, *The Discovery of India*, he also wrote the following:

> (*Quote*) The diversity of India is tremendous. It lies on the surface, and anybody can see it. It concerns itself with physical appearances as well as with certain mental habits and traits. There is little in common, to outward seeming, between the Pathan of the Northwest and the Tamil in the far South. Their racial stocks are not the same, though there may be common strands running through them; they differ in face and figure, food and clothing, and, of course, language . . . The Pathan and Tamil are two extreme examples; the other lie somewhere in between. All of them have still more the distinguishing mark of India. It is fascinating to find how the Bengalis, the Marathas, the Gujaratis, the Tamils, the Andhras, the Oriyas, the Assamese, the Canarese, the Malayalis, the Sindhis, the Punjabis, the Pathans, the Kashmiris, the Rajputs, and the great central block comprising the Hindustani-speaking people, have retained their peculiar characteristics for hundreds of years, have still more or less the same virtues and failings of which old tradition or record tells us, and yet have been throughout these ages *distinctively Indian*, with the same national heritage and the same set of moral and mental qualities . . .
>
> There was something living and dynamic about this heritage which showed itself in ways of living and a philosophical attitude to life and its problems. Ancient India, like ancient China, was a world in itself, a culture and a civilisation which gave shape to all things. Foreign

> influences poured in and often influenced that culture and were absorbed. Disruptive tendencies gave rise immediately to an attempt to find a synthesis. *Some kind of a dream of unity has occupied the mind of India since the dawn of civilisation.* That unity was not conceived as something imposed from outside, a standardisation of externals or even of beliefs. It was something deeper and, within its fold, the widest tolerance of beliefs and customs was practiced and every variety acknowledged and even encouraged . . .
>
> In ancient and medieval times, the idea of the modern nation was non-existent, and feudal, religious, racial, and cultural bonds had more importance. Yet I think that at almost any time in recorded history, an Indian would have felt more or less at home in any part of India, and would have felt as a stranger and alien in any other country. He would certainly have felt less of a stranger in countries, which had partly adopted his culture or religion. Those, such as Christians, Jews, Parsees, or Moslems, who professed a religion of non-Indian origin on coming to India, settled down there, became distinctively Indian in the course of a few generations. Indian converts to some of these religions never ceased to be Indians on account of a change of their faith. They were looked upon in other countries as Indians and foreigners, even though there might have been a community of faith between them. (*Unquote*)

In the lengthy but spirited dissertation (quoted above), Panditji was referring to undivided British India—at that time home to more than 14 major languages (and 33 main dialects)[11] wholly unrelated to one another. The Indian National Congress, of which Panditji was the most frequently-elected president, looked upon the entire subcontinent as a single country, its inhabitants as one people. Its rival political party, the Muslim League, anxious for territorial adjustments to be made on the basis of areas predominantly inhabited by Muslims, hoped to persuade the British to carve out a separate state for them. In fact, in March 1940, the Muslim League had passed a resolution in Lahore (then part of undivided British India) demanding that 'the areas in which the Muslims are numerically in a majority . . . should be grouped to constitute independent states in which the constituent units shall be autonomous and sovereign.'[12]

III. The idea of a parliamentary form of government (like that of Britain's) inspired Indian nationalists, but not Gandhiji: he was impressed by something different (*read footnote 13*)[13]

It was the founding of the Indian National Congress in 1885 as an all-India political party that became a turning point in the formalisation of opposition to—and of dealing with—the British Raj.

The first non-official attempt at drafting a Constitution with a parliamentary system of government for India was in 1895, under the inspiration of Lokmanya Bal Gangadhar Tilak. In a brief preface to what he characterised as a 'Home Rule Bill', Tilak set out the outlines of a Constitution which he wished India to get from the British Government. It was to be called *'Constitution of India Act'*, and it provided for a Parliament of India, i.e., 'an assembly of representatives, official as well as non-official, of *the Indian nation*' wherein 'every citizen may express his thoughts by words or writings and publish them in print without liability or censure except being answerable for abuses that may be committed in the exercise of this right, and wherein no-one shall be sentenced except by a competent authority', and 'wherein the law shall be equal to all'. It also provided for every citizen to have one vote for electing members of Parliament and one vote for electing members of the local legislative council[14]. However, all this (at the time) remained in the realm of wishful expectation.

After Parliament in England had passed the Government of India Act 1858—completing at one legislative stroke the transfer of British power over India from the East India Company to the British Crown—the governance of British India had been conducted by a bureaucracy, entirely non-Indian in composition. Indians had no real part or share in the direction of the government of the country, though they had been repeatedly clamouring for it.[15]

However, after a million Indian soldiers in the British Army fought alongside the British in the First World War (1914-1918)—a large number sacrificing their lives—the British attitude changed, as evidenced by the declaration of policy announced (in Britain's Parliament) by the then Secretary of State for India, Mr Edwin Montagu:

> *(Quote)* The policy of His Majesty's Government with which the Government of India are in complete accord, is that of the increasing association of India in every branch of the administration and the gradual development of self-governing institutions with a view to the progressive realisation of responsible Government in India as an integral part of the British Empire.[16] *(Unquote)*

After the end of the First World War in 1918, this declaration of policy was incorporated in the Preamble, to the British Parliament's Government of India Act (1919), which Dr B. R. Ambedkar had described as '*the Constitution of British India*'[17]. The 1919 Act also incorporated in statute-form—the reforms proposed in the Montagu-Chelmsford Report (Cmnd. 9109)[18], reproducing some of the provisions of an earlier piece of British legislation, viz., the Government of India Act, 1915 (as amended in 1916).

In a treatise—published in 1922—Sir Courtenay Ilbert (Law Member of the Council of the Governor-General) described the Government of India Act 1919 as '*the most adventurous experiment which has yet been tried in India*', and added:

> *(Quote) The ideal aimed at by the British Government in India had previously been a benevolent despotism administered by an intelligent bureaucracy*. That ideal has now to be reconciled with the desire (of the people of India) for self-government with which all Englishmen are bound by their instincts and tradition to sympathise and which no Englishman can afford to condemn.[19] (*Unquote*)

In the mid-1920s, when Britain had a Labour Party Government, India's political leaders—under the inspiration of Sir Tej Bahadur Sapru (a prominent lawyer, economist, and statesman)—sent on to London a comprehensive draft bill for self-government—'A bill to constitute within the British Empire a Commonwealth of India'. The Commonwealth of India Bill, 1925 got introduced in Britain's Parliament, and it provided that 'there shall be a Parliament which shall consist of the Viceroy as the King's representative, a Senate, and a Legislative Assembly'. It also included a clause conferring on citizens fundamental rights: of personal liberty, of security, of property, of freedom of expression, of conscience, of equality before the law, of equality between sexes, and of free elementary education. The bill also stated that every literate citizen—literate in the language of the taluka—over 21 years of age and owning some property or having some income, was to have a vote. After the bill passed its first reading in the House of Commons, it was ordered to be printed, in anticipation of it being enacted into law. But soon after, the Labour Party lost its majority in the House of Commons, and Indian aspirations suffered a setback for several years.

IV. Subsequent events—including the passing by Britain's Parliament of the Indian Independence Act, 1947

In accordance with the recommendations made in the Montagu-Chelmsford Report, the then Conservative Party Government in Britain (in 1928) appointed a commission, headed by Sir John Simon, to report on *'India's progress towards constitutional reforms'*. The Simon Commission—also known as the Indian Statutory Commission—consisted of seven members of Britain's Parliament, then characterised in India as 'all-male, all-white' (since no Indian had been included) and it reflected the attitude of the then Conservative Party Government in the UK, which was not to associate Indians with decision-making in matters relating to political and constitutional progress.[20] In its report, the Simon Commission omitted to endorse the general demand in India for the setting-out of fundamental rights in a Constitution Act. In the early 1930s, there followed three Round Table Conferences in London attended by representatives of all major interests. Dr B. R. Ambedkar, then a representative of what were known as the 'Depressed Classes', also attended. The proposals made at the Round Table Conferences were outlined by the British Government in a White Paper—Proposals for Constitutional Reforms (Cmnd. Paper 4268). Whilst not envisaging 'self-government', the Command Paper mentioned one more stage in what the British were pleased to call 'constitutional progress'. The INC (Indian National Congress) however rejected the proposals stating that:

> *(Quote)* The only satisfactory alternative to the White Paper is a Constitution drawn up by a Constituent Assembly elected on the basis of adult franchise or as near it as possible. [21] (*Unquote*)

Eventually, Britain's Parliament replaced the Act of 1919 with the Government of India Act, 1935[22], which made provision, for the first time, for 'responsible government' (responsible to Indians in India but only at the provincial level, not at the national level). The 1935 Act contained 473 clauses and 16 schedules and is believed to be the longest piece of legislation ever passed in the United Kingdom. Under the 1935 Act, the viceroy, as well as the governors of provinces, were empowered to promulgate laws independently of the legislators (a privilege they did not possess under the 1919 Act)[23]. The 1935 Act (in Part-II) also provided for 'The Federation of India', uniting the governor's provinces in British India with the princely states, by means of a Federal Executive consisting of the governor-general of India and his council of ministers, and a Federal Legislature consisting of two chambers (the 'Council of State' and the 'House of Assembly'). The ruler of each of the princely states was free to accede to the Federation of India by executing an Instrument of Accession (as set out in Section 6 of the 1935 Act). Part-II of the 1935 Act (The Federation of India) could not be implemented, because in the period before 1947, the princely states had second thoughts about joining the Federation. The princes had been advised that their accession to the Federation would turn out to be a '*painful delusion*', and whatever safeguards there were for the rights and interests of the princely states (in the 1935 Act) would disappear since they would be incompatible with the dominion status that was being promised.[24] Granville Austin, in his book, *Cornerstone of a Nation,* has given a slightly different version (page 245):

> *(Quote)*... negotiations concerning the terms of accession by Indian States were to be undertaken by each State separately by the Viceroy of India, as the Crown representative; initiated in 1937 (on the coming into force of the 1935 Act) the negotiations dragged on till the Second World War with the result that none of the Indian States had become members of the Federation. (*Unquote*)

However, since an intermediate court between the High Courts and the Privy Council was acceptable to all political parties, 'the Federal Court of India' (envisaged in the GOI Act, 1935) was set up and began functioning from April 1937.[25]

The provisions of the Government of India Act, 1935, notably Part-II: The Federation of India—'the readymade federal suit' (as Viscount Simon had irreverently called it), served as a convenient framework for free India's draft Constitution, since it accommodated the concept of a unified India.

In fact, those who designed British India's first Constitution rendered yeoman service to generations of post-1947 citizens of free India when they conceived of and introduced 'The Federation of India' in British Parliament's Government of India Act, 1935, since this was the format that was adopted for free India's Constitution of 1950. It also facilitated the erstwhile semi-sovereign, semi-independent Indian states to 'accede' (between 1947 to 1949) to the Independent India that had been set up by the British Parliament's Indian Independence Act, 1947.

The INC (Indian National Congress) as well as the Muslim League had been critical of the 1935 Act, (when enacted) for not meeting the expectations of the people. Pandit Nehru had characterised it as 'a charter of slavery' and 'an attempt to perpetuate the political and economic bondage of India'[26], and yet, both the Congress and the Muslim League had set up candidates who contested elections to the provincial legislatures (under the 1935 Act). The Congress Party was successful in forming governments in some of the provinces (viz., the United Province, the Central Province, the provinces of Bihar, Orissa, and Madras as well as in the province of Bombay).

In the 1940s, in the midst of political deadlock and worsening communal conflict, *several non-official attempts were made at drafting constitutional proposals*[27], but they were ignored by the two major political parties (the Congress and the Muslim League) principally because they did not ensure a strong centralised body that then appeared necessary to govern a country as vast and disparate as India.

In 1942, Sir Stafford Cripps (then Lord Privy Seal in the UK's Labour Party Government) headed a British Government Mission to India, and when in India, he made it clear (for the first time) that Indians should write their own constitution. This was followed, in September 1945, with the Labour Government in the UK announcing that fresh elections would be held in India's provinces in order that the freshly-elected provincial legislatures could act as electoral bodies for India's *Constituent Assembly*. In March 1946, a UK cabinet-level mission visited India, principally to mediate between the Congress and the Muslim League and to help find a middle ground upon which the two major religious communities in the subcontinent could get constitutionally united. But the Cabinet Mission Plan of 1946 for keeping India united failed.

In July 1946, members of the then newly-elected provincial assemblies proceeded to elect delegates to India's Constituent Assembly which commenced its deliberations on 9 December 1946[28] without the participation of the Muslim League, as it had boycotted proceedings in the Constituent Assembly. The representatives of the Muslim League who did take part in the ongoing proceedings of the Constituent Assembly were those who had remained in India after partition; and there were many.

India's constitutional historian, Granville Austin, in his first book, *The Indian Constitution: Cornerstone of a Nation* (Oxford University Press, 1966)[29] has provided the numbers:

> *(Quote)* It is important to remember that the Indian Muslim community had a population of about 100 million of which approximately 65 million became Pakistanis. The 1951 census figures for both countries show India with 35.5 million Muslims and Pakistan with 65 million. (page 6). (*Unquote*)

V. Looking back, were the interests of the Muslims who remained behind in India at the time of partition (and of their progeny) adequately secured and safeguarded?

Not, according to the late Mr Jaswant Singh, then senior cabinet minister in the National Democratic Alliance (NDA), which was in governance at the centre from 1999 to 2004. He noted this in his book, *Jinnah: India, Partition, Independence* (Rupa, New Delhi, 2009). He gave his reasons in a television interview (in August 2009) over CNN-IBN with prominent broadcaster Karan Thapar. Excerpts from a transcript of this interview read as follows:

> **Karan Thapar**: Your book raises disturbing questions about the partition of India. You say it was done in a way 'that multiplied our problems without solving any communal issue'. Then you ask, 'if the communal issue (the principal issue), remains in an even more exacerbated form than before, then why did we divide at all?'
>
> **Jaswant Singh**: Yes, indeed why? I cannot yet find the answer. Look into the eyes of the Muslims who live in India, and you truly see through the pain in which they live—to which land do they belong? We treat them as aliens, somewhere inside, because we continue to ask even after partition: you still want something? These are citizens of India—it was Jinnah's failure because he never advised Muslims who stayed back.
>
> **Karan Thapar**: One of the most moving passages of your biography is when you write of Indian Muslims who stayed on in India and didn't go to Pakistan. You say they are 'abandoned', you say they are 'bereft of a sense of kinship', not 'one with the entirety' and then you add that 'this robs them of the essence of psychological security'.
>
> **Jaswant Singh**: That is right, it does. That lies at the root of the Sachar Committee report.[30]

> **Karan Thapar**: So, in fact, Indian Muslims have paid the price in their personal lives.
>
> **Jaswant Singh**: Without doubt, as have Pakistani Muslims.
>
> **Karan Thapar**: Muslims have paid a price on both sides.
>
> **Jaswant Singh**: I think Muslims have paid a price in partition. They would have been significantly stronger in a united India, effectively so much larger land, every potential is here. Of course, Pakistan or Bangladesh won't like what I am saying.

In a more recent publication, *Scars of 1947: Real Partition Stories,* by Rajeev Shukla (published by Penguin/Viking (2022)), the point of view of Hindu migrants from Pakistan has been presented. Two of the chapters (Chapters 6 and 12) in the book are devoted to stories of the families of two future prime ministers of India: Inder Kumar Gujral and Dr Manmohan Singh. And in the prologue, it is stated:

> *(Quote)* The tragic Partition of India will never be forgotten by the people of the two countries that came into being after this event . . . The story was the same on either side of a hastily created border by the British. Hundreds of thousands of Hindus, Muslims, and Sikhs lost their lives in this mass migration. *People from both countries who lived through Partition and its aftermath have only one hope for generations to come: that such an event never take place again anywhere in the world; that people resolve their differences and not live with so much pain.* (*Unquote*)

The December 28, 1947 issue of the HARIJAN reported that Gandhiji told a packed audience at a panchayat ground in one of India's villages:

> *(Quote)* My voice was not so powerful as it once used to be. There was a time when whatever I said was acted upon. If

I had the original power, not a single Muslim should have found it necessary to migrate to Pakistan from India or a single Hindu or Sikh to leave his home in Pakistan and seek asylum in the Indian Union. (*Unquote*)

VI. Events in and after 1947

In the first half of 1947, developments in India, outside the Constituent Assembly, had a profound impact on the British Government. With the outbreak of large-scale communal riots in various parts of northern India, and the adverse comments of the Muslim League on the Objectives Resolution adopted by the Constituent Assembly (on 22 January 1947)[31], the newly appointed viceroy and governor-general (Lord Louis Mountbatten)—who had assumed charge in March 1947—was convinced that the transfer of power would have to be hastened.

In the first week of June 1947, Lord Mountbatten as viceroy of India announced a plan to partition India.[32] He also intimated that the date of transfer of power to Indians would be advanced from June 1948 (the date previously announced by Mr Attlee in Britain's Parliament) to 15 August 1947, and that on and from that date, Britain would recognise the existence of two independent states on the subcontinent: India and Pakistan. The Indian Independence Act 1947 was drafted and rushed through Britain's Parliament[33], and it declared that there would be two 'dominions' in the subcontinent: the 'Dominion of India' and the 'Dominion of Pakistan' and also gave statutory recognition to the Constituent Assemblies formed in each of the two dominions. Under the Indian Independence Act, 1947, the predominantly Muslim-inhabited areas (East Bengal, West Punjab, Sind, Baluchistan, and the North-Western Provinces) were to go to Pakistan. The rest (which included the provinces of Assam, Bihar, the Central Provinces, Berar, Madras, Orissa, East Punjab, the United Provinces, and West Bengal) were to remain a part of India.

As for the princely states, the 'paramountcy' of the British Crown in relation to Indian states 'lapsed' on 15 August 1947, (under Section 7 of the Indian Independence Act, 1947) leaving their rulers '*finally bereft of all authority, little lost pools of sovereignty, left behind on a barren shore, by the receding tide of history*', as expressed (somewhat exasperatingly) by Malcolm Muggeridge, editor of *Punch*.[34]

Senior Bureaucrat V. P. Menon (who along with Senior Minister Sardar Vallabhbhai Patel was responsible for the successful integration of the princely states with the Union of India) expressed his disappointment with Section 7 of the Indian Independence Act, 1947, describing it as 'the greatest disservice the British had done us as well as the rulers, (because) during the course of a century, the provinces and the States had welded together'. In *The Story of the Integration of the Indian States* (Orient Longmans Ltd., March 1956), a book that the Statesman of Calcutta had described as 'unquestionably one of the most important books of the decade following Indian Independence', its author, V. P. Menon, had written:

> *(Quote)* It seemed necessary that the Prime Minister and the Cabinet should give a free hand to Sardar in dealing with them (the rulers). At its meeting held on 25 June, the interim Cabinet accepted the proposal for the creation of the States Department and on 27 June a press *communiqué* was issued allotting the Department to Sardar. I was named as the Secretary.
>
> I was more than ever convinced that in view of the disposition of some of the rulers to cast in their lot with Pakistan, of a few others to assert their independence, and the keen desire of all to safeguard their sovereignty, some sort of organic bond should be forged between the Government of India and the States if the integrity of the country was to be

> preserved. The States which were geographically contiguous to India must be made to feel legally and morally that they were part of it. (*Unquote*)

VII. Accession of Indian states to the Dominion of India brought into existence by the Indian Independence Act, 1947—and the problem created by the princely state of Hyderabad

Most of the rulers of princely states located in British India were persuaded (or felt compelled, by changed circumstances) to sign Instruments of Accession to the Dominion of India, as was prescribed and provided for in Section 6 of the 1935 Act. A few had also acceded to Pakistan; the state of Junagadh (a state with a predominantly Hindu population but with a Muslim ruler) had also initially acceded to Pakistan.[35]

However, there were problems with the erstwhile *Indian state of Hyderabad.* For generations, it had a Muslim ruler but the population of the state was predominately Hindu—although the civil services, the police, and the army in the state had been manned mainly by Muslims.

The princely state of Hyderabad was located over most of the Deccan Plateau in southern India, covering an area of over 82,000 square miles and occupying a pivotal position in the heart of the country, and was surrounded by the Central Provinces in the north, by Bombay Province in the west, and Madras Province on the east and south. In population, revenue, and (above all) in strategic importance, it was the premier princely state in the country. It had been founded by Mir Qamruddin, the son of a general in the army of Emperor Aurangzeb. Six years after Aurangzeb's death, his successor, Emperor Farrukhsiyar, appointed Mir Qamruddin as viceroy of the Deccan with the title *'Nizam-ul-mulk Feroz Jung'*. In the course of time, Mir Qamruddin made himself virtually independent of Delhi, though he, and his successors after him, did pledge nominal allegiance to the Mughal Emperors. In 1798, the then Nizam gave over to the British the military control of his territories, and in 1858, when the British assumed direct governance of British India, the Nizam pledged his loyalty to the British Government. Since then—geographically, culturally, economically, and even politically—Hyderabad was an integral part of British India. No natural barriers separated the border areas of the state, and its population was homogenous with the population of the surrounding Indian provinces. The princely state of Hyderabad was entirely dependent upon India for its railway, postal, telegraph, and telephone services and its entire system of communications (by land and by air).

At the time of partition, Nizam Usman Ali Khan was the seventh Nizam in the line of succession, having succeeded to the *gaddi* (throne) in August 1911, and in 1918, the British had conferred on him the hereditary title of 'His Exalted Highness', and later, in 1921, the King of England in a letter referred to him as a 'Faithful Ally of the British Government'. On the strength of these titular appendages, the Nizam claimed independence in the internal affairs of his state 'just as much as, the British Government in British India'—a claim that was instantly rejected by Lord Reading, viceroy of India, who informed the Nizam that he did not stand in a category separate from that of rulers of other Indian states.

As early as 1926, the problem with the then princely state of Hyderabad had been foreseen by Sir William Barton, British Resident: '*There can be no doubt that it (Hyderabad) owes its very existence to the British connection . . . Left entirely to himself it is doubtful if the present Nizam would be able to maintain himself for any length of time.*'

Soon after June 1947, the Nizam issued a *firman* (edict) declaring his intention not to be represented in the Constituent Assembly either of Pakistan or of India, making it clear that on 15 August 1947, he would resume the status of an independent sovereign, but when he saw that Section 7 of the Indian Independence Act, 1947 did not permit the grant of dominion status separately to any Indian state, he protested—quite vociferously—but in vain.

Lord Mountbatten had been hopeful that Hyderabad would ultimately accede to India. He explained to V.P. Menon that the main reason why the Nizam had not acceded was because, although the Muslims in the state represented only 15 per cent of the population, they filled almost all the important government posts including those in the army and the police. It was therefore a revolt on their part against which the Nizam had to guard rather than any kind of uprising by the non-Muslims, although the latter represented the vast majority of the state's population. He therefore pleaded that some time should be given to the Nizam to educate this all-powerful minority. On the question of separate dominion status for Hyderabad, however, Mountbatten remained firm. He said that: 'His Majesty's Government would not agree to Hyderabad becoming a member of the British Commonwealth of Nations except through either of the two new dominions.' Since the largest Indian state of Hyderabad (which included Berar) continued to refuse to accede to India—the latter actually raised the banner of revolt—Indian troops (on orders from the interim central government) marched into Hyderabad and Berar. The Nizam characterised this as an 'invasion', but the Government of India treated it as 'police action'—an act of 'liberation' of the people living there. Immediately after the 'police action' and the installation of the military governor's administration in Hyderabad, the Nizam fell in line with other Indian states and signed the instrument of accession. On 23 November 1949, he also issued a firman accepting the Constitution framed by the Constituent Assembly of India as the Constitution of Hyderabad.

The impact of the 'police action' in Hyderabad on the rest of India was 'unreservedly healthy' (as V. P. Menon had observed). It helped to quickly settle the problem of the Indian states and the Government of India was recognised as the paramount authority over the entire territory of India.

VIII. Barring Jammu, Ladakh, and the Valley of Kashmir, the erstwhile Indian states were absorbed into the Dominion of India: and so were the smaller units

- Some of the smaller Indian states were merged into former Indian provinces, and they were later designated *Part A States* in the Constitution of India;[36]
- Some Indian states were grouped together into more viable units, and they were later designated in India's Constitution as *Part B States*; (two of the largest princely states—the state of Hyderabad and the state of Jammu & Kashmir—had been listed in Part B of the First Schedule of the Constitution).[37]
- The remaining units (viz., Ajmer, Bhopal, Bilaspur, Cooch-Bihar, Coorg, Delhi, Himachal Pradesh, Kutch, Manipur, and Tripura) which were chief commissioner's provinces under the Government of India Act 1935 (or were treated as such) were initially described in the Constitution as *Part C States* (later 'Union Territories')[38]. After the Constitution 7th Amendment Act of 1956, and as a consequence of the enactment of the States Reorganisation Act, 1956, the *Union Territories* in the Constitution were mentioned by name: viz., Delhi, Himachal Pradesh, Manipur, Tripura, The Andaman and Nicobar Islands, and the Laccadive, Minicoy, and Amindivi Islands.
- Manipur[39] and Tripura were designated 'State' by the North-Eastern Areas (Reorganisation) Act, 1971. Meghalaya (a part of Assam) was also designated a

'State' by the same Act, whereas Arunachal Pradesh[40] and Mizoram were designated as 'Union Territories' in the year 1986, however, both Mizoram and Arunachal Pradesh were described as 'State' in India's Constitution.

- The erstwhile British Indian state of Sikkim, in the strategic north-east[41], had stayed out; (it was brought into the Union much later in 1975 under Article 2 of India's Constitution).[42]

The Kingdom of Sikkim had been founded by the Namgyal dynasty in the 17th century. It was ruled by Buddhist priest-kings (Chogyals). In the year 1890, it became a princely state of British India, with a political officer of the Imperial Raj stationed in the capital, Gangtok. In the year 1922, Sikkim became a member of the Chamber of Princes (the assembly representing rulers of princely states). And with the lapse of 'paramountcy' under the Indian Independence Act 1947, Sikkim (having its own legislative assembly) became a protectorate of the Dominion of India. In 1974, the Sikkim Assembly passed the Government of Sikkim Act, 1974 establishing a fully responsible government and seeking representation for the people of Sikkim in India's parliamentary system. Later, Sikkim's Assembly passed a resolution expressing its desire to associate with the political and economic institutions of India and seeking representation for the people of Sikkim in India's parliamentary system. It was in pursuance of this resolution that the Constitution 35th Amendment Act, 1974 was passed in India's Parliament, making Sikkim an 'associate state', but, since the status of an 'associate' state was not recognised in India's Constitution, the Constitution 36th Amendment Act, 1975 corrected the error, with retrospective effect, and admitted Sikkim into the Union under Article 2 of the Constitution, making it the twenty-second state in the Republic of

India, and so designated in the First Schedule of India's Constitution.

IX. The Valley of Kashmir—'where hope and history is in hourly collision'[43]—was left out: it was not absorbed into the Dominion of India: the unique relationship of J&K with the Union of India was revealed in the Constituent Assembly only in October 1949:

The *autonomous* state of Jammu and Kashmir (including Ladakh) had been included in the First Schedule to the Constitution of India, 1950 as a Part-B State. But, only Article 1 was to apply to it (under Article 370), as to which other provisions were also to apply to the state and with what exceptions and modifications was left to be determined by presidential orders issued from time to time.

The following is a brief history of the state of Jammu and Kashmir:

i. Jammu and Kashmir (along with Ladakh) had been brought into existence in the year 1846 as a separate state. In the year 1819, Kashmir was conquered by Maharaja Ranjit Singh and till the year 1846, it had a Sikh ruler, whilst Jammu was ruled by a Dogra chief of Rajput descent, until the year 1818 when the principality of Jammu became part of the territory of Rajah Gulab Singh of Kashmir under the Treaty of Amritsar of 1846[44]. This treaty (with the British) recognised and established Gulab Singh as Maharaja, in possession of all the hill country between the Indus and Ravi (rivers) including *Kashmir, Jammu, Ladakh, and Gilgit,* but excluding Lahoul, Kulu, and other areas (including Chamba) which for strategic purposes the British considered advisable to retain. It was with the aid of British troops that Maharaja Gulab Singh became the ruler of

Kashmir. Gulab Singh died in 1857 and was succeeded by his son Ranbir Singh, who in turn was succeeded by Maharajah Pratap Singh. Lt. General Maharajah Sir Hari Singh ascended the gaddi in September 1925 as ruler of Jammu and Kashmir. The state of Jammu and Kashmir always had a preponderance of Muslims. But after partition, the population ratio was affected to some extent, particularly in Jammu, as a result of migration to and from Pakistan. In Ladakh, however, the majority of the people were (and remain) Buddhists. Although Muslims formed the largest single community in the state of Jammu and Kashmir, there were complaints that the majority of the posts both in the government and in the army were being held by Hindus.

ii. In the year 1932, the All Jammu and Kashmir Muslim Conference, with Sheikh Abdullah as its moving spirit, asserted the rights of the Muslim community. Later, it changed its name to the 'National Conference' and, became affiliated to the All India States Peoples' Conference. Repeated campaigns against the Maharajah were launched by the National Conference, and as a consequence, Sheikh Abdullah was imprisoned by the ruler on several occasions.[45]

iii. In 1939, Maharaja Hari Singh promulgated the Jammu and Kashmir Constitution Act 14 of 1939[46]—*an Act to consolidate and amend the law relating to the government of Jammu and Kashmir.*

iv. After the lapse of British paramountcy over princely states (in Britain's Parliament Indian Independence Act, 1947), Maharaja Hari Singh wanted Jammu and Kashmir to be an independent state. But the sudden invasion by an armed group of raiders from Pakistan on 24 October 1947 compelled a change of mind. In return for India's military intervention, the Maharaja signed the Instrument of Accession to the proposed Union of

India on 25 October 1947.[47] Clauses 5, 7, and 8 of the Instrument of Accession read as follows:

> (*Quote*) 5. The terms of this my Instrument of Accession shall not be varied by any amendment of the Act or of the Indian Independence Act, 1947, unless such amendment is accepted by an Instrument supplementary to this Instrument.
>
> 7. Nothing in this Instrument shall be deemed to commit me in any way to acceptance of any future Constitution of India or to fetter my discretion to enter into arrangements with the Government of India under any such future constitution.
>
> 8. Nothing in this Instrument affects the continuance of my sovereignty in and over this State, or save as provided by or under this Instrument, the exercise or any powers, authority and rights now enjoyed by me as Ruler of this State or the validity of any law at present in force in this State. (*Unquote*)

v. The idea of convening a Constituent Assembly for Jammu and Kashmir State had been conceived even before Partition, and probably it would have been implemented but for the invasion of the State (in 1947) by tribesmen from what had become the territory of Pakistan. When the 'National Conference' formed the interim government in the state (under the Jammu and Kashmir Constitution Act of 1939), it was expressly declared (in 1948) that, as soon as normal conditions were restored, steps would be taken to convene a National Assembly based upon adult suffrage, to frame a Constitution for the state[48]. The ultimate convening of the Constituent Assembly in 1951 was the natural outcome of the desire of the people of the state to have a democratic government responsible to a legislature, elected by the people of the state.

vi. In March 1948, Maharaja Hari Singh deputed four representatives of the state to represent the state of Jammu and Kashmir in India's Constituent Assembly.

vii. On 25 November 1948, Maharaja Hari Singh declared in a proclamation 'that the Constitution of India shortly to be adopted by the Constituent Assembly of India shall in so far as it is applicable to the State of Jammu and Kashmir, govern the constitutional relationship between this State and the contemplated Union of India and shall be enforced in the State by me, my heirs and successors in accordance with the tenor of its provisions; *that the provisions of the said Constitution shall, as from the date of its commencement, supersede and abrogate all other constitutional provisions inconsistent therewith which are at present in force in this State'.*[49]

viii. On 20 June 1949, Maharaja Hari Singh issued another proclamation entrusting his powers and functions in relation to the state and its government to his son and heir Yuvaraj Karan Singh.

ix. *On 17 October 1949, in India's Constituent Assembly—which had been in almost continuous session since November 1946—Mr Ayyangar senior member in the Constituent Assembly moved for the adoption of a new Article—***Article 306A:**[50]

> **The Honourable Shri N. Gopalaswami Ayyangar:**
>
> Sir, this matter, the *matter of this particular motion, relates to the Jammu and Kashmir State.* The House is fully aware of the fact that the State has acceded to the Dominion of India. The history of this accession is also well known. The accession took place on the 26 October 1947. Since then, the State has had a chequered history. Conditions are not yet normal in the State. The meaning of this accession is that at present that State is a unit of a federal State,

namely, the Dominion of India. This Dominion is getting transformed into a Republic, which will be inaugurated on 26 January 1950. The Jammu and Kashmir State, therefore, has to become a unit of the new Republic of India.

As the House is aware, accession to the Dominion always took place by means of an instrument which had to be signed by the Ruler of the State and which had to be accepted by the Governor-General of India. That has taken place in this case. As the House is also aware, Instruments of Accession will be a thing of past in the new Constitution. The States have been integrated with the Federal Republic in such a manner that they do not have to accede or execute a document of Accession for the purpose of becoming units of the Republic, but they are mentioned in the Constitution itself; and, in the case of practically all States other than the State of Jammu and Kashmir, their constitutions also have been embodied in the Constitution for the whole of India. *All those other States have agreed to integrate themselves in that way and accept the Constitution.*

Maulana Hasrat Mohani:
Why this discrimination, please?

The Honourable Shri N. Gopalaswami Ayyangar:
The discrimination is due to the special conditions of Kashmir. That particular State is not yet ripe for this kind of integration. It is the hope of everybody here that in due course even Jammu and Kashmir will become ripe for the same sort of integration as has taken place in the case of other States. At present it is not possible to achieve that integration. There are various reasons why this is not possible now, I shall refer again to this a little later.

In the case of the other Indian States or Unions of States there are two or three points which have got to be remembered. They have all accepted the Constitution framed for States in Part-I of the new Constitution and those provisions have been adapted so as to suit conditions of Indian States and Unions of States. Secondly, the Centre, that is the Republican Federal Centre will have power to make laws applying in every such State or Union to all Union and Concurrent Subjects. Thirdly, a uniformity of relationship has been established between those States and Union and the Centre. *Kashmir's conditions are, as I have said, special and require special treatment.*

I do not want to take much of the time of the House, but I shall briefly indicate what the special conditions are. In the first place, there has been a war going on within the limits of Jammu and Kashmir State.

There was a cease-fire agreed to at the beginning of this year and that cease-fire is still on. But the conditions in the State are still unusual and abnormal. They have not settled down. It is therefore necessary that the administration of the State should be geared to these unusual conditions until normal life is restored as in the case of the other States.

Part of the State is still in the hands of rebels and enemies.

We are entangled with the United Nations in regard to Jammu and Kashmir and it is not possible to say now when we shall be free from this entanglement. *That can take place only when the Kashmir problem is satisfactorily settled.*

Again, the Government of India have committed themselves to the people of Kashmir in certain respects. They have committed themselves to the position that an opportunity would be given to the people of the State to decide for themselves whether they will remain with the Republic or wish to go out of it. We are also committed to ascertaining this will of the people by means of a plebiscite provided that peaceful and normal conditions are restored and the impartiality of the plebiscite could be guaranteed. *We have also agreed that the will of the people, through the instrument of a constituent assembly, will determine the constitution of the State as well as the sphere of Union jurisdiction over the State.*

At present, the legislature which was known as the Praja Sabha in the State is dead. Neither that legislature nor a constituent assembly can be convoked or can function until complete peace comes to prevail in that State. We have therefore to deal with the Government of the State which, as represented in its Council of Ministers, reflects the opinion of the largest political party in the State. Till a constituent assembly comes into being, only an interim arrangement is possible and not an arrangement which could at once be brought into line with the arrangement that exists in the case of the other States.

Now, if you remember the viewpoints that I have mentioned, *it is an inevitable conclusion that, at the present moment, we could establish only an interim system. Article 306A is an attempt to establish such a system.*[51]

The mover, Mr Gopalaswami Ayyangar, then went on to *explain* the different parts of Article 306A, and ultimately stated the *effect* of the Article as follows:

The *effect* of this article is that the Jammu and Kashmir State which is now a part of India will continue to be

> a part of India, will be a unit of the future Federal Republic of India and the Union Legislature will get jurisdiction to enact laws on matters specified either in the Instrument of Accession or by later addition with the concurrence of the Government of the State. And steps have to be taken for the purpose of convening a Constituent Assembly in due course which will go into the matters I have already referred to. When it has come to a decision on the different matters it will make a recommendation to the President who will either abrogate Article 306A or direct that it shall apply with such modifications and exceptions as the Constituent Assembly may recommend. That, Sir, is briefly a description of the effect of this article, and I hope the House will carry it.[52]

The President of the Constituent Assembly (Dr Rajendra Prasad) then put the motion to vote:

> The position is that after Article 306, the following Article be inserted . . . The motion was adopted. And Article 306A was added to the Constitution (on 17 October 1949).[53]

x. On 26 November 1949, Dr Ambedkar moved the following motion in the Constituent Assembly:

> That the Constitution as settled by the Assembly be passed.
>
> *The motion was adopted (with prolonged cheers).*[54]

xi. Article 306A was included in Part-XXI of the Constitution (Temporary and Transitional Provisions) and renumbered as Article 370, with the marginal note: 'Temporary Provisions with respect to the State of Jammu and Kashmir'.[55]

X. Article 370 of the Constitution—Analysed

a. *Only Article 1 of the Indian Constitution, along with Article 370, was to apply to the State of Jammu and Kashmir*. By virtue of Article 1, the State of Jammu and Kashmir thus became an *integral part of the Union of India.*[56]

b. All other provisions of the Constitution of India were to be applied to that State *only through Presidential Orders, subject to such exceptions and modifications as the President (of India) may by order specify.*

c. *Clause 1 of Article 370* expressly limited the powers of India's Parliament to make laws for the State of Jammu and Kashmir to three subjects: defence, external affairs, and communications (corresponding to matters specified in the Instrument of Accession governing the accession of the State to the Dominion of India—being the matters with respect to which the Dominion Legislature may make laws for that State); but no such order was to be issued except in *consultation* with the State Government (of Jammu and Kashmir).

d. Such *other* provisions of the Constitution of India were to apply in relation to the State of Jammu and Kashmir 'subject to such *exceptions* and *modifications* as the President may by order specify'; but no such order was to be issued except with the *concurrence* of the State Government (of Jammu and Kashmir).

e. Notwithstanding anything in the provisions of Article 370, the President of India was also empowered (by Clause (3) of Article 370) to declare by public notification that Article 370 '*shall cease to be operative or shall be operative only with such exceptions and modifications and from such date as he (the President) may specify'*—but under the proviso to Article 370 (3), the *recommendations* of the Constituent Assembly of the State *'shall be necessary'* before the President issues such a notification.[57]

XI. Post-Constitutional Events

xii. On 20 April 1951, a proclamation was issued by Yuvaraj Karan Singh regarding the setting up of the Constituent Assembly for framing of a Constitution for the state of Jammu and Kashmir.[58]

xiii. On 14 May 1954[59], in exercise of powers conferred by clause 1 of Article 370 of the Constitution, the president promulgated the Constitution (Application to Jammu and Kashmir Order, 1954) by which additional Article 35A was added to the Constitution.[60] It provided that *notwithstanding anything in the Constitution,* no existing law in force in the State of Jammu and Kashmir, and no law hereafter enacted by the State Legislature inter alia conferring on *permanent residents* special rights and privileges or imposing upon other persons any restrictions as respects—employment under the State Government, acquisition of immovable property in the State, settlement in the State, or right to scholarships and such other forms of aid as the State Government may provide shall be void on the ground that it is inconsistent with or takes away or abridges any rights conferred on the other citizens of India by any provision of this Part.

xiv. On 26 November 1956, the Constituent Assembly of Jammu and Kashmir adopted the Constitution of

Jammu and Kashmir[61]—and the *Kashmir Constitution Act of 1939 stood repealed.*

xv. On 26 January 1957, the Constitution of Jammu and Kashmir 1956 came into force and from 26 January 1957, the Constituent Assembly of Jammu and Kashmir stood dissolved.[62]

XII. The Current Status of the Erstwhile State of Jammu and Kashmir

Although the Constitution of India 1950 had set up an indestructible Union of States, the states and union territories had no permanent existence. Each state (including its territory) could be reorganised (its boundaries altered, its areas increased or diminished) by ordinary law passed by Parliament even though that would result in an amendment of some part of the Constitution.[63] The hope that had been expressed in India's Constituent Assembly, by N. Gopalaswami Ayyangar—which was greeted by cheers—was that:

> . . .. *in due course even Jammu and Kashmir will become ripe for some sort of integration as has taken place in the case of the states.*

It got realised 'in due course'—but only 73 years later—by the Government at India unilaterally introducing a series of "laws" (mentioned below) that had the consequence of the erstwhile state of Jammu and Kashmir ceasing to remain in existence (from 5 August 2019) with its autonomous status deleted, none of which was greeted with cheers by the permanent residents of Jammu and Kashmir!—

1. As from 5 August 2019, a new Article 370 was introduced—*not by an amendment of the Constitution*

but by presidential order—it provided that *all the provisions of the Constitution (as amended from time to time) without any modifications or exceptions would henceforth apply to the territory, and to the people in the state of Jammu and Kashmir.*

2. From 5 August 2019, Presidential Ordinance 272 of 2019 was promulgated by which Article 35A of the Constitution—that had conferred on 'permanent residents' of Jammu and Kashmir certain special rights and privileges 'notwithstanding anything in the Constitution'—stood deleted.
3. In Article 367 of the Constitution (*Interpretation*) the following was added as from 05.08.2019 by public notification issued in the name of the President.

   "To article 367, there shall be added the following clause, namely:

   "(4) For the purposes of this Constitution as it applies in relation to the State of Jammu and Kashmir–

   (a) references to this Constitution or to the provisions thereof shall be construed as references to the Constitution or the provisions thereof as applied in relation to the said State;

   (b) references to the person for the time being recognized by the President on the recommendation of the Legislative Assembly of the State as the Sadar-i-Riyasat of Jammu and Kashmir, acting on the advice of the Council of Ministers of the State for the time being in office, shall be construed as references to the Governor of Jammu and Kashmir;

   (c) references to the Government of the said State shall be construed as including references to the Governor of Jammu and Kashmir acting on the advice of his Council of Ministers; and

(d) in proviso to clause (3) of article 370 of this Constitution, the expression "Constituent Assembly of the State referred to in clause (2)" shall read "Legislative Assembly of the State". (clearly an attempted amendment).

4. From 6 August 2019, the state of Jammu and Kashmir ceased to be a State, upon Parliament passing the Jammu and Kashmir Reorganisation Act No. 34 of 2019—it created two new union territories: the *Union Territory of Ladakh* (comprising Kargil and Leh districts) and the *Union Territory of Jammu and Kashmir* (other than the territory of Ladakh).

   Constitutional challenges to each one of these "laws" of August 5 and 6 (2019)—have been pending in India's Supreme Court and await a hearing in August 2023.

NOTE: Article 370 had been sought to be abrogated by inserting clause (4) in Article 367, by Presidential Notification dispensing with the obligatory condition in the proviso to Article 370(3) which had read:

> "Provided that the recommendation of the Constituent Assembly of the State referred to in clause (2) *shall be necessary* before the President issues such a notification"!

Notes and References:

1. The chapter deals (mainly) with a period before India's Constitution was finally adopted by the Constituent Assembly on 26 November 1949.
2. India, that is Bharat, shall be a Union of States (Article 1).
3. The old Sanskrit name was Himalaya—the abode of snow: stretching across a large part of Asia, immediately to the north of India, in the form of 'great protuberances above the general level of the earth's surface'. The whole of its southern border is named Himalaya, and its northern border, in a much less definite way, is called Kunlun-Shan (or the Kunlun Mountains), one of the longest mountain chains in Asia extending over 3,000 kilometres (1,864.11 miles). Between the Himalayas and the Kunlun Mountains lies the tableland of Tibet, with an average elevation of 4,500 metres above sea level. Neither the Himalayas nor Kunlun-Shan nor the Tibetan tableland have any separate geographical existence, the whole constituting 'one huge agglomeration of mountains', so described by Sir John Strachey in his book: *India* . . . (new and revised edition, 1903, pages 18-19); originally published in the year 1888 by Kegan Paul, Trench, Trubner & Co., London.
4. Not all the inhabitants of Hindustan are Hindus, but a large majority of them profess the Hindu religion; Will Durant tells us in *The Story of Civilization* (Vol. I, Simon and Schuster, New York, 1954, pages 392-93), that: it is out of the derived Persian term 'Hindu' that the invading Greeks had coined 'India'.
5. The Great Rann of Kutch comprises about 11,583 square kilometres (approximately 4472 square miles) between the Gulf of Kutch and the mouth of the Indus River in what is now southern Pakistan.
6. 231 million of whom had been enumerated in the very first census of 1901 in British India. See *Imperial Gazetteer of India*, Volume 1, page 449.

   In the territory of independent India (a much lesser area than British India since it had formerly included what is now the territory of Pakistan and of Bangladesh), the census of 2011 recorded its population as being over 1,210 million or 1.2 billion (which equals 121 crores).
7. The British had listed 562 as 'princely states' even though only about one hundred of them deserved to be so-called. They covered 630,068

square miles of internal principalities and chiefships that lay within the recognised boundaries of British India and were described by Britain's Parliament in 1861 and 1876 as 'provinces and states in alliance with Her Majesty', and in 1889 as 'provinces and states under the suzerainty of Her Majesty'. See *The Native States of India* by Sir William Lee-Warner (1846-1914), published in 1910 by Tulsi Publishing House, New Delhi.

8. Ramachandra Guha—India's 21st-century historian—has this to say about the princely states: 'The princely states were so many that there was even disagreement as to their number. One historian puts it at 521, another at 565. They were more than 500, by any count, and they varied very widely in terms of size and status. At one end of the scale were the massive states of Kashmir and Hyderabad, each the size of a large European country; at the other end, tiny fiefdoms or jagirs of a dozen or less villages.' (From *India After Gandhi,* published by Picador, India, 2017, page 36)

9. Commenting in the year 1930 on 'the Indian States', the Simon Commission (set up in 1928) had observed:

   No account of the conditions of the Indian problem could be adequate which did not include some description of the Indian States. They constitute an outstanding feature which is without precedent or analogy elsewhere. Some of them are countries comparable in size and importance to a British Province; others are much smaller; and at the far end of the scale, we find estates of a few acres owned or shared by petty chieftains and others who exercise no jurisdictional powers . . .

   Numbering in all over 550, they comprised a total area of about 600,000 square miles scattered all over India.

   (Report of the Indian Statutory Commission (Simon Commission), Vol. I, paragraph 101): Extract from Shiva Rao: *The Framing of India's Constitution: A Study,* page 511.

10. He did not then foresee that—a century later—with the signing of the Maastricht Treaty (w.e.f. 1 November 1993), there would be a union of European nations that would be described as the European Union (EU).

11. **At present, 22 major languages that are listed in the Eighth Schedule to the Constitution are spoken and written amongst more than 1,407 million people in India (over 140 crores) who also speak in hundreds of local dialects (called mother tongue—the language that one first speaks as a child).**

12. See The Muslim Case for Pakistan: http://www.columbia.edu/itc/mealac/pritchett/00ambedkar/ambedkar_partition/index.html (University of Columbia).

13. **He was impressed by something different: by what G. K. Chesterton (a prominent English writer of the early 20th century had written in the *Illustrated London News* (18 September 1909), viz., that the idea of Indian nationalists was 'not very Indian and not very national'. 'There is a world of difference,' he wrote, 'between a conquered people demanding its own institutions and the same people demanding the institutions of a conqueror.' Mohandas Karamchand Gandhi (who was in England at the time and was to go to South Africa) was most impressed by this article (see *Collected Works of Mahatma Gandhi* (in 98 Volumes)). In Vol. IX, he had written: '*Indians must reflect over these views of Mr Chesterton and consider what they should rightly demand.*' (Vol. IX, page 425, October 1909).**

14. See B. Shiva Rao's *Framing of India's Constitution: Select Documents*, Vol. I, pages 5-15.

15. But, the Indian Councils Act 1909—based on the Morley-Minto Reforms (John Morley being the Secretary of State for India and Lord Minto the viceroy of India)—did give a limited role to Indians in provincial legislatures.

16. A. C. Bannerjee: *Indian Constitutional Documents,* 2nd edition, Vol. II, page 325.

17. See *Dr Babasaheb Ambedkar Writings and Speeches,* Volume 12 (published by the Government of Maharashtra in 1993).

18. The Montagu-Chelmsford Reforms (briefly known as the Mont-Ford Reforms) introduced self-governing institutions in British India. The reforms took their name from Edwin Montagu, the Secretary of State for India from 1917 to 1922, and Lord Chelmsford, the viceroy of India between 1916 and 1921. The reforms were outlined in the Montagu-Chelmsford Report, prepared in 1918, and formed the basis of the Government of India Act 1919. *The genesis of the Rajya Sabha in the Constitution of India 1950 can be traced to the Montagu-Chelmsford reforms and the Government of India Act, 1919. They provided for the first time for a second chamber to be called the Council of States.*

19. *The Government of India: A Brief Historical Survey of Parliamentary Legislation Relating to India* (published at the Clarendon Press, Oxford, 1922).

20. The visit to India in 1928 of the members of the Simon Commission resulted in widespread protests throughout the country. See *History of Modern India* by Claude Markowitz (published in 2004 by Anthem Press, ISBN: 478-1-84-4331-001-4).

21. It was only in 1942 that Britain (through the Cripps Mission led by Sir Stafford Cripps), accepted that an elected body of India should frame India's Constitution.

22. The Joint Select Committee on the Government of India Bill of 1934 did not view with favour the demand for a constitutional guarantee of fundamental rights to British subjects in India. See Indian Constitutional Reforms (Report of Joint Committee) Hansard H.C. Deb dated 1 November 1934, Volume 293, CC 395-405: where one of the members (J. Jones) stated: 'It seems to me most extraordinary that many members seem to be under the impression that there is an exact comparison between India and England. They are talking about India as though it were a country that had the right to control its own affairs. *We are only giving them a temporary opportunity of expressing their opinion . . .*'

23. The precursor to the Ordinance—making power in India's Constitution.

24. See B. Shiva Rao *Framing of India's Constitution: A Study,* page 25.

25. By the Government of India (Federal Court) Order 1937, dated 29 July 1937, a provision was made for the establishment of the Federal Court of India with a Chief Justice of India and not more than six puisne judges. Appeals from the Federal Court of India were to lie to His Majesty's Privy Council in London. On 24 September 1949, the Constituent Assembly, in its role as independent India's Provisional Parliament, passed the Abolition of Privy Council Jurisdiction Act, 1949, and with effect from 10 October 1949, the jurisdiction of His Majesty's Privy Council (over judgements decrees and orders of the Federal Court of India) ceased, and with the commencement of the Constitution (26 January 1950), the judges of the Federal Court became judges of the Supreme Court of India (Article 374 of the Constitution of India 1950).

26. *Congress Political and Economic Studies No.3: A Brief Analysis of the New Constitution* by Z. A. Ahmed (published in 1937). See also the *Encyclopedia Britannica* (Macromedia), Volume 9, 15th edition, page 430.

27. For instance, in 1944, the communist leader M. N. Roy presented *The Constitution of Free India: A Draft*, which provided for radical decentralisation and for direct democracy through the establishment of a nationwide network of people's committees and for the collective ownership of economic resources. In *Citizenship and Its Discontents: An Indian History* (published by Harvard University Press), the author Niraja Tayal extolled M. N. Roy's draft, describing it as 'by far the most populist and radical of the manifestos of the "new India"'.

    In 1945, a non-political committee, under the chairmanship of Tej Bahadur Sapru (and which included some future members of the Constituent Assembly: M. R. Jayakar, Frank Anthony, John Matthai, and N. Gopalaswami Ayyangar), came up with another set of proposals, incorporated in what became known as the Sapru Report:

    Professor W. Norman Brown, who founded the American Institute of India Studies at Pennsylvania (in an article), opined that the Sapru Committee Report 'appeared to be the most reflective and sustained Indian presentation of constitutional issues that has been published'. W. Norman Brown: 'Indian Constitutional Issue—Far Eastern Survey', 22 May 1946, Vol. 15, No.10, pages 155-158 (on page 153).

    And in 1946, the Gandhian economist, Shriman Narayan Agarwal, wrote: *The Gandhian Constitution of Free India.*

    The only concession made by India's Constituent Assembly to Shriman Narayan Agarwal's Gandhian Constitution was in one of the Directives of State Policy (now set out in Article 40 of the Constitution of India 1950). It provided that the State shall take steps to organise village panchayats and endow them with such powers and authority that may enable them to function as units of self-government.

28. **The Constituent Assembly took two years, eleven months, and seventeen days to complete its historic task of drafting a Constitution for independent India and during this period it held sessions for over 165 working days. The Debates—running into ten thousand printed pages— have been printed by the Lok Sabha Secretariat, New Delhi (6th reprint, 2014) in five books (Book 1 contains Volumes I to VI of the debates, Book 2 contains Volume VII of the debates, Book 3 contains Volumes VIII of the debates, Book 4 contains Volume IX of the debates, and Book 5 contains Volumes X to XII of the debates).**

29. His second book, published in the year 2003, is also a classic. It is titled: *Working a Democratic Constitution: A History of the Indian Experience* (Oxford University Press).

30. Social, Economic, and Education Status of the Muslim Community of India—A Report by the Prime Minister's High Level Committee of November 2006 (https://www.minorityaffairs.gov.in/sites/default/files/sachar_comm.pdf).

31. Constituent Assembly Debates (CAD), Book No. 1, January 1947, page 324.

32. Oxford's professor of colonial history, Reginald Coupland, in his writings, had perpetuated the dominant view of the British Empire as a great civilising experience. But Coupland was also the first to raise the notion of partition, when analysing 'the Indian Problem in depth for his All Souls colleague, Leo Amery, Secretary of State for India', and 'when the idea (of partition) was hurriedly implemented in 1947, it was another fellow of All Souls—a barrister—who had previously never travelled east of Paris (Cyril Radcliffe) who was put in charge of hastily drawing fateful lines that separated Pakistan from India, resulting in 20 million refugees and mass carnage.' (See Fara Dabhoiwala: 'Imperial Delusions' in the *New York Review of Books*, Vol. XVIII, No.11, pages 59-62)

33. The India Independence Bill was introduced in the House of Commons on 4 July 1947 and passed by the House on 15 July 1947. It was passed by the House of Lords the next day on 16 July 1947. Royal assent was granted (by King George VI) on 18 July 1947.

34. The British weekly magazine of satire was published continuously from the year 1841 right through until the year 2002.

35. 'After a brief struggle between India and Pakistan, Junagadh voted to join India in a plebiscite held on 20 February 1948, and became a part of Saurashtra in the then larger state of Bombay—later in 1960, Saurashtra became part of the newly-formed state of Gujarat.' (See Wikipedia)

36. Article 1(2) of the Constitution of India 1950 read: The States and the territories thereof shall be the States and their territories specified in Parts A, B, and C of the First Schedule.

37. The state of Hyderabad, initially a Part B State, was renamed (after the States Reorganisation Act, 1956) as the state of Andhra Pradesh. By the Constitution Seventh Amendment Act, 1956, Article 1(2) was substituted, Parts A, B, and C of the First Schedule were abolished, and all the states and their territories were together specified in the First Schedule of the Constitution. After 1956, the state of Jammu and

Kashmir was also no longer a Part B State but 'a state the territories of which were specified in the First Schedule to the Constitution'.

The State of Jammu and Kashmir with its 84,471 square miles was larger than the state of Hyderabad. But its population of over 4 million people was mostly Hindu in Jammu, and mostly Muslim in the Kashmir valley, and Ladakh (bordering Tibet) with its high mountain ranges was populated by people who were Buddhists.

38. For a fuller account of the Indian states, see Shiva Rao: *The Framing of India's Constitution* (Chapter 18) published by the Indian Institute of Public Administration, New Delhi, 1967, as well as the 'White Paper on Indian States' issued by the Government of India in July 1948.

39. Manipur, when still under a constitutional monarchy, had the unique distinction of having held elections in June 1948 based on adult franchise and in October 1949, the ruler of Manipur, Bodhchandra Singh, merged with the Indian Union.

40. It became part of the state of Assam (in 1950). What is now Arunachal Pradesh got established as the North-East Frontier Agency in 1954.

41. 'Strategic' since Sikkim bordered Tibet at Nathu-La. The pass at Nathu-La (at 14,200 feet)—in Sikkim—gave access to the Tibetan plateau and to the entire Chumbi Valley.

42. Article 2: Admission or establishment of new States. Parliament may by law admit into the Union, or establish, new States on such terms and conditions as it thinks fit.

The Constitutionality of some clauses of Article 371F (Special Provisions with respect to the state of Sikkim) inserted by the Constitution 36th Amendment Act, 1975 were later challenged but were upheld by the majority—with a forceful dissent by Chief Justice L. M. Sharma: *Somnath Poudyal vs. Union of India*—1994 Supp. (1) SCC 325 (4:1).

43. A quote from Pico Iyer's latest book, *The Half Known Life: In Search of Paradise,* published by Riverhead Books (January 2023). In it, the author states that the Valley of Kashmir has paid a steep price for its beauty.

44. The Treaty of Amritsar has been reproduced in Justice A. S. Anand's book, *The Constitution of Jammu & Kashmir: Its Development & Comments,* pages 354-355 (Universal Law Publishing Co. (2010)).

45. In 1946, the Sheikh organised the 'Quit Kashmir' campaign against the Maharajah and, as a result, he was sentenced to a long term of imprisonment, but by this time, he had acquired a considerable hold over the hearts of the people of the State. See *The Story of the Integration of the Indian States* by V. P. Menon (published by Orient Longmans Ltd., March 1956, pages 392-393).

46. The entire J&K Constitution Act, 1939 has been reproduced in Justice A. S. Anand's Book: *The Constitution of Jammu & Kashmir: Its Development & Comments,* published by Universal Law Publishing Co., 6th edition (2010), pages 360 to 379.

47. A complete copy of the Instrument of Accession is reproduced in Justice A. S. Anand's book, *The Constitution of Jammu & Kashmir: Its Development & Comments,* published by Universal Law Publishing Co., 6th edition (2010), pages 358-359.

    But what is of historical interest is the letter of the Maharaja that accompanied the signed instrument of accession and of Lord Mountbatten's reply. They have been recently reproduced verbatim (from the HT Archives) in the *Hindustan Times* issue of 21 October 2022.

48. Proclamation of Maharaja Hari Singh, 5 March 1948.

49. The entire proclamation of 25 November 1948 has been reproduced on page 202 of Justice Jaswant Singh's book, *Jammu and Kashmir: Political and Constitutional Development* (Har-Anand Publications, 1996).

50. **Article 306A (draft amendment) was not included either in the first Draft Constitution prepared by the Constitutional Adviser (Mr B. N. Rau) in October 1947, or in the Draft Constitution prepared by the Drafting Committee (i.e., the revised Draft Constitution of 24 February 1948) submitted to the president of the Constituent Assembly. Article 306A had been separately drafted by the Drafting Committee (as was indicated by the President of the Constituent Assembly).**

51. CAD, Book No. 5, (17 October 1949 to 24 January 1950), pages 423-427.

52. CAD, Book No. 5, (17 October 1949 to 24 January 1950), page 427. A brief summary of this has been recorded in the study volume of *The Framing of India's Constitution* by B. Shiva Rao (pages 552-554).

53. CAD, Book No. 5 (17 October 1949 to 24 January 1950) on page 429.

54. CAD, Book No. 5, Vol. X-XII, page 955.

55. In 2017, a bench of two judges of the Supreme Court of India in *State Bank of India vs. Santosh Gupta* (AIR 2017 SC 25) on page 32, held with reference to the State of Jammu and Kashmir that: '*the quasi-federal structure of the Constitution of India continues, but with differences*'. (The differences were reflected in Article 370)

56. In Part-I—The Union and Its Territory—Article 1 read as follows:

    1. Name and territory of the Union.
        (1) India, that is Bharat, shall be a Union of States.
        (2) [The States and the territories thereof shall be as specified in the First Schedule.]
        (3) The territory of India shall comprise:
            (a) the territories of the States;
            (b) [the Union territories specified in the First Schedule; and]
            (c) such other territories as may be acquired.

    The State of Jammu & Kashmir was included in Part B of the First Schedule (Indian States that had acceded to the Union).

57. **Since 1950, there were three important decisions of Constitution Benches of the Supreme Court of India on the width and scope of Article 370, viz.:**
    (i) In *Puranlal Lakhanpal vs. President of India* (March 1961) reported in AIR 1961 SC 1519 (5J).
    (ii) In *Mohd. Maqbool Damnoo vs. The State of Jammu & Kashmir* (5 January 1972), reported in AIR 1972 SC 963 (5J).
    (iii) In *Sampat Prakash vs. State of Jammu & Kashmir* (10 October 1968) reported in AIR 1970 Supreme Court 1118 (5J).

58. The copy of the proclamation is on pages 203-204 of Justice Jaswant Singh's book, *Jammu and Kashmir: Political and Constitutional Development,* published by Har-Anand Publications (1996).

59. The entire Presidential Order of 1954 has been reproduced in Justice A. S. Anand's book: *The Constitution of Jammu & Kashmir: Its Development & Comments* (Universal Law Publishing Co.), pages 405-417.

60. Printed copies of the Constitution of India 1950 do not show this nor do they reveal the addition of Article 35A—because Article 35A was not added by an amendment to the Constitution of India, but by exercise of Presidential Powers under Article 370.

61. The entire Constitution of Jammu and Kashmir, 1956 has been reproduced in Justice A. S. Anand's book *The Constitution of Jammu & Kashmir: Its Development & Comments* (Universal Law Publishing Co., 6th edition (2010), pages 187 to 352).

62. Pages 286-289 of A. G. Noorani's book, *Article 370: A Constitutional History of Jammu and Kashmir*, published by Oxford University Press (2011).

63. The Constitution of India 1950 has prescribed three separate methods for amending the Constitution:

    (1) by ordinary law, viz., by simple majority in each House of Parliament as provided for in Articles 3 and 4:

    Article 3: Formation of new States and alteration of areas, boundaries or names of existing States—by ordinary law made by Parliament.

    Article 4: Laws made under articles 2 and 3 could provide for the amendment of the First and the Fourth Schedules and for supplemental, incidental, and consequential matters.

    (2) by a special procedure and special majority as prescribed in Article 368 (2) of the Constitution for all other amendments, and;

    (3) additionally, by ratification by States where the amendments involve any change in the following Articles viz. Articles 54, 55, 73, 162, 241, or any change in Chapter IV of Part-V (Union Judiciary), Chapter V of Part-VI (High Courts in the States), or Chapter I of Part-XI (Relations between the Union and the States). Such amendments are required to be passed by Parliament by a special majority and according to the procedure prescribed in Article 368(2); and in addition require to be ratified by not less than one half of the States by resolution to that effect passed by the legislatures of these States before the bills making provision for such amendments are presented to the President for his assent.

Chapter Two

(A) How India's Constitution Almost Never Got Finalised

(B) After the Constitution was finalised and came into force—by whom was it to be interpreted?

The Issue of Language

The most remarkable feature of the debates in the Constituent Assembly was that, because of India's political past, they were conducted almost entirely in English. And despite Hindi being the language of a vast majority of the citizens of India, there was no agreement in the Constituent Assembly as to what should be the national language of the Union of India.

When the British first came, saw, and conquered India in 1774, the first governor-general of Bengal, Warren Hastings, ordered the people of English origin residing in India to acquaint themselves 'to the fullest extent' with Indian languages and culture in order to better associate themselves with (what were then called) 'the Orientals'. The educational policy of Warren Hastings led to the establishment of a famous college at Fort William in Calcutta, where Arabic, Persian, and Sanskrit were taught, and students could avail themselves of courses in Hindu and Muslim laws as well as in English law. This continued for fifty more years, till the mid-1830s, when it was reversed.It was Thomas Macaulay's (now infamous) *Minute on Education*—compiled in the spring of the year 1835—that was responsible for changing the entire course of British educational policy in India. Macaulay favoured English, and the curriculum, in schools, colleges, and elsewhere, was adapted accordingly with fateful consequences, both for the Indians and for the British. For Indians, the changed educational policy no longer produced a learned class imbued with the best that English language and literature could offer, but, rather, an English-speaking secretarial and professional class, *without a tradition of responsibility and power.* In 1942, Jawaharlal Nehru characterised Macaulay's educational policy as: 'education for clerks!'[1] And in 1964, Malcolm Muggeridge (editor of PUNCH), in a broadcast over the BBC, said that 'education was about the worst thing the British did to India,' adding that 'appropriately enough this contributed to our departure.[2]' He then embellished his assertion with a rhetorical query: 'Was it not the enraged and unemployed graduates who chased us out, hurling after us curses, and copies of the *Oxford Book of English Verse?*

Many years before this, C. F. Andrews, a stounch supporter of independence for India and a friend of the Mahatma, expressed different sentiments, with a less rhetorical flourish. In a letter addressed to the 17th viceroy and governor-general of India (the fourth Earl of Minto[3]), he wrote:

> English as the language of education has justified itself, in spite of great drawbacks. *It has had a supreme political justification. It has made India no longer only a geographical expression but a political unity. It has created the hope and the possibility of an Indian Nation.* English history and literature have fashioned the political thought of modern India and fashioned it inevitably on national lines.[4]

When John Morley as secretary of state for India wrote to the Earl of Minto arguing that 'Reforms will not save the Raj but if they don't, nothing else will', the titled Lord pontifically wrote back: 'I am afraid I must utterly disagree. The Raj will not disappear in India as long as the British race remains what it is, because we shall fight for the Raj as hard as, we have ever fought, if it comes to fighting, and we shall win as we have always won!' However, despite this expression of bravado, it was in the year 1909 that the 'Morley Minto Reforms' (so-called) were passed in Britain's Parliament. It was in this colonial background that India's Draft Constitution got framed—in English—by Constitutional Adviser Benegal Narsing Rau (B. N. Rau). It was then discussed and debated in the Constituent Assembly by persons elected by members of already existing legislative assemblies; most of whom were men (372 in number) and only seventeen were women[5], all of them conversant in the English language.

(A) How India's Constitution Almost Never Got Finalised

The Official Language of Choice

With many main indigenous languages and dialects from which to choose, the members of India's Constituent Assembly adopted English (the language of the British conqueror) as the second of the two Official Languages of the Union—the first being Hindi in the Devanagari script. This has been finally set out in Part-XVII of the Constitution (Articles 343 to 351), but not before there had taken place a long-drawn battle of words between diverse groups in the Constituent Assembly; a battle that went on, intermittently, till almost the very end of the proceedings of the Constituent Assembly. The issue of language had assumed overwhelming importance in India's Constituent Assembly, because (like fundamental rights) it affected each and every member. The debates on the subject were fractious and dragged on and on—first, from February to November 1948, and then (after a cooling-off period from January to August 1949) from August 1949 onwards—amidst frayed tempers. There was no agreement on a *national language*, particularly since there were so many differences on what numerals to adopt for Hindi! It was almost after all other articles in the Constitution had been adopted, and at almost the very end of the proceedings that the language issue got resolved in the Constituent Assembly. Professor Granville Austin, who wrote his first book[6] on India's Constitution in 1966, headed his long chapter on 'The Language and the Constitution—as *The Half-hearted Compromise*'; in which the following passage occurs:

> The members of the Constituent Assembly did not attempt the impossible; they did not lay down in the language provisions of the Constitution that one language should be spoken all over India. Yet they could not avoid giving one of the regional languages special status, so they provided, not that there be a 'national' language, but, using a tactful euphemism, that Hindi should be the 'official language of the Union'. Hindi would also be used for inter-provincial communication. For an initial period of fifteen years, however, English was to continue to serve as the official language. *After this time, Hindi would supplant English unless Parliament legislated otherwise.* But English was to be retained for use in the courts and for official texts after the expiration of the fifteen-year period, *until Parliament otherwise legislated.* The provincial governments were permitted to choose one of the regional languages or English for the conduct of their own affairs, and major regional languages were listed in a Schedule to the Constitution (the Eighth Schedule).[7]

Ultimately, the Constituent Assembly formally adopted the language-compromise but only at the end of six hectic weeks between 1 August and 14 September 1949.

Under the 'compromise', Hindi did not supplant English only because 'Parliament legislated otherwise'; the Official Languages Act, 1963, passed by India's Parliament, provided for the continuing use of English beyond the initial 15-year period but tactfully, did not say for how long. As regards the language to be used in courts, English was retained beyond the 15-year period only because India's Parliament did not choose (nor has it so far chosen) 'to legislate otherwise.' In Article 348 (in Chapter Three of Part-XVII [Official Language]), it has been mentioned that the language to be used in the Supreme Court of India and in the high courts, and for bills and acts enacted by Parliament or by legislatures of a state, and for all ordinances promulgated by the President of India or by the governor of a state, and for all orders, rules, regulations, and bye-laws issued under the Constitution or under any law made by Parliament or by the legislature of a state, *'shall be in the English language'* only *'until Parliament by law otherwise provides'*.

English has now continued for more than 70-plus years as one of the two official languages in India and is the language used in all the high courts (though not exclusively)[8] and in the Supreme Court of India exclusively. This has helped to preserve linguistic peace between Hindi and non-Hindi speakers in multilingual India; on the more positive side, the *increased* use of Hindi in India, as well as the *continued* use of English in courts and outside courts—e.g. in the print and electronic media—has helped in fostering a spirit of nationalism. It is also compatible with the increasing spread of the English language around the world.

Christophe Jaffrelot, Professor Indian Politics and Sociology at King's India Institute, London has written:

> "Despite English being criticized as a colonial inheritance and an instrumental knowledge in several quarters, the language remains a vehicle for emancipation for many. The south recognized this aspect of English, while several states in the north tried to abolish the use of the language. English medium education has provided advantages in securing jobs, acquiring skills and entering the service-driven modern economy."

But this is at variance with the official view.

In the year 2022, a parliamentary committee on official languages recommended the use of *Hindi only* as the medium of instruction in central institutions of higher education in Hindi-speaking states, and encouraged the use of *regional languages* in non-Hindi-speaking states. This has once again sparked a controversy—characterised by critics of the BJP (the ruling party in power at the Centre)—as an attempt *to impose Hindi on non-Hindi speaking people.*[9] The Chief Minister of Tamil Nadu very recently warned: "Igniting the embers of the 1965 Anti-Hindi Imposition Agitations would be an unwise move"; he was referring to a series of protests in Tamil Nadu that had ultimately led to the DMK (the political party his father, Mr. Karunanidi headed) coming to power in the State in the year 1967.

In his second book, *Working a Democratic Constitution: The Indian Experience*[10], Granville Austin had this to say about language:

> (*Quote*) Although rarely a source of secessionist sentiment, language was a disruptive issue broadly during the Nehru years. It had aroused such passions in the Constituent Assembly that there is no 'national' language specified in the Constitution, only an 'Official Language': Hindi, for official business conducted by the central government and among governments. And the 'imposition' of Hindi, as the other major language groups thought it, especially in the South, was so fiercely resisted that English has been the legislated substitute for, or alternative to, Hindi since 1950.[11]Language differences, however, have been—and remain—the most significant aspect of the diversity of India. And though diversity is a good thing, language differences have also contributed to the diversification of India—which is not such a good thing.When, in the year 1937, the then Congress 'prime minister' of Madras province, Mr C. Rajagopalachari, had introduced compulsory Hindi in the first three grades of the schools in the Madras presidency, the violent reaction set the tone for anti-Hindi riots that occurred nearly thirty years later, in 1965. (*Unquote*)

Differences in language have now become a part of separate regional identities and have promoted and perpetuated regional distinctiveness. In earlier editions of *The State of the World Atlas*, India had been described as '*a country with a significant linguistic conflict.*' Although this description has not been repeated in the latest edition of that book[12], India continues to remain a land of '*linguistic differences*'. In the past two decades, regional political parties have become more vocal and more dominant in Indian politics. At the centre and in many of the states, the traditional National 'Congress Party'—which in the days of the British Raj had fought hard for and won India's independence (and was advised by Mahatma Gandhi to disband itself after independence; advice which it chose to ignore)—has been transformed from the once most formidable majority party in the country to being just one out of many political parties.

In addition, the Constitution of India also suffers from an excessive emphasis on detail, which could well have been left to ordinary legislation: a fact admitted by Dr Ambedkar in November 1946, when introducing the Draft Constitution to members of India's Constituent Assembly (quoted below):

> As to the accusation that the Draft Constitution has produced a good part of the provisions of the Government of India Act, 1935, I make no apologies. There is nothing to be ashamed of in borrowing. It involves no plagiarism. Nobody holds any patent rights in the fundamental ideas of a Constitution. *What I am sorry about is that the provisions taken from the Government of India Act, 1935 relate mostly to the details of administration.* I agree that administrative details should have no place in the Constitution. I wish very much that the Drafting Committee could see its way to avoid their inclusion in the Constitution. *But this is to be said on the necessity which justifies their inclusion* . . . One is

that the form of administration has a close connection with the form of the Constitution. *The form of the administration must be appropriate to and in the same sense as the form of the Constitution.* The other is that it is perfectly possible to pervert the Constitution, without changing its form, by merely changing the form of the administration and to make it inconsistent with and opposed to *the spirit of the Constitution.*[13]

(B) After the Constitution got finalised and came into force—by whom was it to be interpreted?

(1) Definitely not by all the three organs of the State – only by the Judiciary:

In *Puttaswamy* (a unanimous 2017 decision of a Bench of Nine Judges) – it held that the right of privacy is a fundamental right; it had been contended on behalf of the Union of India that it was only Parliament in its constituent capacity that could introduce a a right of privacy; the contention was rejected by all the nine Judges – as was stated in the concurring judgment of Nariman J –

> ***"........ in our constitution it is not left to all the three organs of the State to interpret the Constitution when a substantial question as to the interpretation of the Constitution arises it is this Court and this Court alone under Article 145(3) that is to decide what the interpretation of the Constitution shall be, and for this purpose, the Constitution entrusts the task to a minimum of five judges of this Court".***

And it was not for the first time that *Puttaswamy* (2017) had so declared. In 1993 in *Supreme Court Advocates-on-Record Association vs. Union of India*: 1993 (4) SCC 441 (Bench of 9 Judges) had held by majority (7:2) (at pages 530-531 paragraphs 83-84) as follows:

(*Quote*) In a democratic polity, the supreme power of the State is shared among the three principal organs—constitutional functionaries - namely, the legislature, the executive and the judiciary. Each of the functionaries is independent and supreme within its allotted sphere and none is superior to the other . . . *Justice has to be administered through the Courts and such administration would relate to social, economic and political aspects of justice as stipulated in the preamble of the Constitution and the judiciary, therefore, becomes the most prominent and outstanding wing of the constitutional system for fulfilling the mandate of the Constitution.*

The constitutional task assigned to the judiciary is in no way less than that of other functionaries - legislature and executive. Indeed, it is the role of the judiciary in carrying out the constitutional message, and it is its responsibility to keep a vigilant watch over the functioning of democracy in accordance with the dictates, directives and imperative commands of the Constitution by checking excessive authority of other constitutional functionaries beyond the ken of the Constitution. In that sense, the judiciary has to act as a sentinel on the qui vive." (*Unquote*)

(2) Under Article 141, "the law declared by the Supreme Court of India shall be binding on all Courts within the territory of India" – i.e. binding on High Courts and binding also on a Bench of two or three Judges of the Supreme Court of India by whom the law had been previously declared: (this is known as the doctrine of *precedent*: "something of the same type that has occurred before").

And Article 144 states: that "all authorities, civil and judicial, in the territory of India shall act in aid of the Supreme Court": which has been interpreted as meaning: "the direction of the Supreme Court is required for completion of the even course of justice". (see 2002 (1) SCC 33).

(3) But When Article 141 says that 'the law declared by the Supreme Court shall be binding on all courts within the territory of India', it does not include the Supreme Court of India.

In *Bengal Immunity Co. Ltd vs. State of Bihar & Ors*: AIR 1955 SC 661 (7J) it was declared (for the first time) that despite the provisions of Article 141 "*in a proper case it is permissible for the Supreme Court to go back upon its previous decision!*" – but only "in a proper case"; In other words the Supreme Court should not lightly dissent from a prior pronouncement of the Court. Article 141 therefore cannot and does not include the Supreme Court itself, (except for the Benches of two or three Judges who have previously so declared the law); and if the Bench of two or three Judges disagrees with the law prevails so declared, it is open to it to request the Chief Justice of India to refer the matter for a final decision to a larger Bench of Judges of the Supreme Court.

(4) The marginal note in Article 145 reads: "*Rules of Court*, etc". Under the Rules of the Supreme Court the Court sits in Benches primarily of two and three judges and in Constitution Benches of five and more Judges. But in this, the concern here is with "etc." (etcetera) in the marginal note to Article 145 – which means "other things; a term usually indicating additional unspecified items" (see Black's Law Dictionary 10th edition page 669)

(5) About these "*other things*"— in *Central Board of Dawoodi Bohra Community and another vs. State of Maharashtra and Anr*: 2005 (2) SCC 673 (Bench decision of five Judges) the legal position was summed up in paragraphs 8, 9 and 12 as follows:

> (*Quote*) (8) In *Raghubir Singh (dead) by Lrs.'s case: 1989 (2) SCC 754* (5J); Chief Justice Pathak pointed out that in

order to promote consistency and certainty in the law laid down by the superior Court the ideal condition would be that the entire Court should sit in all cases to decide questions of law, as is done by the Supreme Court of the United States. Yet, His Lordship noticed, that having regard to the volume of work demanding the attention of the Supreme Court of India, it has been found necessary as a general rule of practice and convenience that the Court should sit in divisions consisting of judges whose number may be determined by the exigencies of judicial need, by the nature of the case including any statutory mandate related thereto and by such other considerations with the Chief Justices, in whom such authority devolves by convention, may find most appropriate. *The Constitution Bench reaffirmed the doctrine of binding precedents as it has the merit of promoting certainty and consistency in judicial decisions, and enables an organic development of the law, besides providing assurance to the individuals as to the consequence of transactions forming part of his daily affairs.*

"(9) Further, the Constitution Bench speaking through Chief Justice Pathak opined that the question was not whether the Supreme Court is bound by its own previous decisions; the question was under what circumstances and within what limits and in what manner should the highest Court overturn its own pronouncements. *In our opinion, what was working in the mind of His Lordship was that being the highest Court of the country, it was open for this Court not to feel bound by its own previous decisions because if that was not permitted, the march of Judge- made law and the development of constitutional jurisprudence would come to a standstill . . .*

"(12) We would like to sum up the legal position in the following terms:-

The law laid down by this Court in a decision delivered by a Bench of larger strength is binding on any subsequent Bench of lesser or co-equal strength.

A Bench of lesser quorum cannot doubt the correctness of the view of the law taken by a Bench of larger quorum. In case of doubt all that the Bench of lesser quorum can do is to invite the attention of the Chief Justice and request for the matter being placed for hearing before a Bench of larger quorum than the Bench whose decision has come up for consideration. It will be open only for a Bench of co- equal strength to express an opinion doubting the correctness of the view taken by the earlier Bench of co- equal strength, whereupon the matter may be placed for hearing before a Bench consisting of a quorum larger than the one which pronounced the decision laying down the law the correctness of which is doubted.

The above rules are subject to two exceptions:

(i) The abovesaid rules do not bind the discretion of the Chief Justice in whom vests the power of framing the roster and who can direct any particular matter to be placed for hearing before any particular Bench of any strength; and

(ii) In spite of the rules laid down hereinabove, if the matter has already come up for hearing before a Bench of larger quorum and that Bench itself feels that the view of the law taken by a Bench of lesser quorum, which view is in doubt, needs correction or reconsideration then by way of exception (and not as a rule) and for reasons it may proceed to hear the case and examine the correctness of the previous decision in question dispensing with the need of a specific reference or the order of Chief Justice constituting the Bench and such listing. Such was the situation in Raghubir Singh & Ors." (*Unquote*)

(6) Article 145(3) reads as follows:

(*Quote*)The *minimum* number of Judges who are to sit for the purpose of deciding any case involving a substantial question of law as to the interpretation of the Constitution or for the purpose of any reference under Article 143 (Power of the President to Consult Supreme Court) *shall be five*".

PROVIDED that, where the Court hearing an appeal under any of the provisions of this Chapter other than article 132 consists of less than five Judges and in the course of the hearing of the appeal the Court is satisfied that the appeal involves a substantial question of law as to the interpretation of this Constitution the determination of which is necessary for the disposal of the appeal, such Court shall refer the question for opinion to a Court constituted as required by this clause for the purpose of deciding any case involving such a question and shall on receipt of the opinion dispose of the appeal in conformity with such opinion. (*Unquote*)

The Proviso to Article 145(3) deals with the contingency of the Supreme Court (Sitting in a Bench of two or three Judges), and in the course of hearing of that Appeal the Court being satisfied that the Appeal involves a substantial question of law as to the interpretation of the Constitution, the determination of which is necessary for the disposal of the Appeal; in which case the Court shall refer the question for opinion to a Court of a Bench of minimum five Judges (i.e. to a Bench of even more than five judges – if necessary) "*for the purpose of deciding any case involving such a question*"; on receipt of the opinion of the Court, it must then dispose of the Appeal in conformity with such opinion.

(7) Sub-Clause (4) of Article 145 deals with a crucial element: "open justice"; Article 145(4) states that that "no judgment shall be delivered by the Supreme Court save in *Open Court*".

Notes and References:

1. Jawaharlal Nehru, *Glimpses of World History*, Oxford University Press, London, 1942, page 434.
2. Malcolm Muggeridge, *Twilight of Empire*, The Listener, Vol. LXXII, 1964, page 966.
3. Nicholas Mansergh, *The Commonwealth Experience*, Weidenfeld and Nicholson, London, 1969.
4. James Dunlop Smith and Martin Gilbert, *Servant of India: A Study of Imperial Rule from 1905 to 1910*, Longmans, London, 1966 edition, p. 132.
5. See *Founding Mothers of the Indian Republic: Gender Politics of the Framing of the Constitution* (Cambridge University Press, 2022) by Achyut Chetan, who teaches at St. Xavier's University in Kolkata: 'All in all, 17 women were elected to the Assembly most of whom were deeply involved in the debates on the drafting of the Constitution of India, for them, securing a foothold in the patriarchal territory ruled by male politicians, statesmen, and lawyers—the founding fathers—was not an easy task (page 43).' The author goes on to say (on page 59) that on the day the Constitution was signed by the members, '. . . there were only 11 women who could officially put their signatures on the grand document of the Indian republic.'
6. Prof. Granville Austin, *The Indian Constitution: Cornerstone of a Nation,* Oxford University Press, UK, 1966.
7. Granville Austin (1968): Chapter 12, pages 265 to 307, on page 266.

8. In some high courts (e.g., the High Court of Uttar Pradesh, the High Court of Madhya Pradesh, and the High Court of Rajasthan) and in one or two additional states north of the Vindhyas, advocates (as well as parties in person) may, if they choose, address the court in Hindi.

9. **In a recent article in the *New York Review of Books*, Volume LXX No. 5, 23 March 2023, Anjum Hasan (Indian novelist) has reviewed the Hindi novel, *Tomb of Sand* by Geetanjali Shree, (translated from Hindi by Daisy Rockwell and published by HarperVia) and has offered the following comment:**

    'There are clumsily forceful official attempts to make Hindi the predominant language of education and administration in a highly multilingual country, leading to, as the well-known Hindi journalist Mrinal Pande recently said, its footprint is growing and its soul shrinking. So as critical as the question of the relative value of each language is this: Can Hindi literature capture the grossly uneven, even misshapen, results of independent India's progress? Forged during that visionary and violent mid-twentieth-century era, in constant conversation with the ideals of nationalism, and then turned into a more artful instrument in the modernist fiction of the 1950s and 1960s, can Hindi reinvent itself again in this messed-up, "topsy-turvy mishmash" of an era without coming across as ingenuous or self-involved? Shree's fiction offers a rousing yes.'

10. Granville Austin, *Working a Democratic Constitution: The Indian Experience,* Oxford University Press, UK, 2000.

11. The nine articles in Part-XVII of the Constitution (Official Language) contain the compromise formula arrived at in the Constituent Assembly.

    14 languages had been listed in the Eighth Schedule of the Constitution as enacted; more have been added since then by Constitutional Amendments. There are now 22 languages listed in the Eighth Schedule pursuant to the recommendations made by the Commission on Official Language set up under Article 344(1).

12. Dan Smith, *The State of the World Atlas,* 10th edition (paperback), February 2021.

13. CAD, Book No.1, 4 November 1946, page 38.

Chapter Three

A Roller-Coaster Ride through Twenty-Five Parts of India's Constitution

Article 394 (along with Articles 5, 6, 7, 8, 9, 60, 324, 366, 367, 379, 380, 388, 391, 392 and 393) came into force on 26th November 1949, and the remaining provisions of the Constitution came into force on January 26, 1950. As enacted the Constitution contained a PREAMBLE and TWENTY-TWO PARTS and as it presently stands—with 105 Amendments—it has remained a Constitution with a PREAMBLE but with TWENTY-FIVE PARTS (additional Part IXA, Part IXB, and Part XIVA); and annexed to the Constitution as enected there were Eight Schedules, there are now Twelve Schedules, annexed to the Constitution.

----------PREAMBLE ----------

WE, THE PEOPLE OF INDIA, having solemnly resolved to constitute India into a SOVEREIGN SOCIALIST SECULAR DEMOCRATIC REPUBLIC and to secure to all its citizens:

JUSTICE, social, economic and political;

LIBERTY of thought, expression, belief, faith and worship;

EQUALITY of status and of opportunity; and to promote among them all

FRATERNITY assuring the dignity of the individual and the unity and integrity of the Nation;

IN OUR CONSTITUENT ASSEMBLY this twenty-sixth day of November, 1949, do HEREBY ADOPT, ENACT AND GIVE TO OURSELVES THIS CONSTITUTION.

The Preamble is the most important part of the Constitution. As was very recently and authoritatively stated in the judgment of a Bench of 9 Judges in K.S. Puttaswamy vs. Union of India – 2017 (10) SCC page 1 at pages 402-403:

> (*Quote*) 105. The Preamble to the Constitution postulates that the people of India have resolved to constitute India into a Republic which (among other things) is Sovereign and Democratic and to secure to all its citizens:
>
>> "JUSTICE, social, economic and political; LIBERTY of thought, expression, belief, faith and worship;
>> EQUALITY of status and of opportunity; and to promote among them all
>> FRATERNITY assuring the dignity of the individual and the unity of the Nation;…
>
> 106. In *Sajjan Singh v State of Rajasthan – 1965 (1) SCR 933 = AIR 1965 SC 845*, Justice Mudholkar alluded to the fact that the Preamble to our Constitution is "not of the common run" as is the Preamble in a legislative enactment but was marked both by a "stamp of deep deliberation" and precision. This was suggestive, in the words of the Court, of the special significance attached to the Preamble by the framers of the Constitution.
>
> 107. In *Kesavananda Bharati v State of Kerala* – 1973 (4) SCC 225 ("*Kesavananda Bharati*"), Chief Justice Sikri noticed that the Preamble is a part of the Constitution. The Preamble emphasises the need to secure to all citizens justice, liberty, equality and fraternity. Together they constitute the founding faith or the blueprint of values embodied with a sense of permanence in the constitutional document. The Preamble speaks of securing liberty of thought, expression, belief, faith and worship. Fraternity is to be promoted to assure the dignity of the individual. The individual lies at the

core of constitutional focus and the ideals of justice, liberty, equality and fraternity animate the vision of securing a dignified existence to the individual. *The Preamble envisions a social ordering in which fundamental constitutional values are regarded as indispensable to the pursuit of happiness. Such fundamental values have also found reflection in the foundational document of totalitarian regimes in other parts of the world. What distinguishes India is the adoption of a democratic way of life, founded on the rule of law. Democracy accepts differences of perception, acknowledges divergences in ways of life, and respects dissent.* (*Unquote*)

PARTS

PART-I: THE UNION AND ITS TERRITORY

PART-II: CITIZENSHIP

PART-III: FUNDAMENTAL RIGHTS

PART-IV: DIRECTIVE PRINCIPLES OF STATE POLICY

PART-IVA: FUNDAMENTAL DUTIES

PART-V: THE UNION

PART-VI: THE STATES IN PART A OF THE FIRST SCHEDULE

PART-VII: THE STATES IN PART B OF THE FIRST SCHEDULE (REPEALED)

PART-VIII: THE UNION TERRITORIES

PART-IX: THE PANCHAYATS

PART-IXA: THE MUNICIPALITIES

PART-IXB: THE CO-OPERATIVE SOCIETIES

PART-X: THE SCHEDULED AND TRIBAL AREAS

PART-XI: RELATIONS BETWEEN THE UNION AND THE STATES

PART-XII: FINANCE, PROPERTY, CONTRACTS, AND SUITS

PART-XIII: TRADE, COMMERCE, AND INTERCOURSE WITHIN THE TERRITORY OF INDIA

PART-XIV: SERVICES UNDER THE UNION AND THE STATES

PART-XIVA: TRIBUNALS

PART-XV: ELECTIONS

PART-XVI: SPECIAL PROVISIONS RELATING TO CERTAIN CLASSES

PART-XVII: OFFICIAL LANGUAGE

PART-XVIII: EMERGENCY PROVISIONS

PART-XIX: MISCELLANEOUS

PART-XX: AMENDMENT OF THE CONSTITUTION

PART-XXI: TEMPORARY, TRANSITIONAL AND SPECIAL PROVISIONS

PART-XXII: SHORT TITLE, COMMENCEMENT, AUTHORITATIVE TEXT IN HINDI AND REPEALS

Annexed to this Constitution: **FIRST SCHEDULE** to **TWELFTH SCHEDULE**

(Please read Chapter-Four: It contains a detailed commentary on the PREAMBLE and on the following concepts—JUSTICE, LIBERTY, EQUALITY, and FRATERNITY.)

----------Part-I ----------

The Union and Its Territories—Articles 1 to 4

Article 1(1) proclaims that India, that is, Bharat, shall be a Union of States. Under India's Constitution, the Union is indestructible, but the States are not. As was observed by the Chairman of India's 15th Finance Commission: 'It is not a confederation of States. It is not a question of holding together but of coming together'[1], (this has been explained in greater detail in Chapter One).

The states and the territories thereof are specified in the First Schedule, **(Article 1(2))**; under **Article 1(3)**, the territory of India comprises:

(a) the territories of the States,

(b) the Union Territories specified in the First Schedule, and

(c) such other territories as may be acquired.

Article 2 stipulates that Parliament may, by law, admit into the Union or establish new States on such terms and conditions as it thinks fit[2]; and Article 3 provides that Parliament may, by law, form new States, increase or diminish the area of any State, and alter the name and boundaries of any State; and Article 4 requires that laws made under Article 2 or Article 3 must contain provisions for amendment of the First Schedule and Fourth Schedule of the Constitution and may contain supplemental incidental and consequential provisions, as may be necessary to give effect to the law already made by Parliament, but no such law should be treated as an amendment of the Constitution for purposes of Article 368 (Power of Parliament to amend the Constitution and the procedure therefor).

Comment

More details are contained in Chapter One.

----------Part-II ----------

Citizenship[3]—Articles 5 to 11

Comment

It was the ideal of a unified India mentioned in the Preamble to the Constitution that inspired the provisions on citizenship. The only definitive feature about citizenship in the Constitution of India 1950 is what Dr Ambedkar had said when introducing the Draft Constitution to members of the Constituent Assembly, viz.:

> The proposed Indian Constitution is a dual polity with a single citizenship. There is only one citizenship for the whole of India. It is Indian citizenship. There is no State citizenship.[4]

By 'dual polity', Dr Ambedkar meant the parliamentary form of government for the union (at the centre) as well as for the states. He considered India's Constitution to be both unitary as well as federal 'according to requirements of time and circumstances'. He had also said that our Constitution-makers had avoided the rigid federal mould in which the US Constitution had been forged.

A common citizenship meant non-discriminatory participation for all citizens in the political life and affairs of the country, since Article 19(1)(d) and (e) of the Constitution had guaranteed to every citizen the right to move freely throughout India and to reside and settle in any part of the country.

Before 26 January 1950, British India had been politically one unit. With the lapse of paramountcy and the loss of protection of the British Crown, the inhabitants of more than 500 Indian states in British India became virtually stateless. The Constitution provided a common citizenship not only for the former inhabitants of British India but also for those in former

Indian states; and with their accession to the Dominion of India in 1948 and 1949, the territory of each of these states became a part of the territory of India.

Between the years 1951 and 2011, each decennial census revealed that from 80 per cent to roughly 84 per cent of the people of India professed some form of the Hindu religion, 10 to 14 per cent of India's population professed Islam, around 2 per cent had been Christian by faith, and less than 2 per cent professed the Sikh religion; Buddhists and Jains—each accounted for less than 1 per cent of India's total population.

On 25 August 2015, the Registrar General of India released the Census 2011 data on population by religious communities: India's total population in 2011 was 121.09 crores with the following composition:

Hindus 96.63 crores (79.8 per cent), Muslims 17.22 crores (14.2 per cent), Christians 2.78 crores (2.32 per cent), Sikhs 2.08 crores (1.7 per cent), Buddhists 0.84 crores (0.7 per cent), Jains: 0.45 crores (0.4 per cent), and Other Religions 0.79 crores (0.7 per cent).[5]

The census for 2021, long overdue, has not been undertaken so far. *The Hindu* reported (in February 2023): 'There is an indication that the census exercise—meant to be completed in 2021 but delayed because of Covid-19—may not be conducted in 2023-24, since the union budget allocation under the Census Survey and Statistics head has been slashed to Rs 1,565 crore from the Rs 3,676 crore allocated in 2022-23.'

Any citizen—Hindu, Muslim, Sikh, Christian, Buddhist, Jain, or any other—is eligible to be elected to any office in the land, including the highest. Since 1950, there have been fifteen presidents of India of which four have been Muslims, one has been Sikh, and India's fifteenth president, elected in 2022, is the first from India's designated tribal communities.[6]

In the wake of the partition of British India, Articles 5 to 9 in Part-II set out who were and who were not, Indian citizens at the commencement of the Constitution, including the rights of persons who had migrated to India from Pakistan, the position of persons who had initially migrated from India to Pakistan and had returned to India under a permit of re-settlement or permanent return, as well as the rights of citizenship of persons of Indian origin residing outside India. Article 10 provided that every person who is or who is deemed citizen of India under Articles 5 to 9 shall continue to be such citizen subject to the provisions of any law that may be made by Parliament; and Article 11 declared that nothing in Articles 5 to 10 will derogate from the power of Parliament to make any provision with respect to acquisition and termination of citizenship and all other matters relating to citizenship.

The Citizenship Act, 1955, passed by Parliament had initially adopted the English Common Law principle of right of citizenship by birth: *jus soli* (right of soil). Later, after 2003, with a large number of persons of Indian origin entering the territory of India from Bangladesh, Sri Lanka, and some African countries, the Citizenship Act provided that every person born in India after 26 January 1950 and before 1 July 1987 did not acquire Indian citizenship at birth, and such person became a citizen (of India) only if at the time of his or her birth either of his or her parents was a citizen of India. This followed the principle of *jus sanguinis* (right of citizenship by blood or consanguinity). Besides, every citizen born in India after 1 July 1987 becomes a citizen by birth only if at the time of his or her birth, both his or her parents were (or are) citizens of India. In addition, persons of Indian-origin cardholders, registered under Government of India notification of 19 August 2002, who were nationals or citizens of certain other countries were by law permitted to apply for overseas citizenship of India—a scheme that has proved beneficial to India.[7]

Under a further amendment made to the Citizenship Act, 1955, the child of an 'illegal migrant' to India born after 1 July 1987 could never become a citizen of India. But in December 2019, this illegal migrant status was lifted w.e.f. 12 February

2019 (under a law yet to be implemented)[8] only for members of the Hindu, Sikh, Buddhist, Jain, or Parsi community, i.e., people who belonged to any of these communities and had entered India illegally from Afghanistan, Bangladesh, and Pakistan. But the illegal migrant status was not lifted for people who had illegally entered India (from the Islamic countries of Afghanistan, Bangladesh, and Pakistan) and belonged to the Muslim community. This was said to contravene the provisions of Article 15(1)[9] of the Constitution, and it was challenged—a constitutional challenge that is pending adjudication in India's Supreme Court.

---------- Part-III ----------

Fundamental Rights—Articles 12 to 35

Article 12: Definition of State.

Article 13: Laws inconsistent with or in derogation of the fundamental rights—are declared void.

Right to Equality

Article 14: Equality before law.

Article 15: Prohibition of discrimination on grounds of religion, race, caste, sex, or place of birth.

Article 16: Equality of opportunity in matters of public employment.

Article 17: Abolition of Untouchability.

Article 18: Abolition of titles.

Right to Freedom

Article 19: Protection of certain rights regarding freedom of speech, etc.

Article 20: Protection in respect of conviction for offences.

Article 21: Protection of life and personal liberty.

Article 21A: Right to education (added wef 01-04-2010).

Article 22: Protection against arrest and detention in certain cases.

Right against Exploitation

Article 23: Prohibition of Traffic in Human Beings and Forced Labour.

Article 24: Prohibition of Employment of Children in Factories, etc.

Right to Freedom of Religion

Article 25: Freedom of conscience and free profession, practice, and propagation of religion.

Article 26: Freedom to manage religious affairs.

Article 27: Freedom as to payment of taxes for promotion of any particular religion—No person is compelled to pay taxes for promotion or maintenance of any particular religion.

Article 28: Freedom as to attendance at religious instruction or religious worship in certain educational institutions—No religious instruction is to be provided in any educational institution wholly maintained out of State funds.

Cultural and Educational Rights

Article 29: Protection of interests of minorities.

Article 30: Right of minorities to establish and administer educational institutions.

Article 31: [Compulsory acquisition of property]—Omitted by the Constitution (44th Amendment) Act, 1978, s. 6 (w.e.f. 20 June 1979).

Saving of Certain Laws

Article 31A: Saving of laws Providing for acquisition of estates, etc.

Article 31B: Validation of certain Acts and Regulations.

Article 31C: Saving of laws giving effect to certain directive principles.

Right to Constitutional Remedies

Article 32: Remedies for enforcement of rights conferred by this Part.

Article 33: Power of Parliament to modify the rights conferred by this Part in their application to Forces, etc.

<u>Article 34</u>: Restriction on rights conferred by this Part while martial law is in force in any area.

<u>Article 35</u>: Legislation to give effect to the provisions of this Part.

PRELIMINARY OBSERVATIONS AND CONCLUSION ON FUNDAMENTAL RIGHTS:

In Modern Constitutions (Oxford University Press: Oxford Paperbacks University Series, Second Edition, 1966) Prof. K. C. Wheare, (noted Constitutional expert) had written:

> "What makes one doubt that the Constitution of India is strictly and fully federal are the powers of intervention in the affairs of the States given by the Constitution to the Central Government and Parliament."

And he went on to observe:

> "In the case of Quasi–Federal constitutions it is probably proper to include the Indian Constitution of 1950."

And in the Oxford Journal of Legal Studies, *it has been categorily stated that in a federation 'it is the apex court that is superior to the federal legislature for settling disagreements over rights'.*[10]

[The doctrine of Judicial Review of all governmental action fits in well in a country with a written constitution (as in INDIA)—but not in ISRAEL, a country that has never had a written constitution. In the context of the present raging controversy in Israel, over Prime Minister Benjamin Netanyahu's plans for a "judicial overhaul", please read—and be enlightened by: (i) an article dated July 13, 2023 by Rivka Weill available at: *https:/verfassungsblog.de;did-isr*, (ii) an article by International Affairs Editor of *The Hindu*, Dr Stanly Johny at page 14 in the Sunday, July 20, 2023 edition of THE HINDU: "why has Israel plunged into a crisis?"; (iii) an article dated July 23, 2023: "What is Israel's reasonableness legislation, and why is it so contentious?" available at *www.ajc.org];* and (iv) Wikipedia: Basic Laws of Israel; (v) *Israel Supreme Court: The Power of Judicial Review*; see *https://www.jewishvirtuallibrary.org/israel-s-supreme-court-and-the-power-of-judicial-review*

The Fundamental Rights Chapter in India's Constitution owes much to the standard-setting UN Charter of October 1945, as well as to the Universal Declaration of Human Rights of December 1948.

When we gave ourselves a written Constitution it was certainly good to provide for Rights enforceable against the State and agencies of the State (as had been done in the Fundamental Rights Chapter): since quite often, the executive and the administration are incapacitated from rendering justice to individual citizens. During the Internal Emergency of June 1975, Union Cabinet Minister Sardar Swaran Singh had been appointed Chairman of the 'Constitution Committee' along with three prominent practising lawyers, its mandate was to clip the powers of the high courts by deleting Article 226 (Power of High Courts to Issue Certain Writs)—the Great Searchlight provision in India's Constitution for ferreting out injustices in individual cases and passing appropriate remedial directions.

Sardar Swaran Singh had then said that when he was a minister in the Punjab Government, he found that as minister, it was just not possible to render justice in individual cases because of the pressures and pulls of politics, and that it was far better that courts were left to do the job. A non-practising lawyer—he was the one person—who set his face against the proposed deletion of Article 226; India's citizens should be truly grateful to him, but not to the lawyer–politicians on that 'Constitution Committee' who were willing to scrap Article 226! Lawyers are endowed with the dual capacity: to rationalise democracy and autocracy: and they do it with equal fervour!

The Constitution envisages JUSTICE (in capital letters) in the Preamble—JUSTICE, economic, social and political—it says justice not just in courts which adjudicate disputes, but justice to all sections of society in their dealings with the state as well as with fellow–citizens. The Fundamental Rights Chapter has enabled courts to bring to account states, state governments and, their officials, but regrettably, in India, we do not have a self-fulfilling Civil Rights Act, as in the USA, where equality and non-discrimination can be enforced in courts by individuals against individuals, firms, and corporations, as well as against the State. The three-tier court-delivery system in India has replicated the British pattern. It is meant only to be resorted to as a last option, when persuasion and negotiation fail. It is necessarily slow and ponderous, perhaps deliberately so. A former Lord Chancellor of England, Lord Hailsham, had this in mind when speaking of legal aid schemes. He said:

> I hope that no one will ever come to think that by the introduction of schemes of this kind, litigation can ever be said to be a good thing. It is, in its nature, an evil and a concession which we make to the follies and wickedness of mankind. It can never be anything else.

Fundamental Rights—Right to Equality (Articles 14 to 18), Right to Freedom (Articles 19, 20, 21, and 22), Right against Exploration (Articles 23 and 24), Right to Freedom of Religion (Articles 25 to 28), Cultural and Educational Rights (Articles 29 and 30), Right to Constitutional Remedies (Articles 32 to 35)—are enforceable against the State (as broadly defined in Article 12) and all laws in force in the territory of India in so far as they are inconsistent with the provisions of Part-III (Fundamental Rights) are (to the extent of their inconsistency) declared to be void (Article 13(1)). The State is also enjoined not to make any law after 26 January 1950 which takes away or abridges the rights conferred by Part-III of the Constitution, and any law made in contravention of this clause is, to the extent of the contravention, declared to be void.

Part-III embodies in India's Constitution what is known as *The Rule of Law* which got established in England with the signing of Magna Carta (1215).[11] The abiding characteristic of Magna Carta (1215) was that it has had the shortest possible life of any historic document because, within months of its signing and sealing, the Great Charter was peremptorily revoked and annulled by the Pope at the prompting of its signatory, King John himself. But the English people know a *good thing* when they see it, and they continue to celebrate the signing of Magna Carta, more than eight centuries after the event! Whenever people are oppressed, fighting for core values, or for human rights, or clamouring for governance under the law, they refer to Magna Carta and quote from it.

For instance, in June 2004, in a celebrated case about Guantanamo Bay—a case that challenged indefinite detentions, tortures and, disappearances, (*Rasul vs. Bush*)—the Supreme Court of the United States, citing a dissent from its earlier 1953 decision, wrote (Justice Stevens writing for the Court):

> Executive imprisonment has been considered oppressive and lawless ever since King John at Runnymede pledged that no free man should be imprisoned, dispossessed, outlawed, or exiled save by judgement of his peers or by the law of the land. The Judges of England developed the writ of habeas corpus largely to preserve these immunities from executive restraint. (345 US 206, 218)

Such evocative ideas are everlasting and whenever resuscitated, get carried forward enthusiastically from one generation to the next. The Great Charter (Magna Carta) has meant less to contemporaries than it has to subsequent generations. Quite early in its history, it became a symbol and a battle cry against oppression, and a battle cry it has remained. The words of the charter need to be respoken again and again as an affirmance of the people's faith in human freedoms, or a reaffirmation of the faith in 'Freedom Under Law'—stirring words that remain engraved on the plaque put up by the American Bar Association at Runnymede.

For us in India, Magna Carta stands for the 'Rule of Law' which is the bedrock of India's Constitution.

Chief Justice Subba Rao had said in *Golak Nath vs. State of Punjab – AIR 1967 S.C. 1643 (6:5)*

> "...But, having regard to the past history of our country, it could not implicitly believe the representatives of the people, for uncontrolled and unrestricted power might lead to an authoritarian State. *It, therefore, preserves the natural rights against the State encroachment and constitutes the higher judiciary of the State as the sentinel of the said rights* and the balancing wheel between the rights, subject to social control. In short, the fundamental rights, subject to social control, have been incorporated in the rule of law."

Though the majority judgment in Golak Nath (1967) stands overruled by *Kesavananda* (1973) (Bench of 13 Judges) the above – quoted dictum of Chief Justice Subba Rao has been specifically incorporated in the Bench decision of Nine Judges (in Puttaswamy – 2017 (5) SCC 1 at page 407 as establishing that "***Fundamental Rights subject to social control have been incorporated (in India) in the rule of law***". As has been stated in the main judgment (of Chief Justice D. Y. Chandrachud) in *Puttaswamy* – 2017 (5) SCC 1 page 1 419 (para 137) – "*A constitutional democracy can survive when citizens have an undiluted assurance that the Rule of Law will protect their rights and liberties against any invasion by the state and that judicial remedies would be available to ask searching questions and expect answers when a citizen has been deprived of these, most precious rights....*"

However, during trying times, like the present; in all places —(not in INDIA alone) the Rule of Law is under much stress: especially in the world of the common law.

To adopt the strict Rule of Law to modern conditions is a difficult task for Judges—first in England itself, and then also in the Commonwealth countries. For instance, in Magna Carta's Chapter 42, the following had been written:

> (*Quote*) In future, it shall be lawful for any man to leave and return to our Kingdom unharmed and without fear, by land or water, preserving his allegiance to us, except in time of war, for some short period, for the common benefit of the realm.
>
> The people that have been imprisoned or outlawed in accordance with the law of the land are excepted from this provision. (*Unquote*)

Thereby hangs a tale—the sad story of the inhabitants of Diego Garcia, an island in the Indian Ocean belonging to the British Indian Overseas Territory (BIOT) of the United Kingdom.

In 1966, the US Government had made a deal with the British Government to purchase Diego Garcia, one of the Islands in the Chagos Archipelago—about one thousand miles south of Mauritius—which was then under the suzerainty of the United Kingdom. The purchase was for establishing a joint UK/US military base there. According to human rights groups, all its 924 inhabitants—British citizens—were either tricked or terrorised into exile. In a challenge to this enforced exile in Britain's High Court, Lord Justice Laws (sitting with another judge in the Queen Bench Division QBD)[12] referred to Magna Carta, Chapter 42, and relying on its terms, declared that exile without due process was prohibited by England's fundamental law. He held that the power to legislate did not include the power to expel all inhabitants. But leave was given to file an appeal. Then in the year 2004, an Order-in-Council (under the royal prerogative) was interposed; it declared that no person had a right of abode in Diego Garcia. In the appeal filed by the government against the decision of the QBD, the 2004 Order-in-Council was invoked, and despite Magna Carta, the House of Lords held by majority (3:2) that the Order-in-Council had the force of law and the enforced exile of inhabitants of Diego Garcia was therefore justified.[13] BUT in a spirited dissent, both Lord Bingham and Lord Mance held that the Order-in-Council of 2004 was ultra vires. They said that it could not be invoked by the government because the royal prerogative had never before been exercised to 'exile an indigenous population from its homeland' and that 'authority negates the existence of such a power'; citing William Holdsworth's celebrated: *History of English Law* Vol. X 393: 'The Crown never had prerogative power to prevent its subjects from entering the Kingdom or to expel them from it.' (The majority—of three judges—in the House of Lords neither referred to nor contradicted the observations of William Holdsworth)

The dissent was in the true spirit of Magna Carta. The majority judgement, having said otherwise, it represented a setback for human rights, because the Rule of Law can only be conceived and fully realised where human rights are fully recognised and respected.

India is a Commonwealth country. It has adopted the Universal Declaration of Human Rights, 1948 drawing on its provisions when framing its 1950 Constitution. India is also a Rule of Law country. However, in the Rule of Law Index (ROLI), 2022, India has been ranked quite low—77 out of 140 countries—by the World Justice Project (WJP), which is a US-based civil society group that rates countries based on the accountability of governments and respect for the fundamental rights of peoples.

Globally, India is also ranked 94 out of 140 countries as far as adherence to fundamental rights is concerned. The overall scores and rankings of the WJP Rule of Law Index 2022[14] range from 0 to 1, where 1 indicates the strongest adherence to the Rule of Law. India's score is 0.50 whilst the score of

India's immediate neighbours is as follows: Afghanistan-0.33, Bangladesh-0.39, Pakistan-0.39, Myanmar-0.36, and Sri Lanka-0.50

In a Rule *of* Law country like India, there is much tension between individual rights protected by the Fundamental Rights Chapter of the Constitution and the good of the general public. A Rule *by* Law country like the Republic of China, for instance, has no such tension as shown by the following example: not that of a thousand people being dishoused (as in the case of Diego Garcia), but of a million people being rendered homeless, without due process, and being uprooted without their consent.

Many years ago, China's Three Gorges Dam project was initiated to tame the mighty and turbulent Yangtze river. It is the world's largest hydropower power generation plant in terms of total installed capacity and annual generation. When completed, it inundated 653 square kilometres of densely populated areas of China, whose inhabitants were peremptorily ordered (without legal recourse to any court of law) to go to other areas to accommodate this mammoth project. But because China is a Rule *by* Law country and not a country governed by the Rule *of* Law (as we know it), its government did not experience any difficulty in 're-settling' over one million people ousted (without their consent) from hearth and home.

I had asked a leading Swiss expert on dams, Prof. Raymond Lafitte, when he was visiting Delhi, as to how he viewed the Three Gorges Dam project. He thought for a while and said that it was a most laudable venture because, just after two decades it would take to build, commission, and operate, fifty million people downstream would be able to cultivate their lands without flooding and be assured of regular releases.

But then I asked, 'What about the over one million people who have been compulsorily deprived of their homes and have to shift elsewhere?

And his reply was: 'Ah, but that *is the price we must pay for future progress.*'

Too high a price in a country governed by the Rule of Law like India that has held periodic general elections every five years ever since 1952. *But progress in a Rule of Law country—like India—is painfully slow as experienced during these past seventy-five years.*

The Three Gorges Dam project in China, though beneficial in the long run, could never be replicated in a country like *India, which is a democracy based on individual rights and freedoms.* It is no use saying that China is not a democratic country. Every country which prides itself as independent stresses, either in its name or its constitution, that it is democratic, and so is the case with the PRC (the People's Republic of China). The difference is that China is not a democracy that concerns itself with individual human rights but with the greater good of an overwhelming majority of its people, i.e., the Benthamite principle of 'the greater good of the greater number'. A project like the Three Gorges Dam or any large beneficial irrigation and power project is just not possible in India since that would involve enormous hardships *in the present* for large groups of people, and in a democracy such as ours, it is the *present* that counts.

In contrast to China's Three Gorges Dam project, I cite the instance of the Narmada Dam project in Gujarat. It was designed in the 1970s to irrigate dry and drought-prone areas in Kutch and Saurashtra. The dam height was to be 455ft—one of the highest in India—which meant that water could be supplied to such far-flung areas. However, the Narmada Dam could not effectively go up to its full height for eight long years (until June 2014) when ultimately permission was received to do so. Meanwhile, Kutch and Saurashtra remained dry and drought-ridden. The Supreme Court of India, in what is called a PIL (public interest litigation), monitored and restricted the height of the dam in a series of orders, i.e., it did not permit raising the height of the dam, until those to be dishoused by the flooding (who were indigenous tribals) had been fairly and adequately rehabilitated, *according to the court and not according to the then governments* (of Gujarat and Madhya Pradesh), and this took eight long years. And since rehabilitation was delayed, justice also got delayed for the people of Kutch and Saurashtra, contrary to Magna Carta.

What is noteworthy about Magna Carta, however, is the English people's attitude to it, which is not a bit uppish or pompous. In fact, in Britain, they also make fun of it whilst following it. Although Magna Carta has been revered through the ages—the English historian Maitland called it 'a sacred text'—the people of England do not regard it as 'sacred', i.e., something immune from criticism or questioning.

In the late 1930s, two Englishmen wrote a book titled, *1066 and All That*. The year 1066 referred (of course) to the Year of the Battle of Hastings; the battle that changed the course of English history because it ended Anglo-Saxon rule and established the rule of the Normans in England. And the years between the year 1066 and 'all that' saw a host of historical events including the signing of Magna Carta and also a spoof on Magna Carta. The spoof has been extremely popular as evidenced by the fact that the book itself has been reprinted at least forty-six times. But the spoof also has a grain of truth in it, viz., *that it was only the rights of the barons that were secured by Magna Carta and not the rights of the common people*. The authors of *1066 and All That* therefore say that by congregating on the Thames, 'the barons compelled King John to sign Magna Carta (The Great Charter) to say:

1. That no one was to be put to death save for some reason *(except the common people)*;
2. That everyone should be free *(except the common people)*; and
3. That the barons should not be tried *(except by a special jury of other barons who would understand)*.'

And the book then goes on to proclaim that Magna Carta 'thus became the chief cause of democracy in England and was therefore a "good thing" for everyone *(except the common people).*'

To continue in the same vein: in India, the first twenty-five years of the working of the Fundamental Rights Chapter (Part-III) was a 'good thing' for everyone (except for the common people of India): simply because Part-IV (Directive Principles of State Policy) had been ignored by lawyers and by the courts.

Conclusion:

In a vast nation like India, despite the declaration of guarantees of fundamental rights, and despite courts striving to uphold and protect them, only so much can be accommodated and protected that does not conflict with the strong sentiments of the vast majority of 'We the People'—an observation that is prompted by the frustration of a decree of the Supreme Court of India upholding the Fundamental Right of *freedom of conscience* under Article 25 of the Constitution, of a very small minority group of citizens, on account of their unpopularity with a large cross section of general public opinion.

The case before the Supreme Court—*Bijoe Emmanuel* (1987)—concerned the adherents of a minuscule sect of Christians known as **Jehovah's Witnesses.** They numbered (and still do) less than a few thousand and lived and live mostly in the state of Kerala. Their children used to attend public schools in the state. In one such school, India's national anthem ('Jana Gana Mana') was regularly sung during the daily assembly. Children belonging to this particular Christian sect stood up respectfully but refused to sing, not because they were opposed to the words or thoughts expressed in the national anthem, but because of the tenets of their religious faith and belief. No one considered this act disrespectful and no one raised any objection until July 1985, when a member of the Legislative Assembly of Kerala, on a visit to the particular public school, noticed this. He then lodged an official complaint that three children (whose parents were Jehovah's Witnesses) did not sing the national anthem at the morning assembly. A commission of inquiry was appointed by the state government, and it reported that the children were law-abiding, showed no disrespect to the national anthem, and stood in respectful silence when it was sung, *but it confirmed that they did not sing*. Consequently, on the instructions of the inspector of schools, the three children were expelled.

A writ petition was filed in the High Court of Kerala, seeking a prohibitory order against the authorities preventing the children from attending the school. The high court rejected the plea. I was consulted and we then took an appeal to the Supreme Court of India, which reversed the verdict of the high court and held that the children did not join the singing of the national anthem in the morning assembly only because of their conscientiously held religious faith, which did not permit them to join in any rituals, except prayers to Jehovah. The apex court noted: 'Jehovah's Witnesses, wherever they are, do hold religious beliefs which may appear strange, even bizarre to us, but the sincerity of their beliefs is beyond question.' The court therefore held that the expulsion violated the fundamental right of freedom of conscience guaranteed in Article 25(1) in Part-III of the Constitution of India. The Supreme Court then directed the authorities to readmit the children to the school and permit them to pursue their studies without insisting on their singing at the morning assembly. The judgement concluded with the following eloquent remarks:

> We only wish to add—our tradition teaches tolerance; our philosophy preaches tolerance; our Constitution practises tolerance; let us not dilute it.[15]

But the public ('We the People') would have none of it. Tolerance in the face of 'unpatriotic' behaviour? Never. The then prime minister (Rajiv Gandhi) expressed shock and amazement at the decision. The then speaker of the Lok Sabha (Balram Jakhar) said he could not understand how anyone who called himself an Indian could refuse to sing the national anthem. There were also murmurs of treason. The then attorney general of India (K. Parasaran) petitioned the Supreme Court of India to review the judgement. The review petition was admitted (at first), but ultimately, the judgement was neither reviewed nor recalled—see 2003 (7) SCC 136 (5J).

Bijoe Emmanuel (1987) *remains good law but only in the law reports! The judgement was unacceptable to a large majority of so-called 'right-thinking' people. The result was that despite the verdict of the highest court, upholding a cherished fundamental right (freedom of conscience), the children were not admitted to any school in Kerala. Unpopular beliefs evoke a great deal of resentment. Jehovah's Witnesses had won their constitutional case in the Supreme Court, but lost their constitutional right, which the decision in the case had affirmed. This has been one amongst some other drawbacks in the working of the Fundamental Rights Chapter (Part-III) in these past seven decades.*

Despite Article 13(1) and 13(2) of the Constitution (declaring VOID all laws and all executive action contrary to fundamental rights) and despite the 'searchlight provisions' in the Constitution (Articles 32 and Article 226) empowering the superior courts to enforce fundamental rights by issuing writs, orders, and directions, when governments at the centre are majoritarian, as well as intolerant of the Opposition, it is useful to recall what Judge Learned Hand[16] *– had said:*

> *(Quote) Liberty lies in the hearts of men and women; when it dies there, no constitution, no law, no court can save it; no constitution, no law, no court can even do much to help it!* [17] ***(Unquote).***

Judge Learned Hand (1872-1961) had enjoyed one of the longest tenures on the Federal Bench of courts in the United States.

Against whom Fundamental Rights in Part-III can be enforced

In *Justice K. S. Puttaswamy vs. Union of India, 2017 (10) SCC 1* - a unanimous verdict of a Bench of Nine Judges - the Supreme Court of India declared '*privacy*' to be constitutionally protected as a facet of Personal Liberty, overruling not only a prior decision of a Bench of eight Judges in *M.P. Sharma vs. Satish Chandra: AIR 1954 S.C. 300*—but also the prior decision in *Kharak Singh vs. State of U.P. AIR 1963 S.C. 1295:* to the extent that it held that the right to privacy was not protected by the Constitution.

In *Puttaswamy* Justice Y.V. Chandrachud had delivered a judgment on his own behalf and on behalf of Justices J. S. Kehar and R.K. Agarwal and Abdul Nazeer and separate *concurring* judgments were delivered by each of the remaining Judges.

It is the concurring Judgment of Justice S. A. Bobde that encapsulates the ratio: as to against whom Fundamental Rights can be enforced (at page 539 of 2017 (10) SCC 1):

> (*Quote*) "397. Once we have arrived at this understanding of the nature of fundamental rights, we can dismantle a core assumption... that a right must either be a common law right or a fundamental right. The only material distinctions between the two classes of rights – of which the nature and content may be the same – lie in the incidence of the duty to respect the right *and in the forum in which a failure to do so can be redressed.* Common law rights are horizontal in their operation when they are violated by one's fellow man, he can be named and proceeded against in an ordinary court of law. Constitutional and fundamental rights, on the other hand, provide remedy against the violation of a valued interest by the 'state', as an abstract entity, whether through legislation or otherwise, as well as by identifiable public officials, being individuals clothed with the powers of the state. It is perfectly possible for an interest to simultaneously be recognized as

> a common law right and a fundamental right. ***Where the interference with a recognized interest is by the state or any other like entity recognized by Article 12, a claim for the violation of a fundamental right would lie. Where the author of an identical interference is a non-state actor, an action at common law would lie in an ordinary court.***
>
> 398. Privacy has the nature of being both a common law right as well as a fundamental right. Its content, in both forms, is identical. All that differs is the incidence of burden and the forum for enforcement for each form." (*Unquote*)

The above cited passages in the concurring judgment of Bobde J. (later, India's 47th Chief Justice) were never dissented from nor adversely commented upon in any of the other judgments in *Puttaswamy*. In fact, in a January 23, 2023 decision of the Supreme Court of India in *Kaushal Kishor vs. State of Uttar Pradesh*, the majority judgment on behalf of four Judges in a Bench of five has approvingly reproduced in extenso the above quoted paragraphs 397 and 398 in *Puttaswamy*: (see 2023 (1) SCALE 225 at page 285)—but then *erroneously* concluded that fundamental rights under Article 19 and Article 21 "*can be enforced under the Constitution against persons other than the State or its instrumentalities*"!

The law today is that where interference with a recognised interest is by the STATE (as broadly defined in Article 12) a claim to enforce a violation of a fundamental right would lie under Part-III of the Constitution - and where the interference of the right is by a non-State actor, an action at common law would lie in the regular courts.

More recently (on April 5, 2023) in the Media One case viz. *Madhyamam Broadcasting Limited vs. Union of India & Ors* [CA No. 8129 of 2022]—reported in 2023 (5) SCALE page 239— Chief Justice Y. V. Chandrachud speaking for the Court in a Bench of two Judges has said:

> "43. Two jurisprudential developments on the interpretation of Part-III of the Constitution must be noticed to understand the impact of constitutionalising the principles of natural justice. The *first*, is the expansion of the meaning of the expression 'procedure established by law'. *The second, is the shift from reading the provisions of Part-III of the Constitution as isolated silos to understanding the overlapping tendencies of fundamental rights"* (as had been expressed in a Bench decision of seven Judges in *Maneka Gandhi: 1978 (1) SCC 248*).

Article 12 defines State and includes the government and the Parliament of India and the government and legislature of each state and all local and other authorities.

Comment:

The Rights to Freedom (under Articles 14, 15, 16, 19, 20, 21, 22, 25, 26, 27, 28, 29, and 30) are against the State, as broadly defined in Article 12.

In November 1948, when draft Article 7 (now Article 12) was debated in the Constituent Assembly, Dr Ambedkar had spelt out the Object of Part-III -

> (*Quote*) The object of the Fundamental Rights is two-fold. First, that every citizen must be in a position to claim those rights. *Secondly, they must be binding upon every authority—* (that is) *upon every authority which has got either the power to make laws or the power to have discretion vested in it.* Therefore, it is quite clear that they must be binding not only upon the Central Government, they must not only be binding upon the provincial government, they must not only be binding upon the governments established in the states, they must also be binding upon district local boards, municipalities, even village panchayats and taluk boards, in

> fact, (binding on) every authority which has been created by law and which has got certain power to make laws, to make rules, or make by-laws (*Unquote*) [18]

[**NOTE**: He did not say they were binding on persons and entities other than the STATES.]

Shortly after the Constitution was enacted, a Constitution Bench of five judges of the Supreme Court of India in *P. D. Shamdasani vs. Central Bank of India* (AIR 1952 SC 59) unanimously held that:

> (*Quote*): Neither Article 19(1)(f) nor Article 31(1) was intended to prevent wrongful individual acts . . . the language and structure of Article 19 and its setting in Part-III clearly show that the article was intended to protect those freedoms against State action (*Unquote*).

And later in 1956, a Constitution Bench of five judges in *Vidya Verma vs. Shiv Narain* (AIR 1956 SC 1108) held that:

> Violation of the right to personal liberty by a private individual is not within the purview of Article 21.

In 1991, India's constitutional historian, H. M. Seervai, in his classic commentary on *The Constitutional Law of India* (4th edition, Vol. I, page 374) summed up the settled position in the following words:

> **Under Article 13(2), it is State action of a particular kind that is prohibited. *Individual invasion of individual rights is not, generally speaking, covered by Article 13(2).* For, although Articles 17, 23, and 24 show that fundamental rights can be violated by private individuals and relief against them would be available under Article 32, still, by and large, Article 13(2) is directed against State action.**

Canada, a Commonwealth country like India, has a written Constitution and its Supreme Court, in its Bench decision of seven Judges had held in *RWDSU vs. Dolphin Delivery Ltd* reported in 1986 (2) Canada, SCR 523, that the (Canadian) Charter of Freedoms (1982):

> . . . does not apply to private litigation completely divorced from any connection with government.

[And yet—as already mentioned above—in the judgement of January 3, 2023 of four Judges in a Bench of five Judges, in *Kaushal Kishor vs. State of Uttar Pradesh*—reported in 2023 (1) SCALE page 225—it was erroneously concluded—disregarding the constitutional mandate of Article 145(3)[19]—that fundamental rights under Article 19 and 21 '*can be enforced (under the Constitution) even against persons other than the State or its instrumentalities*.'!]

There is one other aspect in Article 12: In international law, the STATE includes the judicial wing of the State, *but not in India. In Article 12, the STATE, does not include the Judiciary.*

In *Naresh Shridhar Mirajkar and Ors. vs. State Of Maharashtra* (AIR 1967 SC 1), a judge of the High Court of Bombay had passed an order prohibiting the publication of the evidence of a witness during the trial of a civil suit. A reporter of a weekly (along with other journalists) moved the Supreme Court of India, under Article 32, on the ground that the order passed by the high court violated the fundamental rights of the petitioner to freedom of speech and expression under the Article 19(1)(a). A special bench of nine judges of the Supreme Court of India, by majority (8:1), rejected the petition on the ground that the judiciary was not STATE-: "*the judicial verdict pronounced by a Court in or in relation to a matter brought before it for its decision cannot be said to affect the fundamental rights of citizens under Article 19(1)*".

Under **Article 13**, enacted laws (past, present, and future) inconsistent with or in derogation of fundamental rights are declared to be void.

Comment:

In Article 13, 'law' and 'laws in force' do not include personal law.[20] (See footnote 20 for a definition of personal law.)

In *State of Bombay vs. Narasu Appa* (AIR 1952 Bom. 84), a division bench of the High Court of Bombay, consisting of Chief Justice Chagla and Justice Gajendragadkar, upheld the constitutional validity of the Hindu Bigamous Marriages Act, 1946. The Act had been challenged as contravening fundamental rights guaranteed under Articles 14, 15, and 25. It was argued inter alia that by reason of the Constitution, Muslim personal law, which admitted polygamy (was included in Article 13), had become void and that personal law was 'nothing else than custom or usage'. However, Chief Justice Chagla characterised this as 'erroneous—custom or usage is a deviation from personal law and not personal law itself.' He emphasised that 'the very presence of Article 44 in the Constitution recognises the existence of separate personal laws, and entry no. 5 in the Concurrent List (in the Seventh Schedule) gives power to state legislatures, to pass laws affecting personal law . . .' The scheme of the constitution therefore seems to be to leave personal law unaffected excerpt where specific provision is made with regard to it and to leave it to the legislatures in future to modify and improve it and ultimately put on the statute book a common and uniform code.

Chief Justice Chagla also held that 'personal law' was not included in the expression 'law in force' defined in Article 13(1). Justice Gajendragadker, in his concurring judgement, agreed. He added that personal laws in India owe their origin to scriptural texts and that the framers of the Constitution deliberately refrained from interfering with personal laws and laid down instead a directive principle in Part-IV, Article 44, that endeavour should be made hereafter to secure a Uniform Civil Code throughout the territory of India.

There were some differences of opinion in the High Courts about the applicability of Part-III to personal laws. In 2017, two judges in a bench decision of five judges of the Supreme Court of India doubted the correctness of the ruling in Narasu Appa (1952) in the Triple Talaq case [*Shayara Bano vs. Union of India*—2017 (9) SCC 5J)] but then left it 'to be determined in a suitable case'. Later, in the Sabarimala Temple case, (5J) (4:1)—2019 (11) SCC 1, Justice D. Y. Chandrachud (as he then was)—now Chief Justice of India—has opined that the Bombay High Court decision of 1952 was based on 'flawed premises' and deserved 'detailed reconsideration'. (paragraph 397 of 2019 (11) SCC at page 233).

However, neither the two Justices in the Triple Talaq case , in 2017, (Justice J. S. Kehar and Justice Abdul Nazeer) nor Justice D. Y. Chandrachud in the Sabarimala Temple Case (2019) dealt with the following point may be in the 1952 decision of the High Court of Bombay viz. that if 'personal law' was comprehended within Article 13, then there was no purpose at all for the Constituent Assembly to have enacted Article 44 (in Part-IV) as a directive principle of State policy—(Article 44 reads: The State shall *endeavour to secure* for the citizens a Uniform Civil Code throughout the territory of India). Article 44 postulates and assumes that "personal law" was not included in Article 13.

Right to Equality

Article 14: Equality before law (The State shall not deny to any person equality before the law or the equal protection of the law throughout the territory of India)

Comment:

A detailed commentary on Article 14 is contained in Chapter Four.

Article 15: Prohibition of discrimination on grounds of religion, race, caste, sex, or place of birth, but then it also provides that nothing in Article 15(1) prevents the State from making any special provision for women and children (Article 15(3)); nothing in Article 15(1) prevents the State from making any special provision for advancement of any socially and educationally backward classes of citizens or for scheduled castes and scheduled tribes (Article 15(4)); and nothing in Article 15(1) prevents the State from making special provision for the advancement of any weaker classes of citizens other than the classes mentioned in Articles 4 and 5 (Article 15(6)).[21]

Comment

Article 15(3) extends to women and children, but in *National Legal Services Authority vs. Union of India* (AIR 2014 SC 1863 (2J)), the Supreme Court of India has also given recognition to the rights of the transgender community.

Article 15(1) is more general than Article 16(1) because its operation is not limited to public employment but extends to the entire field of state discrimination. See *Indira Sawhney vs. Union of India* (AIR 1993 SC 477), para 116.

Article 16: It ensures equality of opportunity in matters of public employment (Article 16(1)). But then again, nothing in Article 16 prevents the State from making any provision for reservation of appointments or posts in favour of OBCs (backward classes of citizens) which in the opinion of the State is not adequately represented in the services under the State (Article 16(4)), and nothing in Article 16 prevents the State from making any provision for reservation in matters of promotion with consequential seniority to any class or classes of posts in the services under the State in favour of the scheduled castes and the scheduled tribes which in the opinion of the State are not adequately represented in the services under the State

(Article 16(4A)), and nothing in Article 16 prevents the State from making any provision for reservation of appointments or posts in favour of economically weaker sections of citizens (other than scheduled castes and scheduled tribes), subject to a maximum of ten per cent of the posts in each category (Article 16(6)).

There is a plethora of 'ifs-and-buts' in the Right to Equality guaranteed in Articles 14, 15, and 16 in India's Constitution.

Comment on Reservations and Quotas in Articles 15 and 16

Thomas Piketty in his Brief History of Equality (2022) has stated that "India has gone furthest in the use of quotas and India's continuing experiment in reservations and quotas illustrates the limits of such policy".

After more than 70 years of working of India's Constitution, the complexities that lie buried in the great and elusive doctrine of equality have not yet been resolved.

To what extent and for how long should the fundamental Right to Equality guaranteed in Article 14 accommodate the exceptions contained in one or more of the clauses of Articles 15 and 16? How far does the Constitution, correctly interpreted, direct us to go? Should we go on equalising downwards? The Supreme Court has been concerned with these questions for decades. In a judgement of significance (under Articles 15 and 16) *M. R. Balaji vs. State of Mysore* (AIR 1963 SC 649), Justice P. B. Gajendragadkar (speaking for a Constitution Bench of five judges) said (at page 664):

> . . . efficiency of administration is of such a paramount importance that it would be unwise and impermissible to make any reservation at the cost of efficiency of administration; that was undoubtedly the effect of Art. 335. Therefore, what is true in regard to Art. 15(4) is equally true in regard to Art. 16(4). *There can be no doubt that the Constitution-makers assumed, as they were entitled to, that while adequate reservation under Art. 16(4), care would be*

> *taken not to provide for unreasonable, excessive, or extravagant reservation, for that would, by eliminating general competition in a large field and by creating widespread dissatisfaction amongst the employees, materially affect efficiency. Therefore, like the special provision improperly made under Art. 15(4), reservation made under Art. 16(4) beyond the permissible and legitimate limits would be liable to be challenged as a fraud on the Constitution.* In this connection, it is necessary to emphasise that Art. 15(4) like Art. 16(4) is an enabling provision; it does not impose an obligation, but merely leaves it to the discretion of the appropriate government to take suitable action, if necessary.

But despite this caution, over the years the guarantee of equality, so proudly proclaimed in Article 14, has kept diminishing.

***Inequality** has been a global problem, but it is more profound in India than anywhere else in the world. The World Inequality Report 2022*[22] *(lead author Lucas Chancel) records that 'India stands out as a poor and very unequal country with an affluent elite.'*[23]

In May 1985, in *Vasant Kumar vs. State of Karnataka* (AIR 1985 SC 1495), one of the judges in a Constitution Bench of five judges (Justice D. A. Desai) deplored what he called 'the unending search for identifying socially and educationally backward classes of citizens' and the tendency of persons seeking reservations to aim downwards rather than upwards.

> For a period of three and half decades, the unending search for identifying socially and educationally backward classes of citizens has defined the policymakers, and the interpreters of the policy as reflected in statutes, or executive and administrative orders and has added a spurt in the reverse direction, namely, those who attempted to move upward (Pratilom) in the social hierarchy have put the movement in reverse gear so as to move downwards (Anulom) in order to be identified as a group or class of citizens socially and educationally backward. (page 1499)

Another judge on the bench (Justice Chinnappa Reddy) wrote:

> The paradox of the 'system of reservation' is that it has engendered a spirit of self-denigration among the people. Nowhere else in the world do castes, classes, or communities queue up for the sake of gaining the backward status. Nowhere else in the world is there competition to assert backwardness and to claim 'we are more backward than you'. This is an unhappy and disquieting situation, *but it is stark reality*. (page 1507)

But the stark reality persists! For more than 25 years after the decision in *Vasant Kumar*, there have been several cases decided by the Supreme Court of India on Articles 15 and 16 (as originally enacted with exceptions subsequently added)[24] but none of them had suggested the imposition of a *time limit for reservations*—only a maximum permissible reservation of 50 per cent for socially and educationally backward classes of citizens had been laid down by majority (7:2) in a nine-judge bench decision in *Indira Sawhney vs. Union of India* (AIR 1993 SC 477) and reaffirmed by the Constitution Bench (of five judges) in *Dr Jaishri Laxmanrao Patil vs. Chief Minister and Others* reported in 2021 (8) SCC page 1.

And yet, the Constitution 103rd Amendment Act, 2019 was passed by India's Parliament (in its constituent capacity) providing for an additional 10 per cent reservation for 'economically weaker sections of citizens (EWS) other than scheduled castes, scheduled tribes, and the non-creamy layer of the other backward classes' (both under Article 15 as well as Article 16); a constitutional challenge to the 2019 Amendment was negatived in a November 7, 2022, majority decision of the Supreme Court of India in *Janhit Abhiyan vs. Union of India*—2023 (5) SCC 1 at page 190 (paragraph 221). One of the judges (Justice Bela Trivedi) (concurring with the majority), *proposed a time limit, for reservations,* as a way out of an ultimately casteless society:

(*Quote*) Be it noted that as per Article 334 of the Constitution, the provisions of the Constitution relating to the reservation of seats for the SCs and the STs in the House of the People and in the Legislative Assemblies of the States would cease to have effect on the expiration of a period of eighty years from the commencement of the Constitution. The representation of Anglo-Indian community in the House of the Parliament and in the Legislative Assemblies of the States by nomination, has already ceased by virtue of the 104th Amendment w.e.f. 25 January 2020. Therefore, similar time limit if prescribed, *for the special provisions in respect of the reservations and representations provided in Article 15 and Article 16 of the Constitution, it could be a way forward leading to an egalitarian, casteless, and classless society*. (*Unquote*)

Another judge (Justice J. B. Pardiwala), whilst upholding the constitutional validity of the 103rd Constitutional Amendment, *suggested* that there should be a more effective process of removal of the 'creamy layer' from OBCs.

(*Quote*) Thus, reservation is not an end but a means—a means to secure social and economic justice. Reservation should not be allowed to become a vested interest. *Real solution, however, lies in eliminating the causes that have led to the social, educational, and economic backwardness of the weaker sections of the community . . . As larger percentages of backward class members attain acceptable standards of education and employment, they should be removed from the backward categories so that the attention can be paid toward those classes which genuinely need help*. (see 2023 (5) SCC 1 at page 274 (paragraph 416). (*Unquote*)

My own view is that in order to forestall further amendments prompted by political considerations, and to prevent a spiralling of quotas and reservations in future, the highest court should ensure by its edict that the minimum percentage of seats in educational institutions (including private educational institutions under Article 15) and the minimum percentage of posts in public employment (under Article 16) do not go beyond 50 per cent: otherwise, the goal of Equality guaranteed by Article 14 would become totally illusory.

Amid worldwide concerns about inequality, and amid vacillation by courts in India concerning reservation/quotas, one thing is certain: as long as poverty continues to stalk the land and gross disparities between the rich and poor remain (which over the years are getting even more pronounced with the rich getting richer but the poor are not), the ideal of an *egalitarian* society envisaged in India's basic document of governance remains a pipe dream. Whatever the nation's karma, the founding fathers cannot be faulted for a lack of idealism; they did not visualise a permanent and perpetual reservations policy. It is not because of our Constitution but despite its provisions that we have failed to achieve what were naively assumed in November 1949/January 1950 to be achievable goals. We have abolished untouchability in our Constitution (Article 17), and we had hoped and strived to outlaw social and educational (and even economic) *backwardness.* But the truth is that 'We the People' have yet to eliminate it from our hearts. Only then will the era of *backwardness* in Indian society begin to be on the way out.

Right to Freedom: Article 19

Under Article 19(1)(a): all citizens have the (fundamental) right to freedom of speech and expression

Under Article 19(1)(b): all citizens have (fundamental) right to assemble peaceably and without arms

Under Article 19(1)(c): all citizens have (fundamental) right to form associations or unions or cooperative societies

Under Article 19(1)(d): all citizens have (fundamental) right to move freely throughout the territory of India;

Under Article 19(1)(e): all citizens have (fundamental) right to have the right to reside and settle in any part of the territory of India

Under Article 19(1)(f): as enacted all citizens had the (fundamental) right to acquire, hold and dispose of property. But this provision along with Article 31 (compulsory acquisition of property) was later omitted by the Constitution Forty-Fourth (Amendment) Act 1978, wef 20-06-1979; and with Article 300A providing that "no person shall be deprived of his property save by authority of law".

Under Article 19(1)(g): all citizens have (fundamental) right to practise any profession or carry on any occupation, trade or business.

The freedoms set out in Articles 19(1)(a) to (e) and (g) are made subject to existing laws as well as future laws that impose '*reasonable* restrictions'—reasonable in the opinion of the court—on the exercise of the relevant fundamental rights set out in Articles 19(2) to (6): (see *Mithu v. State of Punjab* – 1985 (2) SCC 277 (5J): where it was stated by the Bench (of 5 Judges): "*it is for the courts to decide whether the procedure prescribed by a law for depriving a person of his life or liberty is fair, just and reasonable*".

Comment on Article 19(1)(a):

(1). Article 19(1)(a) is a pre-eminent fundamental right because it is inextricably linked to India being declared a democratic republic—'a democracy being government of the people via open discussion[25] (as was stated in 1989 (2) SCC 574 at paragraph 36).

But because of the stress on the negative aspects of free speech and expression [in Article 19(2) – 'Nothing in sub-clause (a) of clause (1) shall affect the operation of any existing law or prevent the State from making any law . . . '], the free-speech-and-expression clause has been described as representing a 'fundamental split between the confident aspirations of Article 19(1)(a) and the nervous apprehensions expressed in Article 19(2).[26]

(2) The rule in *New York Times vs. Sullivan* (1964) has been adopted in India: in *R. Rajagopal vs. State of Tamil Nadu & Others – 1994 (6) SCC 632* – a Bench of two Judges of the Supreme Court of India (Justice Jeevan Reddy and Justice Suhas Sen) – held (in paragraphs 11 and 16) that the rule in the U.S. Supreme Court judgment *New York Times Co vs. Sullivan* (1964) – which was "inherently a part of the Right to Privacy" would apply in INDIA as well. In view of Article 19(1)(a), in India the remedy of an action for damages for defamation was simply not available with respect to acts and conduct of public officials relevant to the discharge of their official duties. Of course, where the publication was proved to be false and actuated by malice or personal animosity, the defendant would have no defence and would be liable for damages.

In *New York Times Co. v. Sullivan – 376 U.S. 254 (1964)*— the U.S. Supreme Court had held - unanimously (9:0)—that a libel (defamation) must be measured by the standard that satisfies the First Amendment of the U.S. Constitution (the constitutional guarantee of freedom of speech and of the press). So too in India (in view of the fundamental right to freedom of speech and expression).

Article 19(1)(a) also bars "public officials" or "public figures" from recovering damages for defamation unless they could show that the statement in issue was made with 'actual malice' i.e. with knowledge that it was false or with a reckless disregard of whether it was false or not.

(3.) Very early in the history of India's Supreme Court, in May 1950, in *Romesh Thapar vs. State of Madras*[27] (AIR 1950 SC 124), a Constitution Bench of six judges held (5:1) that the freedom of speech and expression included 'Freedom of propagation of ideas and that Freedom was ensured by the Freedom of circulation'. The majority of five justices on the bench also stated that:

> **Very stringent limits have been set to permissible legislative abridgement of the right to free speech and expression and this was doubtless due to the realisation . . . that freedom of speech and of the press lay at the foundation of all democratic organisation for without free political discussion no public education, so essential for the proper functioning of the processes of popular government is possible.**
>
> A freedom of such amplitude might involve risks of abuse. But the framers of the Constitution may well have reflected—with Madison, who was the leading spirit in the preparation of the First Amendment of the US Federal Constitution—that 'it is better to leave a few of its noxious branches to their luxuriant growth, than by pruning them away to injure the vigour of those yielding fruit' (Quoted in *Near vs. Minnesota* (1931) Vol. 283 US 697).[28]

In the companion case, *Brij Bhushan vs. State of Delhi* (AIR 1950 SC 129 (5:1)), the the (5:1) said: There can be little doubt *that the imposition of pre-censorship on a journal is a restriction on the liberty of the press which is an essential part of the right to freedom of speech and expression declared by Article*

19(1)(a). Citing Blackstone (Commentaries), the majority then concluded that such a restriction (i.e., pre-censorship) did not fall within the reservation under 19(2), since it was an 'unreasonable restriction' even though at the time the case was decided the 'restriction' in Article 19(2) did not have to be 'reasonable'. This requirement came only with the Constitution FirstAmendment Act, 1951.

In *Sakal Papers Ltd. vs. Union of India* (AIR 1962 SC 305 (5J)), a Constitution Bench of the Supreme Court of India considered the constitutional validity of the Newspaper (Price and Page) Act 1956 where it was argued by the Union of India that a diminution of the advertisement revenue could not be regarded as an infringement of the right under Article 19(1)(a). The Court rejected the argument stating:

> If the areas of an advertisement is curtailed, the price of the newspapers will be forced up. If that happened, the circulation will inevitably go down. This would be not remote but a direct consequence of curtailment of advertisements.

And in *Bennett Coleman vs. Union of India* (AIR 1973 SC 106 at 118 (4:1)), the majority judgement held inter alia that the restriction on advertisements directly affected the fundamental right of the citizens under Article 19(1)(a) 'on the aspects of propagation, publication, and circulation'.

In *Tata Press Ltd. vs. Mahanagar Telephone Nigam Ltd.* (AIR 1995 SC 2438 (3J)), it was held that the protection of Article 19(1)(a) was available to the speaker as well as to the recipient of the speech since 'commercial speech' could not be denied the protection of Article 19(1)(a), and as a matter of fact, 'the recipient of the commercial speech may have a deeper interest in the advertisement than advertisement itself'.

The people of India owe a debt of gratitude to journalists—and the Indian press—for being instrumental in expanding the limits of the Free Speech and Expression Clause in India's Constitution as shown below:

- *Express Newspapers Pvt. Ltd. vs. Union of India,* along with eight other national newspapers (1958), filed petitions under Article 32 in the Supreme Court and succeeded in establishing that freedom of speech in Article 19(1)(a) also comprehended the Freedom of the Press in (AIR 1958 SC 578 at page 617), the court said:

> Laws which single out the press for laying upon it excessive and prohibitive burdens which would restrict circulation and ultimately drive the press to seek government aid would be struck down as unconstitutional.

Later cases extended the protection of Article 19(1)(a) to the electronic media as well. (see *LIC vs. Manubhai Shah* (1992) 3 SCC 657 and *Secretary, Ministry of Information and Broadcasting vs. Cricket Association of Bengal* 1995 (2) SCC 161).

- In *Indian Express Newspapers* (along with four other newspapers) *vs. Union of India* (AIR 1986 SC 515 (3J)), Justices Chinnappa Reddy, A. P. Sen, and Venkataramiah held (in a decision of 6 December 1984): Article 19(1)(a) could be invoked even for an indirect invasion of fundamental rights. What was challenged in that case was the levy of import duty on imported newsprint under the Customs Act 1962, which inevitably resulted in the curtailment of the circulation of large newspapers. The judgement of the court (delivered by Justice Venkataramiah) noted 'that freedom of the press' means 'freedom from interference from authority which would have the effect of interference with the content and circulation of the newspaper'.

- In *Express Newspapers Ltd. Union of India reported* in AIR 1986 SC 870 (3J) (a decision of October 7, 1985), the Indian Express had been targeted, and a bench of three judges of the Supreme Court of India gave an expanded meaning to freedom of speech and expression (as well as freedom of the press), holding that even an indirect assault on the freedom of the press would attract the fundamental right in Article 19(1)(a) as well as in Article 14. In that case, the Lessor (a governmental authority) had issued a notice of forfeiture of the lease granted to the Indian Express Buildings on Bahadur Shah Zafar Marg, New Delhi for alleged breaches of the conditions of the lease and for demolition of the buildings. A petition under Article 32 was filed in the Supreme Court of India. It was contended by the Union of India that since the Indian Express was seeking to enforce a contractual right (under the lease), the questions raised could not be decided under Article 32 of the Constitution. All three judges disagreed and Justice A. P. Sen said (when delivering the main judgement) that Article 19(1)(a) was directly infringed—

> (*Quote*) Here the very threat is to the existence of a free and independent press' (paragraph 74).
>
> Here the impugned notices of re-entry upon forfeiture of the lease and of the threatened demolition of the Express buildings are meant to silence the voice of the Indian Express. It must logically follow that the impugned notices constitute a direct and immediate threat to the freedom of the press and are thus violative of Article 19(1)(a) read with Article 14 of the Constitution. It must accordingly be held that these petitions under Article 32 are maintainable (paragraph 77). (*Unquote*)

Companion Justice Venkataramiah held (paragraph 200):

> (*Quote*) The material available in this case is sufficient to hold that the impugned notices suffer from arbitrariness and non-application of mind. They are violative of Article 14 of the Constitution. Hence they are liable to be quashed. It is not necessary therefore to express any opinion on the contentions based on Article 19(1)(a) of the Constitution. (*Unquote*)

And Justice R. B. Mishra (the third judge) said that the impugned notices threatening re-entry and demolition were invalid and of no legal value and must be quashed 'for reasons detailed in the two judgements . . .' (just delivered) (paragraph 205).

- In March 2015, in *Shreya Singal* (2015 (5) SCC 1), a bench of two judges of the Supreme Court of India followed a long line of cases (eg AIR 1951 S.C. 118 (5J) and AIR 1952 S.C. 196 (5J) that had laid down the test for determining the standard of reasonableness of the restrictions under Article 19(2). Section 66A of the Information Technology Act, 2000 penalised speech on the grounds of information being grossly offensive possessing a menacing character, causing annoyance, etc. These restrictions (the court said) did not stand the test of 'reasonableness', and, the Supreme Court struck down section 66A as unconstitutional[29]: laying stress on the phrase "reasonable restrictions" that occured in each sub-clause of Article 19(2).

The importance of Shreya Singhal (2015) is that it has laid down a 'strict-scrutiny standard' for determining the validity of speech restriction. It has also established a clear nexus between vagueness and overreach as a basis for invalidating a speech-restriction clause.

<u>**Article 20**</u>: provides that no person shall be convicted of any offence except for violation of a law in force at the time of the commission of the act charged as an offence; and that no person can be subjected to a penalty greater than that which might have been inflicted under the law in force at the time of the offence; and that no person shall be prosecuted and punished for the same offence more than once; and also that no person shall be compelled to be a witness against himself (Article 20(3)).[30]

Comment on Article 20: Self-Incriminating Statements

In the year 1961, a bench of eleven judges (constituted for the first time to decide a case) had spelt out (by a majority 8:3) a much weaker version of the Fifth Amendment of the US

Constitution: in *State of Bombay vs. Kathi Kalu* (AIR 1961 SC 1808 (8:3)). But ten years later, in *Selvi vs. State of Karnataka* (2010 (7) SCC 263), a bench of three judges of the Supreme Court of India did say that Article 20(3) protected the accused as well as suspects and witnesses from being compelled to make self-incriminating statements, and that if they were compelled to undergo a narcoanalysis test, a polygraph test, and a Brain Electrical Activation Profile (BEAP) such tests would violate the protection conferred by Article 20(3). But in a later bench decision of three judges of the Supreme Court of India, in *Ritesh Sinha vs. State of U.P.* (2019 (8) SCC 1)—following the majority decision in *State of Bombay vs. Kathi Kalu* (1961) (8:3)—it was once again held that a magistrate did have the power to order a person to give a 'voice sample for the purpose of the investigation of a crime.'

Article 21: provides that no person can be deprived of his life or liberty except according to procedure established by law.

Comment:

(A detailed commentary on Article 21 is in Chapter Four).

Suffice it to mention—in this synoptic view of India's Constitution—that the following rights have been held to flow out of Article 21 viz.: the right to go abroad (AIR 1967 S.C. 1836); the right against solitary conferment and the right to freedom from torture (1978 (4) SCC 494); right to legal aid (1978 (3) SCC 544); the right to speedy trial (1980 (3) SCC 526); right against custodial violence (1983 (2) SCC 96); right against public hanging (1989 Supp.1 SCC 264); right to a doctor's assistance at government hospitals (1989 (4) SCC 286); right to shelter (1990 (1) SCC 520); right to a healthy environment (1995 (2) SCC 577); right to compensation for unlawful arrest (1983) (4) SCC 141; right to reputation (2013 (10) SCC 591; right to earn a livelihood (1985 (3) SCC 545.

Such rights are not an exercise in constitutional amendment but only arise out of *interpreting* the right guaranteed by Article 21 of the Constitution – the emphasis on the recognition that the *Constitution places on the individual.*

It is important to note that the word "procedure" in Article 21 covers the entire process by which the deprivation is effected and "*that would include not only the adjectival but also the substantive part of the law*" (See Bachan Singh – 1980 (2) SCC 684). **And as was said by a Constitution Bench of five Judges in Mithu vs. State of Punjab – 1983 (2) SCC 277 - "the last word on the question of justice and fairness does not rest with the legislature".**

NOTE: Although all articles in Part-III could be suspended—during the period of an emergency proclaimed under Article 352—under Article 359(1)—as amended by the Constitution Forty-Fourth (Amendment) Act, 1978 it was expressly provided that neither Article 20 nor Article 21 can be suspended during the period of an Emergency.

Right to Education: Article 21A

Article 21A was inserted for the first time by the Constitution 86th Amendment Act, 2002.

<u>Article 21A</u>: states that the state shall provide free and compulsory education to all children of the age of six to fourteen years in such manner as the state may, by law, determine.

Comment on Article 21A:

Article 45 (in Part-IV) provides as a directive principle of state policy that 'the state shall endeavour to provide within a period of ten years from the commencement of this Constitution for free and compulsory education for all children until they complete the age of 14 years'. In *Unni Krishnan J. P. & Ors. vs. State of Andhra Pradesh & Ors.* (1993)[31], a Constitution Bench of the Supreme Court of India construed this to mean that the right to education (up to the age of 14 years) had matured into a fundamental right.

> *The citizens of this country have a fundamental right to education. The said right flows from Article 21.* This right, however, is not an absolute right. Its content and parameters have to be determined in the light of Article 41[32] and Article 45[33]. *In other words, every child/citizen of this country has a right to free education until he completes the age of 14 years. Thereafter his right to education is subject to the limits of the economic capacity and development of the State.*

And in the year 1996 (in *University of Delhi vs. Anand Vardhan Chandel* reported later in 2000 (10) SCC 648), another Constitution Bench of the Supreme Court of India reiterated and affirmed what had been stated in *Unni Krishnan J. P. & Ors. vs. State of Andhra Pradesh & Ors.*

Inserting Article 21A (a special provision regarding education) in the year 2002 has—in effeect—diluted this declaration of the law by the Supreme Court and has substituted for it a watered-down version because, under Article 21A, the state is not bound to provide free and compulsory education to all children up to the age of 14 years, but only between the ages of 6 to 14 years. And more importantly, even this right is conditional because the obligation of the state to provide free and compulsory education to children between the ages of 6 to 14 is limited to whatever the state chooses to provide by law ("in such manner as the state may by law determine"), this is not even a statutory right. It is only such right as the state by law chooses to give.

As to what sort of education, should be provided, attention is invited to the article 'Cleansing the Past, Creating the Future? Do (History) Books Matter?' by Kumkum Roy (retired professor of ancient history at the Centre of Historical Studies, Jawaharlal Nehru University) in which it has been stated:

> Deletions in the NCERT introductory textbook for history indicate that the slightest allusion to respect for social and cultural differences as an ideal is considered irrelevant.

(The article is reported in www.theindiaforum.in/education/cleansing-past-creating-future-do-history-books-matter).

There is another aspect. By clause (4) of the Constitution 86th Amendment Act, 2002, an additional constitutional duty has been added, viz., the obligation of the state has been substituted by a *fundamental duty* of a parent to 'provide opportunities for education' to his or her child between the ages 6 to 14 years (see Article 51A (k)). One would have thought that it was the fundamental duty of the state to provide opportunities for education and for the parent to avail of that opportunity *if the parent had the means to do so* (most parents in India do not have the means to educate their children).

To have converted a directive principle (Article 45) not enforceable in any court into a fundamental right enforceable against the state looks and sounds commendable, but not in terms of Article 21A because that Article inserted by the Constitution 86th (Amendment) Act, 2002, has diminished what had been previously proclaimed in *Unni Krishnan J. P. & Ors. vs. State of Andhra Pradesh & Ors.* (1993).

As to the need for education, in Irfan Habib's *Maulana Azad—A Life* (India's first education minister) (2023), the author recalls what Professor Romila Thapar had said (and I quote):

> Maulana Azad had advocated the idea of compulsory education for all Indians up to the age of 14. His argument was that basic education should be available to all with an emphasis on rural and girls' education. Citizens cannot discharge their duty to the State unless they are educated. *By basic education, he did not mean memorising basic questions and answers to them. The purpose of education is to learn to think, (she said), about the man who set up the University Grants Commission and the Lalit Kala Akademi...* (*Unquote*)

<u>**Article 22**</u>: It provides for protection against arrest and detention in certain cases; and a constitutional recognition of preventive detention (i.e., jail without trial).

Comment on Protection against Arrest and Detention: BAIL, NOT JAIL

Clauses (1) and (2) of Article 22 confer fundamental rights. They provide that no person can be detained in custody without being informed of the ground of his arrest and he cannot also be denied the right to consult and be defended by a legal practitioner of his choice, and every person who is arrested and detained in custody has the right to be produced within 24 hours of his arrest before the nearest magistrate and no such person can be detained in custody without the authority of such magistrate.

But more needs to be done by lawyers and by the courts to strengthen the constitutional protection afforded by Articles 22(1) and (2):

According to the National Crime Records Bureau (NCRB) as on 31 December 2021, out of a total of 5,54,034 persons in prison, as many as 4,22,165 persons were incarcerated as under-trials, who languish in jails without bail or without the means to apply for bail and waiting for their trial to commence, and (in some cases) waiting for their trial to conclude. 'Bail, not jail' the watchword made famous by Justice Krishna Iyer has remained a pious dream.

In *State of Rajasthan, Jaipur vs. Balchand Alias Baliay*: 1977 (4) SCC at page 308 - Justice Krishna Iyer, speaking in and for the highest Court, observed:

> "The basic rule may perhaps be tersely put as bail, not jail, except where there are circumstances suggestive of fleeing from justice of thwarting the course of justice or creating other troubles in the shape of repeating offences or intimidating witnesses and the like, by the petitioner who seeks enlargement on bail from the Court. We do not intend

> to be exhaustive but only illustrative.....It may well be that in most cases not monetary surety-ship but undertaking by relations of the petitioner or organisation to which he belongs may be better and more socially relevant."

In an article in the *Times of India* (April 2023), Bibek Debroy (Eminent Economist—with a penchant for law reforms) has written:

> According to NCRB, as of December 2021, there were 427,165 under-trials—*11,490 of whom have been in jail for over five years awaiting trial, a sad commentary on criminal justice delivery.*

Sad indeed. But, sophisticated modern technology does help to ensure continuing liberty of the person, as evidenced by the bail-order recently issued by the Supreme Court of India (on July 28, 2023) in a case where there was a statutory presumption of guilt (as there is in UAPA—Unlawful Activities Prevention Act, 1967 and in PMLA—Prevention of Money Laundering Act, 2002 and in the anti-narcotics law)— in one recent case, whilst granting bail, the Court directed the two accused to "keep the location status of their mobile phones active 24 hours a day"! A most useful precedent for courts to follow!

Our laws of incarceration with regard to punishment for crimes are out of date, not in tune with the times; prior attempts at reform have been unsuccessful.

Section 53 of the Indian Penal Code of 1860 provides for five forms of punishment—death; imprisonment for life; simple and rigorous imprisonment for a period; forfeiture of property and fine—there is nothing intervening between imprisonment and fine. Some attempts at innovation had been made in the past, but without success. The Indian Penal Code (Amendment) Bill, 1972 had provided for sentencing alternatives. With the restrictive use of the death penalty ('in the rarest of the rare cases', as the Supreme Court had prescribed) and a limited infrastructure for enlarging on probation, imprisonment was the only punishment available in a wide variety of cases.

This created problems of resource, and it led the Executive to look for non-custodial alternatives. The Indian Penal Code Amendment Bill of 1972 suggested three *new forms of punishment: externment, compensation to victims and public censure*. The Bill was sent to a select committee of Parliament, and in 1978 the committee rejected the proposal for externment as a form of punishment, having regard to its constitutional ramifications. *The subsequent Indian Penal Code Amendment Bill of 1978 introduced in Parliament proposed four forms of punishment: community service, compensation to victims, public censure and disqualification from holding offices in certain types of cases, for example, in white-collar crimes*. But the 1978 Bill never saw the light of day. The blame lies at the door of the lawmakers, and also the Executive, which under our Constitution is empowered to make laws by way of ordinances when Parliament is not in session.

Alternatives to custodial incarceration is the crying need of the hour.

Comment on Preventive Detention Article 22 (3) to (7):

Clauses (3) to (7) of Article 22 have no place in a Fundamental Right Chapter as they do not confer fundamental rights at all —but provide for a denial of fundamental rights because what is said to be available to all persons under Article 22(1) and (2) has been expressly denied to any person, who is arrested or detained under any *law of preventive detention* (such law being made—as regards length of preventive detention—in conformity with Article 22(4)).

It was pursuant to the provisions of Article 22(4) that on 25 February 1950, a month after the commencement of India's Constitution, that Parliament enacted independent and free India's first Preventive Detention Act, 1950 (a law that made provision for jail-without-trial).

The Preventive Detention Act, 1950 was replaced by the Maintenance of Internal Security Act, 1971 (MISA) which after its repeal has been replaced by the Conversation of Foreign Exchange and Prevention of Smuggling Activities Act, 1974 (COFEPOSA). Preventive detention is also provided for in the Prevention of Black Marketing and Maintenance of Supplies of Essential Commodities Act, 1980 and in the National Security Act, 1980.

However, it is comforting that both in the past, as well as more recently, courts have looked upon preventive detention laws unfavourably as mentioned below:

(a) In September, 1965 a year before he became India's Chief Justice (from June 1966 to April 1967), Justice Subba Rao had presided over a Constitution Bench in a case dealing with conditions of preventive detention.[34] Prabhakar Sanzgiri, who had been detained under the Defence of India Rules 1962, had written a book during the period of his enforced idleness. It was a book in Marathi titled, *Inside the Atom,* which was of scientific interest and intended to educate the uninitiated on the quantum theory. It had not even the remotest connection with the defence of India, nor was it a danger to public safety. Prabhakar wanted permission to send the book out for publication. Permission was refused. He had been detained in accordance with law and the right to move the court under Articles 19 and 21 of the Constitution had been suspended (under Articles 358 and 359). This was during the Emergency of 1962 (imposed when the Chinese had first invaded India). On a writ petition filed on behalf of Prabhakar, the Government of Maharashtra justified its order of refusal to permit the book to be published on the ground that when a person was detained, he lost his freedom and could exercise only such privileges as were conferred on him by the order of detention. The Bombay Conditions for Detention Order 1951 regulated the terms of Prabhakar's detention. It did not confer on him the privilege of writing a book and sending it out for publication. There was legal support for the state government's submission to the Court in *A. K. Gopalan's* case decided by a Constitution Bench of the court (4:1) way back in 1950 (and till then still good law).

However, Justice Subba Rao, speaking for the court, brushed aside this objection. He held that there were different aspects of personal liberty. And having forfeited his right to move about freely by reason of the detention order, the detenu had not forfeited his other freedoms and the liberty to write and publish a book was one such freedom that had not been taken away under the Defence of India Rules, 1962. The Bombay Condition of Detention Order laid down restrictions on the liberty of the detenu—this did not mean that he could not exercise his other rights. The Subba Rao Court turned the argument of the state on its head, revealing its absurdity. 'If the argument (for the state) were to be accepted, he wrote, 'this would mean that the detenu could be starved to death if there was no condition that he was to be provided with food.' The court held that the refusal of the authorities to send the manuscript of the book out of the jail for publication was contrary to law.

It was the Constitution Bench decision in *Prabhakar's* case (1968) that influenced a spate of later decisions on preventive detention: In the late 1970s and the early 1980s, in *Hoskot* (1973 (1) SCR 192), in the (two) *Sunil Batra's* cases (1979 (1) SCR 392 and 1980 (2) SCR 557), and in *Francis Coralie* (AIR 1981 SC 746).

b) More recently, on 14 November 2022, the Madurai Bench of the Madras High Court[35] began its judgement in a group of cases as follows: '*The cases on hand gave us a wake-up call and made us ask ourselves as to whether we have become complacent while dealing with preventive detention . . .'* (2022 SC Online Madras 5278) Judges (Justices M. S. Ramesh and N. Anand Venkatesh) have aptly described prevention detention laws as 'a freckle on the constitutional canvas' and gone on to say that it was high time that the court 'starts imposing compensation on the state whenever it interferes with preventive detention orders in deserving cases'. And (in the group of cases before it) the court then concluded:

> We therefore hold that while quashing preventive detention orders, if the court finds that the detention was based on non-existent or irrelevant grounds, the consequence would be that the state would be mulcted in punitive damages for depriving the liberty of the subject, without any lawful justification.

This is a novel but refreshing aspect of the court's antipathy towards preventive detention laws.

(c) Most important is the 10 April 2023 decision (in a criminal appeal) reported in 2023 Vol.5 SCALE 559 (*Pramod Single vs. Union of India & Ors.*) of a bench of two judges of the Supreme Court of India a detention order was passed against the appellant (in *Pramod Singla vs. Union of India & Ors.*) under the COFEPOSA Act. His representation under Article 22(5) having been rejected, Singla filed a writ petition in the Delhi High Court against his detention, and since no relief was granted to him by that court, he approached the Supreme Court of India under Article 136 of the Constitution. The Supreme Court of India set aside the detention order dated 1 February 2022 with the following observations:

(*Quote*) We find it important to note that preventive detention laws in India are a colonial legacy, and have a great potential to be abused and misused. Laws that have the ability to confer arbitrary powers to the state, must in all circumstances, be very critically examined, and must be used only in the rarest of rare cases. *In cases of preventive detention, where the detenue is held in arrest not for a crime he has committed, but for a potential crime he may commit, the courts must always give every benefit of doubt in favour of the detenue, and even the slightest of errors in procedural compliances must result in favour of the detenue.*

At the sake of repetition, we find it important to state that in cases of preventive detention, every procedural irregularity, keeping in mind the principles of Article 21 and Article 22(5) of the Constitution of India, must be adjudged in favour of the detenue. In the present case at hand, the appellant detenue herein has been supplied with illegible documents in a foreign language. It is also important to note that these are the very same documents that the authorities have relied upon to detain the appellant herein.

Preventive detention laws in India are a colonial legacy, and as such, are extremely powerful laws that have the ability to confer arbitrary power to the state. In such a circumstance, *where there is a possibility of an unfettered discretion of power by the government, this court must analyse cases arising from such laws with extreme caution and excruciating detail, to ensure that there are checks and balances on the power of the government.* Every procedural rigidity must be followed in entirety by the government in cases of preventive detention, and every lapse in procedure must give rise to a benefit to the case of the detenue.

> The courts, in circumstances of preventive detention, are conferred with the duty that has been given the utmost importance by the Constitution, which is the protection of individual and civil liberties. This act of protecting civil liberties, is not just the saving of rights of individuals in person and the society at large, but is also an act of preserving our constitutional ethos, which is a product of a series of struggles against the arbitrary power of the British state. (*Unquote*)

Article 23: Prohibition of trafficking in human beings and forced labour

Article 24: Prohibition of employment of children in factories, etc.

Comment on Articles 23 and 24:

Article 23 prohibits trafficking in human beings and also prohibits inter alia 'forced labour'. In *Peoples Union for Democratic Rights vs. Union of India* (1982 (3) SCC 235), the Supreme Court of India held that the practice of forced labour was not limited in its application against the state but was also enforceable against any other person indulging in such practice. And following on this, the court also held (in *Sanjit Roy vs. State of Rajasthan* (1983 (1) SCC 525)) but with only one of the two judges on the bench so holding (Justice Bhagwati) that where workers were not paid minimum wages, this had to be also treated also as forced labour. The other judge on the bench (Justice Pathak) held that paying a labourer wages below the statutory minimum wage was a violation of Article 14.

Right to Freedom of Religion

Article 25: It allows for freedom of conscience and free profession, practice, and propagation of religion.

Article 26: It allows for freedom to manage religious affairs.

Article 27: It allows for freedom as to payment of taxes for promotion of any particular religion.

Article 28: It allows for freedom as to attendance at religious instruction or religious worship in certain educational institutions (no person attending any educational institution recognised by the state or receiving aid out of state funds can be required to like part in any religious that may be imparted in such institution).

Comment:

In the recent *Sabarimala Temple* case reported in (2019) 11 SCC page 1, a Constitution Bench of five judges held by majority (4:1) that:

> (*Quote*) 144.2 Article 25(1), by employing the expression 'all persons', demonstrates that the freedom of conscience and the right to freely profess, practise, and propagate religion is available, though subject to the restrictions delineated in Article 25(1) itself, to every person including women: "The right guaranteed under Article 25(1) has nothing to do with gender or, for that matter, certain physiological factors specifically attributable to women".
>
> 144.4 The impugned Rule 3(b) of the 1965 Rules, framed under the 1965 Act, that stipulates exclusion of entry of women of the age group of 10 to 50 years, is a clear violation of the right of Hindu women to practise their religious beliefs which, in consequence, makes their fundamental right of religion under Article 25(1) a dead letter. (*Unquote*)

But the majority decision was thereafter subjected to a review in the *Sabarimala Temple* case (Review 5 J) reported 2020 (2) SCC page 1, and a review was ordered by a majority (3:2), where seven questions were framed for determination as to the true interpretation of Article 25 and 26, and the seven questions were referred to a larger bench pending the review in the case at hand.

Pursuant to this, in January 2020, a special bench of nine judges was constituted (by the then Chief Justice of India) and the Bench reformulated the questions as follows[36]:

> 2.1 (1) What is the scope and ambit of right to freedom of religion under Article 25 of the Constitution of India?
>
> 2.2 (2) What is the interplay between the rights of persons under Article 25 of the Constitution of India and rights of religious denominations under Article 26 of the Constitution of India?
>
> 2.3 (3) Whether the rights of a religious denomination under Article 26 of the Constitution of India are subject to other provisions of Part-III of the Constitution of India apart from public order, morality, and health?
>
> 2.4 (4) What is the scope and extent of the word 'morality' under Articles 25 and 26 of the Constitution of India and whether it is meant to include constitutional morality?
>
> 2.5 (5) What is the scope and extent of judicial review with regard to a religious practice as referred to in Article 25 of the Constitution of India?
>
> 2.6 (6) What is the meaning of the expression 'sections of Hindus' occurring in Article 25(2)(b) of the Constitution of India?
>
> 2.7 (7) Whether a person not belonging to a religious denomination or religious group can question a practice of that religious denomination or religious group by filing a PIL?

The special bench of nine judges was not able to proceed much further because of the onset of Covid-19 in March 2020 and the Bench has not been reconstituted since then.

Meanwhile in a recent judgement in *Central Board of Dawoodi Bohra Community vs. State of Maharashtra* (2023 (2) SCALE page 617) handed down on 10 February 2023 another bench of five hon'ble judges has referred to a bench of nine judges for reconsideration a prior decision of the Supreme Court of India in *Syedna Saifuddin Saheb vs. State of Bombay* (1962 Supp.2 SCR 496); a decision that upheld (4:1) the right of the spiritual leader of the community of Bohras (the Syedna) to excommunicate its members for serious religious infractions. This reference was made on the ground that the majority decision in *Syedna* (1962) fell within questions 2.3(3) and 2.4(4) framed in *Sabarimala* (quoted above). The decision in *Syedna* (1962) therefore now stands referred to a bench of nine judges (as and when it is reconstituted by the Chief Justice of India).

Cultural and Educational Rights

Article 29(1): It provides any section of citizens residing in the territory of India or any part thereof having a distinct language, script, or culture of its own shall have the right to conserve the same.

Article 29(2): It states that no citizen shall be denied admission into any educational institution maintained by the State or receiving aid out of State funds on grounds only of religion, race, caste, language, or any of them.

Article 30(1): It states that all minorities, whether based on religion or language, shall have the right to establish and administer educational institutions of their choice.

> [Under Article 30(1A)—In making any law providing for the compulsory acquisition of any property of an educational institution established and administered by a minority, referred to in clause (1), the State shall ensure that the amount fixed by or determined under such law for the

acquisition of such property is such as would not restrict or abrogate the right guaranteed under that clause.]

Article 30(2): provides that the State shall not, in granting aid to educational institutions, discriminate against any educational institution on the ground that it is under the management of a minority, whether based on religion or language.

Comment on Article 30:

The following are the leading cases on educational rights of minorities:

(i) In Re: Kerala Education Bill, 1957 presidential reference under Article 143(1) of the Constitution reported in 1959 1 SCR 995 (bench of seven judges) declared the law as to who were to be regarded as 'minorities' in a state:

> Article 30(1) of the Constitution which was a necessary concomitant to Article 29(1) and gave the minorities the right to establish and administer their institutions, did not define the word 'minority' nor was it defined anywhere else by the Constitution, but it was absurd to suggest that a minority or section envisaged by Article 30(1) and Article 29(1) could mean only such persons as constituted a numerical minority in the particular region where the educational institution was situated or resided under a local authority. Article 350A[37] of the Constitution, properly construed, could lend no support to such a proposition. *As the impugned bill (Kerala Education Bill) extended to the entire state, minorities in the state must be determined on the basis of its entire population, and thus the Christians, the Muslims, and the Anglo-Indians would be its minority communities.*

(ii) In *Ahmedabad St. Xaviers College. vs. State of Gujarat & Anr* (bench of nine judges reported in AIR 1974 S.C. 1389 = 1974 (1) SCC 717), the court unanimously held that since decision in the Kerala Education Bill case (1959), Article 30(1) 'covers institutions imparting general secular education': "The object of Article 30(1) is to enable children of minorities to go out in the world fully equipped and it would be wrong to read Article 30(1) as restricting the right of minorities to establish and administer educational institutions of their choice only to cases where such institutions, were concerned with language, script, or culture of the minorities. Article 30 covered (the court said) the entire field of secular education in schools and colleges".

But what the minorities secured in the first two cases got lost in the next case (a decision of a bench of eleven judges that dealt with minority educational institutions (MEIs) for post-graduate courses in medicine, engineering and the like).

(iii) Even though Article 30 had declared that all minorities whether based on religion or language shall have the right to establish and administer educational institutions 'of their choice', in *TMA Pai Foundation* reported in 2002 (8) SCC 481, the court did not grant autonomy to minority educational institutions (MEI) as had been proclaimed in Article 30(1). The difficulty felt by the bench of eleven justices (in *TMA Pai*) was how to reconcile the provisions of Article 30 with the seemingly contrary provisions contained in Article 29(2) (no citizen shall be denied admission into *any educational institution* maintained by the state or receiving aid out of state funds on grounds only religion race, caste, language, or any of them). The inarticulate major premise underlying the decision of the justices who constituted the majority in the eleven-judge bench in *TMA Pai* (at least six judges out of eleven) was the strong suspicion that many of the MEIs were selling seats to the highest bidder and were therefore disentitled to invoke the fundamental right granted to minorities in Article 30. In the very first case (*Kerala Education Reference*, 1959), Chief Justice S. R. Das had warned that the fundamental right to *administer* did not include the right to mal-administer. In the view of most of the judges on the bench (in *TMA Pai*), state-aided MEIs which had established institutions for post-graduate courses in medicine, engineering, and the like were claiming a fundamental right to administer them solely with a view to profiteer from the admission and allotment of seats—in other words to mal-administer. The ultimate majority decision in *TMA Pai* (2002) was not the result of a textual or even a contextual interpretation of Article 30, but was rendered only because of the apprehension of the court that treating the right of minorities as absolute (as Article 30 was worded) would totally negate the claim of the state to regulate MEIs—especially in higher education—and hence the control of the state not only in higher education but at all levels of education was upheld.

The content and ambit of minority rights under Article 30 (for state-aided MEIs) stands diminished after the decision in TMA Pai (2002), since the latter decision has approximated the fundamental right of all minority educational institutions guaranteed under Article 30 to establish and maintain educational institutions to an 'occupation'. Under Article 19(1)(g) of the Constitution, the right to carry on an occupation is (and was) always subject to reasonable restrictions that may be imposed by law in public interest. Fundamental rights of MEIs thus got devalued, because approximating the provisions in Article 30 to the provisions contained in Article 19(1)(g) meant, that, the 'reasonable restrictions' imposed by ordinary law on this fundamental right—permissible under Article 19(6)—had also got subsumed in what was an otherwise unrestricted fundamental right guaranteed under Article 30.

Re: Muslims—In the 30th May 2023 issue of *The Hindu*, it was reported as follows:

> *All India Survey on Education conducted under the Ministry of Education, GOI (2020-2021) presents a dismal picture of the Muslim community.* At a time when the enrolment of scheduled castes, scheduled tribes, and other backward classes (OBCs) in higher education improved by 4.2 per cent, 11.9 per cent, and 4 per cent respectively, compared with 2019-2020, the Muslim community's enrolment declined by 8 per cent, numbering around 1,79,000 students. This unprecedented decline, caused partially by the Covid-19 pandemic, points to the relative economic impoverishment of the community, which forces its talented students to pursue earning opportunities after completing schooling rather than enrolling for higher education, beginning at the graduation level.[38]

Exceptions to and Exemptions from Fundamental Rights

Justice M. Hidayatullah (Judge, Supreme Court of India from 1958-1968) had memorably said that 'ours is the only constitution that needs protection against itself.' Article 31 (A), 31(B) & 31(C) had been added as constitutional amendments as a protection against the enforcement of fundamental rights in Part-III!

Comment on Articles 31A, 31B, and 31C

Article 31A: Saving of laws providing for acquisition of estates and land reform—such laws are exempted from the operation of the Fundamental Rights Chapter.

Article 31A was originally inserted by the Constitution First Amendment Act, 1951 and amended by the Constitution Fourth Amendment Act, 1955 (w.e.f. the commencement of the Constitution). In *Waman Rao vs. Union of India* (1981 (2) SCC 362 (5J)), Article 31A has been held not to damage or destroy the basic structure of the Constitution.

Article 31B: Validation of certain acts and regulations.

According to Article 31B—also added by the Constitution 1st Amendment Act, 1951—none of the Acts originally mentioned (in the Ninth Schedule)—as well as further laws that were added or may be added subsequently in the Ninth Schedule by government—were not to be void nor deemed to be void for contravention of fundamental rights, notwithstanding any judgement decree or order of a court.

Since 1951, the Ninth Schedule stood enlarged to include as many as 284 laws and regulations which were not to be declared void only because of their inclusion in the Ninth Schedule under Article 31B.

Article 31B was initially held valid in *State of Bihar vs. Kameshwar Singh* (AIR 1952 SC 252). However, in *Kesavananda Bharati vs. State of Kerala* (AIR 1973 SC 1461), decided on April 24, 1973 by a special bench of thirteen judges, it was held by majority (7:6) that Parliament had no power to amend the Constitution so as to damage or destroy its basic or essential features or its basic structure; and consequently in *Waman Rao vs. Union of India* (1981 (2) SCC 362), it was held (by a Constitution Bench of five judges) that all amendments to the Constitution that were made before 24 April 1973, by which the Ninth Schedule to the Constitution had been amended from time to time by the inclusion of various acts and regulations therein, were to be regarded as valid and constitutional, but that laws added to the Ninth Schedule *on or after 24 April 1973*, were (and would be in the future also) open to challenge on the ground that they, or any one or more of them, were (or are) beyond the amendment power of Parliament *if it is shown that they damage the basic or essential features of the Constitution or its basic structure.*

Article 31B has been "read down" after the decision of the Bench of 13 Judges (7:6)—*Kesavananda Bharati* (1973) and it is now virtually "a dead letter".

Article 31C[39]: Saving of laws giving effect to provisions in Article 39(a) and 39(b), the Directive Principles of State Policy (in Part-IV).

Article 31C had been added by the Constitution 25th Amendment Act 1971, and it was later amended by the Constitution 42nd Amendment Act, 1974, to save all laws giving effect to all or any of the provisions in Part-IV, but this later amendment has been invalidated as stated below.

In *Kesavananda Bharati* (AIR 1973 SC 1461), the Supreme Court of India had held in a bench decision of thirteen justices (7:6) that Article 31C as enacted in 1971 was valid but that only the following words in Article 31C as enacted in 1971 were invalid, viz., 'and no law containing a declaration that it is for giving effect to such policy (i.e., of securing all or any of the principles in Part-IV) shall be called in question on the ground that it does not give effect to such policy', because whether there was a valid nexus between the Directive Principles of State Policy and the law enacted being in conformity with fundamental rights was a matter to be determined *exclusively* by the courts.

But after the amendment (by enlargement) of Article 31C by the Constitution 42nd Amendment Act, 1976, the Supreme Court, in its later decision in *Waman Rao vs. Union of India* (1981 (2) SCC 362 on page 403) (4:1) held that Article 31C was valid only as it stood prior to its further amendment by Sec.4 of the Constitution 42nd Amendment Act, 1976, i.e., in so far as it protected laws enacted pursuant to the provisions contained in Article 39(b) and (c) in Part-IV (i.e., towards securing that the ownership and control of material resources of the community should be so distributed as to subserve the common good, and also powers ensuring that the operation of the economic system does not result in concentration of wealth).

Judicial Review of Constitutional Amendments: whether in India a Constitutional Amendment Can Be Challenged as Unconstitutional[40]: (Also see Note (1) below as well as footnote No.40)

Initially, in 1951, a Constitution Bench had said NO—all five judges—in *Shankari Prasad vs. Union of India* (AIR 1951 SC 458)[41] ("to make a law which contravenes the Constitution constitutionally valid is a matter of constitutional amendment and as such it falls within the exclusive power of Parliament").

Fourteen years later, a Constitution Bench of five judges once again said no in *Sajjan Singh vs. State of Rajasthan* (AIR 1965 SC 845[42]), but this time, not unanimously: Justice M. Hidayatullah (whilst following the decision in *Sajjan Singh* (1951) as a binding precedent) observed:

> (*Quote*) I find some difficulty in accepting a part of the reasoning in *Shankari Prasad* (1951) . . . I reserve my opinion on that case I apprehend that it depends how wide is the word 'law' . . . I would require stronger reasons than those given in *Shankari Prasad* to make me accept the view that fundamental rights are not really fundamental . . . *The Constitution gives so many guarantees in Part-III that it would be difficult to think that they were the playthings of a special majority.* (*Unquote*)

Justice Mudholkar (whilst also following *Sajjan Singh* as a binding precedent) said:

> I do not regard what this court has said—in *Shankari Prasad*—as the last word . . . and I doubt whether the power to amend could be exercised with respect to *any of the basic features of the Constitution.*

Later on, the question of *whether there were any limitations in the power of amendment* was referred (by Chief Justice Subba Rao) to a bench of eleven judges. The bench decision of eleven judges (presided over by Chief Justice Subba Rao) in *Golaknath (Golaknath vs. State of Punjab* AIR 1967 SC 1643) held—by majority (6:5)—that an amendment of the Constitution was 'law' and if such law took away or abridged the rights conferred by Part-III such amendment was 'void' because of Article 13(2).

However, when the constitutional validity of subsequent Constitutional Amendments—the 24th, 25th, and 29th Amendment Acts (of 1971 and 1972) enacted by Parliament after *Golaknath* (1967)—were once again challenged as unconstitutional, and the reference was heard by a larger bench of thirteen judges in *Kesavananda* (1973). It was held in *Kesavananda* (almost unanimously—12:1) that a constitutional amendment under Article 368 was not 'law' under Article 13, and the majority decision in *Golaknath* (1967) was overruled.

But in *Kesavananda* (1973), it was also held—by a narrow majority (7:6)—that although it was permissible under the power of amendment to effect changes (howsoever important) and to readapt the system to the requirement of changing conditions.

> "It is not permissible to touch the foundations, to alter the basic institutional pattern".

This heralded what is now known as the 'basic structure doctrine' which after the decisions in *Kesavananda* (1973)—as well as in *Raj Narain* (1975)—continues as good law.

The critically decisive paragraphs in *Kesavananda* are to be found in the judgement of Justice Khanna in *Kesavananda* (1973)[43].

Note-(1): The author of an article titled, 'Unconstitutional Constitutional Amendments—The Migration and Success of a Constitutional Idea' (reproduced in the *American Journal of Comparative Law*, Vol. 61, pages 657-717) has concluded as follows:

> *(Quote)* It is clear that the limitations on the amendment power are not identical everywhere. As noted above, each state has its own supra-constitutional principles. Some states have broad limitations on the amending power, others narrow ones. In some states, these limits are enforceable in courts; in others, they are not. This story demonstrates not only that constitutional ideas may migrate through different jurisdictions, but also that these ideas can be redesigned or reshaped in order to accommodate each jurisdiction's unique constitutional setting, history, culture, and design. As Mary Ann Glendon notes, 'the problems confronting different societies are frequently the same, but the solutions are different inasmuch as they must be tailored to the particular needs of each society'. Therefore, the investigation of the limits of amendatory power can be useful not only in shedding light on the concept of 'unconstitutional constitutional amendments' but also in clarifying the constitutional order, culture, and identity of specific states . . .
>
> The spread of the idea of limitations to the constitutional amendment power, coupled with the practice of judicial review of constitutional amendments opens up great opportunities for constitutionalism. The expansion of limits on constitutional amendments and the basic structure

> doctrine can be seen as a straightforward attempt by courts to 'ensure the survival and operation of democratic institutions', while curbing abuse of the amendment power. *(Unquote)*

Note-(2): After his retirement as Chief Justice of India (in April 1967), K. Subba Rao, principal author of the majority judgement in *Golaknath* (1967), (in an address to the Nagpur University in September 1967) whilst speaking on 'Amendments to the Constitution', had said:

> *(Quote)* By describing the power under Article 368 as constituent power, the amendment made does not cease to be one made in exercise of the power under the Constitution. However you may describe the power, the law of amendment is made in exercise of the power under the Constitution. If so looked at the nomenclature given to the power has no relevance to the enquiry.
>
> That apart let me analyse this concept of constituent power. 'The constituent power' is the power to elect representatives charged with the making or changing a Constitution. This power rests with the people. They can elect a Constituent Assembly and confer the power on them. *The Constituent Assembly after making a Constitution becomes functus officio. The said Assembly cannot confer that constituent power on any of the institutions created under the Constitution.* It may confer a wide power of amendment on one of the institutions but that power of amendment is exercised under the Constitution, and therefore is not a constituent power. If the Parliament seeks to change the Constitution otherwise than by law of amendment, it can only seek the help of the people to create a new Constituent Assembly. This the Parliament can do in the exercise of residuary power.[44] (*Unquote*)

For more on judicial review of constitutional amendments, see the detailed discussion on the Union Judiciary in Chapter Six.

<u>Article 32</u>: Remedies for enforcement of rights conferred by Part-III

Comment:

The Supreme Court of India is conferred the power to issue directions or orders or writs including writs in the nature of *habeas corpus, mandamus, prohibition, quo warranto,* and *certiorari* for enforcement of the rights conferred by Part-III as are the high courts under Article 226. In addition, under Article 32(3), Parliament may by law empower any other court to exercise within the local limits of its jurisdiction all or any of the powers exercisable by the Supreme Court (no such law has been so far passed).

The importance of Article 32 in the Constitution had been stressed by Dr Ambedkar in the Constituent Assembly. Speaking on 9 December 1948, he said:

> Now, sir I am very glad that the majority of those who spoke on this article have realised the importance and the significance of this article. *If I was asked to name any particular article in this Constitution as the most important an article without which this Constitution would be a nullity. I could not refer to any other article except this one. It is the very soul of the Constitution and the very heart of it and I am glad that the house has realised its importance . . .*

Speaking particularly about the named writs that the Supreme Court was empowered to issue under Article 32, viz., *habeas corpus, mandamus, prohibition, quo warranto* and *certiorari*, Dr Ambedkar also said:

> . . . It is not that the Supreme Court is left to be invested with the power to issue these writs by a law to be made by the legislature at its sweet will. The Constitution has invested the Supreme Court with these rights and these writs could not be taken away unless and until the Constitution itself

> is amended by means left open to the legislature. *This in my judgement is one of the greatest safeguards that can be provided for the safety and security of the individual. We need not therefore have much apprehension that the freedoms which this Constitution has provided will be taken away by any legislature merely because it happens to have a majority.*[45]

Article 33: Power of Parliament to modify the rights conferred by Part-III in their application to armed forces, etc.

Article 34: Restriction on rights conferred by Part-III while martial law is in force

Comment:

Under the Constitution, members of the armed forces, though citizens, may have their rights curtailed in the wider national interest (Article 33). And even qua all other citizens, there is hidden, within the provisions of Article 34, the possibility of a declaration of martial law in any particular part of the country and that of indemnifying any person in respect of any acts done in connection with the maintenance of restoration of order in any area within the territory of India where such martial law was in force, despite many provocations; but thanks to the wisdom of successive governments, at the centre, 'martial law' has never been resorted to in any part of India.

Article 34 as enacted and in force is primarily concerned with granting indemnity by law in respect of acts done during periods of martial law. The Constitution does not contain a provision authorising a declaration of martial law.

Article 35: Legislation for giving effect to the provisions of Part-III. Notwithstanding anything in the Constitution, Parliament has (and the legislature of a state does not have) the power to make laws with respect to matters set out in Article 16(3)[46], in Article 32(3)[47], and in Articles 33 and 34.

More commentary on different aspects of fundamental rights can be found in Chapter Four which deals with the Preamble and the concepts of Justice, Liberty, Equality, and Fraternity.

---------- Part-IV----------

Parts III and IV together constitute the "conscience of the Constitution". (see Chapter Five).

Directive Principles of State Policy—Articles 36 to 51

Article 36: Definition of State.

Article 37: Application of the principles contained in this Part.

Article 38: State to secure a social order for the promotion of welfare of the people.

Article 39: Certain principles of policy to be followed by the State

Article 39A: Equal justice and free legal aid (added by the Constitution 42nd Amendment Act, 1976).

Article 40: Organisation of village panchayats.

Article 41: Right to work, to education, and to public assistance in certain cases

Article 42: Provision for just and humane conditions of work and maternity relief

Article 43: Living wage, etc., for workers.

Article 43A: Participation of workers in management of industries (added by the Constitution 42nd Amendment Act, 1976).

Article 43B: Promotion of cooperative societies (added by the Constitution 97th Amendment Act, 2011).

Article 44: Uniform Civil Code for the Citizens

Article 45: Provision for early childhood care and education to children below the age of six years.

Article 46: Promotion of educational and economic interests of Scheduled Castes, Scheduled Tribes, and other weaker sections.

Article 47: Duty of the State to raise the level of nutrition and the standard of living and to improve public health.

Article 48: Organisation of agriculture and animal husbandry.

Article 48A: Protection and improvement of environment and safeguarding of forests and wildlife (added by the Constitution 42nd Amendment Act, 1976).

Article 49: Protection of monuments and places and objects of national importance.

Article 50: Separation of judiciary from executive.

Article 51: Promotion of international peace and security.

Comment on Part IV:

Article 36: Definition of "State" (In Part-IV STATE has the same meaning as in Part-III).

Article 37: Application of the principles contained in this Part.

The provisions contained in this Part shall not be enforceable by any court, but the principles therein laid down are nevertheless fundamental in the governance of the country and it shall be the duty of the State to apply these principles in making laws.
The original text of what was to become Article 37 of the Constitution was a liberal adaptation of Article 45 of the Irish Constitution . . . Article 37's claim to fame is that it was introduced during the debates on the draft constitution by and at the suggestion of two out of the 17 women members of the Constituent Assembly, viz., Rajkumari Amrit Kaur and Hansa Mehta.[48]

Article 38: State to secure a social order for the promotion of welfare of the people.

Article 39: Certain principles of policy to be followed by the State. The State shall in particular direct its policy towards securing:

(a) . . .

(b) that the ownership and control of the material resources of the community are so distributed as best to subserve the common good;

(c) that the operation of the economic system does not result in the concentration of wealth and means of production to the common detriment;

(d) . . .

(e) . . .

(f) . . .

Under Article 31C (added by the Constitution 25th Amendment Act, 1971 (w.e.f. 24 April 1972), notwithstanding anything contained in Article 13, no law giving effect to the policy of the state towards securing the matters mentioned in Article 39(b) and (c) shall be deemed to be void on the ground that it is inconsistent with or takes away or abridges any of the rights conferred by Article 14 or Article 19.

The above-stated part of Article 31C has been held not to violate the basic structure or framework of the Constitution.

However, Article 31C (the valid part) in no way bars judicial review as to whether a nexus has been established between the law impugned and the provisions of Article 39(b) and (c), as was held in *Assam Sillimanite vs. Union of India* (AIR 1992 SC 938 (2J)).

Article 44: Uniform civil code for the citizens. The State shall endeavour to secure for the citizens a uniform civil code throughout the territory of India.

Comment on Article 44 (Uniform Civil Code)

A renewed 'push' for a Uniform Civil Code—which many communities perceive as an encroachment into their personal laws and religious-rights is presently under way!

In constitutional democracies based on majority rule, courts lean in favour of minorities, not because minorities are always right—very often they are not—but simply because in the normal political process, they do not have the votes necessary to translate their aspirations into law. In many decisions of our highest court over the years, expression has been given to the popular majoritarian view about the need for a common civil code.[49] In *John Vallamattom vs. Union of India* (AIR 2003 SC 2902), Chief Justice Khare, sitting in a bench of three judges, had said:

> It is a matter of regret that Article 14 of the Constitution has not been given effect to . . . *A common civil code will help the cause of national integration by removing contradictions based on ideologies.*

Permit me however to present a non-populist, minority view:

> Do we really need a uniform civil code? The people—'We the People' (with which our Constitution begins)—have not said so. All that Article 44 states is that the State shall *endeavour to secure* for the citizens a uniform civil code throughout the territory of India, and this provision is expressly made not enforceable in courts (Article 37). Then why do 'WE' (obviously mainly the majority community) feel the need for a uniform civil code for "THEM" (the largest single minority) in matters as private and personal as birth, marriage, divorce, and death? In all other matters—in civil procedure, in criminal procedure, in penal law, in contract, in transfer of property, in evidence—we already have in place a uniform set of laws applicable to all.

It was said of Lord Salisbury[50] (the man who succeeded Benjamin Disraeli as prime minister of England) that it was his firm belief that only uncontentious legislation should be brought before Parliament and if it was controversial, then England was not ready for it. When we think of adopting a common civil code, I would advocate the 'Salisbury approach', because it is with small beginnings that we will ultimately achieve—without rancour or bitterness—what the directive principle of state policy in Article 44 projects as our ultimate national goal. And we are already getting results. Take the example of the Special Marriage Act of 1954. Those who register their marriages under it are entitled to do so without having to renounce their religion (Under the now repealed Special Marriage Act of 1872 parties who wanted a marriage to be registered under that Act were compelled to renounce their religion). And all communities—Hindus, Muslims, Parsis, Christians and Sikhs, Buddhists, and Jains—are now permitted to have a divorce by mutual consent if they have been living separately for one year or more and have mutually agreed that the marriage should be dissolved. They don't need to prove marital misconduct required under their own personal laws (Section 28 of the Special Marriage Act, 1954). Silently, this Act of Parliament has established—without pressure, and by consensus—a uniform law for marriage and divorce, which is not a binding code, but an enabling one. And this is what was intended by Article 44.

If the debates in the Constituent Assembly are read, one will find that the inclusion of Article 44 in its present form had been opposed. The Muslims, the largest single minority, were dissatisfied. And when its representatives proposed amendments to the draft Article to expressly provide that the personal law of any community shall not be changed except with the previous approval of that community, Dr Ambedkar had said the amendments were not necessary. Muslim members (he said) were reading too much into it. It merely said that the state will 'endeavour' to secure a uniform civil code for citizens of the country: 'It does not say,' he said, 'that after the code is framed, the state shall enforce it upon all citizens merely because they are citizens.'

In his concluding remarks on draft Article 35 (now Article 44) during the debate in the Constituent Assembly, Dr Ambedkar had also said:

> (*Quote*) I think they have read rather too much into Article 35, which merely proposes that the State shall endeavour to secure a civil code for the citizens of the country. It does not say that after the Code is framed, the State shall enforce it upon all citizens merely because they are citizens. *It is perfectly possible that the future parliament may make a provision by way of making a beginning that the Code shall apply only to those who make a declaration that they are prepared to be bound by it, so that in the initial stage the application of the Code may be purely voluntary. Parliament may feel the ground by some such method. This is not a novel method. It was adopted in the Shariat Act of 1937 when it was applied to territories other than the North-West Frontier Province.* The law said that here is a Shariat law which should be applied to Mussulmans who wanted that he should be bound by the Shariat Act should go to an officer of the state, make a declaration that he is willing to be bound by it, and after he has made that declaration, the law will bind him and his successors. It would be perfectly possible for Parliament to introduce a provision of that sort, so that the fear which my friends have expressed here will be altogether nullified. I therefore submit that there is no substance in these amendments, and I oppose them.[51] (*Unquote*)

That Muslim personal law causes a *disproportionate* growth rate in the population of Muslims is the most prominent argument for a common civil code. But the published census figures show that the number of Hindus that were registered in the decennial census of 1961 was 366 million, and the figure doubled to 672 million in the published census of 1991 and in the last census of 2011 the figure rose to 966 million. The number of Muslims registered in the decennial census of 1961 was 46 million and the figure also doubled to 95 million in the decennial census of 1991 and in the last census of 2011, the figure rose to 172 million. Obviously, marriage laws had little to do with the increase in either case. But the argument continues to have its protagonists, and it has become a part of both folklore and wordy duels.

Most disputes in the world arise from words, and words reflect an oversimplification of ideas raising false hopes. 'Secularism' is one such word. It means different things to different people and to different political parties. To me, it means something not found in their dictionaries, nor in any common dictionary of the English language. To me, secularism in India means the ability to comprehend and tolerate an infinite variety of social problems, including the absence of a uniform code for marriage, divorce, and succession for a section of its citizens. And I can also tell you what is not secularism. An incapacity for civilised discourse is not secularism. Uncompromising truculence or arrogance is not secularism. *And an enforced regime of personal laws imposed only at the will of the majority is also not secularism.*

When an enlightened section of my own microscopic Parsi community suggested to Prime Minister Indira Gandhi that our then archaic and discriminatory law of intestate succession needed amendment (a Parsi female inheriting only one-half of the share of a Parsi male under the Succession Act 1925), she refused to introduce amending legislation unless there was an overwhelming consensus. This was then attempted over the next few years and it was only when the Parsi Panchayat of Bombay ultimately said that the community unanimously wanted a reform in the law, to treat males and females equally, that the Indian Succession Act of 1925 was amended (in 1991) to bring it in line with the general law of intestate succession—an instance of the application of the 'Salisbury approach'.

There is of course logic in favour of the plea for a *uniform civil code. We do need a uniform civil code,* but only when we, i.e., We the People, are all ready for it, and when we have, in thought and deed, put all acrimony behind us. Till then, as Winston Churchill once said in a speech in the House of Commons (when it was suggested that he rename Government ministries), '*beware of needless innovations, especially when guided by logic*'.

Article 45: Provision for early childhood care and education to children below the age of six years.

Comment :

See the comment on Article 21A.

Article 46: Promotion of educational and economic interests of scheduled castes, scheduled tribes, and other weaker sections.

Comment on Article 46:

Article 46 is to be read with Article 335 (claims of scheduled castes and scheduled tribes shall be taken into consideration, consistently with the maintenance of efficiency of administration, in the making of appointments to services and posts in connection with the affairs of the Union or of a State). *Article 335 is a provision that is often overlooked both by governments, and even by courts when dealing with quotas (under Article 15) and reservations in posts under the state (under Article 16*). Way back in 1963, the Supreme Court of India had said that overlooking or ignoring the provisions in Article 335, was liable to be challenged as a 'fraud on the Constitution'.[52]: AIR1963 S.C. 649 at page 664.

----------Part-IV-A ----------

Fundamental Duties—Article 51A[53]

It shall be the duty of every citizen of India:

(a) to abide by the Constitution and respect its ideals and institutions, the national flag and the national anthem.

(b) to cherish and follow the noble ideals which inspired our national struggle for freedom.

(c) to uphold and protect the sovereignty, unity, and integrity of India.

(d) to defend the country and render national service when called upon to do so.

(e) to promote harmony and the spirit of common brotherhood amongst all the people of India transcending religious, linguistic, and regional or sectional diversities (and thus cementing the bond of Fraternity set out in the Preamble), and to renounce practices derogatory to the dignity of women.

(f) to value and preserve the rich heritage of our composite culture.

(g) to protect and improve the natural environment including forests, lakes, rivers, and wildlife, and to have compassion for living creatures.

(h) to develop the scientific temper, humanism and the spirit of inquiry and reform.

(i) to safeguard public property and to abjure violence.

(j) to strive towards excellence in all spheres of individual and collective activity so that the nation constantly rises to higher levels of endeavour and achievement.

(k) who is a parent or guardian to provide opportunities for education to his child or, as the case may be, ward between the age of six and fourteen years.

Clause (k) was added by the Constitution 86th Amendment Act, 2002. This was linked to the fundamental right added in Part-III, viz., Article 21A.

Comment on Article 51A

Article 51A was inserted in the Constitution during the Internal Emergency of June 1975 - March 1977, and was inspired (presumably) by what Gandhiji had written in a letter to Dr Julian Huxley, director general of UNESCO way back in 1947:

> I learnt from my illiterate but wise mother that all rights to be deserved and preserved came from duty well done.

The letter had been written in a moving train while Gandhiji was travelling to Delhi in May 1947, and was in reply to an invitation to 60 leading personalities throughout the world to define what they thought would form the basis of a 'World Charter of Human Rights'. Defining his view of human rights, Gandhiji wrote in his letter to Dr Huxley:

> 'The right to live accrues to us only when we do the duty of citizenship of the world. Every other right can be shown to be a usurpation hardly worth fighting for.'

Fundamental duties can be enforced not under Part-III nor under Article 226 but by filing suits in civil courts under Section 9 of the Code of Civil Procedure 1908. 'A suit for its maintainability requires no authority of law and it is enough that no statute bars the suit': Ganga Bai vs. Vijay Kumar *(AIR 1974 SC 1176)*

PART-V: THE UNION
and
PART-VI: THE STATES
(dealt with in CHAPTER SIX in this book)

Part-V: THE UNION

- **Chapter I** - THE EXECUTIVE: Articles 52 to 78
- **Chapter II** - PARLIAMENT: Articles 79 to 122
- **Chapter III** - LEGISLATIVE POWERS OF THE PRESIDENT: Article 123
- **Chapter IV** - THE UNION JUDICIARY: Articles 124 to 146
- **Chapter V** - COMPTROLLER AND AUDITOR GENERAL OF INDIA: Articles 147 to 151;

Part-VI: THE STATES

- **Chapter I** - GENERAL: Article 152
- **Chapter II** - THE EXECUTIVE: Articles 153 to 167;
- **Chapter III** - THE STATE LEGISLATURE: Articles 168 to 187;

  Conduct of Business—Articles 188 and 189;

  Disqualifications of Members—Articles 190 to 193;

  Powers, Privileges, and Immunities of State Legislatures and Their Members—Articles 194 and 195;

  Legislative Procedure—Articles 196 to 201;

  Procedure in Financial Matters—Articles 202 to 207;

  Procedure Generally—Articles 208 to 212;

- **Chapter IV** - LEGISLATIVE POWER OF THE GOVERNOR: Article 213
- **Chapter V** - The High Courts in the States: Articles 214 to 232
- **Chapter VI** - SUBORDINATE COURTS: Articles 233 to 237

Part V and Part VI are structured parts of the Constitution—the provisions relating to the working of the Constitution in its various manifestations viz The Executive, The Legislature and The Judiciary

Chapter Seven contains an analysis of and comments on:

(i) Powers and Privileges of Houses of Parliament and of the members and committees thereof and Powers and Previleges of State Legislatures and of members and committees thereof: Articles 105 and 194 (in Parts-V and VI);

(ii) Power of the President of India and of Governors of States to grant pardon etc. and to suspend, remit or commute sentences in certain cases: Articles 72 and 161 (also in Parts-V and VI);

(iii) The Comptroller and Auditor-General of India — the financial ombudsman of the Union and of the States: Articles 147 to 157 (in Part-V);

(iv) Elections and Election Commission: Articles 324 to 329A (in Part-XV)

---------- Part-VII ----------

Article 238: The States in Part B of the First Schedule (repealed)

Part-VII in the Constitution as enacted was repealed by the Constitution Seventh Amendment Act, 1956, w.e.f. 1 November 1956, when all references to Part-A, Part-B, and Part-C States in the Constitution as enacted stood deleted.

---------- Part-VIII ----------

The Union Territories[54]—Articles 239 to 241

This Part now consists of seven articles:

Article 239: Administration of Union Territories.

Article 239A: Creation of local legislatures and/or council of ministers for the union territories.

Article 239AA: Special provisions with regard to Delhi (added by the Constitution 69th Amendment Act, 1991, w.e.f. 1 February 1992).

Article 239B[55]: Power of the administrator of Puducherry to promulgate Ordinances.

Article 239AB: Provision in case of failure of constitutional machinery (also added by Constitution 69th Amendment Act, 1991).

Article 240[56]: Power of the president to make regulations for the union territory of the Andaman and Nicobar Islands, of Lakshadweep, of Dadra and Nagar Haveli, and of Daman and Diu.

Article 241: Parliament 'may' by law constitute a high court for a union territory.

Article 242: Deleted by the Constitution Seventh Amendment Act, 1956.

Comment:

As the position stands at present, the Union Territories are divided into three categories:

i. Union territories without a legislature, viz., Andaman and Nicobar, Lakshadweep, Dadar and Nagar Haveli,

Daman and Diu, and Chandigarh. They are directly administered by the centre.

ii. Union territory of Puducherry for which a legislature has been established by Act of Parliament under Article 239A—the Puducherry Legislative Assembly has power to make laws for the Union Territory of Puducherry with respect to any of the matters in the state list or concurrent list in the Seventh Schedule to the Constitution.

iii. The National Capital Territory of Delhi for which a legislature has been created by the Constitution (Articles 239AA and 239AB).

A union territory is a separate entity under the Constitution. Its administrator is not a constitutional functionary like the governor of a state but is a delegate of the president of India qua the territory and its administrator. And any regulation made by the president for a union territory (e.g. of Puducherry) has the same force and effect as an Act of Parliament (Article 240(2)).

Re: **Delhi**—Article 239AA (special provisions with respect to Delhi) had been added by the Constitution 69th Amendment Act, 1991 and it provided that the Union Territory of Delhi was to be called the National Capital Territory (NCT) with a legislative assembly to be filled by members chosen by direct election from territorial constituencies in the NCT, and with a lieutenant governor (to be appointed by the centre) as its administrator. In other words, Delhi was to be neither a full-fledged state nor a union territory directly administered by the centre, but something in between.

In an earlier case, *Government of NCT of Delhi vs. Union of India & Another* (2018 (8) SCC 501 (5J)), the Supreme Court had held that:

> The assurance by the insertion of Article 239AA by the Constitution 69th Amendment Act, 1991, by exercise of the

> constituent power is not to be (construed) with any kind of rigid understanding of the provision. It is because the exercise of constituent power is meant to confer democratic, societal, and political powers on the citizens who reside within the National Capital Territory of Delhi that it has been granted a special status. (page 555)

And in the light of the prior ruling of the nine-judge bench in *New Delhi Municipal Corporation* (1997 (7) SCC 339), it was also held in 2018 (8) SCC 501 (5J) that:

> It is clear as noonday that by no stretch of imagination, NCT of Delhi can be accorded the status of a State under our present constitutional scheme. The status of NCT of Delhi is sui generis, a class apart, and the status of the Lieutenant Governor of Delhi is not that of a Governor of a State, rather he remains an Administrator, in a limited sense, working with the designation of Lieutenant Governor. (page 647)

But Delhi's hybrid status has resulted in manifold problems, some of which were resolved by the Supreme Court of India in 2018 in *Government of NCT of Delhi vs. Union of India & Another,* but more problems arose in later years as summarised below:

(a) In 2017, in fresh proceedings initiated (CA No.: 2357 of 2017—*Government of NCT of Delhi vs. Union of India),* a Constitution Bench of the court, presided over by Chief Justice D. Y. Chandrachud, handed down its final decision on 11 May 2023. *It decided that the Delhi Government headed by its Chief Minister—and not the Lt. Governor appointed by the Central Government—would control civil services working for the Delhi Government.*[57]

(b) The Constitution Bench also held (on 11 May 2023) that by virtue of Article 239AA of the Constitution, the

National Capital Territory of Delhi (NCTD) has been accorded a *sui generis* status setting it apart from other union territories and that the legislative assembly of the NCTD has the competence over all entries in the State List (List-II of the Seventh Schedule as well as in List-III of the Seventh Schedule except for the excluded entries in List-III). The Constitution Bench held that the Union of India had the executive power only over the three named entries of List-II over which the NCTD did not have legislative competence. More importantly, the court also held that the NCTD had legislative and executive powers over services (i.e., Entry 41 of List-II of the Seventh Schedule) because Part-XIV of the Constitution was applicable to union territories. But all this was short-lived. (see point (c) below)

(c) However on 19 May 2023, the president of India promulgated the Government of National Capital Territory of Delhi (Amendment) Ordinance No. 1 of 2023, stating that as the national capital has 'a unique status and certain distinguishing features' and 'there is a need to promote the national interests without compromising on the democratic aspirations of the residents of Delhi'. The ordinance inserted Section 3A in Article 239AA declaring that 'notwithstanding anything contained in any judgement, order, or decree of any court, the legislative assembly shall have the power to make laws as per Article 239AA except with respect to any matter enumerated in Entry 41 of List-II of the Seventh Schedule of the Constitution of India or any matter connected therewith or incidental thereto'.[58] It also made certain marginal and consequential changes in Article 239AA[59].

(d) The ordinance of May 19 2023, has been promptly challenged in the Supreme Court of India and stands replaced by an Act of Parliament passed in August 2023.

The Ordinance and the Act has put the Lt. Governor back in the driver's seat of governance by giving him the power to take a final call on any decision taken by the Delhi Assembly with respect to **services**. The legal wrangling between the Centre and the Government of the National Capital Territory of Delhi over the contours of their respective powers has been a never ending saga.

(e) Meanwhile, to resolve the wrangle a useful suggestion had been made (*see footnote 60*) that the centre should carve out for itself a separate a Union Territory of New Delhi (i.e., Lutyens' Delhi) to be continued to be administered by the centre, leaving the rest of what is Delhi today—with an approximate population of 16 million people—to become a new full state with its own self-governing machinery of police, etc.[60]

PART-IX: The Panchayats

and

PART-IX-A: The Municipalities

Added by the Constitution Seventy-Third and Seventy-Fourth Amendment Acts, 1992 (w.e.f. 24 April 1993).

Comment:

In evaluating 30 years of the Constitution's 73rd and 74th Amendments of 1992, the monthly magazine, *Seminar*, had brought out a special edition (*Seminar* 763 of March 2023)[61] which highlighted the advantages as well as the shortfalls of the two constitutional Amendments (relating to panchayats and municipalities).

> Not only did these constitutional amendments serve the purpose of decentralisation in the Indian political system, but extensive quotas for historically marginalised groups and women ensured better descriptive representation of these communities than ever before. The two Acts mandated one-third of the total seats in all local bodies to be reserved for women as well as reserved seats for the scheduled castes (SCs), scheduled tribes (STs), and other backward classes ((OBCs) based on the percentage of their populations). These groups gained a share of political power, and this development was marked by the emergence of a new pattern of leadership—*naya netas* (new leaders)—who are independent of traditional power structures.
>
> While this indeed is a sign of greater democratisation at the local level in India, there is another side to this story. Despite the decline in caste hierarchies, there remains abundant evidence of the reproduction of traditional local power structures, even though they may no longer be based on land and ritual distinction exclusively as they once were.

While the participation of women at the polling booth has increased manifold in the past three decades, they continue to remain on the margins as far as nomination as candidates for assembly or general elections are concerned, or for that matter important positions in organisational structure of the party.

The notion that decentralisation will increase participatory governance and lead to improvements in people's well-being is not entirely consistent with documented evidence. There is some truth to the scepticism as to whether the introduction of democratic principles alone can help achieve objectives, without addressing the social and political structures at the local level, especially in areas where a large number of people are dependent upon a small number of powerful local elites.

Local governments in India are a state subject and thus there is a considerable variation across states in the architecture of this model as well as number of items on which local governments can act independently. Different states have followed different trajectories to devolve powers, functions, and responsibilities to the elected representatives. These local bodies continue to have very limited financial and administrative powers.

Many of the deficiencies of Indian politics visible in national and state elections have now become part and parcel of third-tier elections as well. The sheer money and muscle power deployed during these elections is phenomenal. If one calculates the average money spent by a panchayat election candidate, then expenditure incurred per voter is likely to be higher than what Lok Sabha or Vidhan Sabha candidates usually spend. The situation is not very different in municipal elections too.

Researchers have documented that indirect elections at various levels have created a system in which large numbers of candidates, get elected unopposed, mostly supported by the ruling party in the state. It is not surprising then the presidential candidate at different tiers of both urban and rural local governments are mostly relatives of sitting Members of Parliament (MP).

As soon as a change in the ruling regime in the state capital takes place, successful no-confidence motions are brought against many incumbent district and block council presidents.

Local-level politicians remain the primary contact points for most citizens in both urban and rural India. A lot of our understanding about the successes and failures of India's decentralised model, especially in academic circles, largely comes, from rural, and the complexity of urban politics has not received due attention. While there are indeed areas of overlap between rural and urban local bodies, we need to develop new formworks to understand the differences in challenges the local governance structures face in these two contexts.

Part IX: The Panchayats[62]
Articles 243 and 243-A to 243-O

Article 243: Definitions.
Article 243A: Gram Sabha.

Article 243B: Constitution of Panchayats.

Article 243C: Composition of Panchayats.

Article 243D: Reservation of seats.

Article 243E: Duration of Panchayats, etc.

Article 243F: Disqualifications for membership.

Article 243G: Powers, authority, and responsibilities of Panchayats.

Article 243H: Powers to impose taxes by, and funds of, the Panchayats.

Article 243I: Constitution of Finance Commission to review financial position.

Article 243J: Audit of accounts of Panchayats.

Article 243K: Elections to the Panchayats.

Article 243L: Application to union territories.

Article 243M: Part not to apply to certain areas.

Article 243N: Continuance of existing laws and Panchayats.

Article 243O: Bar to interference by courts in electoral matters.

Comment:

The rationale for inserting Part-IX has been stated in Durga Das Basu's, *Shorter Constitution of India* (15th edition 2018, Vol. 2, on page 1293), with appreciation and plaudits to the author of the 15th edition, Justice A. K. Patnaik.

The 73rd Amendment was brought into force on 24.04.1993 to give effect to one of the Directive Principles of State

Policy, namely, Article 40 of the Constitution (Organisation of Village Panchayats). This Amendment came into the Constitution under Article 368 and, therefore, it cannot be said to be a basic feature of the Constitution. Under the enabling provision—the State Legislature is empowered to endow Panchayats with such power and authority to enable them to function as institutions of self-government.[63] What was sought to be done by the 73rd Amendment was to confer constitutional status to District Panchayats, Taluka Panchayats, and Village Panchayats. *A State Legislature, in the light of the constitutional provisions in Part IX, cannot do away with these democratic bodies at the local level nor can their normal tenure be curtailed otherwise than in accordance with law nor can the State Government delay elections of these bodies.*[64]

Part-IX-A: The Municipalities[65]
Article 243P to Article 243ZG

Article 243P: Definitions.

Article 243R: Composition of Municipalities.

Article 243S: Constitution and composition of Wards Committees, etc.

Article 243T: Reservation of seats.

Article 243U: Duration of Municipalities, etc.

Article 243V: Disqualifications for membership.

Article 243W: Powers, authority, and responsibilities of Municipalities, etc.

Article 243X: Power to impose taxes by, and funds of, the Municipalities.

Article 243Y: Finance commission.

Article 243Z: Audit of accounts of Municipalities.

Article 243ZA: Elections to the Municipalities.

Article 243ZB: Application to union territories.

Article 243ZC: Part not to apply to certain areas.

Article 243ZD: Committee for district planning.

Article 243ZE: Committee for metropolitan planning.

Article 243ZF: Continuance of existing laws and Municipalities.

Article 243ZG: Bar to interference by courts in electoral matters.

Comment:

Examining the underlying object of inserting Part-IX-A by the Constitution (74th) Amendment Act, 1992, and highlighting the effective and meaningful role to be played by local bodies in the political governance of the country, the Supreme Court of India in a 2006 judgement had stated:

> The object of introducing these provisions was that in many states the local bodies were not working properly, and the timely elections were not being held and the nominated bodies were continuing for long periods. Elections had been irregular, and many times unnecessarily delayed or postponed, and the elected bodies had been superseded or suspended without adequate justification at the whims and fancies of the state authorities. These views were expressed by the then minister of state for urban development while introducing the Constitution Amendment Bill before the Parliament and thus the new provisions were added in the Constitution with a view to restore the rightful place in political governance for local bodies. It was considered necessary to provide a constitutional status to such bodies and to ensure regular and fair conduct of elections.[66] (2006) 8 SCC 352.

PART-IX-B: The Cooperative Societies
Article 243ZH to Article 243ZT

Part IX-B (containing Articles 243ZH to 243ZT) was inserted by the Constitution 97th Amendment Act, 2011 (w.e.f. 15 February 2012).

Article 243ZH: Definitions.

Article 243ZI: Incorporation of cooperative societies.

Article 243ZJ: Number and term of members of board and its office bearers.

Article 243ZK: Election of members of board.

Article 243ZL: Supersession and suspension of board and interim management.

Article 243ZM: Audit of accounts of cooperative societies.

Article 243ZN: Convening of general body meetings.

Article 243ZO: Right of a member to get information.

Article 243ZP: Returns.

Article 243ZQ: Offences and penalties.

Article 243ZR: Application to multi-state cooperative societies.

Article 243ZS: Application to union territories.

Article 243ZT: Continuance of existing laws.

Comment:

The cooperative movement in India started at the beginning of the 20th century. But cooperatives in India did not have effective autonomy, democratic functioning, or professional management. The National Policy on Cooperatives announced by the Department of Agriculture and Cooperation, Ministry of Agriculture, Government of India (in March 2002), was the basis for the Constitution 97th Amendment Act, 2011, which inserted Part-XI-B in the Constitution (as well as Article 43B in Part-IV).

The right to form cooperative societies is a fundamental right (under Article 19 of the Constitution of India) and with the insertion of Article 43B in the Directive Principles of State Policy (Part-IV) ("the State shall endeavour to promote voluntary formation and autonomous functioning, democratic control and professional management, of cooperative societies"), a new Part-IX-B had been introduced in order to give a constitutional status to cooperative societies.[67]: see AIR 2015 SC 1960.

----------Part-X ----------

The Scheduled and Tribal Areas—Articles 244 to 244A

<u>Article 244(1)</u>: The provisions of the Fifth Schedule apply to the administration and control of the scheduled areas and scheduled tribes in any state other than the states of Assam, Meghalaya, Tripura, and Mizoram. The Fifth Schedule contains provisions as to the administration and control of scheduled areas and scheduled tribes.

<u>Article 244(2)</u>: The provisions of the Sixth Schedule apply to the administration of tribal areas in the states of Assam, Meghalaya6[68], Tripura, and Mizoram. The Sixth Schedule contains provisions as to the administration of tribal areas in the states of Assam, Meghalaya, Tripura, and Mizoram.

<u>Article 244A</u>: Inserted by the Constitution 22nd Amendment Act, 1969, w.e.f. 25 September 1969. Parliament may, by law, form within the state of Assam an autonomous state, comprising any of the tribal areas specified in Part-I of the table appended to paragraph 20 of the Sixth Schedule and create therefore a legislature for the autonomous state and a council of ministers.

Comment:

The Fifth Schedule corresponds to the excluded areas and partially excluded areas, in sections 91-92 of the Government of India Act, 1935 and the Government of India (Excluded and Partially Excluded Areas) Order, 1936 (minus the areas of Assam which are included in the Sixth Schedule). *The reason why special provisions have been made for these areas and for scheduled tribes is that they are culturally different, and that their social and other customs are also different from the rest of India.* (see Constituent Assembly Debates, Vol. VII-Appendix C and D, pages 101-109 and page 157)

The scheduled areas are determined by the President by order and such order may be amended by the President from time to time.

Any amendment of the Fifth Schedule must be made by Parliament.[69] The enumeration of scheduled tribes under Article 342, is by the Constitution (Scheduled Tribes) Order, 1950, as amended by the Scheduled Castes and Scheduled Tribes Amendment Acts 63 of 1956, 108 of 1976, 18 of 1987, and 15 of 1990. A tribe is a scheduled tribe only if included in the President's order under Article 342.

The executive power of the union extends to giving directives to the state regarding the administration of the scheduled areas (paragraph 3). Tribes Advisory Councils are to be constituted to give advice on such matters as the welfare and advancement of the scheduled tribes in the states as may be referred to them by the governor (paragraph 4). Governors of the states in which there are scheduled areas[70] have to submit reports to the president regarding the administration of such areas, annually or whenever so required by the president (paragraph 3).

The governor is authorised to direct that any particular Act of Parliament or of the Legislature of the state shall not apply to a scheduled area or shall apply, only subject to exceptions or modifications. The governor is also authorised to make regulations to prohibit or restrict the transfer of land by, or among members of, the scheduled tribes, regulate the allotment of land, and regulate the business of money-lending. All such regulations by the governor must have the assent of the president (paragraph 5).

In other words, under Schedule Five, it is the governor who is the legislative authority for the scheduled areas and scheduled tribes to which this schedule applies. He makes regulations after consulting the Tribes Advisory Council and submits them to the president for the latter's assent (paragraph 5).

(see also Durga Das Basu's *Shorter Constitution of India* (15th edition, 2018, Vol. 2 by Justice A. K. Patnaik at pages 1987-1988)

Part-XI

Relations between the Union and the States—Articles 245 to 263

Chapter I: Legislative Relations—Distribution of Legislative Powers

Article 245: Extent of laws made by Parliament and by the Legislatures of States. Parliament is to make laws for the whole or any part of the territory of India and the Legislature of a State may make laws for the whole or any part of the State. But no law made by Parliament shall be deemed to be invalid on the ground that it would have extra-territorial operation.[71]

Article 246: Subject-matter of laws made by Parliament and by the Legislatures of States.

1. Notwithstanding anything in clauses (2) and (3), Parliament has exclusive power to make laws with respect to any of the matters enumerated in List-I in the Seventh Schedule (in this Constitution referred to as the 'Union List').
2. Notwithstanding anything in clause (3), Parliament, and, subject to clause (1), the Legislature of any State also, have power to make laws with respect to any of the matters enumerated in List-III in the Seventh Schedule (in this Constitution referred to as the 'Concurrent List').
3. Subject to clauses (1) and (2), the Legislature of any State has exclusive power to make laws for such State or any part thereof with respect to any of the matters enumerated in List-II in the Seventh Schedule (in this Constitution referred to as the 'State List').
4. Parliament has power to make laws with respect to any matter for any part of the territory of India not included

[in a State] notwithstanding that such matter is a matter enumerated in the State List.

Article 246A: Special provision with respect to goods and services tax (inserted by the Constitution 101st Amendment Act, 2016 (w.e.f. 16 September 2016)).

246A: Special provision with respect to goods and services tax.

1. Notwithstanding anything contained in articles 246 and 254, Parliament, and, subject to clause (2), the Legislature of every State, have power to make laws with respect to goods and services tax imposed by the Union or by such State.
2. Parliament has exclusive power to make laws with respect to goods and services tax where the supply of goods, or of services, or both takes place in the course of inter-State trade or commerce.

Explanation:
The provisions of this article, shall, in respect of goods and services tax referred to in clause (5) of article 279A, take effect from the date recommended by the Goods and Services Tax Council.

Article 247: Power of Parliament to provide for the establishment of certain additional courts.

Article 248: Residuary powers of legislation. Subject to Article 246A Parliament has exclusive power to make any law with respect to any matter nor enumerated in the Concurrent List (in the Seventh Schedule) or in the State List in the Seventh Schedule.

Article 249: Power of Parliament to legislate with respect to a matter in the State List in the national interest.

<u>**Article 250**</u>: Power of Parliament to legislate with respect to any matter in the State List if a Proclamation of Emergency is in operation.

<u>**Article 251**</u>: Inconsistency between laws made by Parliament under articles 249 and 250 and laws made by the Legislatures of States.

<u>**Article 252**</u>: Power of Parliament to legislate for two or more States by consent and adoption of such legislation by any other State.

<u>**Article 253**</u>: Legislation for giving effect to international agreements.

<u>**Article 254**</u>: Inconsistency between laws made by Parliament and laws made by the Legislatures of States, wherein laws made by Parliament prevail.

<u>**Article 255**</u>: Requirements as to recommendations and previous sanctions to be regarded as matters of procedure only.

Comment on Articles 245 to 263:

While Articles 245 to 255 deal generally with the distribution of legislative powers, the distribution of administrative powers is dealt with in Articles 256-261.

Like under the Government of India Act, 1935, in the Constitution of India there is a threefold distribution of legislative powers between the Union and the States, affected by the three separate legislative lists in the Seventh Schedule of the Constitution:

List-I or the Union List includes subjects over which the union shall have exclusive powers of legislation, including 98 items or subjects. These include defence, foreign affairs, banks, currency and coinage, union duties and taxes and the like, and the all-embracing entry 97 (any other matter not enumerated in List-II or List-III including any tax not mentioned in either of those Lists).

List-II or the State List comprises 59 items or entries over which the state legislature have exclusive power of legislation, such as public order and police, local government, public health and sanitation, agriculture, forests and fisheries, education, state taxes and duties, and the like.

List-III (or the Concurrent List) gives concurrent powers to the union and the state legislatures over 52 items, such as criminal law and procedure, civil procedure, marriage, contracts, torts, trusts, welfare of labour, and social insurance, economic and social planning.

If any provision of law made by a state legislature (under the Concurrent List) is repugnant to any law made by Parliament (under the Concurrent List) the law made by Parliament (whether passed before or after the state law) shall prevail and the State law shall to the extent of the repugnancy (but so long only as the law made by Parliament continues to have effect) be inoperative (Article 251).

The question of repugnancy under Article 254(1) between a law made by Parliament and a law made by the state legislature arises only in case both the legislations occupy the same field with respect to one of the matters enumerated in the Concurrent List and there is direct conflict between the two laws. It is only when both these requirements are fulfilled that the state law will, to the extent of repugnancy become void.[72]

Article 254 of the Constitution is attracted only when legislation covering the same ground both by the centre and by the state operate in the same field; both of them being competent to enact, i.e., laws mentioned in the Concurrent List (see *Western Coalfields vs. Special Area Development Authority* (AIR 1982 SC 697) (paragraphs 26-29)).

Comment on Laws and Court Decisions and Validating Acts

The legislature is competent to put an end to the finality of a judicial decision and reopen a past controversy, and even to pass a Validating Act to declare to be valid a law that had been pronounced to be void by the court. This is not an exercise of judicial power. The legislature can change the basis on which a decision is given by the court and thus change the law in general. I*t can (and does) render a judicial decision ineffective by enacting a valid law on the topic within its legislative field by fundamentally altering or changing its character retrospectively. But where an Act made by a state legislature is invalidated by the courts on the ground of incompetence to enact it, the state legislature cannot enact a law declaring that the judgement of the court shall not operate; it cannot overrule or annul the decision of a court.*

Differentiating *legislative acts* from *judicial acts*—in a judgement of the Supreme Court of India reported in AIR 1996 SC 1431 *Indian Aluminium Co. vs. State of Kerala* (Bench of two Judges) a resume is given on the distinction between *legislative acts* and *judicial acts*[73]:

(1) In a democracy governed by rule of law, the legislature exercises the power under Articles 245 and 246 and other companion Articles read with the entries in the respective Lists in the Seventh Schedule to make laws which includes power to amend the laws.

(2) Courts in their concern and endeavour to preserve judicial power equally must maintain the delicate balance devised by the Constitution between the three sovereign functionaries.

(3) In its anxiety to safeguard judicial power, it is important not to be overzealous and invalidate valid laws competently made.

(4) The courts, therefore, need to carefully scan the law to find out: (a) whether the vice pointed out by the court and invalidity suffered by previous law is cured complying with the legal and constitutional requirements; (b) whether the legislature has competence to validate the law; (c) whether such validation is consistent with the rights guaranteed in Part-III of the Constitution.

(5) The court does not have the power to validate an invalid law or to legalise impost of tax illegally made and collected or to remove the norm of invalidation. These are not judicial functions—they are the exclusive province of the legislature.

(6) In exercising legislative power, the legislature by mere declaration, without anything more, cannot directly overrule, revise, or override a judicial decision. It can render a judicial decision ineffective by enacting a valid law on the topic within its legislative field *fundamentally altering or changing its character retrospectively*.

(7) It is empowered to give effect to retrospective legislation with a deeming date or with effect from a particular date.

(8) The legislature can change the character of the tax or duty from an impermissible to a permissible tax, but the tax or levy should answer its true character and the legislature is competent to validate such a tax by removing the invalid base for its recovery.

(9) It is competent for the legislature to enact the law with retrospective effect and authorise its agencies to levy and collect the tax on that basis, and make the imposition of levy collected and recovery of the tax valid, notwithstanding the declaration by the court.

(10) *The consistent thread that runs through all the decisions of this court is that the legislature cannot directly overrule a court's decision but has power to make the decision ineffective by removing the basis on which the decision was rendered, consistent with the law of the Constitution, but the legislature must ensure that it has the legislative competence to do this.*

Chapter II: Administrative Relations—General

Article 256: Obligation of States and the Union.

Article 257: Control of the Union over States in certain cases.

Article 258: Power of the Union to confer powers, etc., on States in certain cases.

Article 258A: Power of the States to entrust functions to the Union (inserted by the Constitution 7th Amendment Act, 1956 (w.e.f. 1 November 1956)).

Article 259: Armed Forces in States in Part B of the First Schedule (repealed by the Constitution 7th Amendment Act, 1956, w.e.f. 1 November 1956).

Article 260: Jurisdiction of the Union in relation to territories outside India.

Article 261: Public acts, records, and judicial proceedings.

Article 262: Adjudication of disputes relating to waters of inter-State rivers or river valleys.

1. Parliament may by law provide for the adjudication of any dispute or complaint with respect to the use, distribution or control of the waters of, or in, any inter-State river or river valley.
2. Notwithstanding anything in this Constitution, Parliament may by law provide that neither the Supreme Court nor any other court shall exercise jurisdiction in respect of any such dispute or complaint as is referred to in clause (1).

Comment on Article 262

The exclusive jurisdiction of the Supreme Court of India under Article 131 of the Constitution is excluded once a water dispute is referred to a tribunal constituted under the Inter-State Water Disputes Act, 1956 (see *Tamil Nadu Cauvery vs. Union of India* (AIR 1990 SC 1316).

Article 263: Provisions with respect to an inter-State Council (as a measure of coordination between States.

----------Part-XII ----------

Finance, Property, Contracts, and Suits—Articles 264 to 300 and 300A

- Chapter I: Finance—Articles 264 to 290A.
- Chapter II: Borrowing—Articles 292 to 293.
- Chapter III: Property, Contracts, Rights, Liabilities, Obligations, and Suits—Articles 294 to 300.
- Chapter IV: Right to Property—Article 300A.

Chapter I: Finance—Articles 264 to 290A (Article 291 has been repealed)

Article 264: Interpretation.

Article 265: Taxes not to be imposed save by authority of law.

Distribution of Revenues between the Union and the States.

Article 266: Consolidated Funds and public accounts of India and of the States.

Article 267: Contingency Fund.

Article 268: Duties levied by the Union but collected and appropriated by the States.

Article 268A: Service tax levied by Union and collected and appropriated by the Union and the States, which had been added by the Constitution 88th Amendment Act, 2003, was omitted by the Constitution 101st Amendment Act, 2016, w.e.f. 16 September 2016.

Article 269: Taxes levied and collected by the Union but assigned to the States.

Article 269A: Levy of Goods and Services Tax in the Course of inter-State Trade or Commerce—inserted by the Constitution (101st) Amendment Act, 2016, w.e.f. 16 September 2016.

Article 270: Taxes levied and distributed between the Union and the States.

Article 271: Surcharge on certain duties and taxes for purposes of the Union.

Article 272: [Taxes which are levied and collected by the Union and may be distributed between the Union and the States.] Repealed by the Constitution (80th Amendment) Act, 2000, s. 4.

Article 273: Grants in lieu of export duty on jute and jute products.

Article 274: Prior recommendation of President required to Bills affecting taxation in which States are interested.

Article 275: Grants from the Union to certain States.

Article 276: Taxes on professions, trades, callings, and employments

Article 277: Savings.

Article 278: [Agreement with States in Part-B of the First Schedule with regard to certain financial matters.] Repealed by the Constitution (7th Amendment) Act, 1956, s. 29 and Schedule.

Article 279: Calculation of 'net proceeds', etc.

Article 279A: Goods and Services Tax Council (This provision—known as the GST Amendment—was added by the Constitution 101st Amendment Act, 2016 (w.e.f. 16 September 2016)).

Article 279A: Goods and Services Tax Council

1. The President shall, within sixty days from the date of commencement of the Constitution (101st Amendment)

Act, 2016, by order, constitute a Council to be called the Goods and Services Tax Council.

2. The Goods and Services Tax Council shall consist of the following members, namely:

   (a) the Union Finance Minister—Chairperson.

   (b) the Union Minister of State in charge of Revenue or Finance—Member.

   (c) the Minister in charge of Finance or Taxation or any other Minister nominated by each State Government—Members.

3. The Members of the Goods and Services Tax Council referred to in sub-clause (c) of clause (2) shall, as soon as may be, choose one amongst themselves to be the Vice-Chairperson of the Council for such period as they may decide.

4. *The Goods and Services Tax Council shall make recommendations to the Union and the States on:*

   (a) the taxes, cesses and surcharges levied by the Union, the States and the local bodies which may be subsumed in the goods and services tax.

   (b) the goods and services that may be subjected to, or exempted from, the goods and services tax.

   (c) model Goods and Services Tax Laws, principles of levy, apportionment of Goods and Services Tax levied on supplies in the course of inter-State trade or commerce under article 269A and the principles that govern the place of supply.

   (d) the threshold limit of turnover below which goods and services may be exempted from goods and services tax.

(e) the rates including floor rates with bands of goods and services tax.

(f) any special rate or rates for a specified period, to raise additional resources during any natural calamity or disaster.

(g) special provision with respect to the States of Arunachal Pradesh, Assam, Jammu and Kashmir, Manipur, Meghalaya, Mizoram, Nagaland, Sikkim, Tripura, Himachal Pradesh and Uttarakhand.

(h) any other matter relating to the goods and services tax, as the Council may decide.

5. *The Goods and Services Tax Council shall recommend the date on which the goods and services tax be levied on petroleum crude, high-speed diesel, motor spirit (commonly known as petrol), natural gas, and aviation turbine fuel.*

Note

Article 279A(5) has not been made operational. The GST Council has not recommended the date on which GST will be levied on petroleum products. States do not want to let go of this source of revenue since apart from petroleum products, the only other source of revenue now for the states is potable alcohol. At present, it appears that the GST Council does not want to impose GST on petroleum products because if they do then input tax credit will have to be given, and that may seriously jeopardise the revenues of the States.

6. While discharging the functions conferred by this article, the Goods and Services Tax Council shall be guided by the need for a harmonised structure of goods and services tax and for the development of a harmonised national market for goods and services.

7. One-half of the total number of members of the Goods and Services Tax Council shall constitute the quorum at its meetings.
8. The Goods and Services Tax Council shall determine the procedure in the performance of its functions.
9. Every decision of the Goods and Services Tax Council shall be taken at a meeting, by a majority of not less than three-fourths of the weighted votes of the members present and voting, in accordance with the following principles, namely:
   (a) the vote of the Central Government shall have a weightage of one-third of the total votes cast, and
   (b) the votes of all the State Governments taken together shall have a weightage of two-thirds of the total votes cast, in that meeting.
10. No act or proceedings of the Goods and Services Tax Council shall be invalid merely by reason of:

    (a) any vacancy in, or any defect in, the constitution of the Council; or

    (b) any defect in the appointment of a person as a Member of the Council; or

    (c) any procedural irregularity of the Council not affecting the merits of the case.
11. The Goods and Services Tax Council shall establish a mechanism to adjudicate any dispute:

    (a) between the Government of India and one or more States; or

    (b) between the Government of India and any State or States on one side and one or more other States on the other side; or

(c) between two or more States, arising out of the recommendations of the Council or implementation thereof.

<u>Article 280</u>: Finance Commission

1. The President shall, within two years from the commencement of this Constitution and thereafter at the expiration of every fifth year or at such earlier time as the President considers necessary, by order constitute a Finance Commission which shall consist of a Chairman and four other members to be appointed by the President.
2. Parliament may by law determine the qualifications which shall be requisite for appointment as members of the Commission and the manner in which they shall be selected.
3. *It shall be the duty of the Commission to make recommendations to the President as to:*

(a) the distribution between the Union and the States of the net proceeds of taxes which are to be, or may be, divided between them under this Chapter and the allocation between the States of the respective shares of such proceeds.

(b) the principles which should govern the grants-in-aid of the revenues of the States out of the Consolidated Fund of India.

(bb) the measures needed to augment the Consolidated Fund of a State to supplement the resources of the Panchayats in the State on the basis of the recommendations made by the Finance Commission of the State.

(c) the measures needed to augment the Consolidated Fund of a State to supplement the resources of the Municipalities in the State on the basis of the recommendations made by the Finance Commission of the State.

(d) any other matter referred to the Commission by the President in the interests of sound finance.

4. The Commission shall determine their procedure and shall have such powers in the performance of their functions as Parliament may by law confer on them.

Article 281: Recommendations of the Finance Commission—together with an explanatory memorandum to be laid before each House of Parliament.

Comment on the Finance Commission

The Finance Commission is a constitutional body that offers suggestions on Centre-State finances.

In a quasi-federal system, there needs to be an impartial body that examines the claim of the states to central finance. Hence the need for an independent finance commission. That it should be an impartial body to examine the claims of the states instead of leaving it to the sole discretion of the central government had been emphasised by D. Ambedkar in the Constituent Assembly (see CAD, Volume IX, pages 311-315). But the finance commission is not a permanent body. It has been and is constituted almost regularly at the expiration of every fifth year after the first two years of the commencement of the Constitution (26 January 1950).

Its duty is to make recommendations to the president (i.e., central government) as to a fair and equitable distribution between the union and the states of the net proceeds of taxes to be divided between them and as to the allocation between the states of respective shares of such proceeds. The finance commission also formulates principles that must govern the grant-in-aid of revenues of the state out of the Consolidated Fund of India.

After the Constitution 73rd Amendment Act, 1992 (Panchayats), the Finance Commission is now required to formulate measures needed to augment the Consolidated Fund of a State in order to supplement resources of panchayats within the state, and similarly, after the Constitution 74th Amendment Act, 1992, (Municipalities), the finance commission must periodically consider measures needed to augment the Consolidated Fund of the state in order to supplement the resources of the municipalities within the state.

Every finance commission gets about two years to deliberate on its terms of reference, to consult with the states, and to frame its recommendations which the central government has to place before Parliament together with an action-taken report. The 15th Finance Commission had submitted to the President its report on November 9, 2020 for the five fiscals: 2021-2022 to 2025-2026. The Government of India accepted the report of the Commission and accordingly the STATES are being given 42 per cent of the divisible tax pool of the Centre during the period 2021-22 to 2025-26.

A challenge that faces the 16th Finance Commission (to be appointed later in the year 2023) is that it will coexist with another permanent constitutional body, viz., the Goods and Services Tax Council (the GST Council—set up under Article 279A), the decisions of the GST Council about tax-rate changes would alter the revenue calculations made by the finance commission for sharing fiscal resources; the 16th Finance Commission would therefore have to consider what recourse mechanism can be put in place to revisit the numbers it recommends due to the decisions of the GST Council.

Miscellaneous Financial Provisions

Article 282: Expenditure defrayable by the Union or a State out of its revenues.

Article 283: Custody, etc., of Consolidated Funds, Contingency Funds and moneys credited to the public accounts.

<u>Article 284</u>: Custody of suitors' deposits and other moneys received by public servants and courts.

<u>Article 285</u>: Exemption of property of the Union from State taxation.

<u>Article 286</u>: (as amended by the Constitution 101st Amendment Act, 2016) Restrictions as to imposition of tax on the sale or purchase of goods.

1. No law of a State shall impose, or authorise the imposition of, *a tax on the supply of goods or of services or both*, where such supply takes place:
   (a) outside the State; or
   (b) in the course of the import of the (goods or services or both) into, or export of the (goods or services or both) out of, the territory of India.
2. Parliament may by law formulate principles for determining when a supply of goods or of services or both in any of the ways mentioned in clause (1).[74]

Note:

Prior to the GST Amendment (inserting Article 279A) by the Constitution 101st Amendment Act, 2016 (w.e.f. 16 September 2016), Article 286 had read as follows:

1. No law of a State shall impose, or authorise the imposition of, *a tax on the sale or purchase of goods* where such sale or purchase takes place:
   (a) outside the State; or
   (b) in the course of the import of the goods into, or export of the goods out of, the territory of India.

2. Parliament may by law formulate principles for determining when a sale or purchase of goods takes place in any of the ways mentioned in clause (1).

3. Any law of a State shall, insofar as it imposes, or authorises the imposition of:

   (a) a tax on the sale or purchase of goods declared by Parliament by law to be of special importance in inter-State trade or commerce; or

   (b) a tax on the sale or purchase of goods, being a tax of the nature referred to in sub-clause (b), sub-clause (c), or sub-clause (d) of clause (29A) of Article 366, be subject to such restrictions and conditions in regard to the system of levy, rates, and other incidents of tax as Parliament may by law specify.

Comment on Article 286 (as amended by the Constitution 101st Amendment Act, 2016)

After the GST Amendment (Goods & Services Tax Amendment), w.e.f. 16 September 2016, the words 'sale or purchase of goods and services' in Article 286 (as enacted) stood replaced by the words 'supply of goods and services'.

Article 286 (as amended) has now to be read in conjunction with Article 246A (special provision with respect to goods and services tax). Under Article 246A, the power to levy GST on inter-state trade and commerce vests exclusively in Parliament. Therefore, what was earlier the Central Sales Tax Act (CST) has now become the Integrated Goods and Services Tax Act (IGST). Article 269A has created a legal fiction because the supply of goods and services in the course of import into the territory of India is now deemed to be in the course of 'inter-state trade and commerce'.

A summary of the situation under Article 286 (as amended) as it exists today is set out below:

1. **Only Parliament can—but states cannot—levy GST on supply of goods and services in the course of inter-state trade and commerce.**
2. **Under Article 286—as it stands today—there is a complete prohibition on states to impose any tax on supply of goods and services which takes place outside the state or which takes place in the course of import of goods and services into India.**
3. **Import of goods and services is now subject to IGST (Integrated Goods and Services Tax) in place of the earlier levy of CVD (Countervailing Duty).**

Article 287: Exemption from taxes on electricity.

Article 288: Exemption from taxation by States in respect of water or electricity in certain cases.

Article 289: Exemption of property and income of a State from Union taxation.

Article 290: Adjustment in respect of certain expenses and pensions.

Article 290A: Annual payment to certain Devaswom Funds.

Article 291: Privy purse sums of Rulers. Repealed by the Constitution (26th Amendment) Act, 1971, s. 2.

Chapter II: Borrowing—Articles 292 to 293

Article 292: Borrowing by the Government of India.

Article 293: Borrowing by States.

Chapter III: Property, Contracts, Rights, Liabilities, Obligations, and Suits—Articles 294 to 300

Article 294: Succession to property, assets, rights, liabilities, and obligations in certain cases.

Article 295: Succession to property, assets, rights, liabilities, and obligations in other cases.

Article 296: Property accruing by escheat or lapse or as bona vacantia.

Article 297: Things of value within territorial waters or continental shelf and resources of the exclusive economic zone to vest in the Union.

Article 298: Power to carry on trade, etc.

Article 299: Contracts.

1. All contracts made in the exercise of the executive power of the Union or of a State shall be expressed to be made by the President, or by the Governor of the State, as the case may be, and all such contracts and all assurances of property made in the exercise of that power shall be executed on behalf of the President or the Governor by such persons and in such manner as he may direct or authorise.
2. Neither the President nor the Governor shall be personally liable in respect of any contract or assurance made or executed for the purposes of this Constitution, or for the purposes of any enactment relating to the Government of India heretofore in force, nor shall any person making or executing any such contract or assurance on behalf of any of them be personally liable in respect thereof.

Comment on Article 299

Section 30 of the Government of India Act, 1919, and Section 175 of the Government of India Act, 1935, empowered governments to enter into contracts with parties and Article 299 has maintained this position.

<u>Article 300</u>: Suits and proceedings.

1. The Government of India may sue or be sued by the name of the Union of India and the Government of a State may sue or be sued by the name of the State and may, subject to any provisions which may be made by Act of Parliament or of the Legislature of such State enacted by virtue of powers conferred by this Constitution, sue or be sued in relation to their respective affairs in the like cases as the Dominion of India and the corresponding Provinces or the corresponding Indian States might have sued or been sued if this Constitution had not been enacted.
2. If at the commencement of this Constitution:

(a) any legal proceedings are pending to which the Dominion of India is a party, the Union of India shall be deemed to be substituted for the Dominion in those proceedings; and

b) any legal proceedings are pending to which a Province or an Indian State is a party, the corresponding State shall be deemed to be substituted for the Province or the Indian State in those proceedings.

Comment on Article 300

The contractual liability of the state is the same as that of an individual under the ordinary law of contract.

As regards torts (or civil wrongs), the law of torts has not been codified in India.

i. No action lies against Government for injury done to an individual in the course of exercise of *sovereign functions* of Government.

ii. But in order to claim immunity of action in respect of the tortuous acts of an officer or servant of Government, the State must show not only that it was done in the course of his employment but that in addition the injury was caused in the course of exercise of *sovereign functions*.

Thus, where the driver of a jeep, owned and maintained by the state of Rajasthan for the official use of the collector of a district, drove it rashly and negligently, while bringing it back from the workshop after repairs and knocked down a pedestrian and fatally injured him, it was held that the state can be made vicariously liable for the tortious act, like any other employer.[75]

Suits lie against the government for wrongs done by public servants in the course of their duty as public servants but where contesting parties are different departments of state, it has been held that the disputes are better resolved through a committee of secretaries of the government of India or of the states[76].

Chapter IV: Right to Property—Article 300A

Article 300A: No person shall be deprived of his property save by authority of law.[77]

Comment on Article 300A

Prior to this amendment, the right to property was guaranteed by Article 31 in the Fundamental Rights Chapter, as was the right to own hold and dispose of property (guaranteed by Article 19(1)(f)). Both Articles 19(1)(f) and 31 were deleted by the Constitution 44th Amendment Act, 1978, and New Article 300A was added in Chapter IV (Right to Property). But Article 300A does confer a valuable constitutional right. In fact, it appears from the cases decided under Article 300A that we are almost harkening back to the time when the right to hold and own property was a fundamental right.

In a leading judgement of the Supreme Court (in *Dwarkadas Shrinivas of Bombay vs. Sholapur Spinning & Weaving Co. Ltd.* (AIR 1954 SC 119)), Justice Mahajan—in upholding the right to property and striking down the Sholapur Spinning and Weaving Company Emergency Provisions Ordinance of 1950 as offending Article 31(2), as it existed—had refused to accept the narrow view of 'acquisition' which necessity meant acquisition of title in whole or in part of the property. 'The word acquisition,' Justice Mahajan said in his concurring judgement, 'has quite a wide concept,' and it includes 'the taking of property permanently or even temporarily.' He quoted Shylock who had said in Shakespeare's *Merchant of Venice*:

> You take my house, when you do take the prop
> That doth sustain my house, you take my life
> When you do take the means whereby I live.

Similarly, in Article 300A, where a constitutional right is conferred, a person is deprived of his property even when it is taken by the state for a temporary purpose or for a temporary period.

In *Delhi Airtech Services Ltd. vs. State of Uttar Pradesh* (2011 (9) SCC 354 = AIR 2012 SC 573), the Supreme Court has held that 'some amount of property right is an indispensable safeguard against tyranny and economic oppression of government', and in *Hindustan Petroleum Corporation Ltd. vs. Darius Shapur Chenai* ((2005) 7 SCC 627 = AIR 2005 (5) SC 3520), it was held that deprivation of property has to be for a public purpose and 'reasonable compensation must be paid'.

Besides, as held in *State of Haryana vs. Mukesh Kumar* (AIR 2012 SC 559), a right to property is now not only a constitutional right but also a human right.

And it has been held in *Vidya Devi vs. State of Himachal Pradesh* (AIR 2020 SC 4709) that the compensation for taking property has to be paid by the state.

Besides, 'law' under Article 300A means a validly enacted law and a 'just, fair, and reasonable law'. The word 'law' must be given the same meaning as in Article 21: (see *Delhi Airtech Services Pvt. Ltd. vs. State of Uttar Pradesh* (AIR 2012 SC 573 (2J) on page 593, paragraph 69)

Even the right to receive a premium is treated as a right to property under Article 300A. (see *State of West Bengal vs. Haresh Banerjee* 2006 (7) SCC 651)

And in *State of Jharkhand vs. J. K. Srivastava* (AIR 2013 SC 3383) (Justice Sikri speaking for the court) held that an attempt by the state to take away a part of the pension or gratuity or even leave encashment of its officers or employees without any statutory provision and under the aegis of administrative instructions, is impermissible—*executive instructions not having a statutory character are not 'law' within the meaning of Article 300A.*

---------- Part-XIII ----------

Trade, Commerce, and Intercourse within the Territory of India—Article 301 to 307

Article 301: Freedom of trade, commerce, and intercourse—subject to the other provisions of this Part, trade, commerce, and intercourse throughout the territory of India shall be free.

Article 302: Power of Parliament to impose restrictions on trade, commerce, and intercourse.

Article 303: Restrictions on the legislative powers of the Union and of the States with regard to trade and commerce.

Article 304: Restrictions on trade, commerce, and intercourse among States. Notwithstanding anything in article 301 or article 303, the Legislature of a State may by law:

(a) impose on goods imported from other States 1 (or the Union territories) any tax to which similar goods manufactured or produced in that State are subject, so, however, as not to discriminate between goods so imported and goods so manufactured or produced; and

(b) impose such reasonable restrictions on the freedom of trade, commerce, or intercourse with or within that State as may be required in the public interest, provided that no Bill or amendment for the purposes of clause (*b*) shall be introduced or moved in the Legislature of a State without the previous sanction of the President.

Article 305: Saving of existing laws and laws providing for State monopolies.

Article 306: Power of certain States in Part B of the First Schedule to impose restrictions on trade and commerce (stands repealed by the Constitution (7th Amendment) Act, 1956, w.e.f. 1 November 1956).

Article 307: Appointment of authority for carrying out the purposes of articles 301 to 304.

Comment on Part-XIII

Part-XIII of the Constitution enumerates a set of constitutional limitations on the legislative power of the union and of the states to regulate trade, commerce, and intercourse throughout the territory of India.

In the *Draft Constitution,* finalised by the Drafting Committee, freedom of trade, commerce, and intercourse throughout the territory of India was initially incorporated as one of the fundamental rights in the following words:

> 16. Subject to the provisions of Article 244 of this Constitution and any law made by Parliament, trade, commerce, and intercourse throughout the territory of India shall be free.

Dr Ambedkar had explained to members of the Constituent Assembly that the reason why this had to be included in the Fundamental Rights Chapter was because the Indian states were to join the Dominion of India and be a part of it under the provisions of the Government of India Act, 1935 only on three subjects: foreign affairs, defence, and communications. It was realised that there would be no use in forming an All-Indian Union of States if trade and commerce throughout the territory of India were not free. Hence it was decided in the Draft Constitution to place the article in the Fundamental Rights Chapter. But since all the states (except the State of Jammu and Kashmir for which separate *temporary* provision had been made—Article 370) ultimately joined the Dominion unreservedly and duly signed instruments of accession before November 1949, the Article on trade, commerce, and intercourse throughout the territory of India was transferred to a separate part of the Constitution.

The most recent leading case on PART-XIII is the decision of the Supreme Court of India in *Jindal Stainless Steel Ltd. vs. State of Haryana* reported in AIR 2016 SC 5617, where a bench of nine judges[78] of the Supreme Court of India (7:2) finally dealt with what had always been a vexed question touching the interpretation of Articles 301 to 307, viz:.

> *. . . can the levy of a non-discriminatory tax per se constitute an infraction of Article 301 of the Constitution of India.*

The answer given by the majority was that a non-discriminatory tax does not per se constitute a restriction on the right to free trade, commerce, and intercourse guaranteed under Article 301, and consequently, earlier decisions of the Supreme Court of India (of smaller benches) taking a contrary view were overruled[79].

As regards an additional question as to whether entry tax levied by states would be violative of Article 301 of the Constitution and whether state enactments relating to entry tax have to be tested with reference to both Article 304(a) and 304(b) of the Constitution for determining their validity, the highest court has said that Article 304(b) does not deal with taxes as 'restrictions' and that the restrictions that are referred to in Article 304(b) are non-fiscal in nature. And hence the constitutional validity of any taxing statute must be tested only on the anvil of Article 304(a) and if the law is found to be non-discriminatory, it would be declared to be constitutionally valid without the legislation having to go through the test or the process envisaged in Article 304(b). However, should the statute fail the test of non-discrimination under Article 304(a), it would have to be struck down because what is constitutionally impermissible in terms of Article 304(a) cannot be validated and sanctioned through the medium of Article 304(b). In other words, 'a fiscal statute is open to challenge only under Article 304(a) of the Constitution without being subjected to the test of Article 304(b), either in terms of the existence of public interest or reasonableness of the levy.'

Note

In Durga Das Basu's *Shorter Constitution of India* (15th edition, Vol. 2 by Justice A. K. Patnaik), a useful summary is given of Articles 301-307 (on page 1525).

An altogether different aspect of Articles 301 to 307 is that the protection of Part-XIII of the Constitution is given only to *lawful* trading activities and therefore activities like gambling and trade in liquors are not within the contemplation of Part-XIII. This had been so held in the leading case of *State of Bombay vs. Chamarbaugwala* (AIR 1957 SC 99) (a Constitution Bench decision of five judges) and followed in *Har Shankar vs. Deputy Excise Commissioner* (AIR 1975 SC 1121) and *Khoday Distilleries Ltd. vs. State of Karnataka* (1995 (1) SCC 574).

---------- Part-XIV ----------

Services under the Union and the States—Articles 308 to 323 (including provision for a Public Service Commission—Articles 314 to 323)

Chapter I: Services

Article 308: Interpretation.

Article 309: Recruitment and conditions of service of persons serving the Union or a State.

Article 310: Tenure of office of persons serving the Union or a State.

Article 311: Dismissal, removal, or reduction in rank of persons employed in civil capacities under the Union or a State.

Article 312: All-India services.

Article 312A: Power of Parliament to vary or revoke conditions of service of officers of certain services (inserted by the Constitution 28th Amendment Act, 1972, w.e.f. 29 August 1972).

Article 313: Transitional provisions.

Article 314. [Provision for protection of existing officers of certain services]—Omitted by the Constitution and was repealed by the (28th Amendment) Act, 1972, s. 3 (w.e.f. 29 August 1972).

Chapter II: Public Service Commissions

Article 315: Public Service Commissions for the Union and for the States.

1. Subject to the provisions of this article, there shall be a Public Service Commission for the Union and a Public Service Commission for each State.

2. Two or more States may agree that there shall be one Public Service Commission for that group of States, and if a resolution to that effect is passed by the House or, where there are two Houses, by each House of the Legislature of each of those States, Parliament may by law provide for the appointment of a Joint State Public Service Commission (referred to in this Chapter as Joint Commission) to serve the needs of those States.
3. Any such law as aforesaid may contain such incidental and consequential provisions as may be necessary or desirable for giving effect to the purposes of the law.
4. The Public Service Commission for the Union, if requested so to do by the Governor 1*** of a State, may, with the approval of the President, agree to serve all or any of the needs of the State.
5. References in this Constitution to the Union Public Service Commission or a State Public Service Commission shall, unless the context otherwise requires, be construed as references to the Commission serving the needs of the Union or, as the case may be, the State as respects the particular matter in question.

Article 316: Appointment and term of office of members.

Article 317: Removal and suspension of a member of a Public Service Commission.

Article 318: Power to make regulations as to conditions of service of members and staff of the Commission.

Article 319: Prohibition as to the holding of offices by members of Commission on ceasing to be such members.

<u>Article 320</u>: Functions of Public Service Commissions:

1. It shall be the duty of the Union and the State Public Service Commissions to conduct examinations for appointments to the services of the Union and the services of the State respectively.
2. It shall also be the duty of the Union Public Service Commission, if requested by any two or more States so to do, to assist those States in framing and operating schemes of joint recruitment for any services for which candidates possessing special qualifications are required.
3. The Union Public Service Commission or the State Public Service Commission, as the case may be, shall be consulted:

(a) on all matters relating to methods of recruitment to civil services and for civil posts.

(b) on the principles to be followed in making appointments to civil services and posts and in making promotions and transfers from one service to another and on the suitability of candidates for such appointments, promotions, or transfers.

(c) on all disciplinary matters affecting a person serving under the Government of India or the Government of a State in a civil capacity, including memorials or petitions relating to such matters.

(d) on any claim by or in respect of a person who is serving or has served under the Government of India or the Government of a State or under the Crown in India or under the Government of an Indian State, in a civil capacity, that any costs incurred by him in defending legal proceedings instituted against him in respect of acts done or purporting to be done in the execution of his duty should be paid out of the Consolidated Fund of India, or, as the case may be, out of the Consolidated Fund of the State.

(e) on any claim for the award of a pension in respect of injuries sustained by a person while serving under the Government of India or the Government of a State or under the Crown in India or under the Government of an Indian State, in a civil capacity, and any question as to the amount of any such award, and it shall be the duty of a Public Service Commission to advise on any matter so referred to them and on any other matter which the President, or, as the case may be, the Governor of the State, may refer to them:

Provided that the President as respects the all-India services and also as respects other services and posts in connection with the affairs of the Union, and the Governor, as respects other services and posts in connection with the affairs of a State, may make regulations specifying the matters in which either generally, or in any particular class of case or in any particular circumstances, it shall not be necessary for a Public Service Commission to be consulted.

4. Nothing in clause (3) shall require a Public Service Commission to be consulted as respects the manner in which any provision referred to in clause (4) of article 16 may be made or as respects the manner in which effect may be given to the provisions of article 335.

5. All regulations made under the proviso to clause (3) by the President or the Governor 1*** of a State shall be laid for not less than fourteen days before each House of Parliament or the House or each House of the Legislature of the State, as the case may be, as soon as possible after they are made, and shall be subject to such modifications, whether by way of repeal or amendment, as both Houses of Parliament or the House or both

Houses of the Legislature of the State may make during the session in which they are so laid.

Article 321: Power to extend functions of Public Service Commissions.

Article 322: Expenses of Public Service Commissions.

Article 323: Reports of Public Service Commissions.

Comment on Public Service Commissions:

The framers of the Constitution of India created some constitutional institutions to uphold constitutional values—Public Service Commissions being one of them. Article 315 of the Constitution of India mandates that there shall be a Public Service Commission for the union and a Public Service Commission for each state. Article 320 provides for the functions of the Public Service Commission stating that it is the duty of the Union Public Service Commission and the State Public Service Commissions to conduct examinations for appointments to the services of the union and the services of the state respectively. In relation to certain matters the Union of India and the states are enjoined with the duties to consult the Public Service Commission. With a view to uphold the dignity and independence of the Public Service Commission, the salaries, allowances, and pensions payable to the members or staff of the commission, are directed to be charged on the Consolidated Fund of India and/or the Consolidated Fund of the State. Also, a chairman of Public Service Commission is removable only by following the procedure laid down under the Constitution of India.

The importance of the Public Service Commission and its chairman had been highlighted in *R/o Ram Ashray Yadav, Chairman vs. Bihar Public Service Commission* (AIR 2000 SC 1448 on page 1450):

> (*Quote*) 31. The credibility of the institution of Public Service Commission is founded upon faith of the common man on its proper functioning. The faith would be eroded and confidence destroyed if it appears that the Chairman or the Members of the Commission act subjectively and not objectively or that their actions are suspect. Society expects honesty, integrity and complete objectivity from the Chairman and Members of the Commission. The Commission must act fairly, without any pressure or influence from any quarter, unbiased and impartially, so that the society does not lose confidence in the Commission. The high constitutional trustees, like the Chairman and Members of the Public Service Commission must for ever remain vigilant and conscious of these necessary adjuncts. (*Unquote*)

However, a murkier side of the picture was exposed in yet another decision—*Inderpreet Singh Kahlon vs. State of Punjab* (AIR 2006 SC 2571 on page 2597)—where one of the justices on the bench of two judges of the Supreme Court of India—Justice Dalveer Bhandari (now a sitting judge of the International Court of Justice at the Hague)—had said (about falling standards of rectitude in public life):

> (*Quote*) 107. The founding fathers of the Constitution perhaps in their wildest dreams, could not have visualised that the people who are expected to strictly adhere to constitutional values and guide the destiny of the Nation in times to come would malign and denigrate the system and in the larger public interest would be required to be put behind the bars. The Chairman of the Punjab Public Service Commission is an important constitutional authority.
>
> 108. This case relates to a period when one Revinder Pal Singh Sidhu (in short, R. S. Sidhu) was the Chairman of the Punjab Public Service Commission (herein called the

Commission) from September 1996 to 2002. His clandestine activities and misdeeds reached the pinnacle of degradation and humiliation. Perhaps, no one could have polluted the entire system in greater measure. On 25 March 2002, an FIR was registered at police station, Mohali, under Section 7 read with Section 13(2) of the Prevention of Corruption Act, 1988, in relation to the trap organised in which R. S. Sidhu was caught red-handed accepting a bribe of Rs 5 lakhs.

109. In three days from 17 April 2002 to 19 April 2002, more than Rs 16 crores were recovered from the lockers and the bank accounts of the relations of R. S. Sidhu . . . securities and properties worth about Rs 22 crores were recovered. Out of the said amount, a sum of Rs 1.28 crores was recovered from the house of Jagman Singh. In the history of this country, there may not have been many cases of the Prevention of Corruption Act of this magnitude, where such huge amount was collected. All this amount was collected by R. S. Sidhu in lieu of ensuring recruitment/appointments to various offices of the PCS (Executive Branch), allied services and PCS (Judicial Branch) in the State of Punjab from the prospective candidates.

110. This unfortunate episode teaches us an important lesson that before appointing the constitutional authorities, there should be a thorough and meticulous inquiry and scrutiny regarding their antecedents. Integrity and merit have to be properly considered and evaluated in the appointments. It is an urgent need of the hour that in such appointments absolute transparency is required to be maintained and demonstrated. The impact of the deeds and misdeeds of the constitutional authorities (who are highly placed) affect a very large number of people for a very long time. Therefore, it is absolutely imperative that only people of high integrity merit, rectitude, and honesty are appointed to such constitutional positions. (*Unquote*)

---------- Part-XIV-A ----------

TRIBUNALS — Articles 323A and 323B (Part-XI-A were added by the Constitution Forty-Second Amendment Act, 1976 (w.e.f. 3 January 1977) during the Internal Emergency of June 1975.

<u>Article 323A</u>: Administrative Tribunals:-

1. Parliament may, by law, provide for the adjudication or trial by administrative tribunals of disputes and complaints with respect to recruitment and conditions of service of persons appointed to public services and posts in connection with the affairs of the Union or of any State or of any local or other authority within the territory of India or under the control of the Government of India or of any corporation owned or controlled by the Government.

2. A law made under clause (1) may:

(a) provide for the establishment of an administrative tribunal for the Union and a separate administrative tribunal for each State or for two or more States.

(b) specify the jurisdiction, powers (including the power to punish for contempt) and authority which may be exercised by each of the said tribunals.

(c) provide for the procedure (including provisions as to limitation and rules of evidence) to be followed by the said tribunals.

(d) exclude the jurisdiction of all courts, except the jurisdiction of the Supreme Court under article 136, with respect to the disputes or complaints referred to in clause (1).

(e) provide for the transfer to each such administrative tribunal of any cases pending before any court or other authority immediately before the establishment of such tribunal as would have been within the jurisdiction of such tribunal if the causes of action on which such suits or proceedings are based had arisen after such establishment.

(f) repeal or amend any order made by the President under clause (3) of article 371D.

(g) contain such supplemental, incidental and consequential provisions (including provisions as to fees) as Parliament may deem necessary for the effective functioning of, and for the speedy disposal of cases by, and the enforcement of the orders of, such tribunals.

3. The provisions of this article shall have effect notwithstanding anything in any other provision of this Constitution or in any other law for the time being in force.

<u>Article 323B</u>: Tribunals for other matters

1. The appropriate Legislature may by law provide for adjudication or trial by tribunals of any disputes offences with respect to all or any of the matters specified in clause (2) with respect to which the legislature has power to make laws.

2. The matters referred to in clause (1) are the following, namely:

Comment on Tribunals:

The 45th Amendment Bill, 1978 (introduced after the revocation of the Internal Emergency of June 1975) contained provisions for the repeal of Article 323A and 323B, but they were not passed.

The Law Commission of India, in its Report No. 272 dated October 2017, has given its *Assessment of Statutory Framework of Tribunals in India.* But in my view, Tribunalisation of the legal system has not been a success since the confidence of litigants and of the public remains—as it was before—with the established courts. Tribunlisation and compartmentalisation have generally failed. There is a need for more expertise in benches in established courts, e.g. an arbitration bench, a labour bench, a Constitution Bench, etc., stressing the experience of judges who handle such matters.

The Supreme Court of India in *L. Chandra Kumar vs. UOI* (AIR 1997 SC 1425) (a special bench of seven Judges) held that clause 2(d) of Article 323A, and clause 3(d) of Article 323B[80] to the extent that they excluded the jurisdiction of the Supreme Court under Article 32, and of the high courts under Articles 226 and 227 were unconstitutional, since they adversely affected the *basic structure* of the Constitution, and correspondingly provisions of the Administrative Tribunal Act, 1985 (w.e.f. 2 October 1985), enacted pursuant to the insertion of Articles 323A and 323B), were also declared to be unconstitutional.

However, the bench of seven judges had also held that the tribunals created under Article 323A and Article 323B of the Constitution remained possessed of the competence to test the constitutional validity of statutory provisions and rules but that all decisions of these tribunals would be subject to scrutiny before a division bench of the high court within whose jurisdiction the concerned tribunal was situated, and that the tribunals would nevertheless, continue to act like courts of first instance in respect of the areas of law for which they had been constituted. It would not, therefore, be open for litigants to directly approach the high courts even in cases where they questioned the vires of statutory legislation (except where the legislation that created the particular tribunal was challenged).

In *Madras Bar Association vs. Union of India* (2014 (10) SCC page 1), a Constitution Bench of five judges of the Supreme Court of India declared the National Tax Tribunal

Act of 2005 (an enactment in pursuance of Articles 323A and 323B) as unconstitutional. It was held that the 'basic structure' of the Constitution would stand violated if while enacting legislation pertaining to transfer of judicial power, Parliament does not ensure that the newly created court/ tribunal conforms with the salient characteristics of the court sought to be substituted.

And in the same case, in a (concurring) judgement at page 243, it was held as follows (and this is the true ratio of the case):

> In view of the constitutional scheme and the jurisdiction conferred on this Court under Article 32 and on the High Courts under Article 226 of the Constitution the power of judicial review being an integral part of the basic structure of the Constitution, *no Act of Parliament can exclude or curtail the powers of the constitutional courts with regard to the enforcement of fundamental rights.*

Then, quoting Lord Atkin, in *1931 Appeal Cases 310* (PC), the concurring judgement went on to say that 'time alone will not validate an Act which when challenged is found to be ultra vires, nor will a history of a gradual series of advances till this boundary is finally crossed avail to protect the ultimate encroachment'. The concurring judgement then concluded that the boundaries having been finally (and definitely) crossed, *the National Tax Tribunal Act, 2005 was therefore unconstitutional 'being the ultimate encroachment on the exclusive domain of the Superior Courts of record in India'.*

----------Part-XV ----------

Elections—Articles 324 to 329A

Article 324: Superintendence, direction, and control of elections to be vested in an Election Commission.

1. The superintendence, direction, and control of the preparation of the electoral rolls for, and the conduct of, all elections to Parliament and to the Legislature of every State and of elections to the offices of President and Vice-President held under this Constitution[81] shall be vested in a Commission (referred to in this Constitution as the Election Commission).
2. The Election Commission shall consist of the Chief Election Commissioner and such number of other Election Commissioners, if any, as the President may from time-to-time fix and the appointment of the Chief Election Commissioner and other Election Commissioners shall, subject to the provisions of any law made in that behalf by Parliament, be made by the President.
3. When any other Election Commissioner is so appointed, the Chief Election Commissioner shall act as the Chairman of the Election Commission.
4. Before each general election to the House of the People and to the Legislative Assembly of each State, and before the first general election and thereafter before each biennial election to the Legislative Council of each State having such Council, the President may also appoint after consultation with the Election Commission such Regional Commissioners as he may consider necessary to assist the Election Commission in the performance of the functions conferred on the Commission by clause (1).

5. Subject to the provisions of any law made by Parliament, the conditions of service and tenure of office of the Election Commissioners and the Regional Commissioners shall be such as the President may by rule determine:

   (a) Provided that the Chief Election Commissioner shall not be removed from his office except in like manner and on the like grounds as a Judge of the Supreme Court and the conditions of service of the Chief Election Commissioner shall not be varied to his disadvantage after his appointment.

   (b) Provided further that any other Election Commissioner or a Regional Commissioner shall not be removed from office except on the recommendation of the Chief Election Commissioner.

6. The President, or the Governor of a State, shall, when so requested by the Election Commission, make available to the Election Commission or to a Regional Commissioner such staff as may be necessary for the discharge of the functions conferred on the Election Commission by clause (1).

Article 325: No person to be ineligible for inclusion in, or to claim to be included in a special, electoral roll on grounds of religion, race, caste, or sex.

Article 326: Elections to the House of the People and to the Legislative Assemblies of States to be on the basis of adult suffrage.

Article 327: Power of Parliament to make provision with respect to elections to Legislatures.

Article 328: Power of Legislature of a State to make provision with respect to elections to such Legislature.

Article 329: Bar to interference by courts in electoral matters— 3[Notwithstanding anything in this Constitution 4***—]:

(a) the validity of any law relating to the delimitation of constituencies or the allotment of seats to such constituencies, made or purporting to be made under Article 327 or Article 328, shall not be called in question in any court.

(b) no election to either House of Parliament or to the House or either House of the Legislature of a State shall be called in question except by an election petition presented to such authority and in such manner as may be provided for by or under any law made by the appropriate Legislature.

Comment: on Article 329(b)

Article 329(b) has been pithily described in a Constitution Bench judgment (delivered by Justice Krishna Iyer) as "*the Great Wall of China*" – (*Mohinder Singh Gill vs. Chief Election Commissioner* – AIR 1978 S.C. 851 (5J) – impregnable and not to be by passed even by a high prerogative Writ (under Article 226)! –

> "There is a non-obstante clause in Article 329 and, therefore, Article 226 stands pushed out where the dispute takes the form of calling in question an election, except in special situations pointed out but left unexplored in Ponnuswami." (AIR 1952 S.C. 64)

[**Article 329A**: A special Provision as to elections to Parliament in the case of the Prime Minister and Speaker (inserted by the Constitution 39th Amendment Act, 1975, w.e.f. 10 August 1975).

Clause (4) of Article 329A had been struck down in *Raj Narain vs. Indira Gandhi/Indira Gandhi vs. Raj Narain* in 1975 Supp. SCC page 1. The rest of Article 329A was repealed by the Constitution 44th Amendment Act, 1978, w.e.f. 20 June 1979.]

Comment on the Election Commission:

Article 324 of the Constitution provides for the Election Commission. Article 324(1) vests the 'superintendence, direction, and control of elections' in the Election Commission. Article 324(2) states that '. . . the appointment of the Chief Election Commissioner and other Election Commissioners shall, *subject to the provisions of any law* made in that behalf by Parliament, be made by the President'. Article 324(5)—similarly—authorises the President (by rule) to determine the conditions of service and tenure of office of the Election Commissioners, again 'subject to a law' made by Parliament. With respect to Article 324(5), Parliament did make a law in 1991 (the Election Commission Act of 1991) but with respect to Article 324 (2), no law was ever made.

In *Anoop Baranwal vs. Union of India*, a judgement delivered on 2 March 2023 and reported in 2023(3) SCALE 640 (SC) = 2023 SCC Online SC 216, a Constitution Bench of the Supreme Court held—unanimously—that *the selection of the Chief Election Commissioner as well as of the Election Commissioners (two of them) should be done only by a three-member committee consisting of the prime minister, the leader of the opposition (or the leader of the largest opposition party in Parliament), and the Chief Justice of India*[82].

Whilst altering the constitutionally prescribed mode of selection, the court paid heed to Dr Ambedkar's grave misgivings expressed in the Constituent Assembly on 16 June 16 1949 when introducing draft Article 289[83] (see footnote 83)*.

The Supreme Court also followed what was said in *Vineet Narain's* case (1998), where a bench of three judges of the

* In the Constituent Assembly Debates, Dr Ambedkar had also said: "My provision—I must admit—does not contain anything to provide against nomination of an unfit person to be Chief Election Commissioner or even an Election Commissioner".

Supreme Court of India had directed a somewhat similar requirement for the appointment of the chief vigilance commissioner[84], a direction that later got incorporated (by government itself) in the Central Vigilance Commission Bill No.137 of 1999, introduced in Parliament, and later passed by Parliament into law, viz., section 4 of the Central Vigilance Commission Act No. 45 of 2003.][85]

As regards the relief relating to putting in place a permanent secretariat for the Election Commission of India and charging its expenditure to the Consolidated Fund of India, the Supreme Court only suggested that the Union of India/Parliament may consider bringing in the necessary changes (by law) "so that the Election Commission of India becomes truly independent".

In a separate concurring judgement (2023 (3) SCALE 640), one of the judges, (Justice Rastogi) added (though this was not concurred in by the remaining four judges):

> *It is desirable* that the grounds of removal of the Election Commissioners shall be the same as that of the Chief Election Commissioner that is on the like grounds as a Judge of the Supreme Court subject to the 'recommendation of the Chief Election Commissioner' as provided under the second proviso to Article 324(5) of the Constitution of India.

He also added:

> The conditions of service of the Election Commissioners shall not be varied to his disadvantage after appointment.

Delhi-based lawyer, Gautam Bhatia, has written an article, 'Decoding the Supreme Court's Election Commission Judgement' (on 3 March 2023) and his comment (quoted below) is that the case itself shows 'the weaknesses in the design of the Constitution':

> The Court has altered the present mode of selection where the CEC is appointed by the President on the advice of the Prime Minister . . . In hindsight, the framers' belief that delegation to Parliament would solve the vexing issue of the independence of the EC—instead of constitutionalising it—seems particularly naive, given that the framers were also enshrining a parliamentary system of governance, which almost inevitably throws up dominant executives firmly in control of their parties. Why would those executives give up such a valuable power? History has borne this out, and it has also placed the Court in a difficult situation. Slice it any way you want, what is happening here does *appear* to be a rewriting of the Constitution by the judiciary. In this post, I have attempted to show that the Court's reasoning process to get there is defensible, *but the brute fact remains that this appointment procedure is nowhere present in the Constitution and is—essentially—brought into being by judicial fiat. This makes an attack on the Court by the executive—on grounds of judicial overreach—an inevitability*. And for that, it is the constitutional design that is to blame, because it places the Court in a no-win situation.[86]

Comment on Elections:

In the book, *Every Vote Counts: Story of India's Elections* (published by Harper Collins (2019)), the author, Navin Chawla (Chief Elections Commissioner 2009-2010), writes about elections in India and posed the question:

> *So, what makes India's general elections a focus of attention?*

And he answers it by giving the example of India's first general election held in 1951-1952:

> (*Quote*) It would be too simplistic to attempt to answer this in terms of size and volume alone, for even when the first

> general election was held in 1951-52, India's population stood at 361 million[87] (or 36.1 crores), making it the largest democratic country in the world. At that time, it was certainly about the boldness of the democratic exercise, for there was no shortage of sceptics who were convinced that India's experiment with democracy could not last.
>
> Therefore, the announcement of the first general election (spread over four months) was viewed through this prism as the first step towards India's impending failure. However, the prophets of doom were to be proved wrong. Prime Minister Jawaharlal Nehru's choice of Sukumar Sen as the first chief election commissioner was a very sound one. Inducted from the ICS (the British interested Indian Civil Service) into the mint-new Indian Administrative Service (IAS), it became his task to devise and create an electoral architecture without the benefit of precedent—the British Raj having felt no need for an independent election commission (at any time) for the provincial assembly elections of 1937 (*Unquote*).

Nine elections later, in an article ('On My Mind: The World of India') published in the *New York Times* (1 December 1989), its former Chief Editor, A. M. Rosenthal, made the following ecstatic comment on India's parliamentary elections of November 1989:

> (*Quote*) When India voted, a whole world voted.
>
> A whole world, hundreds of millions of people, speaking in a great orchestra of different languages, praying to different gods, hundreds of principalities, people driven to centuries of war against each other by rulers seeking conquest, foreigners seeking booty, religious zealots seeking blood, educated people by the millions, illiterate peasants by the scores of millions, from mountains through great stretches of plains to southern seas.
>
> Once again, this whole world voted as one nation in a countrywide election, nine times now! (*Unquote*)

More details pertaining to elections have been covered in Chapter Seven. The chapter also discusses the present composition of the election commission, and as to how it could, and why it should be made more independent of the government.

----------Part-XVI ----------

Special Provisions Relating to Certain Classes, Scheduled Castes, Scheduled Tribes, and Socially and Educationally Backward Classes—Articles 330 to 342A

Article 330: It provides for reservation of seats for Scheduled Castes and Scheduled Tribes in the House of the People (Lok Sabha).

Article 331: Representation of the Anglo-Indian Community in the House of the People. The President was empowered to nominate but not more than two members of the Anglo-Indian Community if he was of the opinion that the community was not adequately represented in the House of the People.

Article 332: Reservation of seats for Scheduled Castes and Scheduled Tribes in the Legislative Assemblies of the States.

[Under Article 341/342, the President is to specify by public notification the castes, races, and tribes that are to be deemed to be Scheduled Castes and Scheduled Tribes for the purposes of the Constitution.]

Article 333: Representation of the Anglo-Indian community in the Legislative Assemblies of the States.

Notwithstanding anything in Article 170, the Governor of a State may, if he is of opinion that the Anglo-Indian community needs representation in the Legislative Assembly of the State and is not adequately represented therein, nominate one member of that community to the Assembly.

Article 334: Reservation of seats and special representation to cease after ten years. Notwithstanding anything in the foregoing provisions of this Part, the provisions of this Constitution relating to:

(a) the reservation of seats for the Scheduled Castes and the Scheduled Tribes in the House of the People and in the Legislative Assemblies of the States; and

(b) the representation of the Anglo-Indian community in the House of the People and in the Legislative Assemblies of the States by nomination, shall cease to have effect on the expiration of a period of ten years from the commencement of this Constitution:

Provided that nothing in this article shall affect any representation in the House of the People or in the Legislative Assembly of a State until the dissolution of the then existing House or Assembly, as the case may be.

Comment:

Under Article 334 as enacted the representation of the Anglo-Indian community in the House of the People and in the legislative assembly of the states was to cease to have effect on the expiration of ten years from the commencement of the Constitution. This was later extended from time-to-time up to seventy years from the commencement of the Constitution. *Special representation for the Anglo-Indian community in the House of the People and in legislative assemblies in states, by nomination has therefore ceased to have effect on and from 25 January 2020, but reservations for scheduled castes and scheduled tribes have been continued.* The Statement of Objects and Reasons (for the bill) that became the Constitution 95th Amendment Act, 2009, stated as follows:

(*Quote*) Article 334 of the Constitution lays down that the provisions of the Constitution relating to the reservation of seats for the Scheduled Castes and the Scheduled Tribes and the *representation of the Anglo-Indian community by nomination* in the House of the People and Legislative Assemblies of the States shall cease to have effect on the expiration of the period of 70 years from the commencement of the Constitution. *In other words, these provisions will cease to have effect on the 25 January 2020, if not extended further.*

2. Although the *Scheduled Castes and the Scheduled Tribes* have made considerable progress in the last 70 years, the reasons which weighed with the Constituent Assembly in making provisions with regard to the aforesaid reservation of seats have not yet ceased to exist. Therefore, with a view to retaining the inclusive character as envisioned by the founding fathers of the Constitution, *it is proposed to continue the reservation of seats for the Scheduled Castes and the Scheduled Tribes for another ten years, i.e., up to 25 January 2030.*

3. The Bill seeks to achieve the above objects (*Unquote*).

<u>Article 335</u>: Claims of Scheduled Castes and Scheduled Tribes to services and posts. The claims of the members of the Scheduled Castes and the Scheduled Tribes shall be taken into consideration, consistently with the maintenance of efficiency of administration, in the making of appointments to services and posts in connection with the affairs of the Union or of a State.

<u>Article 336</u>: Special provision for Anglo-Indian Community in certain services.

<u>Article 337</u>: Special provision with respect to educational grants for the benefit of Anglo-Indian community.

<u>Article 338</u>: National Commission for Scheduled Castes.

<u>Article 338A</u>: National Commission for Scheduled Tribes (inserted by the Constitution 89th Amendment Act, 2003, w.e.f. 19 February 2004).

<u>Article 338B</u>: National Commission for Backward Classes (inserted by the Constitution 102nd Amendment Act, 2018, w.e.f. 25 August 2008).

<u>Article 339</u>: Control of the Union over the administration of Scheduled Areas and the welfare of Scheduled Tribes.

<u>Article 340</u>: Appointment of a Commission to investigate condition of backward classes.

<u>Article 341</u>: Scheduled Castes.

1. The President may with respect to any State or Union territory and where it is a State, after consultation with the Governor thereof, by public notification, specify the castes, races, or tribes or parts of or groups within castes, races, or tribes which shall for the purposes of this Constitution be deemed to be Scheduled Castes in relation to that State 2 (or Union territory, as the case may be).
2. Parliament may by law include in or exclude from the list of Scheduled Castes specified in a notification issued under clause (1) any caste, race, or tribe or part of or group within any caste, race, or tribe, but save as aforesaid, a notification issued under the said clause shall not be varied by any subsequent notification.

<u>Article 342</u>: Scheduled Tribes.

1. The President may with respect to any State or Union territory and where it is a State, after consultation with the Governor thereof, by public notification, specify the tribes or tribal communities or parts of or groups within tribes or tribal communities which shall for the purposes of this Constitution be deemed to be Scheduled Tribes in relation to that State (or Union territory, as the case may be).

2. Parliament may by law include in or exclude from the list of Scheduled Tribes specified in a notification issued under clause (1) any tribe or tribal community or part of

or group within any tribe or tribal community, but save as aforesaid, a notification issued under the said clause shall not be varied by any subsequent notification.

<u>**Article 342A**</u>: Socially and educationally advanced backward classes (inserted by the Constitution 102nd Amendment Act, 15 August 2018).

1. The President may with respect to any State or Union territory, and where it is a State, after consultation with the Governor thereof, by public notification, specify the socially and educationally backward classes in the Central List which shall for the purposes of the Central Government, be deemed to be socially and educationally backward classes in relation to that State or Union territory, as the case may be.
2. Parliament may by law include in or exclude from the Central List of socially and educationally backward classes specified in a notification issued under clause (1) any socially and educationally backward class, but save as aforesaid, a notification issued under the said clause shall not be varied by any subsequent notification.
3. Notwithstanding any contained in clauses (1) and (2), every State or Union territory may, by law, prepare and maintain, for its own purposes, a list of socially and educationally backward classes, entries in which may be different from the Central List.

Comment on Part-XVI:

In exercise of the powers conferred by Article 340 (read with the observations in the principal judgement in *Indira Sawhney's* case (1992 Supp.3 SCC 217, paragraphs 652-654)), Parliament had enacted the National Commission for Backward Classes Act, 1993 for the identification of backward classes referred to in Article 16(4) and to make special provisions relating to such backward classes and their reservations for appointment to posts under the Government of India.

The provisions of Article 335 are significant but are often overlooked. In *M. R. Balaji vs. State of Mysore* (AIR 1963 SC 649 at 664 (5J)), it had been stated by Justice P. B. Gajendragadkar that:

> There can be doubt that the Constitution-makers assumed . . . that while making adequate reservation under Article 16(4) care would be taken not to provide for unreasonable, excessive, or extravagant reservation . . . Therefore, like the special provision improperly made under Article 15(4), reservation made under Article 16(4) beyond the permissible and legitimate limits would be liable to be challenged *as a fraud on the Constitution.*

None of the subsequent cases (after 1963) under Articles 15 and 16 (respecting reservations) have ever expressed any dissent from the view taken in *Balaji*, viz., that a special provision for reservation 'beyond the permissible and legitimate limits' would be a *fraud on the Constitution.* However, regrettably, the so-called 'permissible and legitimate limits' have never been definitively laid down by the Supreme Court.

----------Part-XVII ----------

Official Language—Articles 343 to 351

Chapter I: Language of the Union

<u>Article 343</u>: Official language of the Union.

1. The official language of the Union shall be Hindi in Devanagari script. The form of numerals to be used for the official purposes of the Union shall be the international form of Indian numerals.
2. Notwithstanding anything in clause (1), for a period of fifteen years from the commencement of this Constitution, the English language shall continue to be used for all the official purposes of the Union for which it was being used immediately before such commencement:

   Provided that the President may, during the said period, by order authorise the use of the Hindi language in addition to the English language and of the Devanagari form of numerals in addition to the international form of Indian numerals for any of the official purposes of the Union.
3. Notwithstanding anything in this article, Parliament may by law provide for the use, after the said period of fifteen years, of:

   (a) the English language, or

   (b) the Devanagari form of numerals, for such purposes as may be specified in the law.

<u>Article 344</u>: Commission and Committee of Parliament on official language.

Chapter II: Regional Language

Article 345: Official language or languages of a State.

Article 346. Official language for communication between one State and another or between a State and the Union.

Article 347: Special provision that a demand being made, the President may, if satisfied that a substitute portion of the population of a State denies the use of a spoken language to be officially recognised, direct that such language shall also be officially recognised throughout the State or any part thereof relating to language spoken by a section of the population of a State.

Chapter III: Language of the Supreme Court, High Courts, etc.

Article 348: Language to be used in the Supreme Court and in the High Courts and for Acts, Bills, etc., to be English.

Article 349: Special procedure for enactment of certain laws relating to language (operates during the first 25 years for the commencement of the Constitution).

Chapter IV: Special Directives

Article 350: Language to be used in representations for redress of grievances.

Article 350A: Facilities for instruction in mother tongue at primary stage (inserted by the Constitution 7th Amendment Act of 1956, w.e.f. 1 November 1956).

Article 350B: Special Officer for linguistic minorities (inserted by Constitution 7th Amendment 1956, w.e.f. 1 November 1956).

Article 351: Directive for development of the Hindi language.

Comment :

Details pertaining to the Official Language are set out in Chapter Two.

----------Part-XVIII ----------

Emergency Provisions—Articles 352 to 360

Article 352: Proclamation of Emergency; in case of or amend rebellion or external aggression.

Article 353: Effect of Proclamation of Emergency.

Article 354: Application of provisions relating to distribution of revenues while a Proclamation of Emergency is in operation.

Article 355: Duty of the Union to protect States against external aggression and internal disturbance.

Article 356: Provisions in case of failure of constitutional machinery in States.

(1) If the President, on receipt of a report from the Governor[88] of a State or otherwise, is satisfied that a situation has arisen in which the Government of the State cannot be carried on in accordance with the provisions of this Constitution, the President may by Proclamation:

(a) assume to himself all or any of the functions of the Government of the State and all or any of the powers vested in or exercisable by the Governor[89] or anybody or authority in the State other than the Legislature of the State.

(b) declare that the powers of the Legislature of the State shall be exercisable by or under the authority of Parliament.

(c) make such incidental and consequential provisions as appear to the President to be necessary or desirable for giving effect to the objects of the Proclamation, including provisions for suspending in whole or in part the operation of any provisions of this

Constitution relating to anybody or authority in the State:

Provided that nothing in this clause shall authorise the President to assume to himself any of the powers vested in or exercisable by a High Court, or to suspend in whole or in part the operation of any provision of this Constitution relating to High Courts.

(2) Any such Proclamation may be revoked or varied by a subsequent Proclamation.

(3) Every Proclamation under this article shall be laid before each House of Parliament and shall, except where it is a Proclamation revoking a previous Proclamation, cease to operate at the expiration of two months unless before the expiration of that period it has been approved by resolutions of both Houses of Parliament:

Provided that if any such Proclamation (not being a Proclamation revoking a previous Proclamation) is issued at a time when the House of the People is dissolved or the dissolution of the House of the People takes place during the period of two months referred to in this clause, and if a resolution approving the Proclamation has been passed by the Council of States, but no resolution with respect to such Proclamation has been passed by the House of the People before the expiration of that period, the Proclamation shall cease to operate at the expiration of thirty days from the date on which the House of the People first sits after its reconstitution unless before the expiration of the said period of thirty days a resolution approving the Proclamation has been also passed by the House of the People.

(4) A Proclamation so approved shall, unless revoked, cease to operate on the expiration of a period of[90] (six months from the date of issue of the Proclamation):

Provided that if and so often as a resolution approving the continuance in force of such a Proclamation is passed by both Houses of Parliament, the Proclamation shall, unless revoked, continue in force for a further period of 2 (six months) from the date on which under this clause it would otherwise have ceased to operate, but no such Proclamation shall in any case remain in force or more than three years:

Provided further that if the dissolution of the House of the People takes place during any such period of[91] (six months) and a resolution approving the continuance in force of such Proclamation has been passed by the Council of States, but no resolution with respect to the continuance in force of such Proclamation has been passed by the House of the People during the said period, the Proclamation shall cease to operate at the expiration of thirty days from the date on which the House of the People first sits after its reconstitution unless before the expiration of the said period of thirty days a resolution approving the continuance in force of the Proclamation has been also passed by the House of the People:

[92][Provided also that in the case of the Proclamation issued under clause (1) on the 11th day of May 1987 with respect to the State of Punjab, the reference in the first proviso to this clause to 'three years' shall be construed as a reference to[93] (five years).]

[94][(5) Notwithstanding anything contained in clause (4), a resolution with respect to the continuance in force of a Proclamation approved under clause (3) for any period beyond the expiration of one year from the date of issue of such Proclamation shall not be passed by either House of Parliament unless:

(a) a Proclamation of Emergency is in operation, in the whole of India or, as the case may be, in the whole or any part of the State, at the time of the passing of such resolution, and

(b) the Election Commission certifies that the continuance in force of the Proclamation approved under clause (3) during the period specified in such resolution is necessary on account of difficulties in holding general elections to the Legislative Assembly of the State concerned:

[95][Provided that nothing in this clause shall apply to the Proclamation issued under clause (1) on the 11th day of May 1987 with respect to the State of Punjab.]

Article 357: Exercise of legislative powers under Proclamation issued under article 356.

Article 358: Suspension of provisions of Article 19 during emergencies.

Article 359: Suspension of the enforcement of the rights conferred by Part-III during emergencies.

Article 359A: [Application of this Part to the State of Punjab]—Omitted by the Constitution 63rd Amendment Act, 1989, s. 3 (w.e.f. 6 January 1990).

Article 360: Provisions as to financial emergency.

Comment on Article 356:

This article preserves the integrity of the union of states when the president 'on receipt of a report from the governor of a state or otherwise' comes to the conclusion—on the advice of his council of ministers—that the government of a state cannot be carried on in accordance with the provisions of the

Constitution, 'President's Rule' is imposed in that state, i.e., the Union (the Centre) takes charge of the affairs of that state. Powers of the state get restored only after fresh elections take place in the state.

The lead case on Article 356 is *S. R. Bommai vs. Union of India* (1994 (3) SCC page 1) where it was held (by a bench of nine judges) that the scope of judicial review was limited based on *Wednesbury principles.*[96] The view of the majority in *Bommai (1994)* (7:2) has been summed up in a subsequent decision by a Bench of 2 Judges in *A. K. Kaul vs. Union of India* (1995 (4) SCC 73 paragraph 21 at page87) as follows:

(*Quote*)

i. the satisfaction of the President in making a Proclamation under Article 356(1) is justiciable;

ii. it would be open to challenge on the ground of mala fides or on the ground of being based wholly on extraneous and/or irrelevant grounds;

iii. even if some of the materials on which the action is taken is found to be irrelevant, the court would not interfere so long as there is some relevant material sustaining the action;

iv. the truth or correctness of the material cannot be questioned by the Court nor will it go into the adequacy of the material and it will also not substitute its opinion for that of the President;

v. the ground of *mala fides* takes in inter alia situations where the proclamation is found to be a clear case of abuse of power or what is sometimes called a fraud on power;

vi. the court will not lightly presume abuse or misuse of power and will make allowance for the fact that the President and the Union Council of Ministers are the best judge of the situation and that they are also in possession of information and material and that the Constitution has trusted their judgement in the matter; and

vii. this does not mean that the President and the Council of Ministers are the final arbiters in the matter or that their opinion is conclusive.

viii. As to the bar to an inquiry by the court imposed under Article 74(2)[97] of the Constitution (Council of Ministers), all the Nine Judges in *S. R. Bommai* (1994) had held that the said bar under Article 74(2) was confined to the advice tendered by the Council of Ministers to the President and did not extend to the material on the basis of which the advice was tendered and, therefore, Articles 74(2) did not bar the production in court of the material on which the advice of the Council of Ministers had been summed up, was based. (This was however subject to the right to claim privilege against production of the said material under Section 123 of the Evidence Act. (*Unquote*).

In *S. R. Bommai* (1994), though all the nine judges held that the exercise of power under Article 356(1) of the Constitution was subject to judicial review, on the question of justiciability of an order of the President (under Article 356 (1)), the view of the majority of judges (Justice Jeevan Reddy in the lead) was that the principles of administrative law expounded in *Barium Chemicals Ltd. vs. Company Law Board* (AIR 1967 SC 295) for adjudging the validity of on action based on a subjective satisfaction of the authority created by statute would not apply in its entirety when considering the exercise of a constitutional power.

Hence, the sufficiency or correctness of factual aspects in a decision of a constitutional authority cannot be reviewed by the courts.

In a later order of a Bench of five Judges of the Supreme Court of India in *Rameshwar Prasad vs. Union of India* – 2005 (7) SCC 157 (Order), with reasons given (reported in (2006) 2 SCC 1) three of the Justices examined factual aspects of that case and held that the Proclamation of the President under Article 356 was vitiated by mala fides – the Governor (in that case) having clearly misled the President (i.e. the Council of Minister advising the President).

----------Part-XIX ----------

Miscellaneous—Articles 361 to 367

Article 361: Protection of President and Governors and Rajpramukhs.

1. The President, or the Governor or Rajpramukh of a State, shall not be answerable to any court for the exercise and performance of the powers and duties of his office or for any act done or purporting to be done by him in the exercise and performance of those powers and duties:

   Provided that the conduct of the President may be brought under review by any court, tribunal, or body appointed or designated by either House of Parliament for the investigation of a charge under Article 61.

   Provided further that nothing in this clause shall be construed as restricting the right of any person to bring appropriate proceedings against the Government of India or the Government of a State.

2. No criminal proceedings whatsoever shall be instituted or continued against the President, or the Governor of a State, in any court during his term of office.

3. No process for the arrest or imprisonment of the President, or the Governor of a State, shall issue from any court during his term of office.

4. No civil proceedings in which relief is claimed against the President, or the Governor of a State, shall be instituted during his term of office in any court in respect of any act done or purporting to be done by him in his personal capacity, whether before or after he entered upon his office as President, or as Governor of such State, until the expiration of two months next after notice in writing has been delivered to the President or the Governor, as the case may be, or left at his office stating the nature

> of the proceedings, the cause of action therefore, the name, description, and place of residence of the party by whom such proceedings are to be instituted and the relief which he claims.

Comment on Article 361:

Article 361 affords personal immunity from legal action to the heads of state (the president) and to heads of state governments (governors and rajpramukhs) for their official acts (The administrative title of rajpramukhs existed during the period of India's independence from 1947, but it was only upto 1956 that heads of provinces or states were called 'rajpramukhs').

Since the proviso to Article 361 clarifies that 'nothing in the clause shall be construed as restricting the right of any person to bring appropriate proceedings against the government of India or the government of a state', it has been held that where personal mala fides are alleged or the plea is of acting ultra vires, it is not open to the government (central or state) to urge that the same cannot be satisfactorily answered because of the immunity granted and the allegations of mala fides and of ultra vires would have to be answered by the appropriate government (central or state).

Article 361 only bars the issue of a notice by the court to the president/governor, in any suit or legal proceeding it does not bar the scrutiny by the court of the alleged action/inaction on the part of the high-ranking dignitary named in Article 361.

As was held—with unanimity—by a Constitution Bench of five judges of the Supreme Court of India (on 8 September 2005) in *Rameshwar Prasad vs. Union of India* (2005 (7) SCC 157 on page 158):

> The Constitution of India grants immunity to the Governor as provided in Article 361. Article 361(1), inter alia, provides that the Governor shall not be answerable to any court for

> the exercise and performance of the powers and duties of his office or for any act done or purporting to be done by him in exercise and performance of those powers and duties. It is submitted by learned Attorney General and Additional Solicitor General that in view of Article 361(1), this Court may not issue notice to the Governor. *While we accept the submission but, at the same time, it is also necessary to note that the immunity granted to the Governor does not affect the power of the Court to judicially scrutinise the attack made to the proclamation issued under Article 356(1) of the Constitution of India on the ground of mala fides or it being ultra vires. It would be for the Government to satisfy the court and adequately meet such ground of challenge.* A mala fide act is wholly outside the scope of the power and has no existence in the eyes of law. Even, the expression 'purporting to be done' in Article 361 does not cover acts which are mala fide or ultra vires and, thus, the Government supporting the Proclamation under Article 356(1) shall have to meet the challenge. *The immunity granted under Article 361 does not mean that in the absence of the Governor, the ground of mala fides or the Proclamation being ultra vires would not be examined by the Court.*

But in the ultimate decision on merits in *Rameshwar Prasad vs. Union of India: 2006 (2) SCC 1,* it was only three of the judges in the Constitution Bench of five judges (viz. Chief Justices Sabharwal, B. N. Agrawal, and Justice Ashok Bhan) who held that the reports of the governor to the president were actuated by mala fides, and as a consequence, the proclamation under Article 356 was vitiated and it was therefore set aside, but two of the judges (Justices K. G. Balakrishnan and Arijit Pasayat) dissented stating:

> The Governor recommended dissolution on the ground that the majority that has been projected had its foundation on unethical and corrupt means in order to cobble a majority,

but that may be a wrong perception of the Governor, but it was certainly not irrational, irrelevant, or extraneous.

The minority then went on to say that even if it was assumed that the presidential proclamation under Article 356 was ultra vires or unconstitutional, the natural consequence would not be the restoration of the status quo ante. The minority also cautioned the centre that 'it has become imperative and necessary that right persons are chosen as governors if the sanctity of the post of head of the executive of a state is to be maintained.'

Comment on the Judgements in the Bihar Dissolution Case (2005)

Who won? The Government of India certainly did not, because the proclamation of the president (i.e., the central government) dissolving the Bihar Legislative Assembly was struck down (by majority of 3:2). *Who lost?* Only Bihar's governor. Except for a gentle ticking-off, there was an otherwise ominous silence particularly in the majority judgement on the role of the council of ministers (whose duty it was to advise the president). So—or so at least it appears to me—the buck had to stop at what is otherwise called 'the fall-guy', the Governor Mr Buta Singh (who made written reports to the president recommending dissolution of the Bihar Assembly). He was the lowest eminent dignitary in the chain of authority that led to the ultimate decision to dissolve the Bihar Assembly. Should the fall-guy then have resigned? Well, if the majority judgement was to be honoured—and it is the majority judgement that did bind the Union of India—he should have resigned and, to keep the record straight, as a matter of fact, he did.

There are two lessons to be learnt from the judgements delivered in the Bihar Dissolution Case. *First, one must change the system for the removal of governors.* Though governors will continue to be appointed by the centre, 'at the pleasure of President'[98], they do have a fixed tenure of five years and they should only be removed during their period of office in the same way as high judicial functionaries—by impeachment.[99] This would save the central government from the embarrassment of having to get rid of its own appointee but more importantly, it would at the same time ensure greater transparency and probity in public life.

The second lesson has nothing to do with governments or governors, but with judgements. The judgement of the Chief Justice (for himself and his two colleagues) in the Bihar Dissolution Case speaking for the majority as well as the judgements of the two dissenting justices occupy more than 170 pages of the law reports. Senior advocates were asked by the media what the judges had said, because only lawyers can understand and interpret (on occasions, differently) the intricate legal jargon. Each judge has his or her own technique and style of writing. But I would respectfully commend to our justices something that I heard Sir Ninian Stephen say in a lecture in Sydney many decades ago. He was one of Australia's distinguished chief justices (later also its equally distinguished governor general). He said that judgements are delivered in cases mainly for the parties to the cause, but sometimes also for expounding the law where it needed to be expounded, and in this regard, it was essential that the judgement should be clear and more importantly, that it should be widely understood. For this purpose, he suggested that judges themselves should add an opening paragraph to their judgements explaining in a few words what the case was all about and what they had decided. (This is invariably done in judgements of the US Supreme Court). I would respectfully commend this advice for acceptance by justices of India's Supreme Court when delivering judgements of momentous import. And the Bihar Dissolution Case was certainly one of momentous import (since the proclamation signed by the president was set aside).

In the end, the most heartening feature about the judgements in the Bihar Legislative Assembly Dissolution Case handed down on 24 January 2006 was the fact that all five justices held that the decision to dissolve the Bihar Assembly was not beyond judicial review.[100] It is on the parameters of such judicial review (strict according to the minority and not-so-strict according to the majority) and on the conclusions to be drawn from the facts brought on record that the verdict got divided (3:2): As to why the majority did not also fault the chain of command at the higher-level, viz., the council of ministers whose decision it was to dissolve, is not explained. This is the least heartening aspect of the majority judgement. One can only surmise that it was perhaps because no unanimity could be reached by the bench about Governor Buta Singh's reports/recommendations to the centre.

One striking aspect of 'judicial governance' (some say we have too much of it, others that we should have even more) is this lack of unanimity amongst judges. Today (after the Supreme Court (Number of Judges Amendment Act, 2019)), the Supreme Court is to consist of *thirty-four individual justices*[101] who don't all think alike and are not averse to saying so. This is also reflected when they sit in Constitution Benches of five, as they did in the Bihar Dissolution Case. Ralph Waldo Emerson once said that: *'A foolish consistency is the hobgoblin of little minds.'* Even the fiercest critic of our highest court cannot accuse its incumbents of having 'little minds' and that's where the problem begins. How can five judges sitting together drawn from different parts of the country with different backgrounds—thinking differently—be expected to be consistent with one another? The problem of diversity of judicial opinion is a human one like the judicial process itself, which has been appropriately described as 'an educated reflex to facts'. But then the great question remains: how is it (people keep asking) that when the Bihar Dissolution Case concerned itself with facts as brought on the record of the court, two learned justices concluded that the report/recommendation of the governor was not mala fide and accordingly the decision of the central government to dissolve the Bihar Assembly was valid and constitutional, and three other justices (equally learned) on the same set of facts reached the precisely the opposite conclusion, viz., that the recommendation of the governor was mala fide and that consequently the premature dissolution of the Bihar Assembly was unconstitutional? How does one explain this?

The answer is difficult. In a somewhat similar situation, it was attempted many years ago by England's then senior-most judge, Lord Goff, who had travelled to India to deliver the G. S. Pathak Memorial Lectures. In his lecture in Delhi, he said that it was his experience that when a judge approached a particular case before him, he had an instinctive feel for the result in that case. 'This was not a mere hunch,' he said, '*it is the fruit of an amalgam—an amalgam of his knowledge of legal principle, his experience as a lawyer, his understanding of the subtle restraints with which all judges should work, his developed sense of justice, and his innate sense of humanity, and his common sense. A combination of these factors provides experienced judges with a strong instinct for the appropriate legal result in any particular case.*' It could not have been expressed better.

Perceptions differ and the perception of judges (who are human after all) must include inherent built-in attitudes which are well-honed over time from extensive judicial experience. Every judge (as has been rightly said) carries in his knapsack his own 'can't-helps'. And more importantly, attitudes of judges also change over time. Take the case of a distinguished former Chief Justice of India. Sitting as a judge in the Bombay High Court, Justice J. C. Shah invariably accepted the official view propounded in the Indian Evidence Act 1872, that courts should presume that '*official acts are regularly performed*'. He was what lawyers in Bombay then used to call a 'pro-establishment judge'. After he was appointed to the Supreme Court in 1959, he formed a diametrically opposite view that acts of officials are generally suspect, and the statutory presumption was misplaced. This was not because he had any particular antipathy to state officialdom (which included ministers) but because of the judge's increased judicial familiarity with their actions. The lawyers of the Supreme Court then began to call him a 'citizen's judge'.

Both labels were erroneous. The truth is that everyone in every station in life *grows* but in which direction and with what propensity is determined by a whole range of factors too difficult to enumerate and impossible to analyse.

Each one of the justices in the Bihar Dissolution Case was a judge having considerable judicial experience. Literally, thousands of cases that had come up before them for decision had contributed to an accumulated reservoir of knowledge (legal and non-legal) that helped shape each of the individual justices' minds and had conditioned their diverse responses to the facts of the cases brought before them.

On the last day of his sixteen-year tenure, Chief Justice Earl Warren of the United States, who is still the most remembered American judge of the 20th century, made a public statement in which he said: '*We do not always agree on the bench. I hope the court will never agree on all things. I am sure that its virility will then have been sapped, because it is composed of independent judges who have no one to be responsible to except their own conscience.*'

I believe that the awful majesty of the law necessarily takes in its sweep the imponderable uncertainty of the law. And the fact that there were strong dissenting opinions alongside an equally robust majority judgement in the Bihar Dissolution Case augurs well for the independence of India's highest judiciary. I believe that it showed that the Supreme Court was (as it is and remains today) in extremely good health, and I thank God for it!

Comment on the Occupational Hazards of Being a Governor :

The governor of a state appointed for a five-year term—holding office during the pleasure of the president (a euphemism for the central government)—is a constitutional head of the state to which he is appointed. But he (or she) is not in the driver's seat as the man or woman who sits there is the chief minister, who is responsible for all the 'accidents' that occur on the unsure political 'road'. The governor is ordinarily activated only at the instance of his council of ministers. He has no personal responsibility for actions taken in his name either in the state assembly, or in courts.

However, the governor's office does have occupational hazards as when he reports to the President under Article 356 that there is a failure of constitutional machinery in the state and that (what is popularly called) 'President's Rule' should be imposed, he acts here on his own. Similarly, when President's Rule is imposed (as it was done in Bihar on 7 March 2005 and the newly-elected legislative assembly was put in suspended animation), he remains the eyes and ears of the central government and governs the state on its behalf. Whether the state assembly should or should not be prematurely dissolved is a matter on which he must make reports to the centre (the reports are not decisions but recommendations). The council of ministers at the centre considers the report/s and if it thinks it appropriate, it advises the president that the state assembly be dissolved before it has completed its full term of five years. In simplistic terms, this was the scenario dealt with in the Bihar Dissolution Case.

Now, after the judgements have been handed down, the law is clear: whatever the governor does on his own is always subject to judicial review—extremely limited judicial review according to the two dissenting judges and a slightly wider judicial scrutiny according to the three (majority) judges. *Despite Article 361 giving the governor constitutional protection that he 'shall not be answerable to any court for the exercise and performance of power and duties of his office or for any act done or purporting to be done by him in the exercise and performance of those powers and duties', all five judges have now held that his actions can be declared mala fide, if the facts so warrant, and any consequential action of government would be then declared unconstitutional.*

After Governor Buta Singh resigned following the majority verdict, he is said to have complained that he was badly treated by the court. But he had those who supported his actions to blame. Oscar Wilde used to say, 'A true friend stabs you in the front.' The most vocal in supporting Governor Buta Singh's stand, and yet equally insistent that the governor should not be impleaded in the case, was the union government, and it was the union government's contention (based on Article 361) that was upheld by the court in a preliminary order, with ultimately disastrous results for Mr Buta Singh. It was because of 'friends' that Governor Buta Singh did not appear in court or say a word in his defence and not unsurprisingly, he lost (though a little comfort for him was the fact that he lost only by a whisker (2:3)).

The true position now is that where the governor's individual actions are liable to be called in question in courts, the governor would be well advised to waive his constitutional immunity, volunteering a true version of the facts. The Bihar Dissolution Case turned entirely on the perception of individual justices of the facts. It was on an assessment of these facts that the majority of three justices found that the action of the governor was mala fide and for oblique political motives. The two dissenting judges found contrary wise and held that his action was bona fide.

[**NOTE**: In the First Judges Case (*S. P. Gupta* 1982), the administrative decision of the then Chief Justice of India recommending transfer of high court judges had been called in question. The then Chief Justice of India, Y. V. Chandrachud, had filed an affidavit before a bench of seven justices—presided over by one of his senior colleagues—and then chose (ill-advisedly) not to appear any further or be represented by a counsel. The consequence was that some of the justices on that bench, not being able to seek clarifications, found themselves unable to accept the affidavit and said so in their judgements.

The conclusion is that howsoever high you be, when your action is called in question, you must defend your action, personally or through counsel.]

Article 361A: Protection of publication of proceedings of Parliament and state legislatures (inserted by the Constitution 44th Amendment Act, 1978 (w.e.f. 20 June 1979).

1. No person is liable to any proceedings, civil or criminal, in any court in respect of the publication in a newspaper of a substantially true report of any proceedings in either House of Parliament or in any State Legislative Assembly or State Legislative Council unless the publication is proved to have been made with malice:

   Provided that nothing in this clause shall apply to the publication of any report of the proceedings of a secret sitting of either House of Parliament or the Legislative Assembly, or, as the case may be, either House of the Legislature, of a State.
2. Clause (1) shall apply in relation to reports or matters broadcast by means of wireless telegraphy as part of any programme or service provided by means of a broadcasting station as it applies in relation to reports or matters published in a newspaper.

Explanation:

In this article, 'newspaper' includes a news agency report containing material for publication in a newspaper.

Comment on Article 361A:

Prior to 1976, the law on this point was different as between the union and the state legislatures. So far as Parliament was concerned, it had enacted the Parliamentary Proceedings (Protection of Publication) Act, 1956, the substance of which was similar to Article 361A. Then, during the Internal Emergency (June 1975 to March 1977), the government felt that high dignitaries should be protected from defamatory publications in the press, even though they related to reports of proceedings in Parliament. The Parliamentary Proceedings (Protection of Publication) Act of 1956 (24 of 1956) was promptly repealed by an ordinance, followed by a repealing Act of 1976 (passed during the Internal Emergency).

But after the Janata Government came into power (at the end of the Internal Emergency), it reversed the situation by enacting the Parliamentary Proceedings (Protection of Publication) Act, 1977 (15 of 1977). That Act, however, did not extend to state legislatures and in order to give the provisions of the foregoing Act a constitutional footing and to make the same law applicable to the state legislatures, Article 361A was then inserted by the Constitution 44th Amendment Act, 1978.

Parliamentary Proceedings (Protection of Publication) Act, 1977 (15 of 1977) has not been repealed after the insertion of Article 361A in the Constitution. It provides, in short, that newspapers and radio broadcasts would be immune from any civil or criminal liability for publishing any proceedings of either house of Parliament, provided such publication:

i. is a substantially true report of such proceedings;

ii. is not actuated by malice;

iii. is for the 'public good'.

The foregoing Act of Parliament relates only to the publication of proceedings in either House of Parliament. It has no application to proceedings in a state legislature (Parliament has no legislative competence to make any law relating to the powers or privileges of the state legislature in view of Entry 39 of List-II (State List) of the Seventh Schedule to the Constitution) (Powers privileges and immunities of the legislatives assembly and of the members and committees thereof).

Article 361B: Disqualification for appointment on remunerative political post (inserted by the Constitution 91st Amendment Act, 2003, w.e.f. 1 January 2004).

A member of a House belonging to any political party who is disqualified for being a member of the House under paragraph 2 of the Tenth Schedule shall also be disqualified to hold any remunerative political post for the duration of the period commencing from the date of his disqualification till the date on which the term of his office as such member would expire or till the date on which he contests an election to a House and is declared elected, whichever is earlier.

Explanation:

For the purposes of this article:

(a) the expression 'House' has the meaning assigned to it in clause (a) of paragraph 1 of the Tenth Schedule.

(b) the expression 'remunerative political post' means any office:

i. under the Government of India or the Government of a State where the salary or remuneration for such office is paid out of the public revenue of the Government of India or the Government of the State, as the case may be; or

ii. under a body, whether incorporated or not, which is wholly or partially owned by the Government of India or the Government of State, and the salary or remuneration for such office is paid by such body, except where such salary or remuneration paid is compensatory in nature.

Article 362: [Rights and privileges of Rulers of Indian States]—Omitted by the Constitution (26th Amendment)Act, 1971, s. 2 (w.e.f. 28 December 1971).

<u>Article 363</u>: Bar to interference by courts in disputes arising out of certain treaties, agreements, etc., entered into before the commencement of the Constitution by any Ruler of an Indian State.

<u>Article 363A</u>: Recognition granted to Rulers of Indian States to cease and Privy Purses to be abolished (inserted by the Constitution 26th Amendment Act, 1971).

<u>Article 364</u>: Special provisions as to major ports and aerodromes.

<u>Article 365</u>: Effect of failure to comply with, or to give effect to, directions given by the Union, where any State has failed to comply with, or to give effect to, any directions given in the exercise of the executive power of the Union under any of the provisions of this Constitution, it shall be lawful for the President to hold that a situation has arisen in which the Government of the State cannot be carried on in accordance with the provisions of this Constitution.

Comment on Article 365

This is a very important provision as without it, there would have been no means to enforce the directions given under Article 355 (duty of the union to protect states against external aggression and internal disturbance) and Article 356 (provisions in case of failure of constitutional machinery in the states). **It is Articles 355 and 356 read with Article 365 that ensures that the Union is kept intact.**

<u>Article 366</u>: Definitions of expressions used in the Constitution (in all 30 expressions in the Constitution have been defined).

Note:—Article 366(22) had defined 'Ruler' as follows:

> 'Ruler' means the Prince, Chief, or other person who, at any time before the commencement of the Constitution (26th Amendment) Act, 1971, was recognised by the President as the Ruler of an Indian State or any person who, at any

time before such commencement, was recognised by the President as the successor of such Ruler.

Comment on Article 366(22):

In September 1970, orders were issued by the president of India (in respect of each of the rulers of former Indian states) derecognising them as rulers, and consequentially resulting in the stoppage of privy purses being received by them, and for the discontinuance of their personal privileges. The orders were challenged in the Supreme Court in a writ petition and decided by a bench of eleven judges (by majority (10:1)) in *H. H. Maharajadhiraja Madhav Rao vs. Union of India*—reported in AIR 1971 SC 530 (bench of eleven justices)—the court declared that the orders of the president were ultra vires, illegal, and unconstitutional.

<u>Article 367</u>: Interpretation—the General Clauses Act, 1897 applies for the interpretation of the Constitution as it applies for the interpretation of Acts passed by Parliament.

----------Part-XX ----------

Amendment of the Constitution—Article 368

Article 368: Power of Parliament to amend the Constitution and procedure therefor:

1. Notwithstanding anything in this Constitution, Parliament may in exercise of its constituent power amend by way of addition, variation, or repeal any provision of this Constitution in accordance with the procedure laid down in this article.
2. An amendment of this Constitution may be initiated only by the introduction of a Bill for the purpose in either House of Parliament, and when the Bill is passed in each House by a majority of the total membership of that House and by a majority of not less than two-thirds of the members of that House present and voting, 4 (it shall be presented to the President who shall give his assent to the Bill and thereupon) the Constitution shall stand amended in accordance with the terms of the Bill:

   Provided that if such amendment seeks to make any change in:

   (a) Article 54, Article 55, Article 73, 5 (Article 162, Article 241, or Article 279A); or

   (b) Chapter IV of Part V, Chapter V of Part VI, or Chapter I of Part XI; or

   (c) any of the Lists in the Seventh Schedule; or

   (d) the representation of States in Parliament; or

   (e) the provisions of this article,

the amendment shall also require to be ratified by the Legislatures of not less than one-half of the States by resolutions to that effect passed by those Legislatures before the Bill making provision for such amendment is presented to the President for assent.

3. Nothing in Article 13 shall apply to any amendment made under this article.
4. No amendment of this Constitution (including the provisions of Part-III) made or purporting to have been made under this article (whether before or after the commencement of section 55 of the Constitution (42nd Amendment) Act, 1976) shall be called in question in any court on any ground.
5. For the removal of doubts, it is hereby declared that there shall be no limitation whatever on the constituent power of Parliament to amend by way of addition, variation or repeal the provisions of this Constitution under this article.

Amending the Constitution:

The Constitution of India 1950 has prescribed three separate methods for amending the Constitution:

(1) by ordinary law, viz., by simple majority in each House of Parliament as provided for in Articles 3 and 4:

Article 3: Formation of new States and alteration of areas, boundaries or names of existing States—by ordinary law made by Parliament.

Article 4: Laws made under articles 2 and 3 could provide for the amendment of the First and the Fourth Schedules and for supplemental, incidental, and consequential matters.

(2) by a special procedure and special majority as prescribed in Article 368 (2) of the Constitution for all other amendments, and;

(3) additionally, by ratification by States where the amendments involve any change in the following Articles viz. Articles 54, 55, 73, 162, 241, or any change in Chapter IV of Part-V (Union Judiciary), Chapter V of Part-VI (High Courts in the States), or Chapter I of Part-XI (Relations between the Union and the States). Such amendments are required to be passed by Parliament by a special majority and according to the procedure prescribed in Article 368(2); and in addition require to be ratified by not less than one half of the States by resolution to that effect passed by the legislatures of these States before the bills making provision for such amendments are presented to the President for his assent.

As enacted Part-XX, *Article 368*, had the following marginal note: 'Procedure for amendment of the Constitution'.

By the Constitution 24th Amendment Act, 1971 (w.e.f. 5 was substituted: *Power of Parliament to amend the Constitution and the procedure therefor.*

Article 368 (1) and (2) as originally enacted was amended by the Constitution 24th Amendment Act, 1971 (w.e.f. 5 November 1971).

Clauses (4) and (5) had been added by the Constitution 42nd Amendment Act, 1976 (w.e.f. 3 January 1977). However, clauses (4) and (5) as added excluded all judicial review. Clauses (4) and (5) were declared unconstitutional and void as violating the Constitution's 'basic structure' in *Minerva Mills vs. Union of India* (1980 (2) SCC 591).[102]

The only *operative* part of Article 368 are now clauses (1), (2), and (3). Even clause (3) is no longer relevant. It had been inserted by the Constitution 24th Amendment Act, 1971 to get over the judgement of the bench of eleven judges (6:5) in *I. C. Golaknath vs. State of Punjab* (AIR 1967 SC 1643: (6:5)) but the majority decision in *Golaknath* is itself no longer relevant since *Golaknath* has been overruled by the larger bench of thirteen judges (7:6) in *Kesavananda* (1973) (7:6).

----------Part-XXI ----------

Temporary Transitional and Special Provisions

Article 369: Temporary power to Parliament to make laws with respect to certain matters in the State List as if they were matters in the Concurrent List.

Article 370: Temporary provisions with respect to the State of Jammu and Kashmir—deleted in August 2019.

Comment :

For more details, please see Chapter One—it has dealt with (*inter alia*) provisions with respect to the state of Jammu and Kashmir.

Article 371: Special provision with respect to the States of Maharashtra and Gujarat—substituted by the Constitution Seventh (Amendment) Act, 1956, for original Article 371 (w.e.f. 1 November 1956).

Article 371A: Special provision with respect to the State of Nagaland (inserted by the Constitution Thirteenth (Amendment) Act, 1962, (w.e.f. 1 December 1963)).

Article 371B: Special provision with respect to the State of Assam (inserted by the Constitution Twenty-Second (Amendment) Act, 1969, (w.e.f. 25 September 1969)).

Article 371C: Special provision with respect to the State of Manipur (inserted by the Constitution Twenty-Seventh (Amendment) Act, 1971, (w.e.f. 15 February 1972)).

Article 371D: Special provisions with respect to the State of Andhra Pradesh or the State of Telangana (inserted by the Constitution Thirty-Second (Amendment) Act, 1973, (w.e.f. 1 July 1974)).

Article 371E: Establishment of Central University in Andhra Pradesh (inserted by the Constitution Thirty-Second (Amendment) Act, 1973, (w.e.f. 1 July 1974)).

Article 371F: Special provisions with respect to the State of Sikkim (inserted by the Constitution Thirty-Sixth (Amendment) Act, 1975, s. 3 (w.e.f. 26 April 1975)).

Article 371G: Special provision with respect to the State of Mizoram (inserted by the Constitution Fifty-Third (Amendment) Act, 1986 (w.e.f. 20 February 1987)).

Article 371H: Special provision with respect to the State of Arunachal Pradesh (inserted by the Constitution Fifty-Fifth (Amendment) Act, 1986 (w.e.f. 20 February 1987)).

Article 371I: Special provision with respect to the State of Goa (inserted by the Constitution Fifty-Sixth (Amendment) Act, 1987 (w.e.f. 30 May 1987)).

Article 371J: Special provisions with respect to the State of Karnataka (inserted by the Constitution Ninety-Eighth (Amendment) Act, 2012, (w.e.f. 1 October 2013)).

Article 372: Continuance in force of existing laws and their adaptation

1. Notwithstanding the repeal by this Constitution of the enactments referred to in Article 395 but subject to the other provisions of this Constitution, all the law in force in the territory of India immediately before the commencement of this Constitution shall continue in force therein until altered or repealed or amended by a competent Legislature or other competent authority.
2. For the purpose of bringing the provisions of any law in force in the territory of India into accord with the provisions of this Constitution, the President may by order make such adaptations and modifications of such

law, whether by way of repeal or amendment, as may be necessary or expedient, and provide that the law shall, as from such date as may be specified in the order, have effect subject to the adaptations and modifications so made, and any such adaptation or modification shall not be questioned in any court of law.

3. Nothing in clause (2) shall be deemed:

   (a) to empower the President to make any adaptation or modification of any law after the expiration of 1 (three years) from the commencement of this Constitution; or

   (b) to prevent any competent Legislature or other competent authority from repealing or amending any law adapted or modified by the President under the said clause.

Explanation I:

The expression 'law in force' in this article shall include a law passed or made by a legislature or other competent authority in the territory of India before the commencement of this Constitution and not previously repealed, notwithstanding that it or parts of it may not be then in operation either at all or in particular areas.

Explanation II:

Any law passed or made by a legislature or other competent authority in the territory of India which immediately before the commencement of this Constitution had extra-territorial effect as well as effect in the territory of India shall, subject to any such adaptations and modifications as aforesaid, continue to have such extra-territorial effect.

Explanation III:

Nothing in this article shall be construed as continuing any temporary law in force beyond the date fixed for its expiration or the date on which it would have expired if this Constitution had not come into force.

Explanation IV:

An ordinance promulgated by the governor of a province under section 88 of the Government of India Act, 1935, and in force immediately before the commencement of this Constitution shall, unless withdrawn by the governor of the corresponding state earlier, cease to operate at the expiration of six weeks from the first meeting after such commencement of the legislative assembly of that state functioning under clause (1) of article 382, and nothing in this article shall be construed as continuing any such ordinance in force beyond the said period.

Article 372A: Power of the President to adapt laws (inserted by the Constitution Seventh (Amendment) Act, 1956 (w.e.f. 1 November 1956).

Article 373: Power of President to make order in respect of persons under preventive detention in certain cases (i.e. until Parliament makes law with respect to preventive detention under Article 22(7).

Article 374: Provisions as to Judges of the Federal Court and proceedings pending in the Federal Court or before His Majesty in Council (Privy Council).

Article 375: Courts, authorities, and officers to continue to function subject to the provisions of the Constitution.

Article 376: Provisions as to Judges of High Courts.

Article 377: Provisions as to Comptroller and Auditor General of India.

Article 378: Provisions as to Public Service Commissions.

Article 378A: Special provision as to duration of Andhra Pradesh Legislative Assembly (inserted by the Constitution Seventh (Amendment) Act, 1956 (w.e.f. 1 November 1956).

Article 379: Provisions as to provisional Parliament and the Speaker and Deputy Speaker thereof—Repealed by the Constitution Seventh (Amendment) Act, 1956, (w.e.f. 1 November 1956).

Article 380: Provision as to President—Repealed, by the Constitution Seventh (Amendment) Act, 1956 (w.e.f. 1 November 1956).

Article 381: Council of Ministers of the President—Repealed by the Constitution Seventh (Amendment) Act, 1956 (w.e.f. 1 November 1956).

Article 382: Provisions as to provisional Legislatures for States in Part A of the First Schedule—Repealed by the Constitution Seventh (Amendment) Act, 1956 (w.e.f. 1 November 1956).

Article 383: Provision as to Governors of Provinces—Repealed by the Constitution Seventh (Amendment) Act, 1956 (w.e.f. 1 November 1956).

Article 384: Council of Ministers of the Governors—Repealed by the Constitution Seventh (Amendment) Act, 1956 (w.e.f. 1 November 1956).

Article 385: Provision as to provisional Legislatures in States in Part B of the First Schedule—Repealed by the Constitution Seventh (Amendment) Act, 1956, (w.e.f. 1 November 1956).

Article 386: Council of Ministers for States in Part B of the First Schedule—Repealed by the Constitution Seventh (Amendment) Act, 1956 (w.e.f. 1 November 1956).

Article 387: Special provision as to determination of population for the purposes of certain elections—Repealed by the Constitution Seventh (Amendment) Act, 1956 (w.e.f. 1 November 1956).

Article 388: Provisions as to the filling of casual vacancies in the provisional Parliament and provisional Legislatures of the States—Repealed by the Constitution (Seventh Amendment) Act, 1956 (w.e.f. 1 November 1956).

Article 389: Provision as to Bills pending in the Dominion Legislatures and in the Legislatures of Provinces and Indian States—Repealed by the Constitution Seventh (Amendment) Act, 1956 (w.e.f. 1 November 1956).

Article 390: Money received or raised or expenditure incurred between the commencement of the Constitution and the 31st day of March, 1950—Repealed by the Constitution Seventh (Amendment) Act, 1956 (w.e.f. 1 November 1956).

Article 391: Power of the President to amend the First and Fourth Schedules in certain contingencies—Repealed by the Constitution Seventh (Amendment) Act, 1956 (w.e.f. 1 November 1956).

Article 392: Power of the President to remove difficulties.

---------- Part-XXII ----------

Short Title, Commencement, and Repeals—Articles 393 to 395

Article 393: Short Title. This Constitution may be called the Constitution of India.

Article 394: Commencement. This article and articles 5, 6, 7, 8, 9, 60, 324, 366, 367, 379, 380, 388, 391, 392, and 393 shall come into force at once, and the remaining provisions of this Constitution shall come into force on the 26th day of January 1950, which day is referred to in this Constitution as the commencement of this Constitution.

Article 394A: Authoritative text in the Hindi language (inserted by the Constitution (58th Amendment) Act, 1987 (w.e.f. 9 December 1987)).

Article 395: Repeals. The Indian Independence Act, 1947, and the Government of India Act, 1935, together with all enactments amending or supplementing the latter Act, but not including the Abolition of Privy Council Jurisdiction Act, 1949, are hereby repealed.

Notes and References:

1. N. K. Singh, Chairman 15th Finance Commission of India—excerpts from a speech published in the *Indian Express*, 21 April 2022.
2. It is under Article 2 that the erstwhile princely State of Sikkim (then ruled by the Chogyal and with a legislative assembly) was admitted into the Union by the Constitution 36th Amendment Act, 1975 as the twenty-second State in the Republic of India and designated State in the First Schedule to the Constitution.
3. As to what 'Citizenship' truly means in a society mired in deep inequality has been explained by historian Romila Thapar ('The Right to be a Citizen') in the book: *On Citizenship* (published by Aleph, 2021).
4. CAD, Vol. VII, 4 November 1948, page 34.
5. The growth rate of the population between 2001-2011 was 17.7 per cent and the growth rate of the population of the different religious communities between those dates was: Hindus 16.8 per cent, Muslims 24.6 per cent, Christians 15.5 per cent, Sikhs 8.4 per cent, Buddhists 6.1 per cent, and Jains 5.4 per cent.
6. Wikipedia.
7. The finance minister of the government of India publicly stated (as reported in the *Times of India* of 9 January 2023) that 'remittances which came from abroad by Indians who migrated are about 100 billion dollars for the year 2022. This is one of the highest.'
8. By the Citizenship Amendment Act, 47 of 2019, w.e.f. 12 December 2019 (rules are yet to be framed).
9. Article 15(1) provides that the state shall not discriminate against any citizen on grounds only of religion, race, caste, sex, and place of birth or any of them.
10. 'The Federal Case for Judicial Review' (*Oxford Journal of Legal Studies* (2022), No. 42 on pages 733-752).
11. Magna Carta Libertatum (Latin for 'Greater Charter of Freedom') was a royal charter of rights agreed to by King John of England at Runnymede near Windsor on 15 June 1215.
12. *R. (Bancoult) vs. Secretary of State for Foreign and Commonwealth Affairs,* Reported in 2001 (1) Queen's Bench 1067 (Bancoult-I). Another case before the High Court of England and Wales (Louis

Oliver Bancoult or Secretary of State for Foreign Commonwealth Affairs (Bancoult-II)) was similarly decided on 11 May 2006 by Lord Justice Hooper and Justice Cresswell and reported in 2006 EWHC 1038.

13. A decision of the Appellate Committee of the House of Lords given on 22 October 2008 and reported in 2008 (4) All. E. R. 1055. Lord Bingham (in his dissent) relied on Chapter 29 of Magna Carta, which provided that 'No freeman shall be taken or imprisoned, or be diseased of his freehold or liberties or free customs, or be outlawed or exiled . . . but by lawful judgement of his peers, or by the law of the land'—a faint echo of Article 21 of India's Constitution.
14. http://worldjusticeproject.org.

15. Bijoe Emmanuel vs. The State of Kerala (AIR 1987 SC 748): In 2018, this standing up for the National Anthem got revisited in Shyam Narayan Chouksey vs. Union of India - 2018 (2) SCC 575 (3J), in which on September 30, 2016 the Supreme Court of India passed the following interim order:

> "All the cinema halls in India shall play the National Anthem before the feature film starts and persons in the halls are obliged to stand up to show respect to the National Anthem".

However in its final judgment in the case (on January 9, 2018) the interim order was modified:

> "to the extent that playing of the National Anthem prior to the screening of feature film in cinema halls is not mandatory, but optional or directory".

16. Wikipedia.

17. 'The Spirit of Liberty' speech at 'I am an American Day' ceremony, Central Park, New York City, 21 May 1944. Learned Hand (that was his name) was a federal judge and was never appointed by any US President to the country's highest court (the US Supreme Court). He remained chief judge of the US Court of Appeals for the Second Circuit from 1924 to 1951 and passed away in 1961. **The standard biography of Judge Learned Hand is by Gerald Gunther, New York: Alfred A. Knopf, 1994.**

18. 25 November 1948: CAD Book No.2, Vol. VII on page 610.

19. 145. Rules of Court, etc.
    (1) . . .
    (2) . . .
    (3) The minimum number of Judges who are to sit for the purpose of deciding any case involving a substantial question of law as to the interpretation of this Constitution or for the purpose of hearing any reference under Article 143 shall be five:

Provided that, where the Court hearing an appeal under any of the provisions of this Chapter other than Article 132 consists of less than five Judges and in the course of the hearing of the appeal the Court is satisfied that the appeal involves a substantial question of law as to the interpretation of this Constitution the determination of which is necessary for the disposal of the appeal, such Court shall refer the question for opinion to a Court constituted as required by this clause for the purpose of deciding any case involving such a question and shall on receipt of the opinion dispose of the appeal in conformity with such opinion.

20. **'Personal law' has been defined as: 'The law that governs a person's family matters, usu., regardless of where the person goes. In common-law systems, personal law refers to the law of the person's domicile. The idea of the personal law is based on the conception of man as a social being, so that those transactions of his daily life which affect him most closely in a personal sense, such as marriage, divorce, legitimacy, many kinds of capacity, and succession, may be governed universally by that system of law deemed most suitable and adequate for the purpose . . .'**

    See R. H. Graveson, *Conflict of Laws* 188 (7th edition, 1974). The definition is reproduced in *Black's Law Dictionary*, 10th edition, 2014, on page 1326.

    See also Article of Flavia Agnes on 'Personal Law' in the *Oxford Handbook of Indian Constitution,* Oxford University Press (2016), pages 903-920. Senior Lawyer Flavia Agnes has written:

    'When we examine rulings of later decades, we can clearly see the influence of *Narasu Appa* gradually wearing out, with courts increasingly testing personal laws against the touchstone of fundamental rights. The approach adopted has been to either "read down" a statutory provision, to reinterpret it in harmony with Part-III of the Constitution, or to strike down the offending section.'

21. See a 2023 Penguin publication titled, *These Seats Are Reserved: Caste, Quotas, and the Constitution of India* by Abhinav Chandrachud.

22. https://wir2022.wid.world.

23. An Oxfam Report (January 2023) states that taxation of the richest is now higher, and that making billionaires pay their fair share is hugely popular. 'Taxing the rich claws back elite power and reduces not just economic inequality but racial, gender, and colonial inequalities too.' The report lays out how much tax the rich should pay and the tested ways in which governments can raise such taxation. (Oxfam report 2022 is available at https://oxfamlibrary.openrepository.com)

24. Article 15 has been amended first by the Constitution First Amendment Act, 1951, w.e.f. 18 June 1951 and then by the Constitution 93rd Amendment Act, 2005, w.e.f. 20 January 2006 and once again by the Constitution 103rd Amendment Act, 2019, w.e.f. 14 January 2019. Article 16 has also been amended by the Constitution 77th Amendment Act, 1975, w.e.f. 17 June 1995, by the Constitution 85th Amendment Act, 2001, w.e.f. 04 January 2002, and then again by the Constitution 81st Amendment Act, 2000, w.e.f. 9 June 2000, and finally by the Constitution 103rd Amendment Act, 2019, w.e.f. 20 January 2019.

25. So described in *S. Rangarajan vs. P. Jagjivan Ram*—1989 (2) SCC 574 para 36.

26. Lawrence Liang writing on 'Free Speech and Expression in India's Constitution' in the *Oxford Handbook of the Indian Constitution,* edited by Sujit Choudhry, Madhav Khosla, and Pratap Bhanu Mehta (2016) published by the Oxford University Press on page 831.

27. AIR 1950 SC 124 (May 1950) on page 129 (3J): 'Democracy is a form of government by the people *via open discussion.* The democratic form of government itself demands its citizens an active and intelligent participation in the affairs of the community. Public discussion with people's participation is a basic feature and a rational process of democracy which distinguishes it from all other forms of government.'

28. Madison, who was the leading spirit in the preparation of the 1st Amendment of the Federal Constitution, described the practice and sentiment which led to the guarantees of liberty of the press in state constitutions in the following words:

    'In every state probably in the Union, the press has exerted a freedom in canvassing the merits and measures of public men of every description which has not been confined to the strict limits of the common law. On this footing the freedom of the press has stood; on this footing it yet stands . . .

'Some degree of abuse is inseparable from the proper use of everything, and in no instance is this more true than in that of the press. It has accordingly been decided by the practice of the States, that it is better to leave a few of its noxious branches to their luxuriant growth, than, by pruning them away, to injure the vigour of those yielding the proper fruits. And can the wisdom of this policy be doubted by any who reflect that to the press alone, chequered as it is with abuses, the world is indebted for all the triumphs which have been gained by reason and humanity over error and oppression; who reflect that to the same beneficent source the United States owe much of the lights which conducted them to the ranks of a free and independent nation, and which have improved their political system into a shape so auspicious to their happiness? Had "Sedition Acts," forbidding every publication that might bring the constituted agents into contempt or disrepute, or that might excite the hatred of the people against the authors of unjust or pernicious measures, been uniformly enforced against the press, might not the United States have been languishing at this day under the infirmities of a sickly Confederation? Might they not, possibly, be miserable colonies, groaning under a foreign yoke?'

29. See the illuminating article on 'Free Speech and Expression' in the *Oxford Handbook of the Indian Constitution* (2016), pages 814-833, on page 821.

30. Article 20: Protection in respect of conviction for offences.
    (a) . . .
    (b) . . .
    (c) No person accused of any offence shall be compelled to be a witness against himself.

31. (1993) 1 SCC 645 (5J).

32. 41. (Right to work, to education, and to public assistance in certain cases) The State shall, within the limits of its economic capacity and development, make effective provision for securing the right to work, to education and to public assistance in cases of unemployment, old age, sickness and disablement, and in other cases of underserved want.

33. 45. (Provision for free and compulsory education for children) The State shall endeavour to provide, within a period of ten years from the commencement of this Constitution, for free and compulsory education for all children until they complete the age of fourteen years.

34. *State of Maharashtra vs. Prabhakar Pandurang Sanzgiri*—AIR 1966 SC 424 (Bench of five judges).

35. In H.CP. (MD) Nos. 1710 and 1206 of 2022 and Cr.M.P. (MD) No. 12692 of 2022—*Sunitha vs. Addl. Chief Secretary to Government Fort St. George, Chennai* (2022 SCC Online Madras 5278).

36. 2020 (3) SCC pages 52-53—Reasons were given in a separate judgement delivered on 11 May 2020, reported in 2020 (9) SCC 121.

37. Article 350A (inserted by the Constitution 7th Amendment Act, 1956) stated:

    350A. Facilities for instruction in mother tongue at the primary stage. It shall be the endeavour of every State and of every local authority within the State to provide adequate facilities for instruction in the mother tongue at the primary stage of education to children belonging to linguistic minority groups; and the President may issue such directions to any State as he considers necessary or proper for securing the provision of such facilities.'

38. Published in *The Hindu*, 30 May 2023, under the title, 'Muslims lag behind all communities in higher education; U.P. shows worst decline, says study.'

39. Article 31C was added by the Constitution 25th Amendment Act, 1971. Article 31C (first part) is valid according to the majority judgement (7:6) in *Kesavananda Bharati vs. State of Kerala* (1973 SC 1461)—so held also in *Waman Rao vs. Union of India* (1981 (2) SCC 362 on page 398 para 53 (5J)).

40. For other jurisdictions, see the article titled, 'Unconstitutional Constitutional Amendments: The Migration and Success of a Constitutional Idea' by Yaniv Roznai, reported in American Journal of Comparative Law Volume 61 (2013), pages 657-719. The article states: 'the issue has already been debated in numerous countries and is likely to arise sooner or later in many others . . . limitations upon the amendment power is just one example of the broader phenomenon of the *migration of legal ideas*', described in the *Oxford Handbook of Comparative Constitutional Law* (2012) as 'constitutional borrowing'. The German Constitutional Court in the *South West State Case* (1951) BverfGE 14(1951) had stated: 'A Constitution has an inner unity and the meaning of one part is linked to that of other provisions; *a constitution reflects certain over-arching principles and fundamental decisions to which individual provisions of the Basic Law are subordinate.*'

The author of the article 'Unconstitutional Constitutional Amendments' concludes his paper with these words:

'Today, judicial review—and even the annulment—of constitutional amendments, i.e., the phenomenon of "unconstitutional constitutional amendments," is no longer merely a theoretical hypothesis, but rather an existing practice in many jurisdictions.'

41. Chief Justice H. J. Kania, Justice Patanjali Sastri, Justice B. K. Mukherjea, Justice S. R. Das, and Justice Chandrasekhar Aiyar.

42. Chief Justice P. B. Gajendragadkar, Justice K. N. Wanchoo, Justice M. Hidayatullah, Justice Raghubar Dayal, and Justice J. R. Mudholkar.

43. Justice H. R. Khanna also quoted from an article by D. Conrad (a German professor) in *The Indian Year Book of International Affairs* (1966-1967), published in 1970 under the auspices of *The Indian Study Group of International Law and Affairs*, University of Madras, on pages 375 to 430. Conrad had put it as follows:

'The general proposition is the distinction between constituent and constituted power, well-known since the days of the French Revolution. Any constitutional body deriving a power of amendment from the constitution is but power constituted and does not via its function become seized with the nation's constituent power. The constituent power perpetually remains with the nation itself; it is exercised through a special mandate to an ad hoc body charged with the framing of the constitution. The mandate, express or implied, represents the fundamental decisions on the constitutional future taken by the sovereign nation. What the constituent assembly does is to make these decisions explicit, to give them detailed, statutory shape, to "formulate" the constitution.'

44. Reported in AIR 1968 SC (Journal Section) pages 21-28, on page 27.

45. CAD Book No. 2, Vol. VII, on page 953 (9 December 1948).

46. Article 16(3): 16. Equality of opportunity in matters of public employment:

(a) . . .

(b) . . .

(c) Nothing in this article shall prevent Parliament from making any law prescribing, in regard to a class or classes of employment or appointment to an office (under the Government of, or any local or other authority within, a State or Union territory, any requirement as to residence within that State or Union territory) prior to such employment or appointment.

Article 32: Remedies for enforcement of rights conferred by this Part.

(a) . . .
(b) . . .
(c) Without prejudice to the powers conferred on the Supreme Court by clauses (1) and (2), Parliament may by law empower any other court to exercise within the local limits of its jurisdiction all or any of the powers exercisable by the Supreme Court under clause (2).

47. Article 32: Remedies for enforcement of rights conferred by this Part.
    (a) . . .
    (b) . . .
    (c) Without prejudice to the powers conferred on the Supreme Court by clauses (1) and (2), Parliament may by law empower any other court to exercise within the local limits of its jurisdiction all or any of the powers exercisable by the Supreme Court under clause (2).

    Article 33 deals with the amend forces and Article 34 speaks of the restriction of rights conferred by Part-III whilst martial law is in force.

48. See Achyut Chetan who has written a book titled, *Founding Mothers of the Indian Republic,* published by the Cambridge University Press (2022).

49. See AIR 1970 SC 2042, AIR 1995 SC 1531, AIR 2000 SC 3650, and AIR 2003 SC 2902 on page 2913 (Chief Justice Khare). See also article in THE HINDU, July 24, 2023, on the politics of the Uniform Civil Code.

50. Lord Salisbury was prime minister of England from 25 June 1895 to 11 July 1902.

51. CAD Book No. 2, Vol. VII, 23 November 1948, on pages 551-552.

52. See *M/s Balaji vs. State of Mysore* (AIR 1963 SC 649 on page 654 (5J)).

53. Article 51A was added by the Constitution 42nd Amendment Act, 1976 (w.e.f. 3 January 1977).

54. Article 239, 239A, and 239B were substituted by the Constitution Seventh Amendment Act, 1956, w.e.f. 1 November 1956, for original Part-VIII, as enacted headed 'States in Part C of the First Schedule'.

    Article 239AA (Special Provisions with respect to Delhi) and Article 239AB (Provisions in case of failure of constitutional machinery) were added by the Constitution 69th Amendment Act, 1991, w.e.f. 1 December 1992.

55. Added by Constitution Twenty-Seventh Amendment Act, 1971, w.e.f. 30 December 1971.

56. Substituted by Constitution Seventh Amendment Act, 1975, w.e.f. 7 November 1956.

57. A significant comment on the judgement ('Did the Supreme Court truly give the Delhi Government a Big Win?') by Ashish Khetan is available on https://thewire.in/law/supreme-court-delhi-government-union-centre. A more critical comment by M. R. Madhavan, PRS Legislative Research, New Delhi, can be found on the editorial page of *The Hindu* (18 May 2023.

58. In *PUCL vs. Union of India*—judgement of a bench of three judges of the Supreme Court of India—AIR 2003 SC 2863. It has been held that a legislature has no power to declare that the judgement of a superior court is not binding; it is only entitled to change the basis of a judicial decision and not the judicial decision itself.

59. In 2003—two decades ago—with a view to satisfy the aspirations of the people of Delhi, Mr L. K. Advani of the BJP government at the centre introduced in Parliament the State of Delhi Bill 2003, which made Delhi a full state on par with every other state with a nearly non-existent role for the Union government. With this, the BJP hoped to recapture power in the proposed state. However, the then Congress government, headed by Mrs Sheela Dixit, opposed the bill and statehood for Delhi became a dead letter. Subsequently, no central government has ever championed the cause again.

60. The suggestion has been made by Mr Arghya Sengupta, director, Vidhi Centre for Legal Policy, in an article on the editorial page of the *Times of India* of 22 May 2023.

61. Printed and published by Malvika Singh on behalf of the Romesh Raj Trust—Editor Tejbir Singh.

62. Part-IX containing Articles 243, 243A to 243O was inserted by the Constitution 73rd Amendment Act of 1992 (w.e.f. 24 April 1993).

63. *U.P. Gram Panchayat Adhikari Sangh vs. Daya Ram Saroj*, (2007) 2 SCC 138, 144, 152 (paragraph 37).

64. *Gujarat Pradesh Panchayat Parishad vs. State of Gujarat*, (2007) 7 SCC 718, 730-31 (paragraph 24).

65. Part-IX-A containing Articles 243P to 243Z and 243ZA to 243 ZS was inserted by the Constitution 74th Amendment Act 1992 (w.e.f. 1 June 1993).

66. *Kishan Singh Tomar vs. Municipal Corporation of the City of Ahmedabad,* (2006) 8 SCC 352 (Constitution Bench of five judges) paragraphs 12 and 13.

67. See *Vipulbhai M. Chaudhary vs. Gujarat Cooperative Milk Marketing Federation Ltd.*, (2015) 8 SCC 1 = AIR 2015 SC 1960.

68. The autonomous state of Meghalaya was constituted by Parliament in January 1972 and Meghalaya was upgraded to a full-fledged state and placed in Part-I of the First Schedule to the Constitution by Parliamentary law, viz., North-Eastern Areas Reorganisation Act, 1974.

69. *Edwingson Bareh vs. State of Assam* (AIR 1966 SC 1220) (4:1). The Sixth Schedule clearly indicates that the Constitution has delegated to the governor a part of the power conferred on Parliament itself.

70. Such States are Andhra Pradesh, Bihar, Gujarat, Himachal Pradesh, Madhya Pradesh, Maharashtra, Orissa, and Rajasthan.

71. See *National Legal Service Authority vs. Union of India & Ors.* (AIR 2013 SC 2178).

72. *M/s Hoechst Pharmaceuticals Ltd. ss. State of Bihar* (AIR 1983 SC 1019) (Bench of three judges).

73. *Indian Aluminium Co. vs. State of Kerala* (AIR 1996 SC 1431).

74. See Central Sales Tax Act, 1956.

75. See *State of Rajasthan vs. Vidhyawati* (AIR 1962 SC 933, 935, 946 (5J)) holding that of the state should be as much liable for tort in respect of a tortious act committed by its servant or agent within the scope of his employment but wholly disassociated from the exercise of sovereign powers, like any other employer.

76. See *State Bank of India vs. National Housing Bank* (AIR 2013 SC 3478).

77. Inserted by the Constitution 44th Amendment Act 1978, w.e.f. 20 June 1979.

78. The majority view in the nine-judge bench was that of Chief Justice T. S. Thakur, Justices A. K. Sikri, A. M. Khanvelkar, S. A. Bobde, Shiva Kirti Singh, N. V. Ramana and Bhanumati, and the minority view was expressed by Justices Dr D. Y. Chandrachud, and Ashok Bhushan.

79. In *Atiabari's* case (AIR 1961 SC 232) in the *Automobile Transport* case (AIR 1962 SC 1406) and in *Jindal Stainless Steel Ltd. vs. State of Haryana* (AIR 2006 SC 2550).

80. Article 323(A)(d) reads as follows:
'a law made under Article 323(A)(1) (appointment of an administrative tribunal for adjudication and trial of disputes and complaint with respect to public services and only in connection with the affairs of the Union or of any State) may exclude the jurisdiction of all Courts except the jurisdiction of the Supreme Court under Article 136 with respect to the disputes or complaints referred to in clause (b).
Under 323(B)(3)(d):
(3) A law made under clause (1) may –
(a) . . .
(b) . . .
(c) . . .
(d) exclude the jurisdiction of all courts except the jurisdiction of the Supreme Court under Article 136 with respect to all or any of the matters falling within the jurisdiction of the said tribunal.

81. The words 'including the appointment of election tribunals for the decision of doubts and disputes arising out of or in connection with elections to Parliament and to the legislatures of states' were omitted by the Constitution (19th Amendment) Act, 1966, s. 2 (w.e.f. 11 December 1966). Since then, disputes regarding elections are decided in the high courts exercising jurisdiction in the states where the elections are held.

82. This was in keeping with the suggestion made by Mr L. K. Advani, then chairman of the BJP party, in Parliament in a letter dated 2 June 2012 to then PM Dr Manmohan Singh. See also Article in *Indian Express* by Damini Nath in 3 March 2023 issue: 'Ambedkar to Advani: Concern over how poll panel members are picked'.

83. In the Constituent Assembly Draft, Article 289 was amended at the instance of Dr Ambedkar to provide that the appointment of the CEC and other ECs (will be made by Parliament but subject to the provisions of any law made by Parliament. In the course of the debate (CAD Book No.3, Vol. VIII, pages 928-929), Dr Ambedkar expressed his grave misgivings in the following words:

'Now, with regard to the question of appointment, I must confess that there is a great deal of force in what my friend Professor Saksena said that there is no use making the tenure of the Election Commissioner a fixed and secure tenure if there is no provision in the Constitution to prevent either a fool or a knave or a person who is likely to be under the thumb of the Executive. My provision—I must admit—does not contain anything to provide against nomination of an unfit person to the post of the Chief Election Commissioner or the other Election Commissioner. I do want to confess that this is a very important question and it has given me a great deal of headache and I have no doubt about it that it is going to give this House a great deal of headache. In the USA, they have solved this question by the provision contained in Article 2 Section (2) of their Constitution whereby certain appointments which are specified in Section (2) of Article 2 cannot be made by the President without the concurrence of the Senate; so that so far as the power of appointment is concerned, although it is vested in the President, it is subject to a check by the Senate so that the Senate may, at the time when any particular name is proposed, make enquiries and satisfy itself that the person proposed is a proper person. But it must also be realised that that is a very dilatory process, a very difficult process. Parliament may not be meeting at the time when the appointment is made and the appointment must be made at once without waiting. Secondly, the American practice is likely and in fact does introduce political considerations in the making of appointments. *Consequently, while I think that the provisions contained in the American Constitution is a very salutary check upon the extravagance of the President in making his appointments, it is likely to create administrative difficulties and I am therefore hesitating whether I should at a later stage recommend the adoption of the American provisions in our Constitution.*'

Dr Ambedkar considered enacting an Instrument of Instructions to the President on appointments along the lines mentioned in Government of India Act, 1935, but since this was later not agreed to by the Constituent Assembly, ***it was left to Parliament to enact a law to ensure that the Election Commission consisting of the CEC and ECs would be totally independent. The regret is that Parliament has so far not done so: Courts cannot compel legislation—they can only make sugestions.***

84. 1998 (1) SCC 226 on page 269 (paragraph 58).

85. The Second Administrative Reforms Commission, in its report (January 2007), had also recommended a collegium consisting of the Speaker of Lok Sabha, the Leader of the Opposition, the Law Minister and the Deputy Speaker of the Rajya Sabha who should make recommendations to the President regarding the appointment of the CEC and of ECs. But this was not incorporated into law.

86. Entire article available at: https://indconlawphil.wordpress.com/category/free-speech/elections/.

87. *The 1951 Census of India, the first after Independence (and after Partition), placed the figure at 361,088,090 or 36.1 crores.*

In the 2011 census (the last census), the population of India rose to 1 billion 21 million, of which 79.8 per cent were Hindus, 14.2 per cent were Muslims, 2.5 per cent were Christians, 1.7 per cent were Sikhs, 0.7 per cent were Buddhists, and 0.4 per cent were Jains. India's projected population as on July 1, 2023 is 139 crores (1392 million).

The census for 2021 did not take place because of the Covid pandemic, and judged by the budget allocation of 1 February 2023 under the head Census Survey and Statistics (slashed from Rs 3,676 crores to only Rs 1,565 crores allocated in 2022-23), *The Hindu* (India's national newspaper) stated that it *did not see a bright prospect for a census until after the national elections in 2024.*

88. The words 'or Rajpramukh' omitted by the Constitution (Seventh Amendment) Act, 1956, s. 29 and Sch. (w.e.f. 1 November 1956).

89. The words 'or Rajpramukh, as the case may be' omitted by the Constitution (Seventh Amendment) Act, 1956, s. 29 and Sch. (w.e.f. 1 November 1956).

90. Subs. by the Constitution (42nd Amendment) Act, 1976, s. 50, for 'six months' (w.e.f. 3 January 1977) and further subs. by the Constitution (44th Amendment) Act, 1978, s. 38, for 'one year from the date of the passing of the second of the resolutions approving the proclamation under clause (3)' (w.e.f. 20 June 1979).

91. Subs. by s. 50, ibid., for 'six months' (w.e.f. 3 January 1977) and further subs. by s. 38, ibid., for 'one year', respectively (w.e.f. 20 June 1979).

92. Ins. by the Constitution (64th Amendment) Act, 1990, s. 2 (w.e.f. 16 April 1990).

93. Subs. by the Constitution (67th Amendment) Act, 1990, s. 2 (w.e.f. 4 October 1990) and further subs. by the Constitution (68th Amendment) Act, 1991, s. 2 (w.e.f. 12 March 1991).

94. Ins. by the Constitution (38th Amendment) Act, 1975, s. 6 (with retrospective effect) and subsequently subs. By the Constitution (44th Amendment) Act, 1978, s. 38, for cl. (5) (w.e.f. 20 June 1979).

95. Proviso omitted by the Constitution (63rd Amendment) Act, 1989, s. 2 (w.e.f. 6 January 1990) and subsequently ins. by the Constitution (64th Amendment) Act, 1990, s. 2 (w.e.f. 16 April 1990).

96. That is, in *Associated Provincial Pictures Houses Ltd. vs. Wednesbury Corpn.* (1947 (2) All England Report 680 (CA), Lord Greene said in 1948 in the famous *Wednesbury* case (1948 (1) King's Bench 223s) that when a statute gave discretion to an administrator to take a decision, the scope of judicial review would remain limited. He also added that interference was not permissible unless one or the other of the following conditions was satisfied, namely the order was contrary to law, or relevant factors were not considered, or irrelevant factors were considered, or the decision was one which no reasonable person could have taken. Lord Diplock, in *Council for Civil Services Union vs. Minister of Civil Service* ((1983) 1 AC 768) (called the CCSU case), summarised the principles of judicial review of administrative action as based upon one or other of the following, viz., illegality, procedural irregularity, and irrationality.

97. 74. Council of Ministers to aid and advise the President:
    (1) . . .
    (2) The question whether any, and if so what, advice was tendered by Ministers to the President shall not be inquired into in any court.

98. Under Article 156(1), the Governor of a State shall hold office at the pleasure of the President, but notwithstanding his tenure of 5 years, he can be removed from office without cause or reason.

99. Under Article 61, the President too can be removed during his term of office but only by impeachment 'for violation of the Constitution'.

100. In this, they correctly followed the decision of the bench of nine judges of the court in the celebrated *S. R. Bommai's* case (1994 (3) SCC page 1).

101. As of 16 February 2023.

102. The decision in *Kesavananda* (1973) apart, there was much that was correct in what the well-known German Professor Dietrich Conrad had said (in his address to the Banaras Hindu University at Varanasi in February 1965): viz '. . . *any amended body organised within a statutory scheme, howsoever verbally unlimited its power, cannot by its very structure change the fundamental pillars supporting its constitutional authority.*'

Chapter Four

The 'Magnificent Prelude' to the Constitution[1]: Exploring the Preamble and Its Features

The Preamble to a statute is a preliminary statement of the facts or reason which have made the passing of the statute desirable.

The Preamble to India's Constitution is a precursor to Part-III (the Fundamental Rights Chapter). As Justice Mahajan (one of the first judges of the Supreme Court of India) had said (in 1955)[2]:

> We think that the rights declared as fundamental rights are a necessary consequence of the declaration in the preamble that the people of India have solemnly resolved to constitute India into a sovereign democratic republic and to secure to all its citizens, justice, social, economic and political, liberty of thought, expression, belief faith, and worship; equality of status and opportunity . . .

Later, in 1992, in the principal majority opinion (in *Indira Sawhney vs. Union of India,* (bench of nine judges) Justice Jeevan Reddy mentioned that those who wrote the Constitution and finalised it: 'did not rest content with evolving the framework of the State. *They also pointed out the goal and the methodology for reaching that goal; in the preamble, they spelt out the goal and in Parts III and IV, they elaborated the methodology to be followed for reaching that goal.*'[3]

The Preamble to the Constitution now reads:

WE, THE PEOPLE OF INDIA, having solemnly resolved to constitute India into a SOVEREIGN SOCIALIST SECULAR DEMOCRATIC REPUBLIC and to secure to all its citizens:

JUSTICE, social, economic and political;

LIBERTY of thought, expression, belief, faith and worship;

EQUALITY of status and of opportunity; and to promote among them all

FRATERNITY assuring the dignity of the individual and the unity and integrity of the Nation;

IN OUR CONSTITUENT ASSEMBLY this twenty-sixth day of November, 1949, do HEREBY ADOPT, ENACT AND GIVE TO OURSELVES THIS CONSTITUTION.

A *Sovereign* state possesses an independent existence being complete in itself without being merely part of a larger whole to whose government it is subject. The word sovereign 'reminds us that the challenge of subjection of States to international law is an aim as yet only imperfectly realised but it is a doctrine which we simply cannot afford to disregard'.[4]

Socialist and *Secular* were not in the Preamble to the Constitution when enacted; they were added by the Constitution 42nd Amendment Act, 1976.

As mentioned in a recent publication, 'there are many socialisms; in fact in the parlance of Nehru's time, as now, "Indians defined *their* socialism for themselves". Nehru refused to define *socialism*, and the use of the word—without a clear definition—has created a gap that has been filled with, the assumption that Indian socialism could be equated with "Soviet-style planning"'.[5]

The word *Secular*—when added in the Preamble—did not strictly conform to its dictionary meaning, i.e., 'not concerned with spiritual or religious matters'[6], because in India, an overwhelming majority of its people are concerned with spiritual and religious matters, and the Constitution is also concerned with religious matters as all persons have been conferred with the fundamental right 'freely to profess, practise, and propagate religion' (Article 25(1)). However, the word 'secular' in the Preamble corresponds with the sense in which that word has been used in the Dictionaries of Law—e.g., *Jowitt's Dictionary of English Law* (page 1623): *'not spiritual-relating to affairs of the present world'*, and *Black's Law Dictionary* (page 1558): *'worldly, as distinguished from spiritual'*. India's Constitution is not spiritual; it is worldly and concerns itself with the public affairs of India, that is Bharat.

A *Democratic* system is a system in which everyone is equal and has the right to vote. In *Black's Law Dictionary*, 10th edition, page 525 (Editor Bryan A. Garner): this is what is stated about INDIA—

> (*Quote*) India's democracy began with the introduction of universal adult franchise—when the Constitution was enacted India had an electorate of some 170 million people, many of whom could not read or write. India's Constitution, its Election Commission, its legislatures were the *essential hardware* necessary for a democratic system—*but this hardware required software and users and this is where 'the myth of democracy begins to become apparent'* [7]. (*Unquote*)

In a 2023 publication[8], *The Indian President*, its author (K. C. Singh, a former ambassador) has written about what he describes as the 'regression' of democracy:

> (*Quote*) Today, democratic *regression* is underway, not just in India, but also globally. In many nations, governments with a huge majority led by populist leaders have slowly bent the written and unwritten rules which condition the proper functioning of a liberal democracy. ***Freedom House,***

> ***in its 2022 survey, labels as 'free' only 83 out of 210 nations surveyed. It also notes with regret that with India being downgraded to 'partly free', less than 20.3 per cent of the world's population now lives in a 'free country'. This is the smallest proportion since 1995. This year also happens to be the fifteenth consecutive year when Freedom House has reported a decline in democracy.*** (Freedom House, 'Freedom in the World 2022: The Global Expansion of Authoritarian Rule', February 2022). (*Unquote*)

A *Republic* is a system of government in which the people hold sovereign power and elect representatives who exercise that power (*Black's Law Dictionary,* 10th edition, page 1496).

The Preamble in the Draft Constitution had been recommended by the Drafting Committee set up by the Constituent Assembly. Its source was the Objectives Resolution moved in the Constituent Assembly by Pandit Nehru on 13 December 1946 (CAD Book No.1, page 57) and unanimously adopted by the Constituent Assembly on 22 January 1947 (CAD Book No. 1 page 315). The Preamble in the Draft Constitution had been taken up for consideration by the Constituent Assembly only a month before the final adoption of all the Articles of the Constitution, 'in order to ensure that it was in conformity with the draft articles that had been already debated and adopted'[9].

The Cabinet Mission Plan of May 1946 had required the *approval* of India's Constitution by Britain's Parliament; but this became unnecessary, since the Cabinet Mission Plan was not accepted by the political parties in India, and also because the transfer of power had already taken place by Britain's Parliament having passed (on 15 August 1947) the Indian Independence Act of 1947. The Preamble was therefore adopted by the Constituent Assembly—as a part of the Constitution, as had been proposed in the Draft Constitution—by retaining the following words at the end of the final paragraph '. . . do *give to ourselves this Constitution*'.[10]

The Preamble stated upfront that the *goal* of the Constitution was to secure to all its citizens:

> JUSTICE, social, economic, and political;
>
> LIBERTY of thought, expression, belief, faith, and worship;
>
> EQUALITY of status and of opportunity; and to promote among them all
>
> FRATERNITY assuring the dignity of the individual and the unity and integrity of the Nation.

All these were goals far too ambitious to be realised in the first seventy-odd years after independence, but attempts so far made towards achieving these goals are outlined in the rest of this chapter.

Justice: Social, Economic, and Political

Theodore Parker of Massachusetts, USA, a little-known 19th century unitarian minister at a seminar in the year 1853, had said:

> I do not pretend to understand the moral universe. The arc is a long one. My eye reaches but little ways. I cannot calculate the curve and complete the figure by experience of sight. I can divine it by conscience. *And from what I see, I am sure it bends towards justice.*

The above-quoted passage was made famous by American civil rights activist Martin Luther King, who (later, on a celebrated occasion) asked how long it would take to see social justice in the USA, and he famously answered it himself: 'How long? Not long. *Because the arc of the moral universe is long but it bends towards justice.* How long? Not long!'

But it is a *New York Times* bestseller, of 2009, *Justice: What's the Right Thing to Do*[11] that expresses—in capsule form—one of its most relevant and appropriate meanings.

One of the purposes of a written Constitution *is the removal of injustices to the extent possible*, a theme that has been popularised by the Nobel Laureate, Professor Amartya Sen, in his book, *The Idea of Justice:*

> ... the strong perception of manifest injustice applies to adult human beings. What moves us, reasonably enough, is not the realisation that the world falls short of being completely just—which few of us expect—but that there are clearly *remediable injustices around us which we want to eliminate.*
>
> This is evident enough in our day-to-day life, with inequalities or subjugations from which we may suffer and which we have good reason to resent, but it also applies to more widespread diagnoses of injustice in the wider world in which we live. It is fair to assume that Parisians would not have stormed the Bastille, Gandhi would not have challenged the Empire on which the sun used not to set, Martin Luther King would not have fought white supremacy in 'the land of the free and the home of the brave', without their sense of manifest injustices that could be overcome. *They were not trying to achieve a perfectly just world (even if there were any agreement on what that would be like), but they did want to remove clear injustices to the extent they could.*[12]

In India's constitutional scheme, the *social* and *economic* aspects of justice are left primarily to the lawmakers (Parliament and state legislatures). In Article 37, the principles laid down in Part-IV (Articles 38 to 51) are stated to be not only fundamental in the governance of the country, but in addition a duty has been imposed on the state (as widely defined in Article 12)[13] *to apply these principles in making laws.*

As to the *political* aspects of justice, this had been achieved not just on paper (with the inclusion of Article 326: 'Elections to be on the basis of adult suffrage'), but also in practice: since 1952India has been holding periodic elections every five years, to Parliament and to state legislatures.

As to one of many subsidiary meanings of *justice* in the dictionary *(connected with state, government, or public affairs)*, the Constitution has left this aspect of justice to be dealt with by the courts: the Union Judiciary (i.e., by the Supreme Court of India in Chapter IV in Part-V) and by the high courts in the states (in Chapter V of Part-V). In England—where there is no written constitution and there are no entrenched fundamental rights—courts have always presumed that Parliament, *when exercising its law-making function, would act in a manner that does not offend one's sense of justice.* At the start of the twentieth century the Judicial Committee of the Privy Council (the highest court in the British Empire) had said—in *Simms and others vs. The Registrar of Probates* (South Australia), 1900 A.C. 323 at 335 P.C.—that *'the legislature uses words which least offends one sense of justice'.* And later the Judicial Committee of the House of Lords (then, the highest court in Great Britain) had observed in *Cramas Properties Ltd. vs. Connaught Fur Trimmings Ltd.* in 1965 (2) All. E.R. 382 on page 385 (H.L.):

> . . . one must always remember that the object in construing any statutory provision is to discover the intention of Parliament and that there is an even stronger presumption that *Parliament does not intend an unreasonable or irrational result* . . .

Judges of the Supreme Court of India have accepted this *conceptual* aspect of justice, i.e., justice-in-enacted-law, as illustrated in their decision in *Budhan Singh vs. Babi Bux*[14] (1970); the facts of that case were as follows:

> *Babi Bux* (and his family) were ryots[15] (peasant cultivators) under the appellants (*Budhan Singh* and his family) in a village called Machara, near Meerut, in Uttar Pradesh. The site had been taken over by the father of Babi Bux from Budhan Singh's ancestors many years before Babi Bux had put up buildings on that site for residential purposes. During the communal disturbances (before and at the time of partition in 1947), Babi Bux and his family had left the village as a measure of safety, taking shelter with some of their relatives in another distant village in Uttar Pradesh. When conditions improved, they returned to Machara (in the year 1949), and found Budhan Singh in physical occupation of the site, having put up structures on the site on which Babi Bux's residential buildings had stood. The residential buildings had been demolished and the site in question had been included as part of the dwelling house of Budhan Singh. Since Budhan Singh refused to deliver back possession of the site (along with structure), Babi Bux filed a civil suit for possession on 9 January 1951. A few days later—on 26 January 1951—the U.P. Zamindari Abolition and Land Reforms Act 1950 came into force. It provided that after the commencement of the Act, the state government was empowered by notification to declare—as from a date to be specified—that all *estates* situated in Uttar Pradesh shall vest in the state and, as from the date so specified, all such estates would stand transferred to and vest in the state free from all encumbrances. But in respect of *lands* or *buildings,* it was provided—in section 9 of the Act—that they were to be treated as '*settled on the persons who held such lands and buildings*'.

On the above facts, the controversy between the parties in the appeal before the Supreme Court was as to the meaning to be attached to the word 'held' in Section 9. Was the holding contemplated therein a *lawful holding* or a *mere possessive holding, lawful, or otherwise*? And the *finding* of the Court (in 1970) was as follows:

Till about 1947, the respondents were lawfully holding the buildings and the site with which we are concerned in this case as Ryots. They never gave up their possession of the buildings voluntarily. The fact that they vacated those buildings and took shelter with their relations during the time of the communal disturbances cannot be considered as abandonment of the buildings. In law, they continued to be in possession of the buildings. Hence the appellant's entry into the suit site was an unlawful act. In the eye of law, they were trespassers. In demolishing the buildings put up by the respondents, they, committed the offence of mischief. The fact they had put up new structures cannot, under the Transfer of Property Act, enhance their rights to the property. We have no material before us from which we can find out the value of the buildings demolished by them and the value of the buildings put up by them unlawfully. From the description of the buildings given in evidence, it appears that the newly put up building is only a cattle-shed. We are not satisfied that the newly put up building is worth more than the buildings that had been demolished by the appellants. In the circumstances of the case, all that can be said is that the old buildings have been substituted by the new building. Therefore, the owners of the old buildings continue to be the owners of the new building. In that view of the matter, it is not necessary to consider whether if a stranger builds a building on the land of another, the true owner of the land is entitled to recover the land with the building on it. *Equitable considerations* persuade us to hold that when the respondents came back to their village in 1949, they were entitled to recover not only the site but also the building constructed on it by the appellants. *Hence, it should be held that on the date of vesting, the respondents were the owners of the building in question. In law, they were holding the same.*

As to the meaning to be attached to the word 'held' in Section 9, the court said:

> It is necessary to mention that it is proper to assume that the lawmakers who are the representatives of the people enact laws which the society considers as honest, fair, and equitable. The object of every legislation is to advance public welfare . . . Justice and reason constitute the great general legislative intent in every piece of legislation. *Consequently, where the suggested construction operates harshly, ridiculously or in any other manner contrary to prevailing conceptions of justice and reason . . . it would seem that the apparent or suggested meaning of the statute (suggested by Budhan Singh) was not the one intended by the lawmakers. In the absence of some other indications that the harsh or ridiculous effect was actually intended by the Legislature. There is little reason to believe that it represents the legislative intent.*

And the judges then went on to add:

> . . . according to the dictionary meaning the word 'held' can mean either a lawful holding or even a holding without any semblance of right, such as a holding by a trespasser. But the real question was as to what was the legislative intent. Did the Legislature intend to settle the concerned building with a person who was lawfully holding or with any person holding lawfully or otherwise.

The justices were unable to persuade themselves that the legislature intended to ignore rightful persons having legal title to possession and wanted to make a gift of the building to a trespasser, howsoever recently that trespasser might have been there if only he happened to be in physical possession of the building on the date of vesting. As they put it: '*we are unable to discern any legislative policy in support of that construction.*'

The far-reaching principle that was upheld in Budhan Singh vs. Babi Bux[16] was that where the suggested construction of a statute operated harshly, courts in India would assume that the apparent or suggested meaning of the statute was not the one intended by the lawmakers—because it was contrary to justice.

As to how justice is expected to be administered has been indicated in the Constitution itself:

1. in Article 32 (1), and in Article 226(1) (the 'Searchlight Provisions' in India's Constitution); and
2. it is also provided for in Article 142(1) of India's Constitution.[17]

And as to what is involved in the administration of justice has been stated, in eloquent prose, by Justice Vivian Bose (one of the first judges of the Supreme Court of India), when speaking in 1954 for a bench of five justices, said:

> We have upon us the whole armour of the Constitution and walk henceforth in its enlightened ways, wearing the breast plate of its protecting provisions and flashing the flaming sword of its inspiration.[18]

High Prerogative Writs—"*the flaming Sword*"

The High Prerogative Writs that were issued by courts in England and were looked upon in India as 'the whole armour of the Constitution'. These writs have been specifically mentioned in Article 32 (concerning the Supreme Court of India) only for enforcing fundamental rights, and in Article 226 (concerning the high courts in the states) for enforcing not only fundamental rights set out in Part-III but also for 'any other purpose'. In *T. C. Basappa vs. T. Nagappa* (AIR 1954 SC 440), a Constitution Bench of the court had held that the powers of the high courts under Article 226 were not confined to issuing prerogative writs only but also 'something more'.

But a writ proceeding cannot be made a forum for adjudicating civil rights. See *P. R. Murlidharan & Ors. vs. Swami Dharmananda Theertha Padar* (2006 (4) SCC 501 on page 506). And no writ can lie against a private person or body where there is no duty imposed on it by statute or other public duty—as was held in *Praga Tools Corporation vs. C. A. Imanual* (AIR 1969 SC 1306 = 1969 (1) SCC 585): Bench of two Judges—though a contrary view has been recently expressed by four Judges in a Bench of Five Judges in *Kaushal Kishore*; 2023(1) SCALE 225 (4:1): disregarding decisions of at least two Constitution Benches of the Supreme Court of India.

- **Writ of Habeas Corpus or Writ in the Nature of Habeas Corpus**

By means of habeas corpus (Latin for 'that you have the body'), the legal authority, under which a person may be detained, can be challenged. Habeas corpus—also termed writ of habeas corpus and the Great Writ and sometimes, shortened to habeas—is of immemorial antiquity. And after a checkered career in which it was involved in the struggles between the common-law courts and the Courts of Chancery and the Star Chamber, as well as in the conflicts between Parliament and the Crown, the protection of the writ was firmly written into English law by the Habeas Corpus Act of 1679. Today, it is said to be 'perhaps the most important writ known to the constitutional law of England.'

It is a writ employed to bring a person before a court, most frequently to ensure that the person's imprisonment or detention is not illegal (*habeas corpus ad subjiciendum*). In addition to being used to test the legality of an arrest or commitment, the writ may be used to obtain judicial review of:

1. the regularity of the extradition process,
2. the right to bail or the right to the amount of bail, or

3. the jurisdiction of a court that has imposed a criminal sentence.[19]

In India, in *Mohd. Ikram Hussain vs. State of U.P.* (AIR 1964 SC 1625 on page 1630), a bench of five justices (Justice Hidayatullah speaking for the court) had said:

> (*Quote*) The writ of habeas corpus issues not only for release from private detention. At *common law,* a writ of habeas corpus was available to the husband for regaining the custody of his wife if she was wrongfully detained by anyone from him. (*Unquote*)

- **Writ of Mandamus or Writ in the Nature of Mandamus**

Mandamus (Latin for 'we command') is a prerogative order issued in certain cases to compel the performance of a duty.

The common-law order of mandamus was substituted for the writ of mandamus in the UK by the Administration of Justice (Miscellaneous Provisions) Act, 1938, s.7 (see Rules of the Supreme Court, Order 53).

The order of mandamus issues from the Queen's Bench Division where the injured party has a right to have anything done, and has no other specific means of compelling its performance, especially where the obligation arises out of the official status of the respondent. Thus, it is used to compel public officers to perform duties imposed upon them by common law or by statute (e.g., to make a rate) or to compel inferior courts to proceed to matters within their jurisdiction. It is also applicable in certain cases where a duty is imposed by Act of Parliament for the benefit of an individual.

Originally mandamus was the generic name for a class of writs varying in their form and object, but totally different from the later prerogative writ, which, for the sake of distinction, was called a special mandamus. *Ultimately, it became an original writ, issuable by the King's Bench in UK in all cases where there was a legal right, but no other specific remedy.*

The object of a mandamus is to prevent disorder from a failure of justice and a defect of the police, and it should be granted in all cases where the law has established no specific remedy. And the value of the matter in issue, or the degree of its importance to the public, should not be too scrupulously weighed!

The writ of mandamus is of very ancient origin, so ancient indeed that its early history is involved in obscurity. The term mandamus, derived from 'letters missive', seems gradually to have been confined in its application to the judicial writ issued by the King's Bench, which has by a steady growth developed into the present writ of mandamus.[20]

In India, the writ of mandamus had been described by the Supreme Court of India in these words:

> (*Quote*) (7) . . . Normally, a writ of mandamus does not issue to or an order in the nature of mandamus is not made against a private individual. Such an order is made against a person directing him to do some particular thing, specified in the order, which appertains to his office and is in the nature of a public duty (*Halsbury's Laws of England*, Vol. 11, Lord Simonds edition, page 84).
>
> . . . So far as election to an office is concerned, a mandamus to restore, admit, or elect to an office will not be granted unless the office is vacant. If the office is in fact full, proceedings must be taken by way of injunction or election petition to oust the party in possession and a mandamus will go only on the supposition that there is nobody holding the office in question. In *R. vs. Chester Corporation*, 1855-25 LJQB 61 (E), it was held that it is an inflexible rule of law that where a person has been de facto elected to a corporate office, and has accepted and acted in the office, the validity of the election and the title to the office can only be tried by proceeding on a *quo warranto* information. A mandamus will not lie unless the election can be shown to be merely

colourable (see *Shri Sohan Lal vs. Union of India*—AIR 1957 SC 529 on page 532, para 7). (*Unquote*)

- **Writ of Prohibition or Writ in the Nature of Prohibition**

Prohibition was an order issuing out of the high court to restrain an inferior court within the limits of its jurisdiction. It was and is granted in all cases where an inferior court exceeds its power, either by acting where it has no jurisdiction, or where, having a primary jurisdiction, it takes upon itself the decision of something not included within its jurisdiction.

A temporary prohibition (sometimes called a prohibition *quousque*) is operative only until a particular act is done, and is ipso facto discharged on the act being done.

Prohibition in England is issued not only out of the Queen's Bench, but also out of the Courts of Chancery, Exchequer, and Common Pleas. If either the judge or a party proceeds after prohibition, an attachment may be had against him for contempt, at the discretion of the court which awarded it, and an action for damages will lie against him by the party injured.

Where a want of jurisdiction is apparent on the face of the proceedings in an inferior court, the high court is bound to grant a prohibition, although the applicant has acquiesced in the proceedings of the inferior court (*Farquharson vs. Morgan* (1894) 1 Q.B. 552). Prohibition may issue even though there is an alternative remedy (*Channel Coaling Co. vs. Ross* (1907) 1 K.B. 145).[21]

In India, this is how the writ has been described:

> The jurisdiction for grant of a writ of prohibition is primarily supervisory and the object of that writ is to restrain Courts or inferior tribunals from exercising a jurisdiction which they do not possess at all or else to prevent them from exceeding the limits of their jurisdiction. In other words, the object is to confine Courts or tribunals of inferior or limited jurisdiction within their bounds. It is well settled that the

writ of prohibition lies not only for excess of jurisdiction or for absence of jurisdiction but the writ also lies in a case of departure from the rules of natural Justice. (see *Govinda Menon vs. Union of India*—AIR 1967 SC 1274 on page 1277 (para 5))

- **Writ of Quo Warranto or Writ of the Nature of Quo Warranto**

Quo warranto (Latin for 'by what authority') is a common-law writ used to inquire into the authority by which a public office is held or a franchise is claimed. Also termed writ of quo warranto, it is also an action by which the state seeks to revoke a corporation's charter.

Quo warranto means 'by what warrant?' or 'by what authority?', and it was a proceeding to inquire whether authority existed to justify or authorise certain acts of a public character or interest. The proceeding on quo warranto was not one to be used by private parties in the conduct of ordinary litigation.[22]

In India, Justice P. B. Gajendragadkar speaking for a Constitution Bench of five judges in *University of Mysore vs. Govinda Rao* (AIR 1965 SC 491 on page 494), had said:

> Broadly stated, the *quo warranto* proceeding affords a judicial enquiry in which any person, holding an independent substantive public office or franchise or liberty, is called upon to show by what right he holds the said office, franchise, or liberty, if the inquiry leads to the finding that the holder of the office has no valid title to it, the issue of the *writ of quo warranto* ousts him from his office.

- **Writ of Certiorari or Writ in the Nature of Certiorari**

Certiorari (Latin for 'to be more fully informed of') is an original writ which issued out of the Crown side of the Queen's Bench Division and addressed to judges or officers of inferior courts, commanding them to certify or to return the records of a cause depending before them, to the end that justice might be done. It was one of the prerogative writs by which causes and judgements could be removed to the Queen's Bench Division from an inferior court when the former wished to inquire into the latter's jurisdiction.

Certiorari will lie only where there is a lack of jurisdiction or an error of law on the face of the record (*R. vs. Burnham Justices*, ex p. Ansorge (1959) 1 W.L.R. 1041).

The most useful employment of certiorari is to enable the high court to review decisions of ministerial and administrative tribunals where no form of appeal is available. The Queen's Bench Division may quash such decisions for want of jurisdiction, breach of the rules of natural justice (e.g., by bias, see *R. vs. Barnsley Justices,* ex. P. Barnsley and District Licensed Victuallers Association (1960) 2 Q.B. 167), or error on the face of a 'speaking order' (*R. vs. Northumberland Compensation Appeals Tribunal* (1952) 1 K.B. 338). There need not be an actual lis or dispute between two parties (*R. vs. Manchester Local Committee for Legal Aid* (1952) 2 Q.B. 413), but the body making the decision must be under a duty to act judicially (*Nakkuda Ali vs. Jayaratne* (1951) A.C. 66).

The established method by which the Court of King's Bench from the earliest times exercised superintendence over the due observance of their limitations by inferior courts, checked the usurpation of jurisdiction, and maintained the supremacy of the royal courts, was by writs of prohibition and certiorari. A proceeding by writ of certiorari (*cause to be certified*) is a special proceeding by which a superior court requires some inferior tribunal, board, or judicial officer to transmit the record of its proceedings for review, for excess of jurisdiction. It is similar to a writ of error, in that it is a proceeding in a higher court to superintend and review judicial acts, but it only lies in cases not appealable by writ of error or otherwise.[23]

In India, in a classic judgement by Justice B. K. Mukherjea (one of the first judges of the Supreme Court and later, the 4th

Chief Justice of India) speaking for a Constitution Bench of five justices in *T. C. Basappa vs. T. Nagappa* (AIR 1954 SC 440 on page 444), said:

> **(*Quote*) One of the fundamental principles in regard to the issuing of a writ of 'certiorari' is, that the writ can be availed of only to remove or adjudicate on the validity of judicial acts. The expression 'judicial acts' includes the exercise of quasi-judicial functions by administrative bodies or other authorities or persons obliged to exercise such functions and is used in contrast with what are purely ministerial acts . . .**
>
> **. . . The supervision of the superior court exercised through writs of 'certiorari' goes on two points, as has been expressed by Lord Sumner in King vs. Nat. Bell Liquors Limited (1922) 2 AC 128 on page 156(E). One is the area of inferior jurisdiction and the qualifications and conditions of its exercise; the other is the observance of law in the course of its exercise. These two heads normally cover all the grounds on which a writ of 'certiorari' could be demanded. (*Unquote*)**

Fundamental duties—prescribed in newly added Article 51A can only be enforced—as between or against citizens—by the filing of suits in civil courts under Section 9 of the Code of Civil Procedure 1908; as had been declared in *Smt. Ganga Bai vs. Vijay Kumar:* AIR 1974 SC 1126:

> *. . . there is an inherent right (under S.9 CPC) in every person to bring a suit of a civil nature and unless the suit is barred by statute one may at one's peril bring a suit of one's choice. A suit for its maintainability requires no authority of law and it is enough that no statute bars the suit.*

Article 142

In addition, Article 142 of India's Constitution specifically empowers the Supreme Court of India to pass 'such decree or order as is necessary for doing complete *justice* in any cause or matter pending before it'. It reads as follows:

> 142. Enforcement of decrees and orders of Supreme Court and orders as to discovery, etc.—(1) The Supreme Court in the exercise of its jurisdiction may pass such decree or *make such order as is necessary for doing complete justice in any cause or matter pending before it*, and any decree so passed or order so made shall be enforceable throughout the territory of India in such manner as may be prescribed by or under any law made by Parliament and, until provision in that behalf is so made, in such manner as the President may by order prescribe.

A part of Article 142 was taken from Section 210 of the Government of India Act, 1935 (Enforcement of orders of the Federal Court) but with the addition of the following italicised words (viz., '*make such order as is necessary for doing complete justice in any cause or matter pending before it*'). These words had not been included in British India's first Constitution Act (the Government of India Act 1935).

As to how these italicised words in Article 142 have been construed, different justices of the Supreme Court of India have interpreted them differently, at different times, as shown below:

A. On the one hand, there have been decisions of the Supreme Court of India that suggest that in doing 'complete justice', statute law may well be ignored, since when doing 'complete justice' in any cause or matter the overriding consideration, is justice, which cannot be fettered by anything stated in a statute. Thus:

i. In a bench decision (of three justices of the Supreme Court of India) in *Delhi Judicial Service Association and Tis Hazari Court vs. State of Gujarat* (AIR 1991 SC 2176 on pages 2210, 2211), it was said:

> (*Quote*). . . This Court's power under Article 142(1) to do 'complete justice' is entirely at a different level and of a different quality. Any prohibition or restriction contained in ordinary laws cannot act as a limitation on the constitutional power of this Court. Once this Court has seisin of a cause or matter before it, it has power to issue any order or direction to do 'complete justice'. This constitutional power of the apex Court cannot be limited or restricted by provisions contained in statutory law. (*Unquote*)

ii. And in a later bench decision of five judges in *Union Carbide Corporation vs. Union of India* (1991 (4) SCC 584 on pages 634-635) Venkatachaliah J., speaking for the court, had said:

> (*Quote*) *This constitutional power of the Apex Court cannot be limited or restricted by provisions contained in statutory law* . . . no enactment made by the Central or State Legislature can limit or restraint the powers of this Court under Article 142—though while exercising power under Article 142, the Court must take into consideration the statutory provisions regulating the matter in dispute what would be the need to do 'complete justice' in a cause or matter would depend upon the facts and circumstances of each case and while exercising that power the Court *must take into consideration the express*

> *provisions of a substantive statute. Once this Court has taken seisin of a case, cause or matter, it has power to pass any order or issue directions as may be necessary to do complete justice in the matter.* (*Unquote*)

BUT on the other hand:

B. i. equally forceful views have been expressed about the need to conform to statutory law—*at all times*—notwithstanding the conferment of power to do 'complete justice', as has been stated in the following decisions: *Prem Chand Garg vs. Excise Commissioner U.P.* (AIR 1963 SC 996), *Nidhi Kaim vs. State of Madhya Pradesh* (2017 (4) SCC page 1), and *ONGC vs. Gujarat Energy Transmission Corporation* (2017 (5) SCC 42) (the latter was a decision where an un-condonable delay in filing something in Court (and so ordained in enacted law) '*cannot be condoned by recourse to Article 142*'. All these were decisions of benches of three justices of the Supreme Court of India.

ii. There is also a bench decision of five justices of the court in *Supreme Court Bar Association vs. Union of India* (1998 (4) SCC 409) (overruling a decision of three justices of the Supreme Court in *V. C. Mishra* (1995 (2) SCC 584)), in exercise of the Supreme Court's original contempt jurisdiction under Article 129 of the Constitution, as well as its jurisdiction under the Contempt of Courts Act, 1971. In a decision reported in 1998 (4) SCC 409, the Supreme Court of India had said that there is no power or jurisdiction to invoke Article 142 (where the contemnor was an advocate) and where in addition to the punishment warranted under the Contempt of Courts Act, 1971, the advocate had been suspended from practising in courts for a particular period of time. The suspension from practice was a jurisdiction vested exclusively in the Bar Councils under the Advocates Act, 1961—*a case illustrative of the proposition that statute law must always prevail over the court's desire to do complete justice in a given case.*

C. Regrettably, even after the latest bench decision of five justices of the Supreme Court of India in the year 2020—interpreting Article 142—the controversy remains unresolved. In a judgement of great length, covering almost the entire volume of the SCC Report (in the *Ayodhya* case), a Constitution bench of five justices emphasised the overriding interests of justice by equating Article 142 with the traditional time-honoured concept of 'justice, equity, and good conscience', which had been prescribed in India in the early days of the British Raj. In *M. Siddiq (Ram Janmabhumi Temple) vs. Mahant Suresh Das* (2020 (1) SCC 1 on page 664), Chief Justice Gogoi speaking for a bench of five justices did not advert to any of the prior decisions of the court, but only said that Article 142 empowered the court '*to craft outcomes that ensure a just result*', and then concluded as follows:

> (*Quote*) (para 1026) The extraordinary constitutional power to pass any decree or an order which, in the opinion of this Court is necessary for doing complete justice embodies the idea that a court must, by necessity, be empowered to craft outcomes that ensure a just outcome. When a court is presented before it with hard cases, they follow an interpretation of the law that best fits and justifies the existing legal landscape—the constitution, statutes, rules, regulations, customs, and common law. Where exclusive rule-based theories of law and adjudication are inadequate to explain either the functioning of

> the system or create a relief that ensures complete justice, it is necessary to supplement such a model with principles grounded in equitable standards. *The power under Article 142* however is not limitless. It authorises the court to pass orders to secure complete justice in the case before it. Article 142 embodies both the notion of justice, equity, and good conscience as well as a supplementary power to the court to effect complete justice. (*Unqote*)

There has been thus far no judicially-settled meaning of the italicised words in Article 142: '*make such order as is necessary for doing complete justice . . . in a cause or matter pending before it*'. The only 'guide' (if it can be called that) appears to be what the late Ronald Dworkin had recommended[24]. Many years ago, in an article published in the *Harvard Law Review* (headed 'Hard Cases'), he wrote:

> (*Quote*) Some cases raise issues so novel that they cannot be decided even by stretching or reinterpreting existing rules. *So, judges must sometimes make new law, either covertly or explicitly. But when they do, they should act as deputy to the appropriate legislature, enacting the law that they suppose the legislature would enact if seized of the problem.* (*Unquote*)

Dworkin had described this as '*the Hercules technique of adjudication.*'

Personal Liberty

In the Preamble, the goal of JUSTICE is followed by LIBERTY (also in capital letters). In the context of the Fundamental Rights Chapter (Part-III) the expression LIBERTY stands qualified by the word "Personal" (since without the qualification (as stated in Shiva Rao: Framing of India's Constitution (1968) – a STUDY at page 238) "even price control legislation would have been interpreted as interfering with the liberty to contract between seller and buyer!" Article 21 reads:

> 'No person shall be deprived of his life or personal liberty except according to procedure established by law.'[26]

There is a historical background to Article 21. Geographically, India and the United States are miles apart, while in politics and in social thought and aspirations, the two countries are continents apart. What initially brought India nearer to the United States was a shared common-law tradition[27], which both countries inherited from what was at one time called Great Britain. British India was the first country outside the United States where decisions of US State and Federal Courts were referred to in court decisions, not because lawyers in India cited them, but because a few Indian judges took a global view of the legal universe. Sir Ashutosh Mookerjee, the first Indian judge to be appointed to the High Court of Calcutta in the early years of the 19th century, and who later became the first Indian acting chief justice of that court,[28] was one of them. His private library was stocked with American State and Federal Court reports (to which he regularly subscribed) and he frequently made use of them, in his decisions.

The influence of US judges increased considerably after the end of the Second World War and they were frequently consulted by constitution-makers from newly emerging nation-states. I recall that on my visit to Jerusalem (in 1993), I had called on Israel's former Chief Justice, Haim Cohn, a great judge and a friend of both India and the United States. He had been Israel's very first attorney general. He told me that he had been instructed by his prime minister, David Ben-Gurion, to draft a constitution for the new state of Israel, which came into existence in May 1948. On his constitutional pilgrimage to

Washington, Haim Cohn met Justice Hugo Black (of the US Supreme Court) who told Cohn to ensure that the provisions of the Constitution of Israel were sufficiently stringent to control the executive. Cohn then met Justice Felix Frankfurter (another judge of the US Supreme Court) who advised him to draft a constitution for Israel that would severely limit the powers of the judiciary. With such a sharp cleavage of views amongst America's leading justices, Cohn came back and told his prime minister that it was best that Israel stopped experimenting with a written constitution and that only 'Basic Laws' (as they came to be known later) should be passed by the Knesset (Israel's Parliament) amendable by a specified majority of its members. And so it was (and so it has since remained).

At about the same time, India's constitutional adviser, Sir Benegal Rau, had been entrusted with the task of drafting a constitution for independent India. Benegal Rau visited Washington where he discussed with Justice Frankfurter the draft of our life-and-liberty clause, which then read: 'no person shall be deprived of his life or liberty *except according to due process of law*.' Frankfurter was appalled and he told Rau that 'due process' had been one of the major headaches for successive generations of judges of the US Supreme Court. He suggested that India should take as a model the then-recent Constitution of post-war Japan and redraft the clause guaranteeing life and liberty in accordance with this document. On his return home, Rau conveyed to the Constitution Committee (set up by the Constituent Assembly) the advice of Justice Frankfurter and the draft of what is now Article 21 was then altered to read: '*No person shall be deprived of his life or liberty except in accordance with procedure established by law*.' It was this article that was ultimately passed by the Constituent Assembly and, for more than 25 years, that was how Article 21 in India's Constitution was read and interpreted by justices of India's Supreme Court.[29] According to this view, enacted law (whatever was enacted) was sufficient justification for deprivation of a person's life or liberty. This is what a majority of four judges in a bench of five justices (popularly described as a Constitution Bench) had said in *A. K. Gopalan* (1950), a case concerning preventive detention; a decision dutifully followed in several later cases until 1970.[30]

However, during the Internal Emergency imposed on 25 June 1975 (which lasted till 21 March 1977), personal liberties were taken away by enacted law[31], resulting in excessive harassment and oppression of innocent citizens who were left with no legal recourse—particularly since fundamental rights under Article 21 were also 'suspended'—under the provisions of the then unamended Article 359(1)[32]. It was then that a majority of four justices in a bench of five had expressed the following opinion about 'Liberty' (as a concept):[33]

> Liberty is confined and controlled by law, whether common law or statute. It is in the words of (Edmund) Burke a regulated freedom. It is not an abstract or absolute freedom. The safeguard of liberty is in the good sense of the people and in the system of representative and responsible government which has been evolved.

Guided—or more appropriately, mis-guided—by the majority opinion in a decision of England's House of Lords in *Liversidge vs. Anderson* (1942)[34], (a wartime decision, which in England itself had been long since discredited), Chief Justice A. N. Ray (who delivered the principal majority judgement in *ADM Jabalpur*) went on to say:

> Liberty is itself the gift of the law and may by the law be forfeited or abridged.[35]

But Justice H. R. Khanna (the seniormost judge on the bench next to Chief Justice A. N. Ray) dissented—the sole dissent in the case. This was how he looked upon the concept of liberty:

> (*Quote*) Men born to freedom are naturally alert to repel invasion of their liberty by evil-minded persons. [The]

> greatest danger to liberty lies in insidious encroachment by men of zeal, well-meaning but lacking in due deference for the rule of law.
>
> Even in the absence of Article 21 in the Constitution, the State has got no power to deprive a person of his life or liberty without the authority of law. This is the essential postulate and basic assumption of the rule-of-law-and-not-of-men in all civilised nations. Without such sanctity of life and liberty, the distinction between a lawless society and one governed by laws would cease to have any meaning. The principle that no one shall be deprived of his life or liberty without the authority of law is rooted in the consideration that life and liberty are priceless possessions which cannot be made the plaything of individual whim and caprice and that any act which has the effect of tampering with life and liberty must receive sustenance from and sanction of the laws of the land. Article 21 incorporates an essential aspect of that principle and makes it part of the fundamental rights guaranteed in Part-III of the Constitution.
>
> It does not, however, follow from the above that if Article 21 had not been drafted and inserted in Part-III, in that event, it would have been permissible for the State to deprive a person of his life or liberty without the authority of law. (*Unquote*)

The majority view of the Supreme Court (4:1) in *ADM Jabalpur* (1976) was the low watermark in Indian human-rights jurisprudence. It has been compared with the decision of the US Supreme Court in *Dred Scott*[36], where Chief Justice Roger Taney speaking (in 1857) for a majority in the court over which he presided (7:2) had said that a 'Negro' (a term now regarded as offensive), whose ancestors were imported into the US and sold as slaves, could never become a member of the political community formed and brought into existence by the Constitution of the United States. He could never be a 'citizen' of the United States of America. Of this case—*Dred Scott*—John

Paul Stevens (a once long-serving judge of the US Supreme Court) had written (after his retirement from the court):

> . . . the only good thing which can be said about that case is Abraham Lincoln's criticism of it, which, in his famous debates with Stephen Douglas (Lincoln's opponent in the 1860 US presidential elections) received nationalist attention, and helped get him elected President of the United States.[37]

But there is one thing in common between the decisions in *Dred Scott* (1857) and *ADM Jabalpur* (1976) given almost exactly more than a hundred years apart. In each of them, there were powerful dissents: *testimony to the independent thinking of individual justices in the highest courts of two of the largest democracies in the world. (In Dred Scott (7:2) Justices Curtis and McLean had dissented).*

After March 1977, judges in the Supreme Court of India—alerted by how the Internal Emergency had been worked by the executive—took a much closer look at Article 21, and recalling to themselves the excesses of the Internal Emergency era, they said that the words '*procedure established by law*' could not possibly mean *any* procedure whatever established by enacted law. Such procedure had to be one which was not arbitrary or discriminatory, one that would pass muster under Article 14. In other words, *enacted law had to meet the test of reasonableness.*[38] This fresh approach to Article 21 gave a new dimension to human rights guaranteed by the Constitution of India. The term 'due process', which had been deliberately excluded by the framers of the Constitution, was (in effect) substantively reintroduced by a more informed judicial interpretation.

This only shows that the hydraulic pressure of great events does exercise its influence on judicial thinking and helps to shape better decision-making.

The majority decision in *ADM Jabalpur* (1976) was formally and finally overruled only in 2017—unanimously—by a bench of nine judges of India's Supreme Court.[39]

The Supreme Court has also stated (on July 13, 2023) – in Petitioner for Special Leave to Appeal (Criminal) No: 4169/2023 - that an accused could not be made to remain behind bars for an indefinite period even under the Narcotics Drugs and Psychotropic Substances (NDPS) Act, 1985 just because the law required a court's satisfaction that the person was not guilty. In that case a Bench of Supreme Court (Justices Surya Kant and Dipankar Datta) stated:

> (*Quote*) "As regard to the twin conditions contained in Section 37 of the NDPS Act (for grant of bail) learned counsel for the respondent - State has been duly heard. Thus, the 1st condition stands complied with. So far as the 2nd condition re: formation of opinion as to whether there are reasonable grounds to believe that the petitioner is not guilty, the same may not be formed at this stage when he has already spent more than three and a half years in custody. The prolonged incarceration, generally militates against the most precious fundamental right guaranteed under Article 21 of the Constitution and in such a situation, the conditional liberty must override the statutory embargo created under Section 37(1)(b)(ii) of the NDPS Act". (*Unquote*)
>
> **The Supreme Court had also recently observed in its order in yet another case, Mohd. *Muslim v. State (NCT of Delhi)* 2023 Live Law (SC) 260 that "a plain and literal interpretation of the rigorous conditions under Section 37 would make granting of bail impossible." A heartening sign for the future!**
>
> (See https://www.livelaw.in/top-stories/plain-literal-interpretation-of-section-37-ndps-act-would-make-bail-impossible-supreme-court-adopts-prima-facie-test-225204?infinitescroll=1).

But liberty does not stand alone in the Preamble. It includes liberty of *thought* and *expression* (as well as liberty of belief, faith, and worship).

Freedom of speech and expression was declared in Article 19(1)(a) as a fundamental right in almost absolute terms, subject only to a restriction imposed by law in the interests of the *security of the state*. In May 1950, a Constitution Bench of six judges—not the customary five judges who normally sit in a Constitution Bench of the Supreme Court—confirmed this. In the *Cross Roads* case, it was held (by majority of 5:1)[40] that unless a law restricting freedom of speech and expression was directed *solely* against undermining the security of the state, such a law could not fall within the permissible restrictions under Clause (2) of Article 19, *'even if the restrictions which the law seeks to impose may have been conceived in the interest of public order'*. In so holding, the majority of five justices particularly relied on the fact that the word 'sedition' which had previously occurred in Article 13(2) (of the Draft Constitution)—corresponding to Article 19(2) of the Constitution as enacted—had been deliberated omitted before it was finally passed (as Article 19(2)). The five judges said (in the *Cross Roads* case) that the deletion of the word 'sedition' from the draft article:

> *(Quote)... therefore* shows that criticism of government exciting disaffection or bad feeling towards it is not to be regarded as a justifying ground for restricting *the freedom of expression and of the press* unless it is such as to undermine the security (of the State) or tends to overthrow the State ... (*Unquote*)

And in further justification, the court went on to declare:

> *(Quote) A freedom of such amplitude might involve risk of abuse.* But the framers of the Constitution may well have reflected, with Madison who was the leading spirit in the preparation of the First Amendment of the US Federal Constitution that 'it is better to leave a few of its noxious branches to their luxuriant

growth, than by pruning them away to injure the vigour of those yielding the proper fruits. (*Unquote*)

The order banning the circulation of *Cross Roads* in Madras (now Chennai) was quashed. *Days later, Sardar Patel wrote to Prime Minister Nehru that sedition could no longer be a crime.*[41] *And the well-informed statesman was spot-on.*

SEDITION AND FUNDAMENTAL RIGHTS

Contrary to the expectations of Sardar Patel, sedition continued to remain on the statute book (Section 124A, IPC 1860) punishable as a crime. It was invoked in India by the executive (particularly in the states)—far too frequently—particularly in the years 2019, 2020, and 2021 and has posed a standing threat to free speech and expression, especially for the men and women of the Fourth Estate[42], as explained below:

a. In British India, the offence of sedition—the vaguest of all offences known to the criminal law—was one of ancient vintage. With effect from the year 1870, Section 124A of India's Penal Code 1860 read: '*whoever by words, either spoken or written, or by signs, or by visible representation, or otherwise, bring into hatred or contempt or excites or attempts to excite disaffection towards a government established by law in India*' *shall be punished . . .*'

b. In the late 19th century, there were in existence a catena of court decisions on SEDITION (Section 124A IPC). Prominent amongst them was *Tilak's* case (1897)[43], where the Privy Council (the highest court of appeal from court decisions in British India) affirmed that the word 'disaffection' in the section meant 'absence of affection in any degree towards the British rule or its administration or representatives'; significantly, the Privy Council also went on to add: '*exciting of mutiny or rebellion or actual disturbance of any sort was "absolutely immaterial"*.'

c. Prominent amongst those who suffered as a result of the declaration of the law in *Tilak's* case was Mohandas Karamchand Gandhi. In the year 1922, he had been charged with the offence of *sedition* under Section 124A IPC (as explained by the Privy Council in *Tilak's* case) for three of his articles published in *Young India*. Gandhi—astute lawyer that he was—did not contest the charge and that is why the 'Great Trial' (as it later came to be known) ended with a damp squib. He was asked by the presiding judge (Robert Broomfield—later appointed Judge in the High Court of Bombay)—if he wished to make a statement before receiving sentence, and this is what Gandhiji—now famously—said:

> (*Quote*) Section 124A, under which I am happily charged, is perhaps the prince among the political sections of the Indian Penal Code designed to suppress the liberty of the citizen. Affection cannot be manufactured or regulated by law. If one has an affection for a person or system, one should be free to give the fullest expression to his disaffection, so long as he does not contemplate, promote, or incite to violence. *But the section under which Mr Banker (a colleague in non-violence) and I are charged is one under which mere promotion of disaffection is a crime. I have studied some of the cases tried under it, and I know that some of the most loved of India's patriots have been convicted under it. I consider it a privilege, therefore, to be charged under that section.* I have endeavored to give in their briefest outline the reasons for my disaffection. I have no personal ill will against any single administrator, much less can I have any disaffection toward the King's person. *But I hold it to be a virtue to be disaffected toward a government which in its totality has done more harm to India than any previous system.* India is less manly under the

> British rule than she ever was before. Holding such a belief, I consider it to be a sin to have affection for the system. And it has been a precious privilege for me to be able to write that I have in the various articles, tendered in evidence against me. (*Unquote*)

In *The World of Law (1960)*[44]—a treasury of great writing about and in the law since Biblical times— it is recorded:

> Passing sentence on Gandhi, his judge confessed, presented a problem of the utmost difficulty. Though Gandhi was evidently of a noble and even saintly character, quite different 'from any person I have ever tried or am likely to have to try', it was his painful task, since the law is no respecter of persons, to consider him solely in the character of a criminal. In attempting to balance what was due to Gandhi and what was in public interest, he imposed a sentence of six years' imprisonment, two years for each count of the charge. When the sentence was passed, Gandhi said it was as light as any judge would inflict on him, and thanked the court for its courtesy. Then the people moved forward and fell at Gandhi's feet, sobbing. Calm and smiling, he looked over their heads, giving encouragement, and, when his friends had left the court, he was led away to Sabarmati jail.

Days thereafter Gandhi and his colleague (Banker) were transferred to Yerawada Jail in Poona.

d. The law of sedition in India—as was declared in *Tilak's* case (1897)—was applied (inter alia) in the case of Mohandas Karamchand Gandhi. However, after the establishment of a (an intervening) Federal Court of India (by the Government of India Act, 1935) the interpretation of Section 124A IPC underwent a marked change. In an appeal from a conviction under Section

124A IPC by Courts in Calcutta—in *Niharendu's* case—the Federal Court of India presided over by its Chief Justice Sir Maurice Gwyer held[45] (1942) in *Niharendu's case* that if the language of Section 124A were to be read literally 'it would make a surprising number of persons in India guilty of sedition' and added:

> No one however supposes that it is to be read in this literal sense.

And without referring to (and overlooking) what the Privy Council had expressly said (in *Tilak* 1897), the Federal Court then went on to declare that *'the gist of the offence was public disorder or the likelihood of public disorder'*, Niharendu's conviction under S.123A IPC was set aside. And for nearly 15 years, the decision of the Federal Court (1947) remained the law of the land. (until it was overruled by the Privy Council in 1947).

e. In AIR 1944 Bombay 255, a division bench of the High Court of Bombay upheld (on appeal) the magistrate's decision acquitting the accused under S.124A IPC, following the then binding decision of the Federal Court in AIR 1942 FC 22. But the Crown (i.e., the Government of Bombay) obtained from the Privy Council Special Leave to appeal against the judgement of the high court, the purpose of the appeal being to 'challenge the soundness of the decision in AIR 1942 FC 22'.

   In *Emperor vs. Sadashiv* (AIR 1947 PC 82), the Privy Council—two of whose five members had hailed from (and been in India) viz., Sir Madhavan Nair and Sir John Beaumont, former Chief Justice of the High Court of Bombay—set aside the decision of the Bombay High Court. The interpretation of Section 124A in *Tilak's* case was once again authoritatively reiterated by the bench of five judges of the Privy Council, in the case of *Emperor vs. Sadashiv*; who stated:

> (*Quote*) Their Lordships are unable to find anything in the language of either S.124A or the Rule which could suggest that the acts or words complained of must either incite to disorder or must be such as to satisfy reasonable men that that is their intention or tendency. (*Unquote*)

The Privy Council then concluded:

> (*Quote*) . . . their Lordships will only add that the amendments of S.124A in 1898, the year after *Tilak's* case, by the inclusion of hatred or contempt and the addition of explanations 2 and 3 did not affect or alter the construction of the section laid down in *Tilak's* case, and, *in their opinion, if the Federal Court, in AIR 1942 FC 22, had drawn their attention to Tilak's case, they should have recognised it as an authority on the construction of S.124A by which they were bound*... *The Lordships are therefore of the opinion that the decision of the Federal Court in AIR 1942 FC 22 proceeded on a wrong construction of Section 124A Penal Code* . . . (*Unquote*)

The decision in *Tilak's* case (1897) therefore remained once again the law of the land (as to the interpretation of Section 124A IPC) after the 1942 judgement of the Federal Court had been set aside by the Privy Council in 1947.

f. With the commencement of the Constitution of India on 26 January 1950, the Privy Council's interpretation of Section 124A in *Tilak's* case (as explained and expounded *King-Emperor vs. Sadashiv Narayan Bhalerao* (AIR 1947 PC 82) was 'the law in force immediately before the commencement of the Constitution' and it continued unaltered—not because the 1947 decision of the Privy

Council was binding on the Supreme Court of India (in State of Bihar vs Abdul Mazid: 1954 SCR 786at pages 795-796, a Bench of the court had said: "we are in no way bound by the decision of the Privy Council ...") but only because of the operation of a special provision in India's Constitution (viz., Article 372). Article 372 stated that all laws in force in the territory of India immediately before the commencement of the Constitution shall continue in force therein *until altered or repealed or amended by a competent legislature or other competent authority;* and the phrase 'laws in force' included not only enacted law but also judge-made law, since the Supreme Court had said (in the year 1955), that the words 'other competent authority' in the collocation of words: (shall continue in force until altered or repealed or amended by a competent legislature or *other competent authority*) could only mean some other *legislative* authority.[46]

g. And in May 1950, five judges of the Supreme Court of India in a Constitution Bench of six judges in *Romesh Thapar vs. State of Madras* (AIR 1950 SC 124)—already referred to—summed up the law then existing (in paragraph 11 of their judgement) in these words:

> (*Quote*) 11. It is also worthy of note that the word 'sedition' which occurred in Article 13(2) of the draft Constitution prepared by the Drafting Committee was deleted before the article was finally passed as Article 19(2). In this connection it may be recalled that the Federal Court had, in drafting sedition in *Niharendu Dutt vs. Emperor*, 1942 F.C.R 38: (AIR (29) 1942 FC 22: 43 Cr.L.J. 504) held that 'the acts or words complained of must either incite to disorder or must be such as to satisfy reasonable men that that is their intention or tendency', *but the Privy Council overruled that decision and emphatically reaffirmed the view*

expressed in Queen-Empress vs. Bal Gangadhar Tilak, 22 Bom. 112 to the effect that:

> . . . the offence consisted in exciting or attempting to excite in others certain had feelings towards the Government and not in exciting or attempting to excite mutiny or rebellion, or any sort of actual disturbance, great or small—*Emperor vs. Sadashiv Narayan*, 74 I.A. 89: (AIR (34) 1947 PC 82: 48 Cr.L.J. 791).

Deletion of the word 'sedition' from the draft Article 13(2), therefore, showed that criticism of Government exciting disaffection or bad feelings towards it was not to be regarded as a justifying ground for restricting the freedom of expression and of the press, unless it was such as to undermine the security or tend to overthrow the State. (*Unquote*)

h. *But all this was overlooked again,* this time by the Supreme Court of India itself, in *Kedar Nath Singh vs. State of Bihar* (1962). In a spate of criminal appeals arising from the States of Bihar and Uttar Pradesh (*Kedar Nath Singh* (1962)), a Constitution Bench of India's Supreme Court after stating (quite correctly) that Section 124A 'clearly violated' the fundamental right to freedom of speech and expression in Article 19(1)(a), *went on (however) to say that S.124A was not unconstitutional* because of the 1942 decision of the Federal Court and was therefore protected from challenge by the words 'in the interests of public order', words that had been added (by India's Provisional Parliament the erstwhile Constituent Assembly) in Article 19(2) by the Constitution First Amendment Act, 1951.[47]

The decision in *Kedar Nath Singh* (1962) omitted to notice the provisions contained in Article 372, and instead went on to project 'a *direct conflict* between the decisions of the Federal Court (1942) and of the Privy Council (1947)', and therefore went on to hold—erroneously—that 'either view can be taken and can be supported on good reasons'. As a matter of fact, there was no conflict of decisions at all, since the ratio of the Federal Court in *Niharendu's* case[48] was that the gist of the offence under S.124A IPC was 'public disorder or the likelihood of public disorder' and this statement of the law had been specifically disapproved of and overruled by the Privy Council in 1947 long before 26 January 1950 (as was stated in AIR 1950 SC 124). Hence, the 'law in force at the commencement of the Constitution' was that Section 124A had to be interpreted on its own terms without any reference to public order or the likelihood of public disorder, and since S.124A IPC being an 'existing law' was plainly contrary to and in violation of Article 19(1)(a)—the clause that guaranteed the fundamental right to freedom of speech and expression. What had been also overlooked in *Kedar Nath Singh* (1962) was that the word 'sedition' which had been included in the draft of Article 19(2) had been deliberately omitted by the Constituent Assembly when Article 19(2) was finalised.

i. As to how all this had happened, viz., the failure to notice the express overruling of the 1942 decision of the Federal Court by the Privy Council in 1947, and the Supreme Court itself having overlooked the binding majority judgement of a Constitution Bench of six judges (5:1) as well as the provisions of Article 372 of the Constitution of India, cannot be explained; it can only be excused, because as Shakespeare, in one of his tragedies *(Othello)* had famously said: 'But men are men; and the best sometimes forget.'

j. The only bit of refreshing news, however, is that all this became pertinent and relevant, not so long ago, when in a fresh batch of writ petitions filed in the year 2021, when the constitutionality of Section 124A IPC was once again challenged in the Supreme Court by an order dated 11 May 2022 of a bench of the Supreme Court presided over by the then Chief Justice of India, it was directed that the petitions be listed for final determination after the summer vacation, and that '*in the meantime since the rigours of Section 124A IPC are no longer in tune with the current social milieu*', it would be appropriate not to continue the use of the said provision of law (i.e., S.124A IPC) by either central or state governments, till the Constitution Bench of the Supreme Court 're-examines the provisions of Section 124A'.

(k) On 01.05.2023 in W.P. (Civil) No.682 of 2021 - *S.G. Vombatkere vs. Union of India* – in which the prior Order of 11.05.2022 of the three Judge Bench of the Supreme Court of India (presided over the then Chief Justice of India) was passed, the learned Attorney General of India stated to a Bench of two Hon'ble Judges:

> "that in pursuance of Order dated 11.05.2022, the Government has initiated the process of re-examining the provisions of Section 124A of the Indian Penal Code of 1860 and the consultations are at a substantial advanced stage"

In view of this submission a two-judge Bench of the Court presided over by the present Chief Justice, Justice D.Y. Chandrachud directed the proceeding to be posted for August 8th, 2023.

Meanwhile on June 23, 2023 the current Chairman of the Law Commission issued a statement that: "Considering the current conditions in the country, sedition law is the need of the hour...." A bolt from the blue - clearly, he spoke out of turn – The Supreme Court of India is yet to re-examine the Constitutionality of the provisions contained in Section 124A of IPC.

On such re-examination, it is respectfully submitted, the Supreme Court of India ought to hold not only that the 1942 decision of the Federal Court of India (in *Niharendu's* case) had already stood overruled by the Privy Council in 1947 and was no longer good law at the commencement of the Constitution, that the provisions of S.124A were and continue to be inconsistent with the fundamental right of free speech and expression (Article 19(1)(a)) and can no longer be saved from challenge even by the so-called 'public order' exception retrospectively engrafted in Article 19(2) by the Constitution First Amendment Act, 1951. It has been settled law (settled since *Tilak's* case in 1897) that actual disturbance of public order of any sort is 'absolutely immaterial' to bring home the offence of sedition as was defined in Section 124A IPC; consequently it should be now held that on the coming into force of the Constitution of India 1950 Section 124A, being 'existing law' had become inconsistent with Article 19(1)(a) itself and had become void under Article 13(1) of the Constitution.

It is submitted that the decision of the Supreme Court of India in *Kedar Nath Singh vs. State of Bihar*[49] (1962) upholding the constitutionality of S.124 IPC—by relying on the judgement of the Federal Court in *Niharendu's* case (AIR 1942 FC 22)[50]—is glaringly erroneous.

Liberty (in the Preamble) not only includes liberty of thought and expression; it also comprehends liberty of belief, faith, and worship—protected by Articles 25 to 28[51].

The Right to Freedom of Religion is not confined to citizens but covers all persons residing in India. India has been and continues to be, a religiously pluralist society.

On a visit to India some years ago, America's talk-show host, Oprah Winfrey, reportedly said: 'People here don't just talk religion; they live it.'[52] And Deputy Prime Minister L. K. Advani had remarked (in 1990): "I never realised that religiousity is so deeply rooted in the Indian people; it made me realise that if I was to communicate the message of nationalism through the religious idiom, I would be able to transmit it more effectively ... " (A quote from Neerja Chowdhury's latest book—August 2023: "*How Prime Ministers Decide*" at pages 339-340).

The majority of the people (more than eighty per cent in the latest census) profess Hinduism, almost the same percentage did so when the European, the French, the Portuguese, and the British first came to India. Within its borders are also found followers of the major religions of the world. From the matrix of Hinduism had emerged three other great world religions: Jainism, Buddhism, and Sikhism. Christianity came to India many centuries before it reached Europe. Judaism and its adherents had once found a home and refuge in India. The ancient synagogue in Cochin, built in 1568 in the state of Kerala, bears testimony to the tolerance of Indian rulers to adherents of alien faiths.

Religion in India not only means the profession of faith but also encompasses places: temples, gurudwaras, mosques, churches, and synagogues. It includes idols and deities and offerings to them, bathing places, graves, tombs, and properties attached to and owned by religious institutions. All this—faith, worship, ritual, and the secular activities of religious groups—had to be provided for (and were provided for) in the

Constitution, in the Chapter on fundamental rights, which is beyond the reach of legislative or executive interference.

There is no provision in India similar to the First Amendment of the US Constitution which prohibits the 'establishment' of religion by law, simply because in India there is no state religion. This was clarified in 1976 by a constitutional amendment that added the word 'Secular' in the Preamble. In the 'Sovereign, Socialist, Secular Democratic Republic of India', no religious instruction can be provided in any educational institution wholly maintained out of state funds (Article 28(1)), nor can any person be compelled to pay taxes to be used for the promotion or maintenance of any particular religion or religious denomination (Article 27). Similarly, no person attending any educational institution recognised by the state or receiving aid out of state funds can be compelled to take part in any religious instruction imparted in that institution or to attend any religious worship conducted in it without his or his guardian's consent (Article 26(3)). At the same time, all persons (not merely citizens) are equally entitled to freedom of conscience and the right to freely profess, practice, and propagate their religion (Article 25). All religious denominations (there were 183 of them in the 1981 census) and even 'sections thereof' have the fundamental right to establish and maintain institutions for religious and charitable purposes to manage their own affairs in matters of religion and to own, acquire, and administer their properties in accordance with law (Article 26).

The freedom to practice religion and the freedom to manage religious affairs are not, however, absolute; they are subject to *public order*, *morality*, and *health*. The clauses on freedom of religion were modelled on Article 44 of the Constitution of Ireland, 1937. The Supreme Court of India has repeatedly stressed the breadth and the limits of this freedom. Religion includes forms of worship and all religious practices that are (or are believed by the faithful to be) an integral part of the religion[53], even the right of the head of a religious denomination to excommunicate any of its members on religious grounds, has been upheld, provided rules of natural justice are observed.[54] But the right to 'propagate' religion (it has been held) does not include the right of conversion to another faith, since Article 25 guarantees both freedom *from* religion (freedom of conscience) as well as freedom *for* all religions, not preferring any particular one.[55] The decision in *Rev. Stanislaus* (*Rev. Stanislaus vs. State of Madhya Pradesh*—AIR 1977 SC 908)[56], when it held that there was no right to convert failed to have regard to the word 'propagate'[57]—but nevertheless that decision continues to remain good law.

Although every religious denomination enjoys complete autonomy in deciding what rites and ceremonies are essential according to its tenets, the right to manage properties of a religious institution has always been regarded as a secular matter that can be regulated by law.[58] And it is the court that ultimately decides this. In the *Nathdwara Temple* case[59], Justice Gajendragadkar, speaking for a bench of five judges, observed:

> (*Quote*) In deciding the question as to whether a given religious practice is an integral part of the religion or not, the test always would be whether it is regarded as such by the community following the religion or not . . .
>
> In cases where conflicting evidence is produced in respect of rival contentions as to competing religious practices, the Court may not be able to resolve the dispute by a blind application of the formula that the community decides which practice is an integral part of its religion, because the community may speak with more than one voice and the formula would, therefore, break down. This question will always have to be decided by the Court and in doing so, the Court may have to enquire whether the practice in question is religious in character and if it is, whether it can be regarded as an integral or essential part of the religion, and the finding of the Court on such an issue will always depend upon the evidence adduced before it as to the conscience

> of the community and the tenets of its religion. It is in the light of this possible complication which may arise in some cases that this Court struck a note of caution in the case of the *Durgah Committee, Ajmer v. Syed Hussain Ali* , and observed that in order that the practices in question should be treated as a part of religion they 'must be regarded by the said religion as its essential and integral part, otherwise even purely secular practices which are not an essential or an integral part of religion are apt to be clothed with a religious form and may make a claim for being treated as religious practices within the meaning of Art. 26(1)'. (*Unquote*)

'EQUALITY of status and opportunity' follows next in the Preamble—reflected in (and elaborated) by Articles 14 to 18 (as well as Article 29(2))[60] in the Fundamental Rights Chapter (Part-III of the Constitution).

General

The principle of equality before the law is universally recognised. It has become an integral part of the constitutions of most of the civilised countries in the world. Peaslee's classic work[61] (in four volumes) mentions that nearly 75 per cent of the constitutions of the nation states in the world contain clauses about equality. The principle of equality is recognised as one of the fundamental principles of modern democracies, and governments based on the rule of law. In a book published in 1945 (then the first of its kind), Sir Hersch Lauterpacht[62], renowned jurist and president of the International Court of Justice wrote about the pre-eminence of equality in the governance of states:

> The claim to equality before the law is in a substantial sense the most fundamental of the rights of man. It occupies the first place in most written constitutions. It is the starting point of all other liberties.[63]

It is easy to be passionate about inequality which has increased dramatically in many parts of the world over the past two generations. Thomas Piketty, professor at the Paris School of Economics and co-director of the World Inequality Lab, has recently written about it in *Capital in the 21st Century*, with a shorter version published in 2021 titled, *A Brief History of Equality* (published by the Harvard University Press). In it (at pages 190-192), he has described '*the case of India, which is the country that has gone the furthest in the use of quotas*' and has tentatively concluded: '*If the balance-sheet on Indian quotas is on the whole positive, this experiment also illustrates the limits of such a policy . . .*'

Though the principle of equality is universally recognised, its precise content is not clear.

Article 14

The first part of Article 14 of India's Constitution (the State shall not deny to any person Equality before the Law) has been modelled on the concept of the Rule of Law and the second part (the equal protection of the laws) is a concept imported from the Constitution of the United States.

Article 14 has contributed a vast body of case-law:

The article had raised problems for the Supreme Court in the 1950s and 1960s. In *State of West Bengal vs. Anwar Ali Sarkar* (1952) (AIR 1952 SC 123) (decision of a full court of seven judges when the strength of the court at the time was seven judges along with the Chief Justice of India), and in the companion case, *Kathi Raning Rawat vs. State of Saurashtra* (1952) (AIR 1952 SC 75) heard along with *Anwar Ali Sarkar*, a majority of the court (6:1) held that whilst Article 14 forbade class legislation, it did not forbid *reasonable classification*. But one of the judges—Justice Vivian Bose—did not agree. The classification test, he said, was not the only test. He then went on to expound his view that laws of liberty, of freedom, and of protection under the Constitution must be left to assume shape slowly as decision is added to decision. 'They cannot be enunciated in static form by hidebound rules and arbitrarily applied standards or tests.' However, Justice Bose's 'judicial-conscience test' was a cry in the wilderness. His colleagues—and those who succeeded him—preferred the objective tests of *reasonable classification*, which in a later decision in *Ram Krishna Dalmia vs. Shri Justice S. R. Tendolkar* (AIR 1958 SC 538 (5J)) the testss were formalised in a series of six propositions. Since then it became a classic statement of the law on Article 14. There were several other cases as well. And by the end of the first two decades of the working of the Constitution, it was assumed that the problems raised by the Equality Clause had been judicially settled.

But a few years later came a concurring judgement of two justices in a bench of five justices in *Royappa* (1974) (AIR 1974 SC 555) where what is sometimes (disparagingly) called the 'New Doctrine' was first enunciated. This enunciation was by only two of the judges on the bench (Justice Bhagwati and Justice Krishna Iyer), who have left their mark on the decisions of the court. In *Royappa*, it was these two judges who expressed the 'New Doctrine' in the following terms:

> (*Quote*) The basic principle which, therefore, informs both Articles 14 and 16 is *equality and inhibition against discrimination*. Now, what is the content and reach of this great equalising principle? It is a founding faith, to use the words of Bose, J., 'a way of life', and it must not be subjected to a narrow pedantic or lexicographic approach. We cannot countenance any attempt to truncate its all-embracing scope and meaning, for to do so would be to violate its activist magnitude. Equality is a dynamic concept with many aspects and dimensions and it cannot be 'cribbed, cabined, and confined' within traditional and doctrinaire limits. *From a positivistic point of view, equality is antithetic to arbitrariness. In fact, equality and arbitrariness are sworn enemies; one belongs to the rule of law in a republic while the other, to the whim and caprice of an absolute monarch.* Where

an act is arbitrary, it is political logic and constitutional law and is therefore violative of Article 14, and if it affects any matter relating to public employment, it is also violative of Article 16. Articles 14 and 16 strike at arbitrariness in State action and ensure fairness and equality of treatment. (*Unquote*)

A few years later in *Maneka Gandhi's* (AIR 1978 SC 579), six judges in a bench of seven judges (which included Justices Bhagwati and Krishna Iyer) applied (for the first time) the *Royappa* test to the procedure prescribed by law under the Passport Act, 1967, and held that such law, for purposes of Article 21, had to answer the test of reasonableness in order to be in conformity with Article 14. The court said the 'law' (in Article 21) must be *right, just, and fair*, and not arbitrary, fanciful, and oppressive, otherwise such a law would not satisfy the requirements of Article 14. This was a conscious departure from the traditional time-honoured classification test. The old rule was that a law was invalid under Article 14 only if there was discrimination, i.e., only if the classification of persons and things under it was arbitrary and unreasonable. Unreasonableness and arbitrariness of the law per se could not result in the court striking down the law for two reasons: (i) because there was a presumption of the constitutionality of laws enacted by a competent legislature, and (ii) Courts would pay due deference to the will of the legislature and its collective wisdom as to circumstances requiring differential treatment.

But the judgement of the two judges in a bench of five in *Royappa*—was affirmed in *Maneka Gandhi* (1978) (by a bench of seven judges),—*the law itself, (or at least the procedural part of the law), had to be justified before the court as just and fair and not arbitrary, fanciful, or oppressive.*[64] (And Maneka Gandhi was later followed by a Bench of Nine Judges in *Puttaswamy* 2017 (10) SCC page 1.

In 1979, when the validity of a bill (proposed law) had been questioned in a Presidential Reference (under Article 143 of the

Constitution) in *re: Special Courts Bill* (before a bench of seven judges)[65], the justices when handing down their opinion (to the president of India) as to whether the Special Courts Bill—if enacted—would be constitutionally invalid, first applied the tests of classification and (after re-formulating them—now in a set of 13 propositions) the court held that by the application of these tests, the conclusion was irresistible that the classification provided for by the Special Courts Bill as presented was valid, and that no objection could be taken against it. But the court then went on to add—presumably on the basis of *Royappa* and *Maneka Gandhi* (but without specific reference to either of these judgements)—that the provisions in the bill *'appeared'* to their lordships to be 'unfair' and 'unjust' in important respects. And that is how the reference to the president was answered.

A year later, in a challenge to an administrative action—*International Airports Authority* (1979) (AIR 1979 SC 1678)—the dictum that arbitrariness was the antithesis of Article 14 was reaffirmed. And when seven years later, in the *Express Newspapers* case (1986 (1) SCC 133 on page 192), the Solicitor General of India, Mr Lal Narayan Sinha, was critical of the observations in *Royappa* and *Maneka Gandhi* and said that this would mean that all governmental acts not supportable by law would then *per se* be violative of Article 14, the response of the court (in *Express Newspaper*) (speaking through Justice A. P. Sen) was:

> (*Quote*) I am afraid, it is rather late in the day to question the correctness of the landmark decision in the *Maneka Gandhi* (AIR 1978 SC 579) and the innovative construction placed by Bhagwati, J., on Article 14 in the three cases of *Royappa, Maneka Gandhi,* and *International Airport Authority* (AIR 1979 SC 1628), which have evolved new dimensions in the judicial process. (*Unquote*)

And the trend towards 'the new dimensions in the judicial process' has continued since then.

The criticism of textbook writers—and of some judges as well of the doctrine enunciated in *Royappa*—later applied in many decisions concerning statute law—that it was a 'naked judicial usurpation of legislative power' is but a name-calling exercise. It does not take into account the ultimate object of Article 14, which in the end, is to prevent the enactment of wholly unjust laws.

One must not run away with the idea that it is only an overactive judiciary in this country that holds exalted and exaggerated views of the court's supervisory powers over legislation under the equality clause of our Constitution. Similar views have been expressed by distinguished judges abroad. In the Annual F. A. Mann Lecture delivered in the UK in November 1994, Lord Harry Woolf (then Lord of Appeal in Ordinary) said, whilst accepting the absolute supremacy of the British Parliament, that there was need to make a distinction between legislation and 'that which sought to undermine in a fundamental way the rule of law on which the unwritten British Constitution depended'. He was addressing the question as to the validity of a law removing or substantially impairing the entire reviewing role of the high court on judicial review, 'a role which in its origin is as ancient as the Common Law and predates our present form of parliamentary sovereignty and the Bill of Rights'. Lord Woolf didn't then say that he would (as judge) strike down a statutory provision made by Parliament excluding all or, substantially all, judicial review, but this is what he did say:

> (*Quote*) *However, if Parliament did the unthinkable then I would say that the courts be also required to act in a manner which would be without precedent.* Some judges might choose to do so by saying that it was an unrebuttable presumption that Parliament could never intend such a result. I myself would consider there were advantages in making it clear that ultimately there are even limits on the supremacy of Parliament which it is the courts' inalienable responsibility

> to identify and uphold. They are limits of the most modest dimensions which I believe any democrat would accept. They are no more than are necessary to enable the rule of law to be preserved.[66] (*Unquote*)

In 1997, as Master of the Rolls (i.e., as president of the Court of Appeal in the UK), Lord Woolf went a step further by saying (again extra-judicially, in a speech off the bench) that in 'extreme circumstances', English judges could 'disapply' Acts of Parliament by reference to some higher norm of justice (in a substantive, not procedural sense)—a doctrine dormant in the English law since the heyday of Chief Justice Sir Edward Coke in 17th century England.[67] Lord Woolf mentioned two examples of such 'extreme circumstances', viz.: an infinite perpetuation by Parliament of its own life or the enactment of racially discriminatory laws on the Nazi model.

In the United States of America, despite claims to the contrary, its Supreme Court has actively enforced 'values', which a majority of the justices felt were essential in American society, even though these 'values' had no specific textual basis in the Constitution. Courts in the United States control the substance of legislation under the due process clause (the Fifth Amendment)[68] simply on the ground that certain types of lawmaking go beyond 'any proper sphere of governmental activity'. The basic judicial premise for this position is that the taking or deprivation of life, liberty, or property by such a law is unconstitutional simply because 'the Constitution never granted the government the ability to pass such a law'.[69] A manifestation of this recognised exercise of judicial power (in the USA) is the concurring opinion of Supreme Court Justice David Souter in the case of *Washington vs. Glucksberg: 521 US 702* (1997).[70] The question presented in this case was whether the State of Washington's prohibitory law on causing and aiding suicide offended the XIV Amendment to the US Constitution. The court held that it did not, because an examination of the nation's history, legal traditions, and practices revealed that the asserted right to assistance in committing suicide was not 'a fundamental-liberty-interest' protected by the 'due process' clause. In concurring with the majority, Justice Souter referred to the concept of *ordered liberty*—'comprising a continuum of rights to be freed from arbitrary impositions and purposeless restraints'.[71] Justice Souter described the substantive due process guarantees against arbitrary legislative deprivation of liberties as the court's *duty* of giving strict scrutiny to 'a legislative resolution (perhaps unconscious) of clashing principles, each quite possibly worthy in and of itself, but each to be weighed within the history of our values as a people'.[72]

Conclusion:

Though ordinarily substantive laws cannot and ought not to be struck down merely because courts regard them as 'unjustified' or 'unreasonable', there is always an ultimate residual discretion—to be exercised only by and in the highest court—and sparingly of course, to invalidate even substantive provisions of statute laws where such substantive provisions are 'wholly unjust' or 'arbitrary beyond the grounds of reason'. In other words, where they 'shock the judicial conscience' as they did in a now celebrated case under the IPC (the Indian Penal Code): *Mithu vs. State of Punjab* (AIR 1983 SC 473); a decision of a bench of five judges.

Under Section 303 IPC (Indian Penal Code) – Punishment for murder – "whoever being under sentence for imprisonment for life commits murder shall be punished with death". In *Mithu vs. State of Punjab*: AIR 1983 SC 473 – a decision of the Constitution Bench of five Judges of the Supreme Court of India, Chief Justice Y.V. Chandrachud - delivering the judgment on behalf of himself, Justices Fazl Ali, Tulzapurkar and Vardarajan – and following the prior judgments of the Courts in *Maneka Gandhi vs. Union of India*: AIR 1978 SC 597 and in *Bachan Singh vs. State of Punjab*: AIR 1980 SC 898 held Section 303 IPC to be "draconian in severity and relentless and inexorable in operation" and struck it down as unconstitutional and void. In his separate concurring judgment Justice Chinappa Reddy (concurring) stated that since "the light shed by Maneka Gandhi (1978) and Bachan Singh (1980) it is impossible to uphold Section 303 as valid. "Section 303 excludes judicial discretion: *so final, so irrevocable and so irresistible is the sentence of death that no law which provides for it without involvement of judicial mind can be said to be fair, just and reasonable. Such a law must necessarily be stigmatised as arbitrary and oppressive.*"

Accommodating Equality in a Sea of 'Untouchability' and Backwardness.

The provisions relating to 'the Right of Equality' in the Constitution (Articles 14 to 18) reflect the grim reality of a developing country, slowly emerging out of a rigid, caste-bound social system. 'The spirit of the age,' Nehru once wrote, 'is in favour of equality, but practice denies it almost everywhere.' In keeping with the spirit of the age, the Constitution guarantees to all persons the equal protection of the laws and prohibits the state (which includes all lawmaking and law enforcement bodies) from denying to any person equality before the law (Article 14). Equality of opportunity is ensured to all citizens in matters relating to employment or appointment to any office under the state (Article 16(1)), the state cannot discriminate (either generally or in matters relating to public employment) against any citizen on grounds of religion, race, caste, sex, or place of birth (Articles 15(2) and 16(2)), and no citizen can be denied admission into any educational institution maintained by the state or receiving aid out of state funds on grounds of religion, race, caste, or language (Article 29(2)). Nothing in these provisions, however, prevents the state *from making special provisions for what the Constitution regards as 'weaker sections of society'. For them, protective discrimination is recognised and encouraged as a fundamental duty of the state.* Article 46 (in Part-IV, Directive Principles of State Policy) enjoins the state to 'promote with special care the educational and economic interest of the weaker sections of the people and in particular of the Scheduled Castes and the Scheduled Tribes'. It directs the state to 'protect them from social injustice and all forms of exploitation'. The beneficiaries of *preferential treatment* had been indicated up front in the Constitution:

1. Women and children were (and remain) exceptions to the general rule against any form of discrimination (Article 15(3)).
2. Scheduled castes, scheduled tribes, and socially and educationally backward classes of citizens are also exceptions to the general rule against discrimination (Articles 15(4) and 16(4)).
3. The scheduled castes (or 'untouchables') are the largest of these groups. The Constitution enables the state to make special reservations in educational institutions and in public services for backward classes of citizens and to ensure that they are adequately represented insofar as this is consistent with maintaining efficient administration (Article 335)[73]. It also provides for representation in Parliament and in state assemblies for scheduled castes and scheduled tribes and a proportional reservation of seats for them in the lawmaking bodies of the nation (Articles 330 and 331). These provisions for representation were initially intended to operate for a period of only ten years from the commencement of the Constitution (26-01-1950) but they have been extended by Parliament periodically by constitutional amendments, and they continue in force even after seventy odd years of the working of India's Constitution.

Preferential treatment for women and children is easily explained. In every society, children are treated differently from adults. Women constitute nearly 50 per cent of India's population; the majority of them have been an oppressed class.

The personal and customary laws of the Hindus and Muslims imposed special disabilities and constraints on them.[74] '*Na sthree swathanthryam arhati*,' (the woman does not deserve independence) said Manu the ancient law by giver. In ancient times, in a male-dominated society, women were looked upon as chattels, useful only for marriage and the bearing of children. As Sir Henry Maine had pointed out the institution known in Roman law as the perpetual tutelage of women was carried to its logical conclusion in India. 'In India,' Maine wrote in 1861, 'the system survives in absolute completeness, and its operation is so strict that a Hindoo Mother frequently becomes the ward of her own son.'[75]

As to why there Are Special Provisions and Preferential Treatment for Scheduled Castes, Scheduled Tribes, and Other Backward Classes.

For treating adult citizens differently, there must be a reason, because as Isaiah Berlin (noted philosopher and historian) said in a famous essay on the subject: '*The assumption is that equality needs no reason, only inequality does.*'[76]

For preferential treatment for scheduled castes and scheduled tribes and other backward classes, the reason therefore lies in India's history.

In the past, these groups had been disadvantaged for centuries, many of them beyond the pale of law, scheduled castes and scheduled tribes beyond human compassion. For more than 2000 years, 'untouchables' and 'tribals' were treated as if they were not human beings (most of them were dubbed by the British conquerors as 'criminal tribes' (and so treated)); a treatment rationalised by the argument that they and their children were inherently inferior in ability to those born into superior stations in life. As Marc Galanter (law professor and writer) says in his treatise on the subject: '*India embraced equality as a cardinal value against a background of elaborate, and clearly perceived, inequalities*.'[77] More poignantly, Mahatma

Gandhi had said (and only he had the courage to say it) in a speech to the All India Congress Committee in Bombay way back in July 1946:

> (*Quote*) Our sins have a strange way of coming home to roost. We turned a portion of ourselves into pariahs, and today, the whites of South Africa are doing the same to our compatriots there. (*Unquote*)

Gandhiji had no moral compunction in comparing caste discrimination in India with apartheid in South Africa. He was convinced that the consequences and effect of each of these evils were the same.

The Aryans were the first invaders of the land inhabited by the serpent-worshiping Nagas and other ancient tribes in the north and by the Dravidians in the south. The Aryans subjugated India without pretending to elevate it. They wanted land and pasture for their cattle. Slowly, they made their way eastward along the Indus and the Ganges until all Hindustan was under their control. Outnumbered by a subject people whom they considered inferior, the Vedic Aryans sought to preserve their racial identity. In a couple of centuries, however, they were assimilated and absorbed. The first caste division was not by status but by colour.[78] It separated the fair Aryans with long noses from the dark, broad-nosed Dravidians. 'It was,' as Will Durant reminded us, 'the marriage regulation of an endogamous group.'

As Bharat—pictured in the Vedas (2000-1000 BC)[79]—changed to the conditions described in the great Hindu epics—the Mahabharata and the Ramayana (1000-400 BC)[80]—occupations became hereditary and more specialised, and caste divisions were more rigidly defined. First, there were the Kshatriyas (or fighters/warriors), who considered it a sin to die in bed. But as conditions of war gave way to peace and as religion and ritual (largely an aid to agriculture in the face of incalculable elements) grew in importance and complexity, requiring proficient intermediaries between men and the gods, the Brahmins consolidated their position. They alone knew the ancient Sanskrit (the oldest in the European group of languages) and could recite the Vedas. They were thus able to recreate the past and project the future in their own image, moulding each generation into one with greater reverence for the priests, building for their caste a prestige that, in later centuries, gave them a supreme place in Hindu society. Below the Brahmins and Kshatriyas were the Vaishyas—farmers and traders. These three castes (or varnas) were regarded as twice born, the second birth (or regeneration) consisting in the study of the Vedas and in the performance of sacraments. The twice-born status was denied to the fourth varna, the Shudras—or the working class—who made up most of the populace. Over the years, a fifth category long unrecognised in theory, *the outcastes*, emerged, consisting of unconverted native tribes, captives of war, and men and women reduced to slavery as punishment. This small group of the casteless formed the nucleus of what became the world's largest minority: the 'untouchables' (now 'the scheduled castes').

It was not as if the caste principles on which Hindu society was organised were never questioned from within. The religious hegemony of the Brahmins was contested by the Kshatriya noblemen who founded Buddhism. This new religion rejected the predetermination of status by birth and the hierarchical ranking of castes. It became the religion of the kings who ruled India for nearly 900 years. Embraced by the Emperor Ashoka the Great (273-232 BC)—grandson of Chandragupta Maurya—Buddhism gained a foothold in the subcontinent and for over 200 years posed a real threat to Hinduism. Then it became riddled with schisms and sects and was influenced by Hindu pantheistic beliefs. Generations of Hindu culture proved too much for this ascetic, non-theistic religion. Buddha was slowly absorbed into the Hindu pantheon as one of the incarnations of the god Vishnu.[81] During the reign of Harshvardhan (606-648 AD)—the last Buddhist king—the great casteless religion was stamped out in the land of its birth. The oriental scholar, Sir Charles Eliot, had described the denouement in a chilling phrase: '*Brahmins killed Buddhism by a fraternal embrace*.'[82]

The Hinduism that replaced Buddhism was an amalgam of faiths and ceremonies that had four common characteristics:

1. it recognised the caste system;
2. it reaffirmed the leadership of the Brahmins;
3. it accepted the law of karma (destiny) and the transmigration of souls; and
4. it replaced with new gods the deities of the Vedas.

Caste came back into its own and with it the antithesis of 'pure' versus 'impure'. The untouchables—Hindu outcastes—grew in number, particularly with the introduction of new occupations.

By the latter part of the Middle Ages, India was more advanced in agriculture, handicrafts, and commerce than many other countries. To the traditional division of society into four main castes (Brahmins, Kshatriyas, Vaishyas, and Shudras) were added an almost indefinite number of occupational castes. The criteria for the hierarchical status of high or low multiplied a hundredfold with new occupations. For each new activity, it was the Brahmins who determined which aspects were 'low' or 'impure', and the number of outcastes increased even further. Muslim rule brought some changes in Indian society but neither the new language of the courts (Persian) nor the religion of the new rulers (Islam) made any difference to the traditional division of labour organised through specialised groups ranked in a hierarchical order. Thus, caste and untouchability continued to flourish during Muslim rule.

An attempt was made at emancipation when the British came and conquered. The new economic order brought in by the conquerors from the West altered the design of a social system that had retained a remarkable continuity for centuries.

Moreover, with English education, more people became acquainted with modern European and American history, with their concepts of *equality* and of *fraternity*. The beneficiaries of the British system of education, mainly the children of high-caste Hindu families, grew up questioning the principles on which their society was organised. A few cosmetic changes were introduced, such as the Caste Disabilities Removal Act of 1850, but this enactment was a dead letter from the start. Social consciousness had not yet been aroused.

Then, at the beginning of the 20th century, Mahatma Gandhi introduced into the independence movement two new concepts: peaceful non-cooperation with the British (non-violent satyagraha) and a plea for a better deal for the outcastes. Gandhi lived among them and described them as 'Harijans' (children of God). In the liberal spirit of the age, the name stuck. It brought an increasing awareness to the Indian mind of the shame of 'untouchability'. Among the more enlightened of the higher castes, a movement started to do something to relieve the lot of the depressed classes. To uplift them was regarded as an act of compassion, a voluntary righting of the wrongs of many years. But as the benefits of Western-style education permeated downward, the bright young men and women in the society of outcastes also spearheaded a movement that was based not on compassion but on right. The leader of this movement—and its most eloquent member—was Dr B. R. Ambedkar, a Harijan (presently, the word Dalit is used instead of Harijan). Along with Jawaharlal Nehru, Dr Ambedkar was one of the principal architects of the Constitution of India.

This then was what WE, the PEOPLE inherited with independence. This was the state of the nation when the Constitution was adopted in November 1949 and promulgated in January 1950.

Aware of the generations of accumulated and accentuated group inequalities, the Constituent Assembly had adopted a constitutional policy of deliberate preferential treatment for the historically disadvantaged people. First, 'untouchability' was abolished and its practice in any form forbidden (Article 17).[83] The Untouchability Offences Act of 1955 (renamed in 1967 as the Civil Rights Act) adopted legal sanctions in aid of the constitutional prohibition, and then, all temples and religious institutions were thrown open to 'all classes and Sections of Hindus' (Article 25(l)(b)).

A form of apartheid, long practised by the twice-born classes against the untouchables, was abolished, and all citizens became entitled to equal access to shops, public restaurants, hotels, and places of entertainment and to the use of wells, tanks, bathing places, roads, and places of public resort maintained out of state funds or dedicated to the use of the general public (Article 15(2)). Untouchability was not merely a stigma; it was an attitude of mind.

Mere constitutional declarations, however, were not enough. The Constitution therefore recognised, promoted, and encouraged special treatment in educational institutions and employment opportunities for the socially less fortunate classes to any office under the state. It empowered Parliament and state legislatures to make special provisions through ordinary law for the advancement of scheduled castes, scheduled tribes and other backward classes (OBCs) who by reason of their occupational background are socially and educationally backward. Provisions could be made for them, without infringing the equality clauses, for reservation of seats in educational institutions and in posts in public services, at almost all levels. The Constitution had also prescribed an agency and a method for designating scheduled castes and scheduled tribes. The president (i.e., the central government, since all executive action of the Government of India is taken in the name of the president) was empowered to specify the castes, races, or tribes that, for the purposes of the Constitution, would be deemed to be scheduled castes or scheduled tribes within any particular state or union territory (Articles 341 and 342). Once promulgated, these lists could be changed only by an Act of Parliament. The Scheduled Castes Order, promulgated by the president in 1950 (with amendments introduced over the years), proceeded primarily on the basis of 'untouchability', measured by the incidence of social disability combined with economic, occupational, educational, residential, and religious criteria.[84] The Scheduled Tribes Order of 1950—also amended over the years—listed backward tribes in need of preferential treatment.

The scheme of scheduled and tribal areas (under the Government of India Act of 1935) was adopted in the Constitution of India (in Part-X, Articles 244 and 244(A)), and in the Fifth and Sixth Schedules to the Constitution). These designated areas were to be administered as a special responsibility of the governor of the state in consultation with tribal committees and councils. The provisions for scheduled tribes in the Constitution were intended to preserve their separate identities. The aim was a balanced improvement of their condition with such a degree of assimilation as would preserve their distinctiveness and give them a measure of autonomy.

Primitive cultures react sharply to alien interference. Experience has shown that indigenous tribal communities are prepared to adapt themselves to change only on their own terms and in their own time. The constitutional policy for scheduled castes (and scheduled tribes) has been to overcome their disabilities and disadvantages by preferential treatment and to eliminate their distinctiveness by enabling them to share the advantages for lack of which they are still a class apart from other, more advantaged members of Hindu society.

While the categories of scheduled castes and scheduled tribes were constitutionally determined, the socially and educationally backward classes of citizens (also designated for preferential treatment) had been left undefined, even though specifically mentioned in Article 15(4) in 1951.[85]

The first Backward Classes Commission (the Kaka Kalelkar Commission) appointed by the central government submitted its report in 1955, listing 2399 castes as 'socially and educationally backward'. However, the report was not accepted by the government since no objective tests were laid down for identifying OBCs. At that time, the government was opposed to the adoption of caste as a criterion for backwardness; it would have preferred the application of an economic or means test. These 'classes of citizens' were then left to be determined by the states and by the government agencies. *But the states had been singularly remiss in not gathering data over the years to enable a realistic determination (at least in terms of percentages) of these classes of citizens as compared to the rest of the population in the state.* Nor was there much progress in the amelioration of the lot of these classes of citizens. The absence of any constitutionally prescribed or judicially mandated method for identifying OBCs led to much speculative reasoning by different state governments. It also fostered bitterness and dissatisfaction amongst members of these classes as well as from those better-off, i.e., those not belonging to the class of OBCs, who objected to preferential treatment for the backward classes.

The state of Karnataka set up its own commission (in 1972) to investigate and report on backward classes in the state. The report of the Havanur Commission[86] (named after its chairman L. G. Havanur) ignored the principle of caste in the concept of social backwardness and devised a new test: *that of poverty coupled with isolation*. This test cut across the caste system and included as backward classes several groups of temple functionaries (who belonged to higher castes) as well as some Kshatriyas. At the same time, it excluded some groups in the traditionally low castes on the grounds of their economic advancement. The state of Karnataka accepted the report and proceeded to make reservations in accordance with it. As expected, the constitutional validity of the state action (order dated 22 February 1977 accepting the report) was challenged in the High Court of Karnataka by writ petitions (which were partially allowed). The case later reached the Supreme Court of India (*K. C. Vasanth Kumar vs. State of Karnataka* (1985)).[87]

Called upon to frame guidelines for determining 'other backward classes'—for purposes of the Karnataka state's

reservation policy[88]—each of the five justices in K. C. Vasanth Kumar (1985) spoke not only diffidently, but also with different voices, without any unanimity on the vital points of contention, viz.:

1. **whether a policy of reservation of more than 50 per cent for OBCs was permissible in law;**
2. **whether castes should form the basis—or at least an important element—for determining social and educational backwardness; and**
3. **whether in jobs in government requiring high expertise and skill, a policy of reservation, detracting from merit, was permissible.**

(1) On the first point of contention, after the decision of the Constitution Bench of the Supreme Court of India in *Nagaraj vs. Union of India* (2006),[89] the ceiling limit of 50 per cent for backward classes had been (then) regarded by the Supreme Court of India as 'a Constitutional mandate'.[90]

(2) On the second point of contention, after the decision of the Constitution Bench of the Supreme Court of India, in *Ashoka Kumar Thakur vs. Union of India and Ors.* (2008)[91], the court made it (regrettably but abundantly) clear by a majority of 4:1, that *caste* did definitely constitute the basis for determining social and educational backwardness.

(3) But as to the third point of contention, as to whether in jobs in government requiring high expertise and skills, a policy of reservations detracting for merits was permissible—this has not yet been authoritatively dealt with nor answered by the highest court. It has been left—by judicial diktat—to be decided by 'the governments': centre and state.

Two of the judges on the Constitution Bench of five justices in *K. C. Vasanth Kumar vs. State of Karnataka* (decided on 8 May 1985) had said that they were in favour of *a reservations policy having a time limit*.[92] 'Otherwise,' as one of them pointed out, 'concessions tend to become vested interests.'[93] However, the judges were all agreed (and alarmed) about a new trend, viz., that of privileged groups among underprivileged classes monopolising for themselves the preferential benefits intended for the class. Justice Chinnappa Reddy dwelt on this degrading spectacle:

> **The paradox of the system of reservation is that it has engendered a spirit of self-denigration among the people. Nowhere else in the world do castes, classes, or communities queue up for the sake of gaining the backward status. Nowhere else in the world is there competition to assert backwardness and to claim 'we are more backward than you'. This is an unhappy and disquieting situation, but it is stark reality.**

Justice D. A. Desai, who made a fervent plea for the recognition of poverty as a true criterion for backwardness, said that if a survey were made about the benefits of preferential treatment among the undefined economically and socially backward classes, 'it would unmistakably show that the benefits of reservations are snatched away by *"the top creamy layer"*[94] of the backward castes.'

This consideration prompted Chief Justice Yeshwant V. Chandrachud (who had delivered a separate order) to recommend that the test of economic backwardness be applied not only to the other backward classes, but also to scheduled castes and scheduled tribes[95] (rejected in later judgements). Chief Justice Chandrachud had also suggested *that the policy of reservations in public employment, in education, and in legislative bodies should be reviewed once every five years, since it would help the state to rectify the distortions arising out of the implementation of the reservations policy*—a useful suggestion but unfortunately not followed. But since this was only a 'suggestion', it was not implemented (and has not been implemented) by the states. Chief Justice Chandrachud also said (another useful recommendation that has been ignored) that an ongoing process of review would help the people (backward and others) to express their views '*in a continuing public debate on the practical effects of that policy*'.

But the 'continuing public debate' anticipated by Chief Justice Y. V. Chandrachud got foreclosed with Prime Minister V. P. Singh's acceptance in totality of the recommendations of the report of the Second Backward Classes Commission—**the Mandal Commission in August 1990**. In January 1979, the Government of India, by an order issued (under Article 340 of the Constitution), had appointed a Second Backward Classes Commission to investigate the conditions of socially and educationally backward classes within the territory of India. The commission was known (and will be long remembered—both by its protagonists and its antagonists as well) as 'the Mandal Commission', named after its chairman B. P. Mandal, a former chief minister of Bihar. *Its recommendations were to change the entire course of the social history of India.*

The report of the Mandal Commission, which came in December 1980, said that the 'reservations' envisaged in Article 15(4) applied to socially and educationally backward classes, not to economically backward ones and concluded that in view of the permanent stratification of society in a hierarchical caste order, low-caste status had a direct bearing on a person's social backwardness. The report overlooked the fact that sub-clauses (3), (4), and (5) of Article 15 did not expressly provide for reservation. It envisaged '*any special provision*' for the advancement of socially and educationally backward classes of citizens or of scheduled castes and scheduled tribes, such as special wide-ranging scholarships and other ameliorative measures for improving standards, and any like provisions that the genius of lawmakers could devise for ensuring advancement amongst the 'classes of citizens' (including scheduled castes and scheduled tribes) mentioned in the three subclauses of Article 15. When reservation of posts was intended to be provided for by the framers of the Constitution that word was advisedly mentioned only in Articles 16(4), (4A) and (4B).

The report of the Mandal Commission mentioned some startling data. It extrapolated from the census figures of 1931 (the last and only available decennial census that had recorded the caste status of Hindus) and concluded that the 'derived' percentage of population of other backward classes (both Hindus and non-Hindus) was as high as 52 per cent of the total population of India, with the scheduled castes and scheduled tribes accounting for an additional 22.5 per cent.[96] The commission then recommended a 27 per cent reservation in favour of the OBCs (in addition to 22.5 per cent already existing in favour of SCs and STs) as also several measures for improving the conditions of backward classes. In its report, the commission stated that the representation of OBCs in government services and public employment was only 13 per cent and their representation in 'plum' jobs (Class I posts) a meagre 4.7 per cent to 6 per cent. Statistics, when skilfully presented, dispel complacency. The OBCs were greatly agitated. But the central government looked the other way. With a characteristic lack of sensitivity, the government of the day took no action whatever, although the report (1980) itself had been ritualistically laid before Parliament and discussed there on one brief occasion in 1982 and again on another occasion in 1983.

Marc Galanter in the preface to the paperback edition (1991) of *Competing Equalities: Law and the Backward Classes in India* (published by Oxford University Press, New Delhi—originally published in 1984 by the University of California Press, Los Angeles) criticised the Mandal Commission report of 1980:

> (*Quote*) The appearance of precision in applying the Commission's criteria is undermined by a serious methodological flaw. These caste groups have not been counted in the census since 1931;[97] the extrapolation of community population figures for half a century on the assumption that all communities experienced equal growth rates renders suspect many of the Commission's findings about relative conditions. (*Unquote*)

However, according to an uncorroborated report published in the *Times of India* (31 August 2010), it is stated that regardless of the recommendations of the Mandal Commission of a 27 per cent reservation in posts in the services under the state, only 7 per cent of the seats had been filled by OBCs till the year 2010.

It was only later, in August 1990, when under the government of Prime Minister V. P. Singh, an office memorandum dated 13 August 1990[98] was sprung upon the nation (to the surprise of many and to the delight of the steadily increasing members belonging to the OBCs[99]). It lit the match that started a conflagration that many believed would lead to real 'social justice'. The prime minister himself added fuel to the fire when he spoke in Parliament on 25 September 1991, somewhat deprecatingly, about merit.

> (*Quote*) We talk about merit. What is the merit of the system itself? That the section which has 52 per cent of the population gets 12.55 per cent in government employment. What is the merit of the system? That in Class I employees of the government it gets only 4.69 per cent for 52 per cent of the population in decision-making at the top echelons . . . it is not even one-tenth of the population of the country; in the power structure it is hardly 4.69 per cent. I want to challenge first the merit of the system itself before we come and question . . . whether on merit to reject this individual or that. *And we want to change the structure basically,*

consciously, with open eyes. And I know when changing the structures, there will be resistance… (*Unquote*)

(Quoted in the Order of the Supreme Court of India in the case of *Indira Sawhney vs. Union of India and Ors.*, AIR 1993, SC 477, para 21, page 514)

From this time on, the structural matrix of 'social justice' got radically changed. And, as expected, there was resistance (there is always resistance to change). There were widespread protests in certain northern states and a serious disturbance to law and order involving damage to private and public property. Some people lost their lives by self-immolation. Petitions were filed in the Supreme Court, the leading Writ Petition No. 930 of 1990 (under Article 32 of the Constitution) titled *Indira Sawhney vs. Union of India and Ors.* questioned the constitutional validity of the office memorandum. The writ petition was admitted, and (with a view not to aggravate matters further) the operation of the memorandum was temporarily stayed by an interim order of the court, reflecting a truism attributed to Justice Benjamin N. Cardozo (noted US jurist): 'The great tides and currents which engulf the rest of men do not turn aside in their course and pass the judges by.'

Soon after the general elections held in May-June 1991, there was a change of government at the centre, and a second office memorandum was issued on 25 September 1991 (modifying the earlier one), which gave some weightage to economic factors and to poverty—though only in name. This office memorandum (which was stated to come into force with immediate effect) declared:

1. Within the 27 per cent of the vacancies in civil posts and services under the Government of India reserved for SEBCs (socially and educationally backward classes), preference shall be given to candidates belonging to the poorer sections of the SEBCs. In case sufficient number

of such candidates are not available, unfilled vacancies shall be filled by the other SEBC candidates.

2. 10 per cent of the vacancies in civil posts and services under the government of India shall be reserved for other economically backward sections of the people who are not covered by any of the existing schemes of reservation.
3. The criteria for determining the poorer sections of the SEBCs or the other economically backward sections of the people who are not covered by any of the existing schemes of reservations are being issued separately.
4. The office memorandum of even number, dated 13 August 1990, was deemed to have been amended to the extent specified by the one of 25 September 1991. (The criteria mentioned in (iii) above have not been listed, issued or published at any time)

The group of writ petitions was first heard by a Constitution Bench presided over by Chief Justice Ranganath Misra. After sometime, the petitions were referred to a 'special bench' of nine justices 'to finally settle the legal position relating to reservations'. The reason given was that 'several judgements of this Court have not spoken in the same voice on this issue and a final look by a larger bench in our opinion should settle the law in an authoritative way'.

However, expectations raised in the referral order were dashed by the decision subsequently rendered, by a majority, in the bench of nine justices![100]

In the course of judgements, different judges spoke in different voices on judgements running into more than 500 closely printed pages. 'The law', regarding reservation for backward classes, was adverted to in the *Indira Sawhney* case but not expounded in any 'authoritative way' as had been initially intended in the order of reference, save in one particular, viz., that Article 16—as then framed—did not include reservation at promotion levels. But then treating this as a lacuna and not as a constitutional impediment, India's Parliament (in its constituent role) added Clause (4A) to Article 16, by the Constitution 81st Amendment Act 2000, expressly permitting the state to prescribe reservations for OBCs even after the initial stage of appointment to posts under the union or the state. *On the vital points raised in Indira Sawhney, there did emerge a majority view (6:3), but the opinion of the majority was not expressed firmly nor in peremptory language*. This is what the majority said:[101]

- That neither the Constitution nor the law prescribes the procedure or method of identification of backward classes; nor was it possible or advisable for the Court to lay down any such procedure or method.
- That it must be left to the appointed authorities to identify backward classes, and so long as the identification (by a survey) covered the entire populace no objection could be taken to it.
- That it was not necessary for a class to be designated as a backward class [and] that it was similarly situated to the Scheduled Castes and Scheduled Tribes; backward classes of citizens could not be identified only and exclusively with reference to economic criteria.
- That the distinction made in the office memorandum of 25 September 1991 between 'poorer sections' and others among the backward classes was not invalid 'if the classification is understood and operated as based upon relative backwardness among the several classes identified as Other Backward Classes'.
- That the adequacy of representation of a particular class in the services under the State was a matter within the subjective satisfaction of the appropriate Government: *not to be ordinarily interfered with by Courts on judicial review.*

Foreclosing judicial review was (and has been) a most perilous step. One of America's longest serving justices in the history of the US Supreme Court, Justice William Douglas—his term lasted 36 years and 209 days—had wisely observed that '*judicial review gives time for the sober second thought*'.

In the Constituent Assembly itself, Dr Ambedkar had indicated what he perceived as the court's role in the determination of reservations for OBCs.[102] He had said that the rule of equality of opportunity must not get destroyed by the magnitude of the reservation prescribed by the executive authorities. This is how he put it:

> (*Quote*) My honourable friend, Mr T. T. Krishnamachari (a member of the Constituent Assembly who went on to become the union finance minister in 1957), asked me whether this rule (viz., that a backward community is that which is backward in the opinion of the government) will be justiciable. It is rather difficult to give a dogmatic answer. *Personally, I think it would be a justiciable matter.* If the local Government included in this category of reservations such a large number of seats, I think one could very well go to the Federal Court and the Supreme Court and say that the reservation is of such a magnitude that the rule regarding equality of opportunity has been destroyed and the court will then come to the conclusion whether the local Government or the State Government has acted in a reasonable and prudent manner. (*Unquote*)

In the majority judgement of Justice Jeevan Reddy—in *Indira Sawhney*—concurred in by separate judgements of Justices S. R. Pandian and P. B. Sawant, only the first part of Dr Ambedkar's speech was quoted, which read:

> (*Quote*) Somebody asked me: 'What is a backward community?' Well, I think anyone who reads the language of the draft itself will find that we have left it to be determined

> by each local Government. A backward community is a community which is backward in the opinion of the Government . . . (*Unquote*)

But the part (set out earlier)—the more pertinent, the more relevant part—where the architect of the Constitution had opined that it was a justiciable matter, was not even mentioned in the principal judgement of Justice Jeevan Reddy (on behalf of himself and three other justices) nor in the concurring judgements of Justices Pandian and Sawant. *In Indira Sawhney, a great opportunity to lay down the limits beyond which the government could not go was passed over.*[103]

Where the court could have, and should have, spoken authoritatively, it refrained from doing so, particularly in that portion of its judgement dealing with 'whether reservations are anti-meritarian'? Whilst correctly holding that 'it may not be said that reservations (per se) are antimeritarian', the court (majority) did say that there were certain services and positions where, whether on account of the nature of the duties attached to them or the level (in the hierarchy) at which they obtain, 'merit alone counts'. But then the court went on to simply caution that 'in such situations, it may not be advisable to provide for reservations' and it was for the Government of India (the court said) to consider and specify the service and posts to which the rule of reservation shall not apply.

Again, even after enumerating in detail the services and posts where (in the opinion of the majority) 'there should be no rule of reservation' in certain services (mentioned in detail in the judgement of Justice Jeevan Reddy), viz.:

> (*Quote*) . . . in defence services, in technical posts in establishments engaged in research and development including those connected with atomic energy and space, in teaching posts of professors, in posts in super-specialities in medicine, engineering and other scientific and technical subjects, in posts of pilots and co-pilots in Indian Airlines and Air India. (*Unquote*)

The court (majority) went out of its way to add:

> (*Quote*) The list given above is merely illustrative and not exhaustive. It is for the Government of India to consider and specify the service and posts to which the rule of reservation shall not apply, but on that account the implementation of the impugned Office Memorandum dated 13 August 1990 cannot be stayed or withheld. (*Unquote*)

The passages quoted above, in my view, indicate an almost conscious abdication—by the majority—of its solemn duty of upholding the constitutional guarantee of Equality before the Law and the Equal Protection of the Law.

The concept of equality in our Constitution has two distinct dimensions. First, it embodies the principle of non-discrimination(Articles 14, 15(1), (2), and 16(2)), and second, at the same time, it obligates the state to take affirmative action for ensuring that unequals (the downtrodden, the oppressed, and the have-nots) in society are brought at a level where they can compete with others (the haves of society) (Articles 15(3), (4), (5), 16(4), (4A), (4B), 39, 39A, and 41).[104] But as to which 'dimension' is the more important in a given case, and as to what should be the balancing factor in the broad conspectus of the equality provisions, are only for the highest court in the country to say. It could not—it simply cannot—be left for the government to provide or for commission appointed by the government to determine.

It is true that Marc Galanter has offered a philosophical justification for the lack of a strong consistent judicial approach in the field of (what he describes as) 'compensatory discrimination':[105]

> (*Quote*) Compensatory discrimination offers a way to leaven our formalism without entirely abandoning its comforts. The Indian example is instructive: India has managed to pursue a commitment to substantive justice without allowing

> that commitment to dissolve competing commitments to formal equality that make law viable in a diverse society with limited consensus. The Indian experience displays a principled eclecticism that avoids suppressing the altruistic fraternal impulse that animates compensatory policies, but that also avoids being enslaved by it. From afar it reflects to us a tempered legalism—one which we find more congenial in practice than in theory. (*Unquote*)

As mentioned before, Thomas Piketty, in his *Brief History of Equality* (2022), has taken a different view. '*India,*' he writes, '*has gone furthest in the use of quotas*' *and India's continuing experiment in reservations and quotas 'illustrates the limits of such a policy.*'[106]

But whatever the view 'from afar' (sometimes, distance does lend enchantment to the view), the experience of others, within India, has been far more pragmatic and realistic and it has been forcefully expressed in the following terms:

> (*Quote*) **From being an instrument of egalitarianism, the reservation policy is now seen as the most blatant expression of what has come to be known as 'vote-bank politics'. This is particularly so in regard to reservations for the OBCs in the post-Mandal scenario, where the most contentious controversies are centred. It is precisely here that affirmative action seems to be falling short.** ***Addressing one injustice or inequality at the cost of causing others will only politicise society further, not make it more equitable or egalitarian. Both Parliament and the court must critique reservation policies and legislation from a constitutional understanding of inclusive and integral justice.***[107] (*Unquote*)

What is sorely lacking in India is the critique by the country's highest court. It is precisely because Indian society is so diverse and there is little or no consensus (as Galanter says) that an effective judicial pronouncement by the Supreme Court would have provided a very helpful guide, and, more importantly, it would have served as a most useful check. The court, when called upon to lay down the 'law', unfortunately, yielded to the temptation of not firmly saying either yea or nay. If only the majority in *Indira Sawhney* (and it was a learned, experienced, and distinguished majority) had set the goalposts and had specified what could or could not be done in the matter of 'reservations', its exposition in its judgement would then have been regarded as 'law', binding on all under Articles 141 and 144 of the Constitution.[108] Instead, there have been only bits of advice and recommendations from the court, which, since they were not expressed in authoritative terms, have been largely ignored.

In *Indira Sawhney* (1992), in para 861 of the majority judgement, the following directions were given:

1. That the Government of India and each of the State Governments and the Administrations of Union Territories would within four months constitute a permanent body for entertaining, examining and recommending upon requests for inclusion and complaints of over-inclusion and under-inclusion in the lists of other backward classes of citizens—the advice tendered by such body being ordinarily binding upon the Government; and
2. Within four months the Government of India would specify the bases, apply the relevant and requisite socio-economic criteria to exclude socially advanced persons/ sections ('creamy layer') from Other Backward Classes and the implementation of the impugned Office Memorandum of 13 August 1990 would be subject to exclusion of such socially advanced persons ('creamy layer').

The directions were complied with. Pursuant to these directions, Parliament then passed the National Commission for Backward Classes Act 1993,[109] in which the term 'backward classes' was defined exhaustively as meaning such backward classes of citizens other than the scheduled castes and the scheduled tribes, as may be specified by the central government in the list, i.e., the list prepared by the Government of India from time to time for purposes of making provisions for the reservation of appointments or posts in favour of backward classes of citizens which, in the opinion of that government, are not adequately represented in the services under the Government of India and any local or other authority within the territory of India or under the control of the Government of India. The list is an ongoing one to be revised (with inclusions or exclusions) every 10 years based on the advice of the Backward Classes Commission. But the 'advice' of the commission is declared to be 'ordinarily binding upon the central government' (Sections 9 and 11).[110]

There is no guidance either from Parliament or the Supreme Court as to the governing legal principles. The central government is now empowered (under Section 11) to include in the list 'new backward classes', but on what criteria is not stipulated. The National Commission for Backward Classes Act 1993 has conferred far-reaching powers on the commission. *Parliament has also viewed Articles 15 and 16 as distinct and separate provisions, independent even of the main equality clause (Article 14), overlooking prior Constitution Bench decisions rendered by the Supreme Court,*[111] *which have held that the 'three provisions (Articles 14, 15, and 16) form part of the same constitutional role of guarantees and supplement each other.* By the 1992, judgement in *Indira Sawhney* and since the enactment of the National Commission for Backward Classes Act 1993, the highest court has denied itself its constitutional function as the guardian of equal protection under the law—a right solemnly guaranteed by Article 14 of the Constitution of India.

In balancing 'equal treatment' and 'compensatory discrimination', Indira Sawhney *(followed in subsequent decisions) has left it to politicians and administrators as to how far they could go.* It was only in *Nagaraj vs. Union of India*

(2007)[112] that a Constitution Bench of the Supreme Court of India said (for once, boldly and not timidly), but only in respect of one aspect of 'reservations', viz., *that the ceiling limit of 50 per cent reservation for backward classes, was, and is 'a constitutional mandate'.*[113]

After a debate in Parliament that ultimately resulted in the passing of the Constitution 93rd Amendment Act 2005, another lingering doubt was cleared: *in the criteria for determining OBCs, economic backwardness was out* (Paradoxically, it was brought in again by the Constitution 103rd Amendment Act of 2019). In 2005, the newly added Article 15(5) had reproduced the language previously used in Article 15(4) in 1951. Parliament reaffirmed that it is the advancement of socially and educationally backward classes of citizens (not economically backward classes of citizens) that was the ultimate aim and goal of India's Constitution. After the Constitution 93rd Amendment Act 2005, Parliament passed the Central Education Institutions (Reservation in Admission) Act 2006 (assented to by the President in 2007 Act 5 of 2007). Section 3 provided for reservation of 15 per cent seats for scheduled castes, 7.5 per cent per cent for scheduled tribes, and 27 per cent for other backward classes[114] in central educational institutions, i.e.:

1. Universities established or incorporated by or under Central Acts.
2. Institutions of national importance set up by Acts of Parliament.
3. Deemed universities under Section 3 of the University Grants Commission Act.
4. Institutions maintained or receiving aid from the Central Government.
5. Educational institutions set up by the Central Government under the Societies Registration Act 1860. (Act 5 of 2007, however, all this is not to apply to minority educational institutions)

In *Ashoka Kumar Thakur vs. Union of India and Ors.* (2008), the constitutional validity of Article 15(5)—added by the Constitution 93rd Amendment Act 2005—was challenged before a bench of five justices of the Supreme Court on the ground that it was contrary to the 'basic structure of the Constitution', because the thrust of our Constitution was to establish a casteless society. However, the challenge was negatived (4:1).[115] The court held that Article 15(5) was valid to the extent that it has permitted reservation for socially and educationally backward classes in state (or state-aided) educational institutions with the exclusion of the 'creamy layer' from amongst the OBCs. *However, the mode or method to be adopted for such exclusion was not prescribed either by Parliament or by the judges.* Justice R. V. Raveendran (in a separate judgement, concurring with the majority) went on to add:

> (*Quote*) Failure to exclude the 'creamy layer' from the benefits of reservation would render the reservation for other backward classes under Act 5 of 2007 unconstitutional.[116] (*Unquote*)

In other words, failure to exclude 'the creamy layer' would violate the basic structure of the Constitution.[117]

Ashoka Kumar Thakur vs. Union of India (2008) was not a unanimous judgement of the Constitution Bench of five justices. The judge who dissented was in a (brave) minority of one. At the very commencement of his separate judgement, Justice Dalveer Bhandari (now a judge in the International Court of Justice) posed what he rightly described as 'the fundamental question':

> (*Quote*) 361. The fundamental question that arises in these writ petitions is: Whether Article 15(5), inserted by the 93rd Amendment, is consistent with the other provisions of the Constitution or whether its impact runs contrary to the constitutional aim of achieving a casteless and classless society.

362. On behalf of the petitioners, Senior Advocate, Mr F. S. Nariman, eloquently argued that if Article 15(5) is permitted to remain in force, then, instead of achieving the goal of a casteless and classless society, India would be converted into a caste-ridden society. The country would forever remain divided on caste lines. The Government has sought to repudiate this argument. The petitioners' argument, however, echoes the grave concern of our Constitution's original Framers.

363. On careful analysis of the Constituent Assembly and the Parliamentary Debates, one thing is crystal clear: our leaders have always, and unanimously, proclaimed with one voice that our constitutional goal is to establish a casteless and classless society. (*Unquote*)

He then dealt with the question posed in para 361 in succeeding paragraphs (537-560) of his judgement and concluded as follows:

(*Quote*) 605. In conclusion, the First Parliament, by enacting Article 15(4), deviated from the original Framers' intent. They passed an amendment that strengthens rather than weakens casteism. If caste-based quotas in education are to stay, they should adhere to a basic tenet of secularism; they should not take caste into account. Instead, exclusively economic criteria should be used. For a period of 10 years, other factors such as income, occupation, and property holdings, etc., including caste, may be taken into consideration and thereafter only economic criteria should prevail. (But) *Indira Sawhney* (1992) has tied our hands. I nevertheless believe that caste matters and will continue to matter as long as we divide society along caste lines. Caste-based discrimination remains. Violence between castes occurs. Caste politics rages on. Where casteism is present, the goal of achieving a casteless society must never be forgotten. Any legislation to the contrary should be discarded. (*Unquote*)

Justice Bhandari's regret that 'caste-based discrimination remains' is a cry of distress—albeit in the wilderness—and a courageous appeal (as in the case of all dissents) to 'the brooding spirit of the future'. *But after the majority decision (4:1) in Ashoka Kumar Thakur (2008), whatever the Preamble may say, the vision of a secular society can no longer be said to be the true aim of our written Constitution.* A great opportunity was missed by the court to steer the ship of state into casteless waters. It is the Supreme Court of India itself that has helped to perpetuate the division of Indian society along caste-based lines. Alas, who will—who can—guide the guardians?

This is one of the more difficult—as yet unanswered—questions in the life of a nation now nearly 75 years old. Even today, no one is quite sure as to what equality of educational and job opportunities truly means.[118] Here's why:

1. **It can hardly be argued that once a backward class, always a backward class as this would defeat the very purpose of special provisions made in the Constitution for the advancement of the backward classes, and for enabling them to come to the level of, and to compete with, the 'forward' classes, as equal citizens.**
2. **To continue to confer upon 'advanced sections' of the backward classes (designated as the 'creamy layer') the special benefits amount to treating equals unequally. It undoubtedly violates the provisions of the Constitution (Article 14 read with Article 16).**
3. **Since there is no judicially recommended criteria evolved of these 'advanced sections' amongst the OBCs, there is room for 'executive change of opinion' (a euphemism for 'administrative manipulation for political purposes'). And it is happening. The game of 'moving the goalposts' is in play, 'Advanced sections' of backward classes are now sought to be placed on an 'upward sliding' scale. For instance, initially**

the then existing ceiling for 'creamy layer'—a mere administrative determination—had been fixed at an annual income of Rs 4.5 lakh per annum, but (if news reports are to be believed and there are a proliferation of them[119]) the then Congress-led government at the centre was trying to 'reach out' to OBCs by drastically relaxing the figure placed by the executive on the judge-invented concept of 'creamy layer'. It was no longer to be at Rs 4.5 lakh per annum; it has been fixed (in the metros) at Rs 12 lakh per annum. This means that OBCs with an income of Rs 1 lakh per month would become eligible for job reservation in the public sector, and there is also expected to be a corresponding upward revision for OBCs in the non-metros at Rs 9 lakh per annum.

4. To rank 'advanced sections' of the backward classes with the rest of the backward classes equally violates the right to equality of the rest in those classes. It would amount to treating unequals equally. This will lead to perverting the objectives of the special constitutional provisions, since the 'forwards' among the backward classes will be thereby facilitated to 'gobble up' (or appropriate) all the special benefits, to the exclusion and at the cost of the rest in their own class—keeping the rest of the really backward classes (e.g., at present, those earning below Rs 4.5 lakh per annum) in a state of 'perpetual backwardness'. *But a state of perpetual backwardness is certainly not envisaged in our Constitution.*

5. *Taking out or weeding out the 'forwards' from among the backward classes is therefore mandated (by dicta of the Supreme Court) as obligatory under the Constitution, but unfortunately as to how and within what time this has to be ensured has not been indicated.* Only the Supreme Court can devise a realistic and practicable

scheme and time frame, which would then have to be enforced by agencies of the state as law declared by the Supreme Court, binding on all. The American courts have said that a time frame is vital because it affects the equal-protection principle, and they have even legislated (judicially) about it. Justice Sandra O'Connor expressed the view of the majority of the US Supreme Court (5:4) when she wrote (in the case of the Michigan Law School's admission policy—*Grutter vs. Bollinger*, 2003 539, US 306 =* 156 L. Ed. 2d 304, 341) as follows:

> Race-conscious admissions policies must be limited in time. This requirement reflects that racial classifications, however compelling their goals, are potentially so dangerous that they may be employed no more broadly than the interest demands. Enshrining a permanent justification for racial preferences would offend this fundamental equal-protection principle. We see no reason to exempt race-conscious admissions programs from the requirement that all governmental use of race must have a logical end point.

But the Supreme Court of India has not said a word about the time frame for weeding out the 'forwards' from among the backward classes. It needs to.

6. There has been thus far too much dithering on this subject. What will help, I believe, is a constant and assiduous gathering of data, a continuous process of objective re-evaluation of progress registered by the 'underdog' categories, a more focused preferential treatment for the disadvantaged and vulnerable, and (above all) a broader constitutional vision (on the part of India's Supreme Court as well as India's Parliament)

of a more inclusive and egalitarian society—together with a firm articulation of this—lest an otherwise deserving policy of 'reservations' (for OBCs) be degraded into a vote-catching exercise leading ultimately to 'reverse discrimination'.

FRATERNITY had been added by the Drafting Committee in the Preamble since 'the need for fraternal concord and goodwill was never greater than now . . .'[120]. The humanitarian concept had its origin in Article 1 of the UN Declaration of Human Rights of 1948, to which the sovereign Republic of India had subscribed, and to which India was also a signatory. This article read:

> All human beings are born free and equal in dignity and rights. They are endowed with reason and conscience and should act towards one another in a spirit of brotherhood.

But 'Fraternity' is not mentioned in any of the enacting Parts of the Constitution, and regretably 'the spirit of brotherhood' it envisages is not widely practised.

Notes and References:

1. Justice Vivian Bose (one of the first justices of the Supreme Court of India) had described the Preamble as 'a magnificent prelude' in *Virendra Singh vs. State of Uttar Pradesh* (AIR 1954 SC 447, page 454, paragraph 34), bench decision of five judges.
2. In *Behram Khurshed Pesikaka vs. State of Bombay* (AIR 1955 SC 123, page 146, paragraph 52).
3. (1992) Supplement SCC 217 on page 631.
4. *Brierly's Law of Nations*, 7th edition, 2012, page 46.
5. See *Nehru's India: A History in Seven Myths* by Taylor C. Sherman, Princeton University Press (November 2022).
6. 'As Indian secularism took shape in the 1940s, it acquired a meaning as a term that could encompass reference of Hinduism and justify special protection for Dalits.' Taylor C. Sherman, *Nehru's India* (2022), page 72.
7. A theme developed in a book most recently published. See Taylor C. Sherman's *Nehru's India: A History in Seven Myths* (2022).
8. *The Indian President* by K. C. Singh, Harper Collins Publications India (2023).
9. See B. Shiva Rao, *Framing of India's Constitution: A Study,* pages 130-131.
10. Ibid., pages 131-132.
11. By Michael Sandel, who has been teaching political philosophy at Harvard University, USA, since 1980.
12. In the Preface to *The Idea of Justice*, Penguin Books, New Delhi, 2009.
13. Article 12. Definition: In this Part (i.e., Part-III), unless the context otherwise requires, 'the State' includes the Government and Parliament of India and the Government and the Legislature of each of the States and all local or other authorities within the territory of India or under the control of the Government of India.
14. AIR 1970 SC 1880—also reported in 1969 (2) SCC 481: a bench decision of Justices K. S. Hegde and A. N. Ray; Justice Hegde speaking for the court.

15. Ryot (or raiyat) is a general economic term used throughout India for peasant cultivators but with variations in different parts. While zamindars were landlords, raiyats were tenants and cultivators, and served as hired labour. A raiyat was primarily defined as someone who had acquired a right to hold land for the purpose of cultivating it, whether alone or by members of his family, hired servants, or partners.

16. The principle had been laid down in two prior decisions of the court in AIR 1966 SC 1191 and AIR 1966 SC 1879, and later restated in *Bharat Petroleum Corporation Ltd. vs. Maddula Ratnavalli & Others,* 2007 (6) SCC 81 (Parliament is presumed to have enacted a reasonable statute).

17. Article 32: Remedies for enforcement of rights conferred by this Part.

    (1) The right to move the Supreme Court by appropriate proceedings for the enforcement of the rights conferred by this Part is guaranteed.

    (2) The Supreme Court shall have the power to issue directions or orders or writs, including writs in the nature of *habeas corpus, mandamus,* prohibition, *quo warranto,* and *certiorari,* whichever may be appropriate, for the enforcement of any of the rights conferred by this Part.

    Article 226: Power of High Courts to issue certain writs.

    (1) Notwithstanding anything in article 32, every High Court shall have power, throughout the territories in relation to which it exercises jurisdiction, to issue to any person or authority, including in appropriate cases, any Government, within those territories directions, orders or (writs, including writs in the nature of *habeas corpus, mandamus,* prohibition, *quo warranto,* and *certiorari,* or any of them, for the enforcement of any of the rights conferred by Part-III and for any other purpose).

    Article 142: Enforcement of decrees and orders of Supreme Court and orders as to discovery, etc.

    (1) The Supreme Court in the exercise of its jurisdiction may pass such decree or make such order as is necessary for doing complete justice in any cause or matter pending before it, and any decree so passed or order so made shall be enforceable throughout the territory of India in such manner as may be prescribed by or under any law made by Parliament and, until provision in that behalf is so made, in such manner as the President may by order prescribe.

18. *Virendra Singh and Others vs. State of U.P.* (AIR 1954, SC 447, page 454, paragraph 34).

19. See *Black's Law Dictionary* (10th edition) by Bryan A. Garner, published by Thomson Reuters (2014), page 825.

    The common law of England was the law is force at the time of the Constitution and continues in India under Article 372.

20. See *Jowitt's Dictionary of English Law* by The Late The Right Honourable The Earl Jowitt and Clifford Walsh, Solicitor (2nd edition, Volume 2, pages 1139-1140, published by Sweet & Maxwell Ltd. London, 1977). See also *Black's Law Dictionary* (10th edition) by Bryan A. Garner (published by Thomson Reuters (2014), page 1105).

21. See *Jowitt's Dictionary of English Law* by The Late The Right Honourable The Earl Jowitt and Clifford Walsh, Solicitor (2nd edition, Volume 2, page 1443, published by Sweet & Maxwell Ltd. London, 1977).

22. See *Black's Law Dictionary* (10th edition) by Bryan A. Garner (published by Thomson Reuters (2014), page 1447).

23. See Jowitt's *Dictionary of English Law* by The Late The Right Honourable The Earl Jowitt and Clifford Walsh, Solicitor (2nd edition, Volume 1, page 307, published by Sweet & Maxwell Ltd. London, 1977) and See *Black's Law Dictionary* (10th edition) by Bryan A. Garner (published by Thomson Reuters (2014), page 275-276).

24. Ronald Dworkin, 'Hard Cases' (*Harvard Law Review*, Vol. 88 No.6 (April 1975), pages 1057-1109); a reproduction of an inaugural lecture by Ronald Dworkin given at Oxford in June of 1971.

25. There are other matters as well: in the Fundamental Rights Chapter that deals with liberty, viz., Right to Freedom (Articles 19, 20, 21, 21A, and 22(1) and 22(2); Right Against Exploitation (Articles 23 and 24); Right to Freedom of Religion (Articles 25, 26, 27, and 28); and Cultural and Educational Rights (Articles 29 and 30).

26. For a scholarly account of Article 21, see *Liberty After Freedom* by Rohan J. Alva, published by Harper Collins (2022).

27. *The common law tradition (what is popularly called judge made law) has been defined as 'a monument slowly raised like a coral reef from the minute accretions of past individuals of whom each built upon the relics which his predecessors left and, in his turn, left a foundation upon which his successors might work' (Vol. 35, 1922, Harvard Law Review*

479) (a review of Benjamin Cardozo's famous book: The Nature of the Judicial Process).

28. Sir Ashutosh Mookerjee was a judge of the High Court of Calcutta from 1904 to 1923 and acted as its Chief Justice in 1920 for a period of six months.

29. Initially, the Constitution Bench decision in *A. K. Gopalan vs. State of Madras*, AIR 1950, SC 27 (majority of 4:1) was a case concerning preventive detention (provided for in Article 22). But one judge (Justice Fazl Ali) dissented with the majority view in *A. K. Gopalan*.

30. *A. K. Gopalan* (majority view) was disapproved in a bench decision of eleven judges (10:1) in *R. C. Cooper vs. Union of India* (AIR 1970 SC 564): the *Bank Nationalisation* case.

31. MISA: Maintenance of Internal Security Act of 1971.

32. Article 359: Suspension of the enforcement of the rights conferred by Part-III during emergencies:

    Where a Proclamation of Emergency is in operation, the President may by order declare that the right to move any court for the enforcement of such of the rights conferred by Part-III as may be mentioned in the order and all proceedings pending in any court for the enforcement of the rights so mentioned shall remain suspended for the period during which the Proclamation is in force or for such shorter period as may be specified in the order.

33. *ADM* (additional district magistrate) *Jabalpur vs. Shivkant Shukla*, AIR 1976, SC 1207.

34. *Liversidge vs. Anderson*, 1942, Appeal Cases, 206.

35. Chief Justice A. N. Ray in *ADM Jabalpur*, AIR 1976, SC 1207, page 1223, paragraph 27.

36. Scott vs. Sandford (Dred Scott case—7:2). 60 US, 393, 404-406, 419-420 (1857): "One of the most important cases in American constitutional history. It played a major role in precipitating the Civil War, it provided a basis for far-reaching interpretation of substantive due process; and it stirred deep-seated emotions in the saga of race-relations in the United States. When scholars evaluate Justice Roger Taney's overall contribution to American jurisprudence they rank him in spite of Dred Scott among the greats.": a quote from page 1003 in the 'Oxford Companion to the Supreme Court of the United States' (2005) – Edited by Kermit Hall and two others.

37. John Paul Stevens: *Five Chief Justices* (Little Brown and Company, New York, 2011, page 20).

38. The majority view in *A. K. Gopalan* (1950) was also dissented from in *Maneka Gandhi vs. Union of India*, AIR 1978, SC 597, page 659, paragraph 120: the unanimous opinion of a bench of seven justices. This view in *Maneka Gandhi* was later reaffirmed in 2007 by a bench of nine justices in *I. R. Coelho vs. State of Tamil Nadu*, AIR 2007, SC 861-874 and 875, paragraphs 58 and 59.

39. *Justice K. S. Puttaswamy (Retd) and Another vs. Union of India & Ors.*, 2017 (10) SCC 1, page 419, paragraphs 137, 138, and 139 (Justice D. Y. Chandrachud speaking for the court).

40. *Romesh Thapar vs. State of Madras* (AIR 1950 SC 124).

41. Sardar Patel to Jawaharlal Nehru, 3 July1950, in Sardar Patel's correspondence, Vol. X, page 358.

42. In modern use, the term Fourth Estate is applied to the Press, with the earliest use in this sense was described by Thomas Carlyle in his book, *On Heroes, Hero-Worship, and the Heroic in History.* 'Burke said there were Three Estates in Parliament; but, in the Reporters' Gallery yonder, there sat a Fourth Estate more important far than they all.'

43. (1897) 25 Indian Appeals 1: Tilak's case; Lokmanya Tilak was amongst the stalwarts of the freedom struggle.

44. Edited by Ephraim London, pages 465-466, published by Simon and Schuster, New York (1960).

45. AIR 1942 FC 22.

46. *Edward Mills Co. vs. State of Ajmer,* AIR 1955 SC 25 on page 31 (referring to the same set of words: '. . . other competent authority' in Article 13(3) of the Constitution).

47. AIR 1962 SC 955 (Bench of five judges).

48. These words had been added in Article 19(2) by India's Provisional Parliament (which had functioned as India's Constituent Assembly till November 1949) by the Constitution First Amendment Act, 1951.

    For a critical commentary of India's First Constitutional Amendment of 1951, see *Sixteen Stormy Days: The Story of the First Amendment of the Constitution of India* by *Tripurdaman Singh* (published by Vintage, Penguin Random India House (2020)) as well as *Rohan J. Alva's* (second) book titled, *A Constitution to Keep: Sedition and Free Speech in Modern India* (published in 2023 by Harper Collins Publishers India). Alva's approach is that S.124A cannot be treated as a 'reasonable' restriction on the fundamental right guaranteed under Article 19(1)(a) 'because of the serious harm it inflicts on the ability of people to engage in free political speech' and that an 'innocent threat to public order can never be the justification for a law on sedition'.

49. AIR 1962 SC 955.

50. AIR 1942 FC 22.

51. Article 25: Freedom of conscience and free profession, practice, and propagation of religion; Article 26: Freedom to manage religious affairs; Article 27: Freedom as to payment of taxes for promotion of any particular religion; Article 28: Freedom as to attendance at religious instruction or religious worship in certain educational institutions.

52. Quoted in *The Hindu,* Sunday, 22 January 2012.

53. *Commissioner of Hindu Endowments vs. L. T. Swamine,* AIR 1954 SC 853 (a classic decision of a full bench of seven judges at a time when the strength of the highest court was seven judges plus the Chief Justice). The court refused to follow *Davis vs. Beason* 133 US 333, 342, where the Supreme Court of the United States held that cults and forms of worship of a particular sect were not matters of religion. In holding that matters or religion included acts done in pursuance thereof, the Supreme Court of India preferred the views of the High Court of Australia (Chief Justice Latham) interpreting Section 116 (the religious freedom clause) of the Australian Constitution, in *Adelaide vs. Commonwealth* 66 CLR 127).

54. *Saifuddin Saheb vs. State of Bombay*, AIR 1962 SC 853.

55. See *Framing of India's Constitution* by B. Shiva Rao, page 261.

56. In *Rev. Stainislaus vs. State of M.P.* the Constitution Bench said:

> 'It has to be appreciated that the freedom of religion enshrined in the Article is not guaranteed in respect of one religion only, but covers all religions alike, and it can be properly enjoyed by a person if he exercises his right in a manner commensurate with the like freedom of persons following the other religions. What is freedom for one, is freedom for the other, in equal measure,

and there can therefore be no such thing as a fundamental right to convert any person to one's own religion' (page 911).

57. In the draft article approved by the Minorities Sub-Committee (and later by the Constituent Assembly), the right to propagate religion had been deliberately added so as to guarantee to proselytising religions (like Christianity and Islam) the right to preach religion with the object of conversion.

58. *Durgah Committee Ajmer vs. Syed Hussain Ali*, AIR 1961 SC 1402, *Nathdwara Temple* case, AIR 1963 SC 1638 on page 1660 (Gajendragadkar).

59. AIR 1963 SC 1638.

60. Article 14 (as enacted): Equality before law; Article 15 (with amendments): Prohibition of discrimination on grounds of religion, race, caste, sex, or place of birth; Article 16 (with amendments): Equality of opportunity in matters of public employment; Article 17: Abolition of 'Untouchability'; Article 18: Abolition of titles; Article 29(2) states that no citizen shall be denied admission into any educational institution maintained by the State or receiving aid out of State funds on grounds only of religion, race, caste, language, or any of them.

There is a large volume of case-law both on Article 14 and as well as on Articles 15 and 16.

Article 15 has been amended on several occasions by the Constitution First Amendment Act, 1951 w.e.f. 18 June 1951 (by adding Article 15(4)) by the Constitution 93rd Amendment Act w.e.f. 20 January 2006 (by adding Article 15(5)), and by the Constitution 103rd Amendment Act, 2019 w.e.f. 14 January 2019 (by adding Article 15(6)). The 103rd Constitutional Amendment (advancement of 'weaker sections' other than classes mentioned in 15(4) and 15(5)) was challenged, but its provision was upheld as constitutional in a 7 November 2022 decision of a bench of five judges (3:2) in Janhit Abhiyan vs. Union of India *(W.P. 55 of 2019): 2023 (5) SCC1.*

Article 16 has also been amended on several occasions by the Constitution 77th Amendment Act, 1955 (w.e.f. 17 June 1995) (by adding Article 16(4A)) by the Constitution 85th Amendment Act, 2001 (w.e.f. 17 June 1995) (by addition of the words of 'promotion' in Article 16(4A)); by the Constitution 81st Amendment Act, 2000 (w.e.f. 9 June 2000) (by addition of Article 16(4B)); and by the Constitution 103rd Amendment Act, 2019 (w.e.f. 14 January 2019) (by adding Article

16(6)) (challenge to the 103rd Constitutional Amendment has been upheld (3:2) in November 2022).

61. Amos Peaslee (1887-1969), international lawyer and author of the four volume, *Constitution of Nations*.

62. Sir Hersch Lauterpacht was a scholar-judge who expanded the frontiers of law. It was he who expounded for the first time what came to be known as 'the modern view' of international law which was that states, through primarily the subject of international law, were not exclusively so—a view which he introduced into the 8th edition of *Oppenheim's International Law* (the first edition that he edited).

63. *International Bill of the Rights of Man* by Prof. Hersch Lauterpacht (1945).

64. On the well-settled principle laid down in judgements of the US Supreme Court. In *Whitney vs. California* 274 US 373 = 71 L. Ed. 1095. Justice Brandeis concurring had said: 'it is settled that the due process clause of the 14th Amendment applies to method of substantive law as well as to matters of procedure. Thus, all fundamental rights comprised within the term "liberty" are protected by the Federal Constitution from invasion by the States. The right of free speech, the right to teach and the right of assembly ace of cause fundamental rights . . . These may not be denied or abridged. But although the rights of free speech and assembly are fundamental, they are not absolute. Their experience is subject to restriction if the particular restriction proposed is required to protect the state from destruction or from serious injury, political or economic or moral.' That the necessity which is essential to a valid restriction does not exist unless speech would produce or is intended to produce a clear and imminent danger of some substantive evil which the state constitutionally may seek to prevent has been settled. See *Schenck vs. United States*, 249 US 47 = 62 L. Ed. 476, 463.

65. AIR 1979 SC 478 = (1979) 1 SCC 380.

66. The lecture is reported in 'Droit Public – English Style', *Public Law*, 1995, pages 57-71.

67. Of how, in the 17th century, England's Chief Justice (quite literally) kept his head. On Sunday morning, 10 November 1607, there was a remarkable interview in Whitehall between Sir Edward Coke, Chief Justice of the Common Pleas, and King James I of England. We have

only Coke's account of the interview and not the King's, but there is no reason to doubt its essential authenticity. The question between them was whether the King, in his own person, might take what causes (or cases) he pleased. In the words of Chief Justice Coke: 'Then the King said that he thought the law was founded upon reason as well as the Judges; to which it was answered by me, that true it was that God had endowed His majesty with excellent science and great endowments of nature, but His majesty was not learned, in the laws of his realm of England, and causes which concern the life, or inheritance, or goods, or fortunes of his subjects (which) are not to be decided by *natural reason* but by the *artificial reason and judgement of law*, which law is an act which requires long study and experience before that a man can attain to the cognisance of it; and that the law was the golden metwand and measure to try the causes of the subjects; and which protected His Majesty in safety and peace: with which the King was greatly offended, and said, that then he should be under the law, which it was treason to affirm (as he said): to which I said that [Henri de] Bracton saith, *quod Rex non debt esse sub-homine sed Deo at lege*. 'The King ought not to be under man, but under God and the law.' R. F. V. Heuston: *Essays in Constitutional Law,* 2nd edition, Stevens & Sons, London, 1964, pages 32-33. While referring to Coke's account of his interview with the King, Heuston says, 'that it would be hard to find a single paragraph in which more of the essence of English constitutional law and history can be found.'

68. The Fifth Amendment provides inter alia that no person shall be deprived 'of life, liberty, or property without due process of law . . .'

69. John E. Nowak and Ronald D. Rotunda: *Constitutional Law,* Hornbook Series, 4th edition, West Publishing Company, Eagan (Minnesota, USA), 1991, page 340.

70. 521 US 702, 1997.

71. *Washington vs. Glucksberg,* 521 US 702, 1997, pages 765-66 = 138 Lawyers Edition 2d 772 (816).

72. 521 US 702, 1997, page 764.

73. In recent times, however, the provisions of Article 335 have been constantly overlooked—and often not addressed.

74. Their social condition has improved vastly thanks to the spate of statutory enactments indigenous movements for their emancipation

have helped to create an increasing awareness among women of their rights, and the facilities available for enforcing them.

75. H. S. Maine, *Ancient Law,* Oxford University Press, London, 1950, page 127; first published 1861.

76. Isaiah Berlin: *Two Concepts of Liberty,* Oxford University Press, London, 1958.

77. Marc Galanter: *Competing Equalities: Law and the Backward Classes in India,* University of California Press, Los Angeles, 1984. See also Louis Dumont: *Homo Hierarchicus: An Essay on the Caste System,* University of Chicago Press, Chicago, 1970.

78. Will Durant: *Story of Civilization,* Vol. I, Simon and Schuster, New York, 1935, page 398. The early Hindu word for caste was varna (colour). The Portuguese later translated it as casta, from the Latin castus (pure).

79. The word 'Veda' means knowledge; literally, a book of knowledge. Of the many Vedas that existed, only four have survived: the Rig Veda, or knowledge of the hymns of praise; the Sama Veda, or knowledge of the melodies; the Yajur Veda, or knowledge of the sacrificial formulas; and the Atharva Veda, or knowledge of the magic formula. Each of these is divided into four sections:

    (1) the hymns;
    (2) the Brahmanas, or manuals of ritual, prayer and incantation for the priests;
    (3) the Aranyakas, or 'forest texts' for hermit saints; and
    (4) the Upanishads, which describe the mysteries of the unintelligible world.

    They are the oldest extant commentaries on the philosophy and psychology of the human race.

80. These great epics are the most famous and best-loved of ancient Hindu literature. The Mahabharata resembles the Greek epic the Iliad, being the story of a great war fought by gods and men and occasioned partly by the loss of a beautiful woman from one nation to another. The Ramayana resembles the other Greek epic, the Odyssey, and it tells of the hero's hardships and wanderings and his wife's patiently waiting for a reunion with him.

81. Brahmins even adopted Buddhist practices as their own; under pressure of the ethics of renunciation preached by Buddhism (and Jainism), a majority of the Brahmins changed to a vegetarian diet and

'renounced' all forms of meat. Since then, they have regarded caste Brahmins who ate meat as impure. The caste system conceptualised 'purity'. (See Louis Dumont: *Homo Hierarchicus: An Essay on the Caste System,* University of Chicago Press, Chicago, 1970, pages 55-56)

82. Sir Charles Eliot: *Hinduism and Buddhism: An Historical Sketch,* Vol. 3, Routledge & Kegan Paul, London, 1921, page 147.

83. This article and others—Article 15(2), free access to public places; Article 23(1), prohibition of forced or bonded labour; and Article 24, prohibition of employment of children in factories, mines, or hazardous occupations—are primarily directed against individual groups and citizens and accordingly are enforceable against them.

84. The Scheduled Castes Order applies only to Hindus and a part of the Sikhs. In 1950, Dalit Sikh castes (Mazhabis, Ramdasias, Kabirpanthis, and Sikligars) were placed in the Schedule Castes Order; the remaining Dalit Sikh castes were added in 1956. Those among the traditionally depressed classes of India (Hindu outcastes) who have embraced Buddhism, Jainism, Islam, or Christianity and members of other non-Hindu religious groups do not qualify for preferential treatment as scheduled castes, although they may qualify under the other constitutionally recognised (but undefined) category, viz., OBCs. Although the Supreme Court has rejected the inclusion of Buddhists in the meaning of 'Hindu' (AIR 1965, SC 1179), in 1990, neo-Buddhists were included. But Muslim and Christian Dalits are still struggling (and agitating for their inclusion in the Scheduled Castes Order).

85. Added by the Constitution First Amendment Act 1951 by India's first Parliament—the same body (Constituent Assembly) that framed the Constitution of India 1950.

86. Report dated 19 November 1975.

87. Meanwhile, the Rane Commission (headed by C. V. Rane), in the state of Gujarat, appointed (in 1981) to recommend identifying tests for the socially and educationally backward classes in the state, had also submitted its report to the state government. It also ignored castes and subcastes in listing the socially and educationally backward classes and concluded that, for an initial period of 10 years, it should be assumed that those who belonged to the lower castes or subcastes but who were individually and financially well off did not suffer from any social and educational backwardness. The financial criterion

adopted was an annual family income of over Rs 10,000. Those with family incomes less than that figure would become beneficiaries of Articles 15(4) and 16(4) of the Constitution. The state government's acceptance of this recommendation and its decision to increase the percentage of reservations from about 30 per cent to nearly 50 per cent sparked a series of riots in the state in the summer of 1985, threatening to spread even beyond Gujarat.

88. During the hearing of *Vasanth Kumar*, the state of Karnataka agreed to appoint a commission afresh and therefore requested the justices on the Supreme Court Bench to frame guidelines. This was so stated by Chief Justice Yeshwant V. Chandrachud at the beginning of his judgement:

> My learned brethren have expressed their respective points of view on the policy of reservations which, alas, is even figuratively, a burning issue today. We were invited by the counsel not so much as to deliver judgements but to express our opinion on the issue of reservations, which may serve as a guideline to the Commission which the Government of Karnataka proposes to appoint, for examining the question of affording better employment and educational opportunities to Scheduled Castes, Scheduled Tribes, and other backward classes. A somewhat unusual exercise is being undertaken by the Court in giving expression to its views without reference to specific facts. But institutions profit from well-meaning innovations.

89. 2006 (8), SCC 212.
90. Also, in *Indira Sawhney and Ors. vs. Union of India* (1992) Supp. 3 SCC 217, a bench decision of nine judges (6:3). But after the majority decision of November 2022 of the Supreme Court of India in *Janhit Abhiyan vs. Union of India: 2023 (5) SCC 1* (bench of five Justices (3:2)) upholding the Constitutional validity of the 103rd Constitution Amendment Act, 2019, the ceiling limit of 50 per cent is no longer a mandate.

91. 2008 (6), SCC 1.

92. See 1985, Supp. SCC 714, page 723, paragraph 2, Chief Justice Chandrachud.

93. Ibid., page 736, paragraph 31, Justice D. A. Desai.

94. There has been no such survey undertaken even till date. In *State of Kerala vs. N. M. Thomas,* AIR 1976, SC 490 (bench of seven judges), Justice Krishna Iyer coined the expression ('the top creamy layer').

95. *K. C. Vasanth Kumar vs. State of Karnataka,* 1985 (Supp.), SCC 714, paragraph 2, page 723. But this suggestion was later categorically rejected both in *Indira Sawhney vs. Union of India and Ors.*, 1992, Supp. 3, SCC 684 (by a bench of nine judges (6:3)) and again in *Ashoka Kumar Thakur* 2008, 6, SCC 1, page 511 (by a bench of five judges).

96. Paragraph 12.19 of the Mandal Commission report reads:

> Systematic caste-wise enumeration of the population was introduced by the Registrar General of India in 1881 and discontinued in 1931. In view of this, figures for caste-wise population beyond 1931 are not available. But assuming that the inter se rate of growth of the population of various castes, communities, and religious groups over the last half a century has remained more or less the same, it is possible to work out the percentage that all these groups constitute of the total population of the country.

97. They have till date still not been counted.

98. Office Memorandum:

Subject: Recommendations of the Second Backward Classes Commission (Mandal Report) Reservation for Socially and Educationally Backward Classes (SEBC) in services under the Government of India.

(1) In a multiple-undulating society like ours, early achievement of the objective of social justice as enshrined in the Constitution is a must. The Second Backward Classes Commission, called the Mandal Commission, was established by the then government with this purpose in view, which submitted its report to the Government of India on 31 December 1980.

(2) Government have carefully considered the report and the recommendations of the Commission in the present context regarding the benefits to be extended to the socially and educationally backward classes as opined by the Commission and are of the clear view that at the outset, certain weightage has to be provided to such classes in the services of the Union and their Public Undertakings. Accordingly, orders are issued as follows:

(i) 27 per cent of the vacancies in civil posts and services under the Government of India shall be reserved for SEBC.

(ii) The aforesaid reservation shall apply to vacancies to be filled by direct recruitment. Detailed instructions relating to the procedures to be followed for enforcing reservation will be issued separately.

(iii) Candidates belonging to SEBC recruited on the basis of merit in an open competition on the same standards prescribed for the general candidates shall not be adjusted against the reservation quota of 27 per cent.

(iv) The SEBC would comprise in the first phase the castes and communities which are common to both the list in the report of the Mandal Commission and the State Governments' lists, a list of such castes/communities is being issued separately.

(vi) The aforesaid reservation shall take effect from 7 August 1990. However, this will not apply to vacancies where the recruitment process has already been initiated prior to the issue of these orders.

(3) Similar instructions in respect of public sector undertakings and financial institutions including public sector banks will be issued by the Department of Public Enterprises and Ministry of Finance, respectively.

Sd/-(Smt. Krishna Singh) Joint Secretary to the Govt. of India.

99. **The population growth in India has been quite staggering and with it, the corresponding swelling numbers of the backward classes. According to the latest census, India's population rose from 533 million in 1971 to 665 million in 1981, to 838 million in 1991, to 1025 million in 2001 and to over 1200 million in the census of 2011. According to World Population Review (WPR) India's population was 1.41 billion as of the end of 2022 and currently India is home to 1425 million people based on latest United Nations data-projection. In September 2021 data collated by the PEW Research Centre had projected that India's population had more than tripled in six decades following Partition!**

100. 1992 Supp 3 SC 217 to page 772 (bench of nine judges (6:3)).

101. Justice B. P. Jeevan Reddy on behalf of himself and Chief Justice M. H. Kania, Justice M. N. Venkatachaliah, and Justice A. M. Ahmadi—concurred in by Justices S. R. Pandian and P. B. Sawant—those concurring had delivered separate judgements. The dissenting justices—Justices T. K. Thommen, Kuldeep Singh, and R. M. Sahai—did not agree that the office memorandum of 13 August 1990, which had been upheld by the majority, was valid. They were

in favour of declaring it to be unenforceable; according to them, reservation was a remedy only for historical discrimination and its continuing ill-effects whilst other affirmative action programmes were intended to redress discrimination of all kinds, whether current or historical.

102. Constituent Assembly Debates, 8 November 1948, Vol. 7, page 702.

103. It ultimately also led to the Constitution 103rd Amendment Act, 2019 (In November 2022 its constitutional validity has been upheld by a majority in a Constitution Bench decision (3:2)).

104. See *Union of India vs. Pushpa Rani,* 2008 (9), SCC 242, paragraph 39, page 271 (Justice B. N. Agrawal and Justice G. S. Singhvi).

105. Marc Galanter: *Competing Equalities, Law and the Backward Classes in India,* University of California Press, Los Angeles, 1984, page 567. The same passage is repeated in the paperback Indian edition, Oxford University Press, New Delhi, 1991.

106. Brief History of Equality, pages 190-192

107. Rudolf C. Heredia: 'Quotas and Minority Rights: Recapturing the Constitutional Vision', *Economic and Political Weekly,* 23 July 2011, Vol. XLVI, pages 66-67.

108. Articles 141 and 144 of the Constitution read as follows:
   - (i) 141. Law declared by Supreme Court to be binding on all courts. The law declared by the Supreme Court shall be binding on all courts within the territory of India.
   - (ii) 144. Civil and judicial authorities to act in aid of the Supreme Court: All authorities, civil and judicial, in the territory of India shall act in aid of the Supreme Court.

109. A permanent body was to be set up known as the National Commission of Backward Classes.

110. Functions of the Commission:
   - (a) The Commission shall examine requests for inclusion of any class of citizens as a backward class in the lists and hear complaints of over-inclusion or under-inclusion of any backward class in such lists and tender such advice to the Central Government as it deems appropriate.
   - (b) The advice of the Commission shall ordinarily be binding upon the Central Government.

   11. Periodic revision of lists by the Central Government:

(1) The Central Government may at any time, and shall, at the expiration of 10 years from the coming into force of this Act and every succeeding period of 10 years thereafter, undertake a revision of the lists with a view to excluding from such lists those classes who have ceased to be backward classes or for including in such lists new backward classes.

(2) The Central Government shall, while undertaking any revision referred to in subsection (1), consult the Commission.

111. R. K. Sabharwal vs. State of Punjab, 1995 (2) SCC 745; *Arijit Singh vs. State of Punjab,* 1996 92) SCC 215; *Indira Sawhney vs. Union of India,* 2000 (1) SCC 168 (creamy layer); *Nagaraj vs. Union of India,* 2006 (8) SCC 212 (five judges); *Jarnail Singh vs. L .N. Gupta,* (2018) 10 SCC 396; *B. K. Pavitra vs. Union of India,* (2019) 10 SCC 129; *Dr Jaishri Laxmanrao Patil vs. Chief Minister of State,* (2021) SCC Online 362 (judgement of May 2021).

112. AIR 2007, SC 71.

113. Unfortunately followed by State and Central governments more in the breach than in the observance.

114. 'Other Backward Classes' are defined in the Act (Act 5 of 2007) as meaning 'a class or classes of citizens who are socially and educationally backward and are so determined by the Central Government'.

115. 2008 (6), SCC 1.

116. 2008 (6), SCC 1, paragraph 650, page 711.

117. The court also held, in keeping with the unanimous decision of a bench of seven judges in *P. A. Inamdar vs. State of Maharashtra* (2005), that the exclusion of minority educational institutions from the purview of Article 15(5) was valid, but the question of validity (i.e., the constitutional validity) of the inclusion of private unaided institutions within the purview of Article 15(5) was 'left open'; soon to be 'closed' by the decision of two justices (in a bench of three) in *Society for Unaided Private Schools of Rajasthan vs. Union of India and Anr.* The judgement, dated 12 April 2012, has held that it was constitutionally permissible to include private unaided educational institutions within the purview of Article 15!

118. A Constitution Bench of five judges, upholding the constitutional validity of the Constitution 103rd Amendment Act 2019 was sharply divided (3:2) even in the year 2023.

119. For instance:

   (1) 'OBC Creamy Layer Ceiling Raised', *The Economic Times*, 17 November 2011, page 2;
   (2) 'Cutoff for OBC "Creamy Layer" May Be Raised to Rs 7 Lakh/ Year', *The Times of India*, 11 June 2012;
   (3) 'OBC Creamy Layer Ceiling May Go Up to Rs 6 Lakh/Yr', *Hindustan Times*, 13 June 2012;
   (4) 'Cabinet to Consider Raising Creamy Layer Ceiling to Rs 6 Lakh a Year, *The Hindu*, 14 June 2012;

120. B. Shiva Rao: *Framing of India's Constitution*, Vol. III, page 510.

Chapter Five

The Conscience of the Constitution: Directive Principles of State Policy (Part-IV) read with Fundamental Rights (Part-III)

Part-IV of the Indian Constitution owes its inspiration to the 1937 Constitution of Eire (Ireland) which contained Directive Principles of State Policy. Articles 36 to 51[1] in Part-IV of India's Constitution treated directive principles as 'fundamental to the governance of the country', as had been explained by Dr Ambedkar in the Constituent Assembly:

> *Because we did not want merely a parliamentary form of government to be instituted through various mechanisms provided in the Constitution, without any direction as to what our economic ideal, as to what our social order ought to be, we deliberately included the Directive Principles in our Constitution.*[2]

'*Fundamental Rights*' (in Part-III) and '*Directive Principles*' (Part-IV) were put together by the Constituent Assembly in the hope that Indian society would be brought closer to the Constitution's goals (expressed in the Preamble). For example, Article 46 in Part-IV (Promotion of educational and economic interests of Scheduled Castes, Scheduled Tribes and other weaker sections of the people) was the goal and the *method for reaching that goal* was set out in Part-III, viz., in Article 15 (Prohibition of discrimination of grounds of religion, race, caste, sex, or place of birth) as well as in Article 16 (Equality of opportunity in matters of public employment).

But in the first two decades of the working of the Constitution, this *hope* remained unfulfilled because whilst the right to move the Supreme Court by appropriate proceedings for the enforcement of the rights conferred by Part-III had been guaranteed (along with provisions enabling the Supreme Court to issue writs directions and orders 'for their enforcement' (Article 32(1)), Directive Principles of State Policy (in Part-IV) had been expressly declared to be *'not enforceable by any Court'* despite they being 'fundamental in the governance of the country' (Article 37). Besides the language used in Article 13 (vis-a-vis 'Fundamental Rights') that 'the State shall not make any law which takes away or abridges the rights conferred by this Part (Part-III) and any law made in contravention of this Clause shall to the extent of the contravention be void' was quite definite and peremptory. Hence, for quite a long while, DPSPs (Directive Principles of State Policy) were treated by India's Supreme Court somewhat like *'parchment barriers'* (a phrase used by James Madison of the United States in the Federalist Papers). In an opinion expressed (in 1958) by India's highest court, it was said that *'the State should certainly implement the directive principles but it must do so in such a way that its laws do not take away or abridge the fundamental rights, for otherwise the protecting provisions of Chap. III will be a mere "rope of sand".*[3]' And even a judge as liberal as Justice Krishna Iyer—in a bench decision of the court handed down in the year 1976—had visualised only a limited role for Directive Principles when he wrote:

> (*Quote*) Statutory interpretation in the creative Indian context, may look for light to the lodestar of Part-IV of the Constitution, e.g., Articles 39(a) and (c) and Article 43, where two judicial choices are available, the construction

in conformity with the social philosophy of Part-IV has preference. *Mumbai Kamgar Sabha vs. M/s Abdulbhai & Ors.* reported in AIR 1976 SC 1455 at page 1465. (*Unquote*)

The perceived imbalance between the provisions contained in Part-III and in Part-IV got restored, but only gradually and over time:

(a) It was in the year 1980, that Chief Justice Y. V. Chandrachud (speaking for a Constitution Bench of five judges of the Supreme Court), in *Minerva Mills vs. Union of India* (1980 (3) SCC 625), expressed (in eloquent prose) what the court conceived to be the vision of the Founding Fathers:

> 56. (on page 654): The significance of the perception that Parts III and IV together constitute the core of commitment to social revolution *and they, together, are the conscience of the Constitution* . . . In other words, the Indian Constitution is founded on the bedrock of the balance between Parts III and IV. *To give absolute primacy to one over the other is to disturb the harmony of the Constitution. This harmony and balance between fundamental rights and directive principles is an essential feature of the basic structure of the Constitution.*[4]

He then went on to add:

> 57. This is not mere semantics. The edifice of our Constitution is built upon the concepts crystallised in the Preamble. We resolved to constitute ourselves into a Socialist State which carried with it the obligation to secure to our people justice-social, economic, and political. We, therefore, put Part-IV into our Constitution containing directive principles of state

policy which specify the socialistic goal to be achieved. We promised to our people a democratic polity which carries with it the obligation of securing to the people liberty of thought, expression, belief, faith, and worship; equality of status and of opportunity and the assurance that the dignity of the individual will at all costs be preserved. *We, therefore, put Part-III in our Constitution, conferring those rights on the people. Those rights are not an end in themselves but are the means to an end. The end is specified in Part-IV.* Therefore, the rights conferred by Part-III are subject to reasonable restrictions and the Constitution provides that enforcement of some of them may, in stated uncommon circumstances, be suspended. *But just as the rights conferred by Part-III would be without a radar and a compass if they were not geared to an ideal, in the same manner the attainment of the ideals set out in Part-IV would become a pretence for tyranny if the price to be paid for achieving that ideal is human freedom.* One of the faiths of our founding fathers was the purity of means . . . *The goals set out in Part-IV have, therefore, to be achieved without the abrogation of the means provided for by Part-III. It is in this sense that Parts III and IV together constitute the core of our Constitution and combine to form its conscience. Anything that destroys the balance between the two parts will ipso facto destroy an essential element of the basic structure of our Constitution.* (on page 654)[5].

(b) In the year 1992, in the principal majority judgment of the Supreme Court of India—a judgment delivered by Justice B. P. Jeevan Reddy; a bench decision of nine Hon'ble Judges (7:2) in *Indira Sawhney Anr. vs. Union of India & Ors.* (1993 Suppl. (3) SCC 217)—the role of the Preamble was also directly linked with Parts III and IV, viz., that the Preamble in the Constitution spelt out the *goal* and both Part-III and Part-IV set out the *methodology for reaching that goal.*

> *(Quote) Forty and three years ago was founded this republic with the fourfold objective of securing to its citizens justice, liberty, equality, and fraternity.* Statesmen of the highest order—the like of which this country has not seen since—belonging to the fields of law, politics, and public life came together to fashion the instrument of change—the Constitution of India. They did not rest content with evolving the framework of the State; they also pointed out the *goal,* and the methodology for reaching that goal. *In the Preamble, they spelt out the goal and in Parts III and IV, they elaborated the methodology to be followed for reaching that goal.* (*Unquote*)

(c) The precise methodology to be followed by the courts was later—much later—fine-tuned. In the authoritative opinion of the court, in a unanimous bench decision of nine Hon'ble Judges of the Supreme Court of India—in *I. R. Coelho vs. State of Tamil Nadu* (2007 (2) SCC 1 = AIR 2007 SC 861) where Chief Justice Sabharwal (speaking for the court) reaffirmed in para 49 (on page 80) what had been already said earlier in 1980, viz.:

> (*Quote*) . . . **The goals set out in Part-IV have, therefore, to be achieved without the abrogation of the means provided for by Part-III. It is in this sense that Parts III and IV together constitute the core of our Constitution and combine to form its conscience. Anything that destroys the balance between the two parts will ipso facto destroy the essential element of the Constitution . . . the matters have to be decided not by metaphysical subtlety, nor as a matter of semantics, but by a broad and liberal approach. We must not miss the wood for the trees.**[6] (*Unquote*)

(d) Ten years later, Dr Justice D. Y. Chandrachud, while delivering a unanimous judgment of the Constitution Bench of (nine judges of the Supreme Court) in *K. S. Puttaswamy vs. Union of India* (2017 (10) SCC 1), upheld the right of privacy as a fundamental right under India's Constitution and went on to add (in para 125 on page 411-412) that 'as had been held in *Minerva Mills (1980)*':

> . . . both Parts III and IV of the Constitution had emerged as inseparably intertwined without a distinction between the negative and positive obligations of the State. The Constitution in this view, is founded on 'the bedrock of the balance between Parts III and IV' and to give absolute primacy to one over the other would be to disturb the harmony of the Constitution.

(e) *In essence, therefore the goals set out in Part-IV had to be achieved without abrogation of the means provided for in Part-III.*

Notes and References:

1. Part-IV—Directive Principles of State Policy.
   Article 36: Definition of State.
   Article 37: Application of the principles contained in this Part.
   Article 38: State to secure a social order for the promotion of welfare of the people.
   Article 39: Certain principles of policy to be followed by the State;
   Article 39A - Equal justice and free legal aid.
   Article 40: Organisation of village panchayats.
   Article 41: Right to work, to education and to public assistance in certain cases.
   Article 42: Provision for just and humane conditions of work and maternity relief.
   Article 43: Living wage, etc., for workers.

Article 43A: Participation of workers in management of Industries.
Article 43B: Promotion of co-operative societies.
Article 44: Uniform civil code for the citizens.
Article 45: Provision for early childhood care and education to children below the age of six years.
Article 46: Promotion of educational and economic interests of Scheduled Castes, Scheduled Tribes and other weaker sections.
Article 47: Duty of the State to raise the level of nutrition and the standard of living and to improve public health.
Article 48: Organisation of agriculture and animal husbandry.
Article 48A: Protection and improvement of environment and safeguarding of forests and wildlife.
Article 49: Protection of monuments and places and objects of national importance.
Article 50: Separation of judiciary from executive.
Article 51: Promotion of international peace and security.

2. CAD, Vol. VII, page 494, 19 November 1948.

3. *Mohd. Hanif Quareshi & Others vs. The State of Bihar*, AIR 1958 SC 731, paragraph 12 (a judgment of a Constitution Bench of five judges).

4. It was for this reason that the words that had been added by the Constitution 42nd Amendment Act, 1976 at the end of Article 31C to indicate that directive principles should have priority over fundamental rights were struck down as unconstitutional and void.

5. In *Minerva Mills* (AIR 1980 SC 1789), a Constitution Bench of the Supreme Court held that clauses (4) and (5) added to Article 368 by Parliament by the Constitution 42nd Amendment Act, 1976 damaged the basic and essential feature of the Constitution. Clauses (4) and (5) of Article 368 read as follows:

   368 (4) No amendment of this Constitution (including the provisions of Part-III) made or purporting to have been made under this article (whether before or after the commencement of section 55 of the Constitution 42nd (Amendment) Act, 1976) shall be called in question in any court on any ground.

   For the removal of doubts, it is hereby declared that there shall be no limitation whatever on the constituent power of Parliament to amend by way of addition, variation or repeal the provisions of this Constitution under this article.

6. See also page 98 (paragraph 101) of *I. R. Coelho vs. State of Tamil Nadu* 2007 (2) SCC 1.

Chapter Six

The Executive, the Legislature, and the Judiciary (Part-V and Part-VI of the Constitution)

The Westminster system or the Westminster model is a type of parliamentary government that incorporates a series of procedures for operating a legislature. This concept was first developed in England. Key aspects of the system include an executive branch (made up principally of members of the legislature, that is responsible to the legislature), the presence of parliamentary opposition parties in Parliament (and State Legislatures), and a ceremonial head of state (at the Centre) who is different from the head of government. The Westminster system originates from the Palace of Westminster, the current seat of Parliament in the United Kingdom and is often contrasted with the wholly-presidential system that originated and prevails in the United States of America, and with the semi-presidential system, based on the government in France.

In the case of the more recent constitutions on the Westminster model—unlike earlier prototypes—they include a chapter dealing with fundamental rights and freedoms. India's constitution has been framed on the Westminster model, i.e., on a parliamentary system, together with a chapter on Fundamental Rights (Part-III).

In a judgement delivered in 1974, a bench of seven judges of the Supreme Court of India[1] had written:

> (*Quote*) Our Constitution embodies generally the Parliamentary or Cabinet system of Government of the British model both for the Union and the States. Under this system, the President is the constitutional or formal head of the Union and he exercises his powers and functions conferred on him by or under the Constitution with the aid and advice of his Council of Ministers. (*Unquote*)

India's parliamentary system of government, though British inspired—ever since the 19th century—has Swadeshi origins[2] as nationalists in British India had expressed their preference for an elected Parliament in what was hoped would be a free India.

However, the parliamentary system is by no means the most effective method of governance. Malcolm Muggeridge, editor of that once famous (now-extinct) magazine *Punch,* had said that: 'the best form of government, *is despotism, tempered with assassination; and since the latter can never be ensured, we have to reluctantly abandon despotism as the most effective form of governance, and pick the next best.*'

Browsing through Part-V of the Constitution one may be misled into believing that there is a delicate balance between the 'three great organs of state', by the very neat arrangement of the topics, viz.: with separate provisions relating to the *Union Executive,* in Chapter I (Articles 52 to 78); separate provisions relating to *Parliament* in Chapter II (Articles 79 to 122); a separate provision relating to *Legislative Powers of the President* in Chapter III (Article 123); provisions in relation to the *Union Judiciary* in Chapter IV (Articles 124 to 146); and finally, in Chapter V, provisions relating to the Constitutional Ombudsman (Financial), viz., the *Comptroller and Auditor-General of India* (Articles 147 to 151).

The Union Executive consists of the president of India (Article 52) (along with a vice-president, who is to act as president in the event of any vacancy in the office of the president or during the president's absence (due to illness or any other case) (Article 63). The Union Executive also includes the council of ministers with the prime minister at the head, to 'aid and advise the president who shall, in the exercise of his functions, act in accordance with such advice' (Article 74). The Union Legislature consists of the president at the head, with two Houses of Parliament to be known respectively as *the Council of States* and the *House of the People* (Article 79). The Council of States (Rajya Sabha) consists of twelve members to be nominated by the President (nominated members) and not more than 238 representatives of the (now) 28 states[3], elected by the elected members of legislative assemblies in each state; the representatives of the Nine Union Territories[4] in the Council of States are to be chosen as Parliament prescribes by law (Article 80). The House of the People (Lok Sabha) consists of 530 members, chosen by direct election from different territorial constituencies in the states, with not more than 20 members to represent the union territories chosen in such manner as Parliament prescribes (Article 81).

[**NOTE:** The new Parliament building inaugurated on **28 May, 2023** has three upper florrs with a built-up area of 64,500 sqm. The Lok Sabha Chamber will now have 888 seats, increased from the existing 540, with the option of expanded seating up to 1272. The Lok Sabha will be used for joint sittings of both Houses, in the absence of a Central Hall, which had been the hallmark of the old Parliament building.]

The other integral part of the union, the Judiciary, consists of the Supreme Court of India (Article 124)—the final interpreter of India's Constitution and the laws—as well as the final appellate authority from all decisions of the high courts in the states. It is also the *exclusive* forum for adjudicating all disputes between two or more states, and between the Government of India and one or more states, in so far as such disputes involve any question (whether of law or fact) on which the existence or extent of a legal right depends (Article 131).

There is a similar division of functions in each of the states (set out in Part-VI). For every state, there is a legislature that consists of the governor (not elected, but appointed by the centre and holding office at the president's 'pleasure' (Article 153)), together with two Houses of Legislature respectively in the states of Andhra Pradesh, Bihar, Maharashtra, Karnataka, Tamil Nadu. Telangana, and Uttar Pradesh (U.P.) and with one House in the remaining states (Article 168).

Governors in the States

Whilst the constitution was being finalised, it was apprehended that the office of the governor would be controlled by the political party at the centre. The issue was a source of conflict between Pandit Nehru and Sardar Patel; the latter preferred governors to be elected by the people of the state. Initially, Sardar Patel's view was favoured. The June 1947 report of the Provincial Constitution Committee ('on the principles of a Model Provincial Constitution')[5] stipulated that 'for each province, there shall be a governor to be elected directly by the people on the basis of adult suffrage'.

And later in October 1947, the Draft Constitution of the Constitutional Adviser (B. N. Rau) provided:

> 111. In each Province, there shall be a Governor who shall be elected in the manner provided in the next succeeding section.
>
> 112. The Governor of a Province shall be elected by direct vote of all persons who have the right to vote at a general election for the Legislative Assembly of the Province.

And the Draft Constitution prepared by the Drafting Committee (February 1948) also provided alternatives:

> 131. The Governor of a State shall be elected by direct vote of all persons who have the right to vote at a general election for the Legislative Assembly of the State.

Alternatively:

> *131. The Governor of a State shall be appointed by the President by warrant under his hand and seal from a panel of four candidates to be elected by the members of the Legislative Assembly of the State, or, where there is a Legislative Council in the State, by all members of the Legislative Assembly and of the Legislative Council of the State assembled at a joint meeting, in accordance with the system of proportional representation by means of the single transferable vote and the voting at such election shall be by secret ballot.

Some of the members of the committee were strongly in favour of this alternative, because they considered that the co-existence of a governor elected by the people and a prime minister responsible to the legislature might lead to friction and consequently, a weakness in the administration.

But at later stages of the proceedings in the Constituent Assembly, it was felt that the co-existence of an *elected* governor, and an *elected* chief minister, responsible to the state legislature, would lead to friction and might weaken the administration. And so, the concept of an elected governor was given up, in favour of a *nominated* governor picked by the Centre.

During the debates in the Constituent Assembly, some members had expressed concern that central control over governors posed a risk to India's democracy. For example, Pandit Hriday Nath Kunzru (president of the Servants of Indian Society) said (prophetically forseeing the future!):

> (*Quote*) . . . I think, Sir, that it should be clearly realised, lest there should be serious conflicts between the Central Government on one side and the Provincial Governments on the other . . .

> If you entrust the Central Executive with power to exercise control over the Provinces in all important matters, and make them fall in line with the policy of the Centre, there is the serious danger of the country falling under a dictatorship.[6] (*Unquote*)

Ultimately, Dr Ambedkar summed up the position[7] as follows:

> (*Quote*) It has been said, in the course of the debate, that the argument against election is that there would be a rivalry between the Prime Minister and the Governor, both deriving their mandate from the people at large. Speaking for myself, that was not the argument which influenced me because I do not accept that even under election, there would be any kind of rivalry between the Prime Minister and the Governor, for the simple reason that the Prime Minister would be elected on the basis of policy, while the Governor could not be elected on the basis of policy, because he could have no policy, not having any power. *So far as I could visualise, the election of the Governor would be on the basis of personality*: is he the right sort of person by his status, by his character, by his education, by his position in the public to fill in a post of Governor? In the case of the Prime Minister, the position would be: is his programme suitable, is his programme right? *There could not, therefore, be any conflict even if we adopt the principle of election . . .*
>
> *The thing that I want to tell the House is this: that the real issue before the House is not nomination or election, but what powers you propose to give to your Governor*. If the Governor is a purely constitutional Governor with no more powers than what we contemplate expressly to give him, he has no power to interfere with the internal administration of a Provincial Ministry. (*Unquote*)

The position ultimately adopted by the Constituent Assembly was that *'the Governor of a State shall be appointed by the President by warrant under his hand and seal'* (Article 155).

When considering the working of the Constitution of India, 1950, the Sarkaria Commission on Centre-State Relations (1987) recommended as follows:[8]

> 4.4.03 . . . that a person to be appointed as a Governor should satisfy the following criteria:
>
> (i) He should be eminent in some walk of life.
>
> (ii) He should be a person from outside the State.
>
> (iii) He should be a detached figure and not too intimately connected with the local politics of the State; and
>
> (iv He should be a person who has not taken too great a part in politics generally, particularly in the recent past.

These recommendations (and they are only 'recommendations') were also reiterated in the majority judgement of the Supreme Court in the *Rameshwar Prasad* (2006 (2) SCC 1 (3:2)) and once again in the Punchhi (Second) Committee report on Centre-State Relations (1987)—March 2010 on page 63. But all this has not yet been translated into law.

More dangerous to India's democracy is that the Constitution remains ambivalent about the *powers of the governor.* It does oblige governors to follow the 'advice' of the state's chief minister (Article 163), but the constitution is silent in key areas, viz.:

(i) *Who is to be appointed chief minister?* (Article 164 only states that 'the Chief Minister shall be appointed by the Governor').

(ii) *When should the governor summon a session of the state assembly?* The only provision as to sessions of

state legislatures (Article 174) is that the governor shall from time to time 'summon the House at such time and place as he thinks fit but that six months shall not intervene between the last sitting in one session and the date appointed for first sitting in the next session' (Article 174).

(iii) ***When should the governor exercise his power to dissolve the state legislative assembly?*** **Article 174 only states that 'the Governor may time to time dissolve the Legislative Assembly'; and**

(iv) ***Currently, and more importantly, when and within what time frame should the governor approve or reject bills passed by state legislatures?*** **(Article 200)**

The report of (Second) Commission on Centre-State Relations (March 2010)—the Justice Punchhi Commission—had recommended that there should not be a delay of more than 6 months from the date when the bill passed by the assembly is submitted to the governor for his assent, but again, this recommendation has not yet been translated into substantive law.

In each and every state, there is a council of ministers with the chief minister at the head to aid and advise the governor in the exercise of his functions—*except where the governor is by or under the Constitution required to exercise his functions in his discretion* (Article 163(1)), as in the case of the administration and control of tribal areas and scheduled areas under provisions set out in the Fifth and Sixth Schedules of the Constitution[9]. The extremely limited situations where the discretionary power of the Governor can be exercised independent of, or even contrary to the aid and advice of the council of ministers, have been laid down by the Supreme Court of India in *Nabam Rebia and Bamang Felix vs. Deputy Speaker, Arunachal Pradesh Legislative Assembly and others* (2016 (8) SCC 1), viz:

> *(Quote) Firstly,* when Constitution expressly provides for the same. *Secondly,* where a constitutional provision could not be construed otherwise on a legitimate interpretation of the same. *Thirdly,* where Court has laid down that such discretion is available to the Governor. The Governor has no freedom to determine when and in which situation he can take a decision to exercise his discretion independent of, or, contrary to the aid and advice of the Council of Ministers—hence Article 163(2) must be read subject to Article 163(1).[10] *(Unquote)*

In the end, since there are bound to be differences of opinion between governors and chief ministers, it has been very recently—once again—suggested that India's democracy would be 'safer' if both the chief minister and the governor were elected directly by the people.[11] But this would now require a constitutional amendment.

For more on governors, see the comment on Article 361 of the Constitution in Chapter Three.

The President

There is one significant balancing feature in India's Constitution, little realised at times, and definitely much less appreciated, and that is in the function of the president (India's head of state). The office of the president under India's Constitution is an elected one. The president of India is a constitutional functionary having no political power, unlike the president of the USA. But in the United States of America, there is what is known as *a-growing-better-with-age theory* of presidential history. And this is so in India as well, but the extent of the powers exercised by heads of state in each country depends on how that country's written constitution is worked.

Under India's Constitution, the president, although a constitutional head of state, is by no means a cipher or a rubber stamp of the central government and as a matter of fact, in one of the books on the president, his/her role has been described as that of a 'quiescent volcano'.[12]

India's head of state has been compared with the constitutional position of the Crown in England. As had been stated, by Walter Bagehot in elegant prose some 150 years ago:

> To state the matter shortly, the Sovereign has, under a constitutional monarchy, three rights—*the right to be consulted, the right to encourage, and the right to warn*. And a king of great sense and sagacity would want no other. He would find that his having no other would enable him to use these with singular effect. He would say to his (First) Minister: '*The responsibility of these measures is upon you. Whatever you think best must be done. Whatever you think best shall have my full and effectual support. But you will observe that for this reason and that reason what you propose to do is bad; for this reason and that reason what you do not propose is better. I do not oppose, it is my duty not to oppose; but observe what I warn.*' Supposing the king to be right, and to have what kings often have, the gift of effectual expression, he could not help moving his Ministers. *He might not always turn his course, but he would always trouble his mind.*[13]

It was the architect of India's Constitution, Dr B. R. Ambedkar, who had said in the Constituent Assembly: '*like the English king, our president will have not only Bagehot's three rights (the right to advise, to warn, and to be consulted), but also the prerogative powers of appointing the prime minister and the dissolution of the House*'.[14]

India is a quasi-federal polity with a parliamentary system of government. Since there is no set theory of federalism, federalism in India has characteristics that are associated both with unitary and non-unitary forms of government. Under our constitutional scheme, there is a clear distribution of legislative and executive powers between the union and the states, though the powers of the states are so hedged in by restrictions that they have no independent 'political sovereignty'. This had been affirmed, way back in 1963, by a majority of judges (5:1) in a Constitution Bench decision of the Supreme Court (in the case of the *State of West Bengal vs. the Union of India*).[15] The crucial question there was whether or not the centre, in exercise of its powers of *eminent domain*,[16] could acquire properties owned by a state. Chief Justice B. P. Sinha, speaking for himself and four other justices, held that it could. 'It would be difficult to hold,' he noted, 'that Parliament which is competent to destroy a State, is, on account of some assumption as to the sovereignty of the State, incompetent effectively to acquire by legislation property owned by the State for governmental purposes.' As mentioned earlier, Professor K. C. Wheare, a noted constitutional expert, had written:[17]

> (*Quote*) What makes one doubt that the Constitution of India is *strictly and fully federal*, however, are the powers of intervention in the affairs of the States given by the Constitution to the Central Government and Parliament. (*Unquote*)
>
> (He therfore characterised it as Quasi-federal).

The above quote was approvingly cited by India's Supreme Court in *S. R. Bommai vs. Union of India* (AIR 1994 SC 1918=1994 (3) SCC 1 (9J)).

In India's *quasi-federal polity*, there is a head of state at the centre whose job it is to keep the 'ship of state' (the union) on an even keel. There is also a governor at the head of each state. At the centre, the head of state has hardly ever 'rocked the boat',[18] except during some periods of the first presidency of Dr Rajendra Prasad.

Amongst all our presidents, the role of Dr Rajendra Prasad, India's first head of state (who was in office for two successive terms—from 26 January 1950 to 13 May 1962), was a bit stormy and turbulent. In office (of president during the first full decade)—India's only head of state to be so elected for two successive terms—Dr Prasad had strong views about the role of president. Having the 'gift of effective expression' (as Bagehot would have said), his views did frequently 'trouble the mind' of India's first prime minister, Jawaharlal Nehru. And in private, Prasad often complained to Minoo Masani, his friend and compatriot in the Constituent Assembly, that Nehru did not allow him to exercise the powers which he was sure he had under the document they together had passed in the Constituent Assembly. Years later, Masani wrote that Rajendrababu did not have the force of Nehru's personality, gave in too readily, and yet went on grumbling (as he gave in) saying: 'this is not the way we framed the Constitution.' Masani added, '. . . when people (ask) what is wrong with this Constitution, I say nothing is wrong; what is wrong is us, we have destroyed the Constitution because people in Delhi love power too much to tolerate either a *strong president* or a *strong state*.'[19]

Even during his second term in office, Dr Rajendra Prasad was not quite convinced that he was simply a constitutional head of state. In 1960, in a speech to the Indian Law Institute in New Delhi, he said that our Constitution contained no provision '*which, in so many words, lays down that the president is bound to act on ministerial advice*.'[20] An assertion, which though legally doubtful, caused a stir, and as constitutional historian Granville Austin put it: '*It set the presidential fox among the constitutional geese*.' But the press had reacted most favourably to Rajendra Prasad's statement!

In a book titled, *The Indian President*, by K. C. Singh (Harper Collins, 2023), it is stated (at page 4):

> (*Quote*) The debate in the Constituent Assembly then turned to examining the Indian president's mode of election and whether it should be direct or indirect. Dr Ambedkar said that in view of India's large population, then 317 million,

it seemed unjustified to hold a separate direct election as the post did not provide 'immense power', like the post of the US president. Prof. K. T. Shah was not convinced and said: 'The President will function only in an emergency; he will (however) function, not ornamentally only.' He added that he cannot just be a 'gramophone of the PM'. To this, Ambedkar retorted: 'What is the position of the President of the Indian Union? He is, if Prof. K. T. Shah were to examine other provisions of the Constitution, only a figurehead. He is unlike the US President, Ambedkar added, and, if at all, the Indian prime minister provides that equivalence . . .

(At page 10, 11 and 12): Dr Prasad, in a note to his secretary on 21 March 1950[21], posed the vital question: Under what circumstances, if any, can the president act independently? He widened the query by arguing that this action can be of three kinds:

(a) It may be against the advice given.
(b) It may be taken without waiting for seeking advice.
(c) It may have to be taken when a minister refuses to give advice.

"Dr Prasad then raised more pointed questions under four heads. First, what was the ambit of Article 53(2) of the Constitution, which vests the 'supreme command of the Defence Forces of the Union' in the president? Second, what is the role of the president in securing the independence of certain organs or functionaries that are expected to act independently, uninfluenced by the executive? These include, as outlined above, the judiciary, the Comptroller and Auditor General (CAG) of Accounts, the Union Public Service Commission (UPSC), and the then the lone election commissioner. Dr Prasad wondered what was expected of his office to ensure that these entities maintained their independence and fairness. Finally, he reasoned that his assent to a bill becomes meaningless if he must act totally on the advice of the very ministry that has enacted that bill.

"These notes were seen by Prime Minister Jawaharlal Nehru who referred them to the then Attorney General M. C. Setalvad. The initial reaction of the Attorney General was that even though the president of India was like the British sovereign, his position could not be considered totally akin as he was elected by the people, albeit indirectly. The president could, therefore, influence the council of ministers by his discretion, advice and suggestions. On receiving the advice of the Attorney General on 24 January 1951, the President instructed his secretariat as follows:

> The position of the President is more or less the same as that of the King of England in constitutional matters, and in all matters, he has to act with the advice of his Council of Ministers. It has been pointed out, however, that it is open to him to influence the Council of Ministers by his advice."

"Dr Prasad then wondered at what stage such advice must be tendered and concluded: 'It means my secretariat has not only to be vigilant and keep itself informed about the activities, administrative as well as legislative, of the Central Government, but also about the legislative activities of the State Governments." (*Unquote*)

Over the past seventy-plus years, in the life of almost every President of India, there have been occasions when he/she has exercised his/her individual powers of persuasion—his/her 'right to warn' (as Bagehot put it). It is only in critical times—in crisis situations—that the true mettle and personality of the person occupying the highest office in the land gets revealed.

The gravest crisis in his time that had been faced by any President in India was, that to which Dr Fakhruddin Ali Ahmed had been exposed. He was elected president in August 1974 and died in office (on 11 February 1977) before completing his five-year term. The 'gravest crisis' he was confronted with was when he was asked to sign (without prior cabinet consultation or approval) the Proclamation of Internal Emergency of 25 June 1975, promulgated under Article 352 (Proclamation of Emergency), the direct and inevitable consequence of which was the rounding-up of his own (the president's own) erstwhile friends and compatriots. They were preventively detained overnight in civil prisons spread across the country.

[NOTE:
Preventive Detention had been expressly provided for (strangely), in the Fundamental Rights Chapter (Part-III) of the Constitution—Article 22(4) to (7), and pursuant to Article 22(4) to (7) independent India's first Preventive Detention Act was passed in India's Parliament in February 1950!]

One of the lessons of the Internal Emergency (which lasted from 26 June 1975 till March 1977) had been not to place excessive reliance on constitutional functionaries. It was because the president so readily agreed to sign the Proclamation of Emergency on the night of 25 June 1975, even before the union cabinet (council of ministers) knew anything about it, that three years later (after the revocation of the Emergency in March 1977), a Constitutional Amendment was introduced and passed by the newly elected Parliament—the Constitution (44th Amendment) Act 1978—which declared that in the future, a president was not empowered to sign a Proclamation of Emergency without a prior cabinet decision, i.e., unless the decision of the council of ministers (that such a proclamation be issued) had been communicated to him *in writing* (Article 52(3)).

But the signing of the Emergency Proclamation in June 1975 by President Dr Fakhruddin Ali Ahmed at the behest of some high officials in government was not just an aberration occasioned by the Internal Emergency. High constitutional functionaries including ministers have failed to fulfil their allotted functions not only when times were bad, but at other times as well, as instanced below:

- In the general elections of March 1977, (for instance) the Janata Government was swept into power, on a tidal wave of protest against the 'Internal Emergency'. And promptly, a circular was issued in April 1977 by Mr Charan Singh, then home minister in the government of Prime Minister Morarji Desai, and letters were also addressed to chief ministers of nine states[22] asking them to recommend dissolution of state assemblies, and seek a fresh mandate from the electorate on the ground that the electorate had *virtually* rejected the candidate of the ruling party in those nine states at the Lok Sabha elections held in March 1977, *even though in respect of the legislatures in some of the nine states, their constitutionally prescribed term of five years had not yet expired.* It was a pressure tactic—a show of strength by the centre not warranted by any of the provisions of the Constitution. But as with some pressure tactics, it worked. When the constitutional validity (and propriety) of the circular was challenged by the state of Rajasthan (along with six other states) in the Supreme Court of India, the court upheld it as a direction that had to be complied with (by a majority of 6:1).[23] It was only 17 years later that the court had second thoughts. In *S. R. Bommai* (1994)[24], a bench of nine judges of the same court (now differently composed), which had previously put its imprimatur on undemocratic and unconstitutional executive action, differed from its own prior decision (of a seven-judge bench) in the case of the *State of Rajasthan*, but, alas, *too late for it to make any difference whatever, the prior decision having already worked itself out.*

- Another instance was in early 1980, when the Janata Party wave had petered out (and a mid-term poll ordered) and Mrs Indira Gandhi was voted back to power. Relying on the Supreme Court judgement in the *State of Rajasthan vs. Union of India* (of May 1977)—which was then still good law—Prime Minister Indira Gandhi instructed her home minister (then Mr Zail Singh) to draft a proclamation under Article 356 for dissolution of nine state assemblies, imposing what is commonly known as 'President's Rule' in each of the states. Mr N. Sanjeeva Reddy (who had been elected president in July 1977 and continued in office till July 1982 in succession to President Fakhruddin Ali Ahmed) did sign the proclamation '*with hesitation*' (as he later said). His explanation was: '*Given the precedent how could I say no? But I told Indira that Morarji had been wrong in principle and to dissolve again was still wrong.*'[25]

During the Internal Emergency (of June 1975 to March 1977), when many members of Parliament belonging to opposition parties were preventively detained (in prison), the government of the day rushed through Parliament with the Constitution (42nd Amendment) Bill 1976. One of its provisions substituted a new clause for Article 74(1). It now read:

> (*Quote*) There shall be a Council of Ministers with the Prime Minister at the head to aid and advise the President *who shall, in the exercise of his functions, act in accordance with such advice.* (*Unquote*)

What was previously left to a 'play-in-the-joints' was now a constitutional mandate.

After the 1976 Amendment, the role of India's head of state was intended to be confined to that of a purely titular functionary: a rubber stamp; the president must have no 'elbow room'; the president must act according to the wishes of his ministers. But when the Janata Government came to power (at the end of the Internal Emergency, after the March 1977 elections), it got passed in Parliament the Constitution 44th Amendment Act (in the year 1978)—an amendment that softened the blow. A proviso was added to the substituted Article 74(1) which read:

> Provided that the President may require the Council of Ministers to reconsider such advice, either generally or otherwise, and the President shall act in accordance with the advice tendered after such reconsideration.

It was this proviso that restored to the high office, the dignity and respectability to which India's head of state was entitled. (See the chapter on 'The President as Arbiter' in K. C. Singh's book, *The Indian President* (HarperCollins Publishers India, 2023, at pages 19 to 45).

Given below are two instances of how the proviso that had been added to Article 74(1) has worked—under the watchful eyes of conscientious heads of state.

1. *First instance:* At the time when the 10th Lok Sabha had been, all but in name, dissolved, the government under Prime Minister Narasimha Rao placed two ordinances for promulgation (under Article 123) before then President Shankar Dayal Sharma (who was president from 25 July 1992 to 25 July 1997), namely, one for shortening the period of poll campaigns (at elections) from three weeks to two weeks, and the other to extend reservations in public employment (under Article 16) to Dalits (not just Dalits who were Hindus but also Dalits professing the Christian faith). Relying on the newly-added proviso to Article 74(1) of the Constitution,

President Shankar Dayal Sharma sent back the draft ordinances to the government, with a note (dated March 19, 1996) that read:

> I would like to inform you that independent of the relative intrinsic merits of the Ordinances proposed, promulgating these Ordinances would appear to be inappropriate and contrary to the canons of Constitutional propriety in view of circumstances existing at this particular juncture.

Since nothing a president says or does in our country remains a secret, the contents of the communication of President Sharma to the prime minister became widely known. And the wisdom and sagacity of a president (even though a constitutional head of state) often trumps the political compulsions of an elected government. That is how a constitutional democracy functions, and must function. The government of the day dropped the proposed ordinances and did not press for their promulgation, worried as always, by the three opening words in the Constitution: WE THE PEOPLE.

2. The *second instance* that I recall is when Mr I. K. Gujral was prime minister (from 21 April 1997 to 19 March 1998). This was during the presidentship of Mr K. R. Narayanan (president of India from July 1997 to July 2002). The council of ministers headed by Mr Gujral had sent on to the president for promulgation a proclamation under Article 356 (Provision in case of failure of constitutional machinery in States) for the imposition, in the state of Bihar, of what is commonly known as 'President's Rule'. Acting under the proviso to Article 74(1), President Mr K. R. Narayanan returned the draft proclamation to the government for its reconsideration, giving (as he always did) elaborate reasons for his view. Again, this became widely known

> and the union government under Mr Gujral wisely refrained from reaffirming it and sending it back to the President, since if he had done so, the public (WE THE PEOPLE) would have been against him. Thus, in politics, we can see that discretion is often the better part of valour.

The above examples show that the president provides the window (perhaps the only window or opening) in that wall of separation that divides those in governance from the rest of the people.

Even after the Constitutional Amendment obliging him to act in accordance with the reconsidered advice given by his council of ministers, there is no prescription in constitutional law as to the time when the president is to act as also in the case of assent by the president under Article 111 to a bill passed by both Houses of Parliament (which is a constitutional precondition to it becoming law). No time is prescribed[26]. And at present, time appears to run in the president's favour, as an astute President Giani Zail Singh (president of India from July 1982 to July 1987) realised and used it to an advantage.

When the Post Office Bill 1987, passed by both Houses of Parliament, had been submitted to him for his assent, there was much criticism of one of its provisions, viz., *the one that permitted an interception by the government of the day of all communications through the mail.* Zail Singh paused and harkened to public opinion. He could sense the public outrage and responded to it by not giving his assent. And before demitting office, he wrote on the files that he hoped that his successor would not clear the bill.[27] As a consequence, the public outcry against the bill gathered greater momentum, and it lay unsigned even on successor-President Venkataraman's desk. The latter then expressed his own displeasure at the bill, and returned it to the prime minister of the day (Mr V. P. Singh) in January 1990. Later, the bill was once again tabled in the

Rajya Sabha, where presumably, it still remains officially, and only in name a pending bill but in actuality, a parliamentary relic.[28]

All of this illustrates how a head of state could (and should) successfully 'choke-off' unpopular legislation by doing *just nothing*, by a calculated process of deliberate inaction. This also illustrates how an unpopular and a regressive measure can presumably be successfully prevented from becoming constitutional law—by exploiting one of the deliberate silences in the Constitution (viz., as to within what time a bill passed by both Houses of Parliament should be assented to by the president). No one suggested that President Zail Singh (popularly known as 'Gianiji') had defied Parliament and no one moved for his impeachment.[29] The obvious reason of course was that Gianiji had the firm backing of public opinion.

The British Constitution is not written. But it also recognises (by convention) that the British Monarch (King or Queen)—on rare but important occasions—is entitled to intervene in public affairs in a way that may be decisive. As England's constitutional historian, Walter Bagehot, used to say, '*The greatest wisdom of a constitutional King would show itself in well-considered inaction.*'

Much later—on 25 February 2005—I personally witnessed a bit of constitutional statesmanship by President A. P. J. Abdul Kalam (president of India from 25 July 2002 to 25 July 2007) when he delivered his address to both Houses to herald in a new session of Parliament. The Constitution provides for the right of a president to address the Houses of Parliament (Article 85), and it is customarily done at the beginning of each session. It does not say who is to prepare the address, and this is determined by *constitutional convention*. Since the president acts only on the advice of his council of ministers (Article 73(1)), the address is always prepared by the government of the day (So too in the states, the governor's address is always prepared by his council of ministers). But on the morning of 25 February 2005, President Kalam made a departure—he had with him the full text of the written speech prepared by the government—

and he ultimately read it, *but he did not begin with it*. He chose to begin with a poem in Tamil, a poem composed not by the government of the day but by himself, just the previous night. It was called: 'Where Are We?'

Where are we?
Where are we now, dear friends,
In the Maha Sabha that shapes our history,
The call of heart beats of Indian people,
People ask us, people ask us;
Oh! Parliamentarians, the sculptors of Mother India,
Lead us unto light, enrich our lives.
Your righteous toil is our guiding light,
If you work hard, we all can prosper.
Like King, so the people,
Nurture great thoughts, rise up in actions,
May righteous methods be your guide;
May you all prosper ever with Almighty's grace.

The poem was a veiled criticism of parliamentarians and their erstwhile manner of functioning—politely but firmly expressed in verse. It was meant as a gentle exhortation from the people's president to the country's representatives not to walk out of the House (as they frequently did and continue to do) but to work hard and do their job. And since the president could not alter the text of his address to both Houses of Parliament, he devised the expedient of saying (what he had to say) in verse—in Tamil—translated over the headphones, and I assure you it was well-received. Once again, an instance of an enlightened head of state taking advantage of one of the great silences in the Constitution to slightly amend a Constitutional convention and exhort the people's representatives to perform their task as parliamentarians with honesty of purpose and with dedication. No one could fault him since he had expressed the sentiments of the vast majority of Indians.

The president of India, as its First Citizen, has the constitutional right, and correspondingly, the duty to interpose in public affairs of great moment, giving of his wisdom—privately, never publicly; quietly, never with fanfare. An elected president—like India's president—notionally represents the collective will of the people, and he can use it (and must use it) to temper the occasional excesses of its elected representatives.

I believe that on those very rare occasions, when Parliament (or the government) chooses to do something which the president of India believes to be unconstitutional, or even morally wrong or improper, it is the president's right and duty to intervene and to make known his views. An illustrative instance in point would be an excessive prolongation (by a proposed constitutional amendment) of the life of an existing Parliament, which would keep in office a government whose normal term has run out, a government anxious to avoid elections. Article 83 of the Constitution, therefore, provides that the House of People (the Lok Sabha) unless sooner dissolved shall continue for five years from the date appointed for its first meeting 'and no longer', and the expiration of the said period of five years shall operate as a dissolution of the House.

But how must a president as a constitutional head of state express his disapproval? It was a former Chief Justice of Pakistan who provided the answer, decades ago. He was asked by his country's president (during Pakistan's initial experiment with Western-style democracy) whether he could constitutionally refuse to give his assent to a bill passed by the National Assembly (Pakistan's first Constitution after independence was like ours—fashioned on the Westminster model). Chief Justice Munir's answer went something like this:

> (*Quote*) If you think it is a matter of the gravest importance, and you cannot in all conscience accept the measure presented to you, you can, and you must (if you are true to your oath) refuse assent—but having refused assent you must then resign; the system must go on; people will

> know why you resigned, and will sort things out with their Governments. (*Unquote*)

Pearly words of wisdom. They show how important, and how potentially effective is the great office of the president in a parliamentary democracy, but they also show that the words of the Constitution though important are never decisive, because the silences in our constitutional law speak louder than words, and with an enlightened president, this helps to maintain the balance.

The Legislature and the Executive

The president of India at the centre and the governor in the states are also an integral part of the legislature (of Parliament at the centre and of legislative assemblies in the states). Article 79 (in Part-V) states that there shall be a Parliament for the union 'which shall consist of the president and two Houses . . . to be known respectively as the Council of States (Rajya Sabha) and the House of the People' and Article 168 (in Part-VI) provides that for every state there shall be a legislature 'which shall consist of the governor and the House (or Houses) of legislature'.

The word 'president' and the word 'governor' whenever occurring in the Constitution are euphemisms. They do not, in fact, mean the president acting on his own or the governor acting on his own. Instead, they mean (at the centre) the council of ministers with the prime minister at the head who acts in the name of the president, and in the states, the council of ministers with the chief minister at the head in each state who acts in the name of the governor of the state.

The governor in each and every state is appointed by the centre, unlike the president and vice-president who are elected. The governor holds office 'at the pleasure' of the president (i.e., the president acting with the aid and advice of his council of ministers) (Articles 155 and 156), which (incidentally) helps to keep the union firmly in place. But the downside of this is that it also enables the government at the centre (if so minded and when so minded) to unduly interfere with the functioning of governments in states, especially when it is headed by a rival political party.

As was stated by a Constitution Bench of the Supreme Court (in 2018):

> (*Quote*) The Constitution makers envisaged and adopted a limited role for the President as the nominal head of the Indian State and imposed sanctions on his or her constitutional authority by making them bound by the decisions of the Council of Ministers generally. A similar role was adopted for the Governor in the States.
>
> Collective responsibility under our Constitution is based on a 'slightly modified version' of the British cabinet system. There is a direct relationship between collective responsibility and the form of government envisaged by the Constitution. The President was designated as the titular head of Government. *The founding fathers and mothers*[30] *of the Constitution adopted the convention which made the President generally bound by the advice of the Council of Ministers. (Unquote)*

(see *NCT of Delhi vs. Union of India, 2018 (8) SCC 501, at pages 674 and 676).*

Likewise, when Article 53(3) states that the supreme command of the defence forces of the union 'shall be vested in the president', it is purely ceremonial; the actual command of the defence forces is (and remains with) the defence minister, who along with other members of the council of ministers, (with the prime minister at the head) is 'collectively responsible' to the House of People (i.e., the Lok Sabha) (Article 74).

And Article 123 in Part-V and Article 213 in Part-VI confer on the president and on the governor in each state (executive heads) legislative functions as well.

In India, the power to promulgate ordinances (a legislative power) has been deliberately conferred on the chief executive at the centre (Article 123) and on the governor (the chief executive) in the states (Article 213) and is to be exercised only when Parliament or state legislatures are in recess (i.e., not in session). In England, the executive has no such power to legislate by ordinance except when a state of emergency is declared. And the executive has no independent power of legislation in any other country in the Commonwealth, not even in Ireland under the Irish Constitution, from which many parts of India's Constitution have been drawn. Even the US President (the most powerful head of state in a democracy) does not possess this power. This law-making power of the executive (by means of ordinances) had its origin in the first Constitution Act of British India, viz., the Government of India Act, 1935, from which the relevant provision was lifted into India's Constitution.

The ordinance-making provisions establish—at the very start—a tilt in the balance of powers and functions in India's Constitution. They emphasise that it is the executive branch which is in the driving seat of government. And again, as if to stress the dominance of the executive, there is no period prescribed in our Constitution for the duration of sessions of Parliament or of state legislatures; that is left entirely to the elected governments (both at the centre and in the states) as to when the Houses of Parliament and the legislatures in the state are to be summoned—and for how long. It is determined by the executive (the council of ministers with the prime minister at the head).

India's Constitution thus envisages—both at the centre as well as in the states—an *all-powerful executive* with the prime minister and his council of ministers (at the centre) and the chief minister and his council of ministers (in the states). It is they who set the agenda for all legislative business when the elected bodies are not in session (for several months each year). It is *they* who are empowered to make laws (through ordinances) and take all executive action pertaining to subjects within their legislative competence.

But the executive under our Constitution is like a full-blown balloon; it is dependent—for the air within it—on the elected legislatures: the House of the People at the centre and the state assemblies in the states. The executive remains omnipotent only so long as the council of ministers retain the confidence of the elected representatives (in the Lok Sabha at the centre and in the legislative assembly in the states) and once that is lost, the air in the balloon gets deflated, and the government has to resign or call fresh elections; which is the essence of *ministerial responsibility*. And it is ministerial responsibility that lies at the heart of the parliamentary form of government.

Again, subject to ministerial responsibility to the elected body, the executive (i.e., the council of ministers) can do all that the legislature can do, as had been highlighted within a few years of India's Constitution being enacted. In *Rai Sahib Ram Jawaya Kapur And Ors. Vs. The State of Punjab* (1955 2 SCR 225 = AIR 1955 SC 549), Chief Justice B. K. Mukerjea, speaking for a Constitution Bench of five judges (and therefore authoritative), had said that the Indian Constitution did not recognise the doctrine of separation of powers *in its absolute rigidity*. 'Our Constitution though federal in its structure,' he said, 'is modelled on the British Parliamentary system where the executive is deemed to have the primary responsibility for the formulation of governmental policy and its transmission into law-though the condition precedent to the exercise of this responsibility is in the executive retaining the confidence of the legislative branch of the state. The executive function comprises both the determination of the policy as well as carrying it into execution.' In *Rai Sahib Ram Jawaya Kapur* case (1955)[31], it was pointed out that Articles 73 and 162 of the Constitution expressly declare that the executive power of the union (and the executive power of the state) extends to matters with respect to which Parliament and state legislatures respectively have the power to make laws. *Hence, there is no necessity at all for enacted law to support executive action, either at the centre or in the states.*

But howsoever powerful the executive—and it is extraordinarily powerful particularly at the centre—the purse strings are controlled by Parliament, and not by the executive. All revenues received by the Government of India and all other monies received by and on behalf of the Government of India must go into a Consolidated Fund of India (Article 114) and likewise in the states (Article 204). And no monies can be withdrawn from the Consolidated Fund of India (or firm out of the Consolidated Fund of a state) except under appropriation made by law—but only *enacted* law, which means this cannot be done by ordinance, either by the president at the centre or by the governor in the states (Articles 114(3) and 204(3))[32]. Expenses of government can only be met by means of a bill introduced in the elected House of the People in Parliament (and in the elected legislative assembly in the state) and such a bill must provide for the appropriation of money from out of the Consolidated Fund (of India or of the state) and the bill has to be passed by the people's elected representatives. *So, the true reason why Parliament meets and conducts union government business, and state legislatures meet and conduct state government business, is primarily because the control of the purse strings is with the elected representatives of the people and not with the executive. This is one of the hallmarks of a parliamentary system of government.*

Purse strings apart, the power of the executive to determine most of what Parliament enacts is a fact of modern political history—true not only in India but also in parliamentary systems of government elsewhere. Lord Hailsham[33], many years after retirement from his high office as Lord Chancellor, coined a new word for the British Parliament. He described it as not 'Legislature' but *'Executature'—a legislative body under the control of the executive.* This is not an exaggerated description.

Council of Ministers

Ministerial power today is parliamentary power and real parliamentary power lies with the ministers. Hardly any bill introduced by a private member ever becomes law during the 50 to 100 day sessions of Parliament each year. The Lok Sabha in 2019 met for 57 days, 56 days in 2020, 59 days in 2021, and in 2022, for 56 days (figures given by the head of PRS Legislative Research in the *Hindustan Times* of 2 January 2023). Mondays to Thursdays and half of Fridays are taken up with government business, and Friday afternoon is reserved for private members' bills. But hardly any bill introduced by a private member is passed. The motions are gone through as a form of a debating exercise in order to draw the attention of the government of the day to some glaring inadequacies in existing laws. Bills continue to be drafted by bureaucrats in accordance with the wishes of the ministers. They are introduced and shepherded through Parliament by the concerned ministers. And not too much happens in their passage through Parliament, except when bills are referred to committees when a more detailed scrutiny is made. Substantive amendments are rare exceptions and are passed only because the minister accepts them or because the amendment represents a compromise across the political party spectrum. The theory that governments put into execution what legislation has confided to it is good only in theory; In practice, it is the government that makes laws, and through its majority requires the Houses of Parliament to consent to them. Long ago, in the year 1867, Walter Bagehot, the shrewd political analyst of his age, wrote, that:

> (*Quote*) The efficient secret of the English Constitution may be described as the close union, the nearly complete fusion, of the executive and legislative powers. No doubt by the traditional theory, as it exists in all the books, the goodness of our Constitution consists in the entire separation of the legislative and executive authorities, but in truth, its merit consists in their singular approximation. The connecting link is the cabinet. By that new word we mean a committee of the legislative body selected to be the executive body. The legislature has many committees, but this is its greatest.[34] (*Unquote*)

This is an accurate description of India's Constitution—both in theory and in practice.

That Parliament has wishes to which it requires governments to conform is a myth, not justified by the working experience of a parliamentary system of government. It is governments that have wishes and policies to which, through their majority, they require Parliament to conform. Then again by authorisation under statute, ministers and executives and bureaucrats frequently legislate—by proxy: *delegatus non potest delegare* (a delegated authority cannot again delegate to others) remains only in the books as an ancient Latin maxim. Courts generally find sufficient reason to uphold nearly all forms of delegated legislation.

The Union Judiciary

Next in Part-V comes *the Union Judiciary*—Articles 124 to 146.

This is where the balance shifts again, but like the glaciers in the Himalayas, the shift is hardly visible. It is the place where the 'Executature' (to use Lord Hailsham's phrase) is called to account and asked to justify its action under the law. The imbalance gets balanced—even if only on a case-to-case basis—by the excesses of administrative action being judicially corrected and executive lapses being prodded into inaction by judicial diktat.

The most significant feature of the Constitution of India then is the area extent and nature of the jurisdiction of India's Supreme Court. It is all-pervasive. Laws enacted by India's Parliament and by state legislatures—all executive action taken in the name of the president at the centre—and in the name of the governor in the states are finally and authoritatively interpreted and corrected by the courts (the high courts and ultimately, the Supreme Court). The law declared by the Supreme Court of India is binding (under the Constitution) on all courts and authorities in the country but not on the Supreme Court itself. This was so held on a purposive interpretation of Article 141[35] in a 1955 judgement of a Constitution Bench of the Supreme Court. In *Bengal Immunity vs. State of Bihar* (AIR 1955 SC 661) (bench of five judges), it was stated:

> Article 141, which lays down that the law declared by the Supreme Court shall be binding on all courts within the territory of India, *quite obviously* refers to Courts other than the Supreme Court.

Not obvious—but deliberately purposive. And only in the interests of the future development of constitutional law.

There is virtually no area of legislative or executive activity that is beyond the highest court's scrutiny. It is the ultimate court of appeal in all civil and criminal cases. Its writ extends to all two million square miles of Indian territory, and over its now considerably more than 1417 million inhabitants (as estimated in the year 2022). India was far more manageable—and better governable—in 1950 when the Constitution was enacted with only 330 million people!

The Supreme Court of India

Article 124(1) in the Constitution of India as enacted provided that there shall be a Supreme Court of India "consisting of a Chief Justice of India and until Parliament by law prescribes a larger number of not more than seven other Judges". By a series of Supreme Court Number of Judges Amendment Acts the number of Judges in India's Supreme Court has increased periodically and today stands at THIRTY-FOUR Judges – unlike the Supreme Court of the USA: which originally consisted of six Justices – and after the year 1790 the total number of Justices changed six times before arriving at the current total of NINE—from the year 1869. There have been seventeen Chief Justices in the history of the U.S. Supreme Court, since the first Chief Justice John Jay in 1789. The current Chief Justice John Roberts has been in office since 2005.

In India since 1950 there have been Fifty Chief Justices with India's first Chief Justice being Sir Harilal Kania. The current Chief Justice of India India's 50th Chief Justice, Justice D.Y. Chandrachud assumed office in November, 2022.

It was in the 1880s that Chief Justice Melville Fuller of the US Supreme Court instituted the tradition of the judicial handshake – a tradition that exists even today when the Nine Justices of the Supreme Court of the U.S. gather together to go on the bench or to meet in conference: each justice shakes the hands of the other Eight Justices – a tradition that is followed "to remind the justices that despite their differences all members of the Court share a unity of purpose". (See Oxford Companion of the Supreme Court of the U.S.) (Oxford University Press, Second Edition page 1153). There is no such tradition in India – though I do recall that Chief Justice Y.V. Chandrachud (CJI from 1978-1985) after concluding each day's hearing in Court, and on the Judges leaving the Court-room, would courteously express his thanks to each one of his colleagues who sat with him that day!.

The Supreme Court of India supervises the decisions not only of the high courts in the states (there are 22 high courts for the

28 states and nine union territories) but also over all tribunals (central and state) functioning in different parts of India. And it does this through its extraordinary jurisdiction conferred by Article 136[36]—of granting special leave to appeal from any decision or order of any court or tribunal in the country. The Supreme Court of India and the high courts in the states are also empowered by the Constitution to issue all manner of writs, orders, and directions not only for the enforcement of a wide range of fundamental rights guaranteed under Part-III of the Constitution (Article 32) but also in addition 'for any other purpose' (Article 226).

The Supreme Court is also invested with a special advisory jurisdiction (Article 143)[37] to answer questions of law or of fact of public importance that may be referred to it by the president of India, i.e., in effect, by the central government—a jurisdiction not invoked, especially when the centre wants to pass on to judges a 'hot political potato'. But the court is aware of this as well. It is not bound to answer a presidential reference, and it may respectfully decline to do so, as it did in the now famous reference of the Ayodhya dispute. The question posed to the court by the executive in the presidential reference was:

> Whether a Hindu temple or any Hindu religious structure existed prior to the construction of the Ram Janmabhoomi-Babri Masjid (including the premises of the inner and outer courtyards of such structure) in the area on which the structure stood?

The Constitution Bench of five judges—though divided (3:2) on the constitutional validity of the Act of Parliament known as The Acquisition of Certain Area at Ayodhya Act, 1993—were unanimous in (respectfully) declining to answer the reference.[38]

At the inaugural sitting of India's Supreme Court in New Delhi on 28 January 1950, India's first Chief Justice, Sir Harilal Kania had said that the foremost task of the judges would be to interpret the Constitution, but 'in no narrow spirit' and 'with an enlightened liberality', and not in 'a spirit of formal or barren legalism'. The reported judgements of the court interpreting the Constitution over the last seventy-odd years have been—*generally speaking*—in tune with the course charted out for it by India's first Chief Justice. '*Generally speaking*', because, as in the life or any institution, the Supreme Court too has had its dark moments, like during the 19-month period of the Internal Emergency of June 1975, which came to be known (because of its unpopularity) as 'the Phoney Emergency'. 'Phoney' also because the Emergency, was contrived, the executive power to declare it (under Article 352) was invoked only to rescue a prime minister who had lost an election petition filed against her in the Allahabad High Court. During that so-called Internal Emergency (from 26 June 1975 to March 1977), fundamental rights were suspended, draconian laws were enacted, and judges in the highest court (with a few notable exceptions) buckled under the fiats of a seemingly omnipotent executive. However, in the period after March 1977 (when the Emergency was lifted with a change of government at the centre), there emerged a remarkable resurgence of enlightened liberalism. In retrospect, the years after Mach 1977 have been the best years of the court. One of the unintended benefits of the Emergency regime was the spurt in judicial activism and intervention, and an enlargement of the scope of judicial review. In one decision after another, since March 1977, the court has built around itself (step-by-step, case-by-case) a virtually impregnable fortress of judicial inviolability.

In the early years of the working of India's Constitution, the Supreme Court had consistently held that whatever was intended by the framers of the Constitution was expressed in the language used in its provisions and that there was no scope for intendment, and the court eschewed a positivist approach when interpreting constitutional provisions. No attempt was made to ferret into the crevices of the Constitution, to plumb the depths of its silences so as to ascertain a judge-oriented meaning. That was to come only in later years, when the confidence of the court in the wisdom of the legislatures had been consistently weakened, and *when the legal presumption of executive acts being regularly performed had worn thin.*[39] The late 1970s and early 1980s marked a turning point in the way in which the court looked at and read the Constitution. Consistent legislative and executive encroachments on judicial power ultimately alerted the court to its true role—that *of the conscience keeper of the nation*. It was only after this realisation that the judges in the highest court embarked on a 'broadly expansive' interpretation of the constitutional provisions.

The first notable example of this was in the matter of the judicial review of Constitutional amendments—Amendment of the Constitution (Article 368) and the Doctrine of Basic Structure.

In the first twenty-odd years of the promulgation of India's Constitution, India's Supreme Court faced a dilemma. The higher judiciary (the Supreme Court and high courts in the states) was empowered under the Constitution to invalidate not only executive orders but also legislative enactments that violated any part of the fundamental rights guaranteed in Part-III of the Constitution (Article 13(1) and (2)), but whether courts were also empowered to adjudicate on the validity of constitutional amendments passed with the requisite special majority where the procedure prescribed in Article 368—*Power of Parliament to amend the Constitution and the procedure therefore*—had been followed, was something on which the Constitution was silent. With one single political party (the Congress Party) consistently returned to power at each general election since 1952 and returned with a two-thirds majority (at least up to 1989)[40], the judges of the Supreme Court kept plumbing the depths of silence in the world's longest Constitution, searching for *some* limitation on the amending power.

As to *how* and *when* they found it is set out below:

(a) The background to the Constitution First Amendment Act, 1951 passed by the Constituent Assembly, acting as India's Provisional Parliament, was that the Congress Party, commanding as it did a comfortable majority of seats both in Parliament and in several state legislatures, had carried out certain measures of agrarian reform in the states by enacting legislation in the form of Zamindari Abolition Acts.[41] The validity of these Acts came to be challenged in writ petitions filed in the high courts under Article 226 of the Constitution on the ground that they contravened the Fundamental Rights conferred by Part-III of the Constitution, including the Fundamental Right to Equality (Article 14) as well as the Fundamental Right to Property (Article 31), viz., the right to insist that property acquired by the state could only be so acquired for a *public purpose and only on payment of just compensation*. The High Court of Patna had held that the Bihar (Abolition of Zamindari) Act was unconstitutional, but the High Courts of Allahabad and Nagpur had upheld the validity of the corresponding abolition-of-zamindari; laws enacted by the states of Uttar Pradesh and Madhya Pradesh (and appeals from each of those decisions were pending in the Supreme Court).

(b) To put an end to all this litigation and to remedy what the Union Government considered to be '*certain defects brought to light in the working of the Constitution*', the Constitution First Amendment Bill was introduced, and ultimately passed, by an overwhelming majority of India's 'Provisional Parliament'. Whilst Article 31A (saving of laws providing for the acquisition of estates, etc.) protected land reform laws from attack under Article 14, as well as under Article 19(1)(f) (the fundamental right to hold and dispose of property), and Article 31 (Right to Property), Article 31B was also introduced (and passed) as an all-embracing exception to the entire chapter on Fundamental Rights.[42]

(c) Reacting to the addition of Articles 31A (saving of laws providing for the acquisition of estates, etc.) and Article 31B (validation of laws placed in the Ninth Schedule of the Constitution), the zamindars (landlords of vast tracts of land in different parts of India) filed petitions in the Supreme Court (under Article 32) challenging the provisions of the Constitution 1st Amendment Act, 1951 as *'unconstitutional and void'*. Five justices of the Supreme Court of India—India's first Chief Justice Sir Harilal Kania presiding over the Constitution Bench—in *Shankari Prasad vs. Union of India* (1951)—found little difficulty in deciding the matter. In a brief but unanimous judgement,[43] the court held that *'to make a law which contravenes the Constitution constitutionally valid is a matter of constitutional amendment and as such falls within the exclusive power of Parliament'*. The petitions filed by the zamindars were dismissed.

(d) But, as written constitutions grow in age, those whose duty it is to interpret them get wiser—and more circumspect. 14 years after *Shankari Prasad* (1951), several writ petitions (including one titled: *Sajjan Singh vs. State of Rajasthan* (1965) were filed challenging (on this occasion) the constitutional validity of the Constitution (17th) Amendment Act 1965. This latter Act had placed (pursuant to the enabling provisions of Article 31B) several state laws in the Ninth Schedule, in order to make them valid even if they contravened the provisions of the Fundamental Rights Chapter, including the Right to Equality and the Fundamental Right to Property. Once again, a Constitution Bench of five justices (Chief

Justice P. B. Gajendragadkar now presiding) dismissed the writ petitions. Three of the judges on the bench (the Chief Justice and justices K. N. Wanchoo and Justice Raghubar Dayal) held that the power of amendment was plenary and included the power to take away or amend all or any of the fundamental rights guaranteed in Part-III of the Constitution.[44] Two of the remaining justices on the bench were not so sure, although they agreed that the petitions deserved to be dismissed (on the basis of the earlier Constitution Bench decision of the court in *Shankari Prasad* (1951). *They also gave reasons for their doubts*. Justice Hidayatullah said that Article 368 did not give the power to amend *any* provision of the Constitution and added that 'the Constitution gives so many assurances in Part-III that it would be difficult to think that they were the playthings of a special majority'. And Justice Mudholkar stated that he would prefer to reserve his opinion as to whether the previous decision in *Shankari Prasad* (1951) was right ('I do not regard what this court has held in that case as the last word'). He also went on to say that so long as the Preamble of the Constitution stood unamended, it would have to be considered whether the power to amend could be exercised with respect to any of 'the basic features of the Constitution'. (Almost a premonition of the later 1973 majority decision in *Kesavananda Bharati* (7:6))

(e) Justice K. Subba Rao of the Supreme Court of India had liberal views on fundamental rights. He believed that it was an oxymoron to say that fundamental rights could ever be taken away or abridged. 'How could anything described as "fundamental" in the Constitution itself be ever taken away or abridged by an amendment to it?' he often queried. So, when Justice K. Subba Rao assumed the office of Chief Justice of India in 1966, citizens were emboldened to file writ petitions (once again) challenging the validity of, viz., the Constitution First Amendment Act 1951 (which had introduced Article 31A and 31B in the Constitution), and the Constitution Fourth Amendment Act, 1955[45] (amending Articles 31A and adding more central and state Acts in the Ninth Schedule) as also the provisions of the Constitution Seventeenth Amendment Act 1964 (that added as many as 43 central and state laws in the Ninth Schedule). The principal writ petition filed under Article 32 *(Golaknath vs. State of Punjab*[46]*)*, when presented to a bench presided over by Chief Justice K. Subba Rao, was admitted and straightway referred to a larger bench of eleven justices for final disposal.

(f) The bench decision of eleven judges in *Golak Nath* held that there was nothing in the Constitution that prevented the Supreme Court from departing from a previous decision of its own if it was satisfied with its error and its baneful effect on the general interest of the public. It also held (by a narrow majority of 6:5) that an amendment of the Constitution was 'law' within the meaning of Article 13 of the Constitution, and that if a 'law', *including an amendment to the Constitution*, took away or abridged the rights conferred by Part-III, or any part thereof, it was void under Article 13(2) of the Constitution. In *Golaknath,* a majority of six justices (in a bench of eleven judges) denied to Parliament the right to take away or abridge any of the fundamental rights in Part-III of the Constitution, in the future since (according to the majority) even amending the Constitution by an Act of Parliament (in its constituent capacity) was 'law' under Article 13. *At the same time, all eleven judges upheld the constitutional validity of the Constitution First Amendment Act of 1951, the Constitution Fourth Amendment Act of 1955, and Constitution Seventh Amendment Act of 1964 (even though according to the majority of justices (6:5), these enactments abridged fundamental rights) only because of the doctrine of stare decisis, i.e., the law declared in earlier decisions of the Supreme Court of India in* Shankari Prasad *(1951) and in* Sajjan Singh *(1965).*

(g) At first, the reaction in Parliament to the majority decision in *Golak Nath* (1967) was one of surprise. After the decision in the *Privy Purse* case (1970), when the Supreme Court in a bench decision of eleven justices (10:1) had struck down as invalid a presidential order abolishing the titles of erstwhile princes of the former Indian states together with their privy purses,[47] Mrs Gandhi as prime minister had advised the president (somewhat in pique) to dissolve the Fourth Lok Sabha and call for general elections. And in the elections of March 1971, Mrs Gandhi and her Congress Party came back to power with an even larger majority than before. And the mood of the newly constituted Parliament now changed—*from one of surprise to one of defiance.*

In a somewhat delayed response to the Supreme Court's majority decision in *Golak Nath* (1967), the newly elected Parliament passed, in quick succession, the following laws amending the Constitution:

- The Constitution (24th) Amendment Act 1971: an Act to enable Parliament in its constituent power to amend all and any part of the Constitution including the chapter relating to Fundamental Rights and also providing that nothing in Article 13 shall apply to any amendment of the Constitution.
- The Constitution (25th) Amendment Act 1971 which introduced Article 31C to provide in the Constitution that no law giving effect to the policy of the State towards securing the principles specified in Clause (b) or Clause (c) of Article 39 shall be deemed

to be void on the ground that it is inconsistent with or takes away or abridges any of the rights conferred by Articles 14, 19, or 31.

- The Constitution (29th) Amendment Act, 1972: an Act which added two State enactments in the Ninth Schedule, parts of which had been previously struck down by the High Court of Kerala, and the High Court decision had been already upheld in the Supreme Court of India.

The Supreme Court's response to this fresh batch of constitutional amendments was to refer the challenges (to these constitutional amendments)—this time to a bench of thirteen judges.

In the case decided in April 1973,[48] (a bench of thirteen judges), one of the justices (delivering his judgement in that case) said:

> The largest bench sat for the longest time to decide issues of grave moment not only to the future of this country but to the future of democracy itself.

The case was titled *His Holiness Kesavananda Bharati vs. State of Kerala*[49], but it is better known as *'Kesavananda'* or as *'the Fundamental Rights Case'*. The bench of thirteen judges was sharply divided. Six judges (viz., justices A. N. Ray, P. Jaganmohan Reddy, D. G. Palekar, K. M. Mathew, M. H. Beg, S. N. Dwivedi, and Y. V. Chandrachud) held that the power of amendment of the Constitution conferred by Article 368 was wide and unfettered and it reached every part and every provision of the Constitution including the chapter on fundamental rights. Six other Justices (viz., Chief Justice S. M. Sikri and justices J. M. Shelat, K. S. Hegde, A. N. Grover, and A. K. Mukherjea) held that the power of amendment was limited, *but they were not all agreed on the extent of such limitation.* The court was thus evenly divided. But it was Justice H. R. Khanna's judgement that tilted the balance. (The great Justice H. R. Khanna whose portrait hangs in Court No.2, where he sat till he was superseded—the 'Second Supersession'—in January 1977, by not being appointed Chief Justice of India though the next senior-most on the bench)[50]

Justice H. R. Khanna held that the power of amendment under Article 368 was plenary, that it included the power to amend various articles of the Constitution, and that it was not fettered by any provision in Part-III (the Fundamental Rights Chapter), that no fundamental right (only because it was 'fundamental') could claim immunity from the amending process, and that the power to amend included within itself the power to add, alter, or repeal the various articles of the Constitution. *But he also held (and this is now the ratio in the Fundamental Rights case) the power to amend under Article 368, wide as it was, did not include the power to abrogate the Constitution or to alter its basic structure or framework.*

A summary of the judgement of the special bench of thirteen justices in *Keshvananda Bharti* was issued after the judgement had been delivered. It is reproduced only in the Official Law Reports in 1973 (Suppl.) SCR 1, and the summary was signed only by Chief Justice S. M. Sikri and justices J. M. Shelat, K. S. Hegde, A. N. Grover, P. Jaganmohan Reddy, D. G. Palekar, H. R. Khanna, A. K. Mukherjea, and Y. V. Chandrachud. In the summary, it was recorded (inter alia, on pages 1001-1002):

> *(2) Article 368 does not enable Parliament to alter the basic structure or framework of the Constitution.*

Two of the justices who had signed the summary—Justice D. G. Palekar and Justice Y. V. Chandrachud—were judges who did not agree with the views of the majority of seven judges (viz., Justices S. M. Sikri, J. M. Shelat, A. N. Grover, K. S. Hegde,

A. K. Mukherjea, P. Jaganmohan Reddy, and H. R. Khanna). They signed the summary acknowledging that it was in fact the majority view. But four of the remaining justices (A. N. Ray, K. K. Mathew, M. H. Beg, and S. N. Dwivedi) did not sign the 'summary'—an event that prompted some lawyers as well as academics to initially opine that the summary did not and could not truly reflect the majority decision. But a later decision of 1993 by a Constitution Bench of five judges put an end to the controversy. In *Raghunathrao Ganpatrao vs. Union of India* (AIR 1993 SC 1267), in a unanimous Constitution Bench decision of five justices, the entire summary of conclusions (including paragraphs (2) quoted above) has been reproduced verbatim as recording correctly what was decided in *Kesavananda Bharti* (1973).

Judge Benjamin Cardozo (1870-1938) distinguished U.S. Supreme Court Judge had famously said:

> **"the Power to declare the law carries with it the power and within limits the duty to make law where none exists; the Judge legislates (but) only between gaps"**

In reading implied limitations in the amending power, India's Supreme Court had certainly made new law. The narrow majority view (7:6) in *Kesavananda* (1973) was criticised as an assertion of naked political power in the guise of judicial interpretation. Frankly, it was, it upset the balance of powers in the Constitution. By propounding the basic structure theory, the guardians of the Constitution (it was said) had at one bound become guardians over the Constitution. Constitutional adjudicators had assumed the role of constitutional governors. Again, the criticism had much validity. With the Congress Party having an overwhelming majority in Parliament, the country might have moved into a state of grave constitutional crisis. But then fate intervened.

The wheel of fortune turned, almost by a fortuitous event, *in the court's favour*. Prime Minister Indira Gandhi lost the election petition filed against her in the Allahabad High Court in June 1975; the extraordinary had happened: a prime minister in office with a commanding majority in Parliament had been unseated. She filed an appeal in the Supreme Court. And whilst her appeal in the Supreme Court of India was pending, the Constitution Thirty-Ninth Amendment Bill, 1975, was hastily drafted—aided and abetted by prominent lawyers—and even more hastily passed; all in three days in August of that fateful year when Mrs Gandhi's appeal was scheduled to be heard by the court. The power to amend the Constitution was invoked by Parliament actually to strike out an item listed for final hearing (on 12 August 1975) before the Supreme Court, viz., the Election Appeal of Mrs Gandhi. *It surprised many that the Constitution Thirty-Ninth Amendment Act, 1975 had actually provided*—in a new Article 329A—six clauses as follows:

- The first three clauses of Article 329A dealt with future elections to Parliament of persons holding the office of prime minister or speaker at the time of the election, or who were appointed to these offices after their elections to Parliament. They were aimed at depriving the courts of their jurisdiction to try election petitions in which the election of the prime minister or of the speaker was challenged.
- *The fourth clause (Clause (4) of Article 329A) completely freed the disputed election of Prime Minister Indira Gandhi from the restraints of all election laws.* It declared such an election valid notwithstanding any judgement.
- The fifth clause ordered that any appeal or cross-appeal pending before the Supreme Court shall be disposed of on the assumption that the judgement under appeal was void, and that the findings contained in the judgement never had any existence in the eye of law, and that the election declared void by the judgement of the Allahabad High Court would continue to be valid in all respects.

- And Clause (6) provided that Article 329A shall have precedence over the rest of the Constitution.
- It was principally the constitutional validity of the fourth clause that had been contested by the respondents in the Supreme Court of India.

With the addition of Article 329A, it was obvious that the judgement of Justice Sinha of the Allahabad High Court (in the election petition) was attempted to be reversed not by a decision of the highest court but by a constitutional amendment; an attempt to somehow preempt the Supreme Court from deciding Mrs Gandhi's election appeal. *Fortunately, in* Indira Gandhi *vs.* Raj Narain/Raj Narain vs. Indira Gandhi *(1975 Supp. SCC page 1 = AIR 1975 SC page 1590), the court resisted the crude attempt. Mrs Gandhi's election appeal in the Supreme Court was ultimately decided unanimously in her favour (on the merits of the election appeal) but not before holding Article 329A(4) to be unconstitutional and void.* As for the rest of the clauses (the first three clauses and the fifth and sixth clauses) in Article 329(A), they were later repealed by India's Parliament by the Constitution Forty-Fourth Amendment Act, 1978 (w.e.f. 20 June 1979). ***Indira Gandhi vs. Raj Narain/Raj Narain vs. Indira Gandhi***[51] **(1975) helped to cement the foundation that was laid down (by a narrow majority) in *Kesavananda* (1973)—viz. the basic structure theory.**

The *post-mortem*—Before the judgement of 7th November 1975 in *Indira Gandhi vs. Raj Narain/Raj Narain vs. Indira Gandhi* was handed down, the Union of India had filed an application for a reconsideration of *Kesavananda Bharati's* case. But it proved abortive and ended as a 'damp squib'[52]. A bench of thirteen judges was specially constituted on 10 November 1975 (by then Chief Justice A. N. Ray) for considering—inter alia—*as to whether the power of amendment of the Constitution was restricted by the theory of basic structure and framework as propounded in Kesavananda Bharati case (1973).* And this new bench of thirteen judges consisted of the following judges, viz., Chief Justice A. N. Ray and justices H. R. Khanna, K. K. Mathew, M. H. Beg, Y. V. Chandrachud, P. N. Bhagwati, V. R. Krishna Iyer, P. K. Goswami, R. S. Sarkaria, A. C. Gupta, N. L. Untwalia, M. Fazl Ali, and P. N. Singhal)—the last eight judges having been appointed to the Supreme Court of India after the decision in *Kesavananda* (1973). The new bench of thirteen judges assembled on 10 November 1975, when an objection was raised to the union government's application for reconsideration of *Kesavananda's* case on the ground that no case had been made out for such reconsideration. Arguments by Counsel N. A. Palkhivala were heard for two entire days and ultimately, on the morning of 12 November 1975, as soon as the bench of thirteen judges again reassembled, Chief Justice Ray curtly announced in open court that the bench was dissolved. All this has been recorded not in any law report since there was no decision in the case but by India's constitutional historian, Mr H. M. Seervai, in his book: *Constitutional Law of India* (Vol. 2) 4th edition on page 1957 with the following pertinent comment:

> (*Quote*) This sequence of events would suggest that Ray CJ realised, before 10 November 1975, that his brother judges in the election case were not likely to depart from the theory of the basic structure; and it would also suggest that the two days' hearing before the bench of thirteen judges satisfied him that the doctrine of the basic structure would not be reconsidered by the present bench.[53] (*Unquote*)

By yet another decision of a bench of five judges in *Minerva Mills vs. Union of India* (AIR 1980, SC 1789), and finally, and irrevocably, by a bench decision of nine justices in *I. R. Coelho vs. State of Tamil Nadu* (AIR 2007, SC 861)[54], the basic structure theory was unanimously reaffirmed.

Ronald Dworkin (1931–2013)—renowned academic jurist—had a theory about the legitimacy of judicial governance. *Present-day judges, he had said, who may have had nothing to do with the written Constitution when it was framed, by reason of their position as judges have become—and must act like—partners with the framers of the Constitution in an ongoing project (since it is, and always will be, an ongoing project), viz., to interpret a historical document in the best possible light.*[55]

In *Indira Gandhi vs. Raj Narain* (1975), a Constitution Bench of the Supreme Court had read the Constitution of India 'in the best possible light'. It had held—under compulsion of a monstrous law—that free and fair elections were a fundamental part of the Constitution and so fundamental as to be beyond the reach of the amending power. This decision constitutes the high-water mark in the assertion of the court's judicial power, in the teeth of a very determined majoritarian regime. If the pernicious fourth clause of the Thirty-Ninth Constitution Amendment had been upheld, Indian democracy would not have long survived.

The basic structure theory has now come to stay—because of political compulsions—and also because of parliamentary acquiescence.

At first, for a continuous period of 25 years—since March 1977 till 2014—no single political party in India had secured a two-thirds representation in Parliament nor anything approximating to it (which was and is a necessary requirement for the passage in Parliament of each and every constitutional amendment). After 2014, however, when INDIA did have a majoritarian government (and from 2019 a super-majoritarian government) at the centre, those in power were moved by the fact that even Parliament had put its imprimatur on the *basic structure theory*. The Constitution Forty-Fourth Amendment Act, 1978, passed by Parliament—in its constitution-amending capacity—expressly provided that the fundamental right guaranteed by Article 20 (that no person can be convicted of an offence except for violation of a law in force at the time of the offence, that no person could be prosecuted and punished for the same offence more than once, and that no person accused of an offence could be compelled to be a witness against himself) and the fundamental right under Article 21 (fundamental right to life and liberty) *could never be suspended even during an emergency, since the rights conferred by Articles 20 and 21 were basic to the Constitutional framework.*

In the period after 1973/1975, the basic structure theory has not been disturbed. *it* has been kept in place for an additional reason as well: *by not being invoked by the judges too often,* and also, by not being permitted to be invoked for striking down ordinary legislation by Parliament. In *Bhim Singh vs. Union of India* (bench of five judges), Justice Krishna Iyer (for the majority) declared (1981 (1) SCC 166) on page 186 that:

> 20. The question of a basic structure being breached cannot arise when we examine the vires of an ordinary legislation as distinguished from a constitutional amendment.

And it was more authoritatively held in *Kuldip Nayar vs. Union of India*—2006 (7) SCC 1—(where a bench of five judges) (para 107) said:

> The challenge to a law made, within its legislative competence, by Parliament on the ground of violation of the basic structure of the Constitution is thus not available.

Prof. Granville Austin has written (in his book, *Working a Democratic Constitution: The Indian Experience*) that the non-event (the abortive attempt at a post-mortem of *Kesavananda* (1973)) was when the court definitively asserted and retained to itself the custody and control of the Constitution, which in the 1970s was in grave danger of being taken over by a majoritarian Parliament.

Apart from the decision in *Indira Gandhi vs. Raj Narain* (1975), the basic structure theory has been so far invoked by the Supreme Court of India to *strike down constitutional amendments* in the following cases:

(i) In *P. Sambamurthy & Anr. vs. State of Andhra Pradesh* (1987 (1) SCC 362), a Constitution Bench of five judges held that a provision introduced in the Constitution (by way of amendment) conferring power on a state government to modify or annul a final order of an administrative tribunal was violative of the basic structure doctrine since it was against the basic concept of justice stated in the Preamble. Accordingly, the offending provision in Article 371D(5) along with the proviso was declared to be unconstitutional and void.

(ii) Ten years later, in *L. Chandra Kumar vs. Union of India* (AIR 1997 SC 1125), a Constitution Bench of seven judges held that some of the clauses of Article 323A and Article 323B (inserted by the Constitution (42nd) Amendment Act, 1976) were invalid (as violating the basic structure of the Constitution) in so far as they excluded the jurisdiction of the Supreme Court of India under Article 32 of the Constitution and the jurisdiction of high courts (under Articles 226 and 227 of the Constitution) in respect of decisions given by administrative tribunals set up under Article 323A. In *L. Chandra Kumar* (1997), it was also stated as under:

> We also hold that the power vested in the High Courts to exercise judicial superintendence over the decisions of all Courts and Tribunals within their respective jurisdictions is also part of the basic structure of the Constitution. This is because where the High Courts are divested of all other judicial functions apart from that of constitutional interpretation, is equally to be avoided. (Page 231)

> . . . The Tribunals are competent to hear matters where the vires of statutory provisions are questioned. *However, in discharging this duty, they cannot act as substitutes for the High Courts and the Supreme Court which have, under our constitutional setup, been specifically entrusted with such an obligation. Their function in this respect is only supplementary and all such decisions of the Tribunals will be subject to scrutiny before a Division Bench of the respective High Courts.* (Page 232).

(iii) The decision in *L. Chandra Kumar* was reiterated with approval by Justice Rohinton Nariman in his concurring judgement—in a bench decision of five judges—in the case of the National Tax Tribunal Act, 2005 in *Madras Bar Association vs. Union of India* (2014 (10) SCC 1) on pages 231-232 (whilst differing with reasons given in the principal judgement of the court). The true ratio of this case is established in the concurring judgement.

(iv) And two years later, in *Supreme Court Advocates-on-Record vs. Union of India* (2016 (5) SCC 1), it was held (by majority 4:1) that the Constitution (99th Amendment) Act, 2014 (along with NJAC Act No. 40 of 2014) substituting an entirely new system of appointment of judges of the higher judiciary to the one that prevailed under the collegium-system-of-appointment (as declared in a bench decision of nine judges in 1993 (4) SCC 441) interpreting Articles 124 and 217 of the Constitution) was ultra vires the basic structure of the constitution. The NJAC Act No. 40 of 2014—made an integral part of the constitutional amendment—had left the choice of making recommendations to government (for the appointment of judges to the Supreme Court and to the high courts) not only to the three senior-most judges of the Supreme Court (including the Chief

> Justice of India), but had also conferred on persons who were not judges at all—but were non-lawyer, non-judge members of the newly-constituted National Judicial Commission—a veto power as regards recommendations so made for the appointment of judges to the Supreme Court and to the high courts.[56]

The basic structure theory initially propounded (in 1973 in *Kesavananda*) was the response of an anxious and activist court to its experience with the working of India's Constitution during its first 25 years. It was an auxiliary precaution taken against the possible tidal wave of majoritarian rule. In the life of a nation as in the life of an individual, it is good to make provision for the future. In *Kesavananda* (1973) and in the *Indira Gandhi Election* case (1975), the highest court took care to make adequate provision for the future, when India would revert again to majoritarian rule. And when majoritarian rule came post-2014—with a super-majoritarian government at the centre post-2019—those in power did not forget (and in any case were constantly reminded) that it was a majoritarian government at the centre that had unconstitutionally imposed the Internal Emergency of June 1975 to March 1977.

A second instance of the highest court acting as the conscience keeper of the nation has been in the manner of appointment of judges in the Supreme Court and in the high courts.

The Constitution had prescribed—until the 99th Constitutional Amendment of 2014 intervened—that appointments of high court judges and judges of the Supreme Court were to be made only after prior *consultation* with the Chief Justice of India and such other judges of the Supreme Court or high courts as the president may determine (Articles 124 and 217 of the Constitution). And in the past, as a matter of convention, though not as a matter of constitutional compulsion, the advice given by the Chief Justice of India (who was always consulted) had been accepted by successive governments. But then, in the year 1981,[57] a bench of seven judges of the Supreme Court held (by majority 4:3)—later it came to be known as the *First Judges Case*—that the last word in such appointments was with the executive; in other words, with the Government of India. Power grows by what it feeds on. No sooner had it been so held by the Constitution Bench in the *First Judges Case* that the last word on the appointment of judges was with the government of the day than the (then) central government began to ignore the advice given or recommendation made by the Chief Justice of India as to the person to be appointed judge of a high court or judge of the Supreme Court. And the government proceeded to appoint judges to the high courts in such a way that they were effectively on probation—their tenure extended from three to six months at a time—and a scheme was also propounded by the central government for the transfer of high court judges from one high court to another (permitted by Article 222 only after 'consultation' with the Chief Justice of India by Article 222, for apparently administrative reasons) as was the intention underlying the Article. But the scheme propounded enabled the government to 'punish' particular judges for rendering decisions unfavourable to government. These moves were challenged before the Supreme Court of India.

It was in this background—in October 1993—that a larger bench was constituted, in what has come to be known as the *Second Judges Case*[58] to consider the correctness of the decision in the *First Judges Case* (1981). This bench of nine Judges held (7:2) that the majority decision of 1981 by the bench of seven judges (4:3)[59], in the *First Judges case*, was erroneous, and it was overruled.

It is not often that a bench of nine Judges is constituted (please see Footnote No.59) The majority (of the bench of nine Judges) also said that Article 214 regarding the appointment of judges to high courts (and correspondingly Article 124 regarding the appointment of judges to the Supreme Court) was not to be interpreted literally, but that a contextual and purposive construction was to be preferred. Before 1993, the 'balance'—in the judicial branch—was always understood to be the last word on what was the law with the judges of the highest court, but as to their appointment as judges on the court (high court or Supreme Court) that was to be made by the president (or in other words by the central government) after consultation with the Chief Justice of India (whose views had been sought and invariably accepted). This delicate balance now shifted. Appointments to the Higher Judiciary henceforth were to be determined by the higher judiciary itself. This somewhat 'revolutionary' interpretation (as it had been described)—though judges and lawyers preferred to call it a 'contextual' and a 'purposeful' interpretation—had been adversely commented upon even by judges abroad when they came and spoke in India. 'Where Angels Fear to Tread' was the trenchant title of a speech on the subject by Robin Cooke (Lord Cooke of Thorndon) which speech he delivered when he visited New Delhi. Cooke was a distinguished judge from New Zealand, so distinguished that he was appointed not only to the Privy Council (as senior judges from courts in the Commonwealth often were) but he was also appointed as a Lord of Appeal in Ordinary in the judicial committee of the House of Lords (England's then highest court of appeal). Those who read his criticism of the *Second Judges Case* were conscious of the fact that he really intended to say (with Alexander Pope), '*Fools rush in where angels fear to tread*', but on second thoughts restrained himself, and adopted as the title of his lecture only the latter half of the quote!

But Lord Cooke notwithstanding—on a later presidential reference (in the year 1998)—in another nine-judge bench (in what later came to be known as the *Third Judges Case*)[60], all nine judges were unanimous. It was asserted that what the majority had said in the *Second Judges Case* (7:2) was absolutely correct, and that there was no need to depart from the *purposeful* interpretation of Articles 124 and 217[61], something that recalled to others another adage (suitably adapted), viz.: *power,* wheresoever it resides (in the instant case it was with the judiciary), *grows by what it feeds on.*

Past and present law ministers had been (and continue to be) convinced, that the articles in the Constitution regarding the appointment of judges to high courts and the Supreme Court needed to be put back on their feet—once again—not by restoring the status quo ante but by replacing the articles with a well-structured National Judicial Commission. But the National Judicial Commission envisaged by the 99th Constitution Amendment Act 2014—and the law that accompanied it—was not at all a well-structured one. It was skewed because it permitted the final decision of judicial members of the NJAC to be vetoed by non-legal members of the National Judicial Commission. The government did not suggest any alternative, and the court felt compelled to strike down the 99th Constitution Amendment.

Bibek Debroy, chairman of the Economic Advisory Council to India's Prime Minister (along with Aditya Sinha) had recently written a perceptive and pertinent article (in the *Times of India*, 13 February 2023) in which they said:

> What the Supreme Court struck down in 2016 was a specific form that the National Judicial Commission took; *with better form and content NJAC might not have been struck down.* On such a serious matter, in hindsight, it is a bit surprising that NJAC was legislated with its deficiencies. In hindsight, it is also a bit surprising that Supreme Court didn't ask for a better version of NJC to be drafted, though in fairness the petition was about NJAC.

And Debroy's (along with Aditya Sinha's) article ended with the words:

> *We need a better method of appointing (and transferring) HC Judges, and SC Judges. The warts are too evident.*

As a matter of fact, there was a *better method* of appointing (and transferring) high court judges and appointing

Supreme Court judges. It had been drafted and proposed by India's retired Chief Justice, M. N. Venkatachaliah, who (as chairman of the National Commission to review the working of the Constitution (NCRWC)) had made the following recommendations (in place of what had been prescribed in Articles 124 and 217), viz., that a National Judicial Commission shall be constituted of only 5 members—the Chief Justice of India and as well as two other judges of the Supreme court next in seniority to the Chief Justice of India, along with the union minister of law and justice and one eminent citizen to be nominated by the president in consultation with the prime minister. It was to be the duty of the Commission (NJC) to make recommendations of persons for appointment of judges of the Supreme Court, chief justices, and judges of high courts and also to make recommendations for the transfer of judges of high courts (including chief justices) from one high court to another. It also provided that the recommendations of the NJC (with three senior-most judges of the Supreme Court of India in the majority) *'shall be binding'*. Thereafter, the then NDA Government (with the BJP in the majority) introduced the Constitution 98th Amendment Bill, 2003 (Bill No. 41 of 2003) in Parliament, which provided for appropriate amendments in Articles 124 and 217 (for appointment of judges in the Supreme Court and of chief justices and judges of the high courts in the states) as well as appropriate amendments in Article 222 (for transfer of judges, including chief justices, from one high court to another).

The only reason why this bill was not passed was because shortly after it was introduced, it lapsed on account of the calling of national elections. *And it was never reintroduced in this form.*

I am proud of our judges past and present, but then I must also say this with a caveat. Whilst I believe that judges of great learning will make good judges, and even some judges not of great learning but endowed with felicity of expression and strong common-sense will also make good judges—*but this is only if they have the right judicial attitudes*. Because it is only right attitudes that make for just decisions, as you will see from what is stated below.

I was witness, after the Internal Emergency of June 1975, to a (regrettable) change of attitude in judges which, for me, was alarming. Before the Internal Emergency of June 1975, I had appeared as a Law Officer of the Union of India in a group of matters in the High Court of Delhi for the central government, where preventive detention orders were served on persons, who were later acknowledged to be smugglers, were challenged in a series of writ petitions under Article 226. The matters went on for many days and judgement was ultimately reserved. It was then delivered by the high court on a Friday: the grounds of detention, the judgement said, were insufficient in law to sustain the orders of detention and all the detention orders were quashed and set aside. In the late afternoon of that fateful Friday (high courts and the Supreme Court being closed on all Saturdays and Sundays), I interrupted a part-heard matter that was being heard by a Constitution Bench (of five judges) of the Supreme Court presided over by then Chief Justice A. N. Ray and orally requested that their Lordships stay the order of the Delhi High Court (which had been pronounced earlier in the day)—on my undertaking that a SLP (Special Leave Petition) would be filed in the morning of the following Monday. The interchange that then took place was as follows:

> ***Chief Justice:*** But Mr Solicitor, this is a matter of personal liberty, and we have neither the judgement nor any application from the government and we cannot on a mere oral application grant a stay.
>
> ***Nariman:*** It is only for two days. The judges of the high court had reserved judgement several weeks ago and delivered it on a Friday. Hence, the request.

Chief Justice: We cannot help that. In matters of personal liberty, we cannot grant a stay.

Nariman (gnashing his teeth): As your Lordship pleases.

There was a furore in government at the Delhi High Court judgement and order, and consternation at the Supreme Court's refusal to interfere. The then finance minister and law minister said that Article 226 (the ample writ jurisdiction of the high courts under our Constitution) needed to be forthwith amended *(As a matter of fact, it was so amended during the Internal Emergency of June 1975 to March 1977).* Anyhow, pursuant to and in obedience to the judgement and order of the high court the detainees were released, amidst much jubilation in Bombay and in Delhi. And having been released from *preventive detention* (i.e., detention without trial) in law, they could not be rearrested even if the judgement was stayed or ultimately set aside. All this was in March or April 1975. Although I was then disappointed by the attitude of the judges, I tried to convince myself—as Chief Justice Ray had said—that this was a matter of personal liberty and on personal liberties, there could be no compromise. But see what happened later.

A day after the Proclamation of Internal Emergency of 26 June 1975, I resigned from my post of Additional Solicitor General of India. The Supreme Court was then on summer vacation. When the court reopened in July 1975—the first week after the reopening—I happened to be present in the same Chief Justice's court when on an oral application by the then Solicitor General of India, Mr Lal Narayan Sinha, the same bench of judges *on an oral application* stayed a judgement of the Bombay High Court, which had not yet been shown to the judges (but about which they were only orally informed). The case concerned a group of municipal councillors in the Municipal Corporation of Bombay who had been preventively detained under the Maintenance of Internal Security Act (MISA) (the preventive detention law then current). There was a mayoral election to take place at which the Congress Party had nominated its candidate. If those councillors who had been detained under the preventive detention law had been permitted to exercise their franchise and to vote, the Congress would have lost the mayoral election. A writ petition had been filed in the Bombay High Court, on their behalf, contending that they had not lost their right to vote (even though preventively detained), and consequently, they should be permitted to exercise their vote either at the detaining centre or brought under guard to the voting centre. This application—which seemed eminently reasonable—was granted by the High Court of Bombay. This was on a Monday and the decision was reported in the newspapers the following day. It was on the morning thereafter that then the Solicitor General of India appearing for the union government in the Supreme Court, without any papers, without a copy of the judgement, *orally* asked the judges for a stay of the judgement of the High Court of Bombay. *The same Supreme Court, the same Chief Justice, (and to the best of my recollection the same set of judges) granted a stay of the bench decision of the high court, and the result was that the municipal election went ahead, and the Congress party's nominee for mayor was duly elected.*

So much for the court's abiding concern for personal liberty during the Internal Emergency of June 1975. As Judge Learned Hand—the greatest amongst America's Federal Judges—had said: *"I often wonder whether we do not rest our hopes too much upon constitutions, upon laws and upon courts. These are false hopes; believe me, these are false hopes. Liberty lies in the hearts of men and women; when it dies there, no constitution, no law, no court can even do much to help it"*. (The Spirit of Liberty." A speech given by Judge Learned Hand in 1944 in celebration of I Am an American Day.)

Notes and References:

1. *Shamsher Singh vs. State of Punjab*—AIR 1974 SC 2192 (bench of seven judges).

2. The first non-official attempt at drafting a Constitution with a parliamentary system of government for India was in the year 1895 under the inspiration of Bal Gangadhar Tilak. Later, in the mid-1920s, under the inspiration of Sir Tej Bahadur Sapru, India's political leaders sent to London a comprehensive draft bill for self-government which got introduced in Britain's Parliament as the Commonwealth of India Bill 1925 but could not be made an Act because the Labour Government in Britain that introduced the Bill, lost its majority in the House of Commons (for more details, see Chapter one).

3. Andhra Pradesh, Assam, Bihar, Gujarat, Kerala, Madhya Pradesh, Tamil Nadu, Maharashtra, Karnataka, Odisha, Punjab, Rajasthan, Uttar Pradesh, West Bengal, Nagaland, Haryana, Himachal Pradesh, Manipur, Tripura, Meghalaya, Sikkim, Mizoram, Arunachal Pradesh, Goa, Chhattisgarh, Uttarakhand, Jharkhand, and Telangana.

4. Delhi, The Andaman and Nicobar Islands, Lakshadweep, Dadra and Nagar Haveli, Daman and Diu, Puducherry, Chandigarh, Jammu and Kashmir, and Ladakh.
   Union Territories are divided into three categories:
   1. Union Territories without legislatures—comprising Andaman and Nicobar, Lakshadweep, Dadra and Nagar Haveli, Daman and Diu, and Chandigarh.
   2. Union Territory for which legislature has been established by Act of Parliament under Article 239A, viz., Puducherry.
   3. Union Territory which has a legislature created by the Constitution (Articles 239AA and 239AB)—consists of The National Capital Territory of Delhi.

5. Shiva Rao: *The Framing of India's Constitution (Select Documents)*, Vol. II, pages 656-657 (27 June 1947).

6. CAD, Book No. 3, Vol. VIII, pages 439-440 (30 May 1949).

7. CAD, Book No. 3, Vol. VIII, pages 468-469 (30 May 1949).

8. Sarkaria Commission Report on Centre-State Relations (1987), Part I, pages 115-116.

9. It is the governor of each state who has to administer and control 'scheduled areas' in states (other than in the states of Assam,

Meghalaya, Tripura, and Mizoram) but only on directions given by the union executive (Article 244 read with the Fifth Schedule). Tribal areas in the states of Assam, Meghalaya, Tripura, and Mizoram are to be administered by district and regional councils (with the assistance of tribal councils) in accordance with rules made by the governor, under provisions set out in the Sixth Schedule (Article 244(2) read with Article 275(1)).

10. 163. Council of Ministers to aid and advise Governor:
    1. There shall be a Council of Ministers with the Chief Minister at the head to aid and advise the Governor in the exercise of his functions, except in so far as he is by or under this Constitution required to exercise his functions or any of them in his discretion.
    2. If any question arises whether any matter is or is not a matter as respects which the Governor is by or under this Constitution required to act in his discretion, the decision of the Governor in his discretion shall be final, and the validity of anything done by the Governor shall not be called in question on the ground that he ought or ought not to have acted in his discretion.
    3. The question of whether any, and if so what, advice was tendered by Ministers to the Governor shall not be inquired into in any court.

11. See *Why India Needs the Presidential System* by Bhanu Dhamija. *Twitter: @BhanuDhamija.*

12. So described in H. N. Pandit: *The PM's President: A New Concept on Trial*, S. Chand & Co., New Delhi, 1974, page 3.

    See also *The Indian President: An Insider's Account of the Zail Singh Years* by K. C. Singh, Harper Collins Publishers India (2023). In it, the author states:

    > The similarity between the oaths of the US and the Indian presidents raises a question. If Indian presidents are merely a cabinet rubber stamp, how can they abide by their oath? In particular, do they have no power to act if the Constitution is subverted in spirit and sometimes, even in letter, by the government? This aspect assumes even greater importance if the Supreme Court is reluctant to intervene.

13. Walter Bagehot: *The English Constitution* (republished in 1991 by Fontana Press, London, page 113). Bagehot (1826-1877) was an English journalist and essayist who wrote extensively about

government. His book, *The English Constitution* (1867), explored the unwritten constitution of the United Kingdom. Even, today, *The Economist* carries a weekly current affairs commentary titled, 'Bagehot', that is named in his honour and analyses life and politics in the tradition of Walter Bagehot.

14. CAD, Vol. VII, page 1158, November 1948 to January 1949.

15. *State of West Bengal vs. Union of India*—AIR 1963, SC 1241 (bench of six judges (5:1))—with a powerful dissent by Justice Subba Rao who pleaded for an adherence to federal principles, but his dissent has remained till today a lone voice in the judicial wilderness. Justice Subba Rao. was a champion of state rights as shown by his concluding remarks:

    "To conclude: The Indian Constitution accepts the federal concept and distributes the sovereign powers between the coordinate constitutional entitles, namely, the Union and the States. This concept implies that one cannot encroach upon the governmental functions or instrumentalities of the other, unless the Constitution expressly provides for such interference. The legislative fields allotted to the units cover subjects for legislation and they do not deal with the relationship between the two coordinate units functioning in their allotted fields. This is regulated by other provisions of the Constitution and there is no provision which enables one unit to take away the property of another except by agreement. The future stability of our vast country with its unity in diversity depends upon the strict adherence of the federal principle, which the fathers of our Constitution have so wisely and foresightedly incorporated therein. This court has the constitutional power and the correlative duty, a difficult and delicate one, to prevent encroachment, either overtly or covertly, by the Union on the State field or vice versa, and thus maintain the balance of the federation. The present is a typical case where the court should stop the Union from overstepping its boundary and trespassing into the State field. *I would, therefore, hold that the impugned Act, in so far as it confers a power on the Union to acquire the lands owned by the State, including coal mines and coal-bearing lands, is ultra vires."*

16. Eminent domain has been authoritatively defined (in *Black's Law Dictionary*, Ninth Edition, Thomson West, 2009, Eagan, Minnesota, page 601) as: 'The inherent power of a governmental entity to take privately owned property, esp. land, and convert it to public use, subject to reasonable compensation for the taking.'

17. In *Federal Government* by K. C. Wheare, Oxford University Press (1967).
18. Figuratively meaning 'to cause trouble when none is welcome' or 'to disturb a situation that is otherwise stable and satisfactory'.
19. Minoo Masani: *Of Four Real Leaders: Some Reminiscences*, which was written in 1994 but published posthumously in 2011 (after Masani passed away on 27 May 1998).
20. An assertion not in keeping with Article 74(1) even as originally enacted. Article 74(1) of the Constitution read: 'There shall be a Council of Ministers with the Prime Minister at the head to aid and advice the President in the exercise of his functions'.
21. Valmiki Choudhary, *President and the Indian Constitution* (New Delhi: Allied Publishers, (1985), pages 68, 69, and 71).
22. Bihar, Haryana, Himachal Pradesh, Madhya Pradesh, Orissa, Punjab, Rajasthan, Uttar Pradesh, and West Bengal.
23. *State of Rajasthan vs. Union of India*, AIR 1977 SC 1361 (bench of seven judges (6:1)); Justice Fazal Ali, however, dissenting.
24. *S. R. Bommai vs. Union of India*, AIR 1994, SC 1918, 2072-2073 (bench of nine judges: interpreting Article 356).
25. Granville Austin: *Working a Democratic Constitution: The Indian Experience*, Oxford University Press, New Delhi, 1999, page 536.
26. **However, the Justice Punchhi Commission on Inter-State Relations had recommended in its report (of 31 March 2010) that assent to a bill should not be held up either by the president of India (under Article 111) or by a governor in a state (under Article 200) beyond six months; a recommendation which, till date, has not yet been translated into constitutional law.**
27. *Memoirs of Giani Zail Singh: The Seventh President of India,* Har Anand Publications, New Delhi 1997, page 279.
28. Granville Austin: *Working a Democratic Constitution: The Indian Experience,* Oxford University Press, New Delhi, 1999, pages 513-514.
29. The impeachment of a president is provided for in Article 61.
30. Achyut Chetan: *Founding Mothers of the Indian Republic: Gender Politics of the Framing of the Constitution,* published by Cambridge University Press.

31. *Rai Sahib Ram Jawaya Kapur & Ors. vs. State of Punjab* (1955 (2) SCR 225 = AIR 1955 SC 549).

32. Article 114: Appropriation Bills (at the Centre).
    (1) . . .
    (2) . . .
    (3) Subject to the provisions of Articles 115 and 116, no money shall be withdrawn from the Consolidated Fund of India except under appropriation made by law passed in accordance with the provisions of this article.
    Article 204: Appropriation Bills (in the States).
    (1) . . .
    (2) . . .
    (3) Subject to the provisions of Articles 205 and 206, no money shall be withdrawn from the Consolidated Fund of the State except under appropriation made by law passed in accordance with the provisions of this article.

33. Quintin McGarel Hogg, Baron Hailsham of St Marylebone, KG, CH, PC, FRS (9 October 1907-12 October 2001), known as the 2nd Viscount Hailsham between 1950 and 1963, at which point he disclaimed his hereditary peerage. He was a British barrister and Conservative Party politician who served as Lord Chancellor from 1970 to 1974 and again from 1979 to 1987.

34. Walter Bagehot: *The English Constitution* (published in 1867).

35. Article 141: Law declared by Supreme Court to be binding on all courts—The law declared by the Supreme Court shall be binding on all courts within the territory of India.

36. Article 136: Special leave to appeal by the Supreme Court.
    (1) Notwithstanding anything in this Chapter, the Supreme Court may, in its discretion, grant special leave to appeal from any judgement, decree, determination, sentence, or order in any cause or matter passed or made by any court or tribunal in the territory of India.
    (2) Nothing in clause (1) shall apply to any judgement, determination, sentence, or order passed or made by any court or tribunal constituted by or under any law relating to the Armed Forces.

37. *The first time Article 143 was invoked was in 1951—the presidential reference in the matter of the* Delhi Laws: *(1951) SCR 747. In the past 70-odd years, only twelve references in all have been so far made to the Supreme Court by the president, i.e., by the central government.*

38. *Ismail Faruqui vs. Union of India,* 1994 (6) SCC 360 (5J)

39. A presumption that had been set out in enacted law in British India—Section 114 of the (Indian) Evidence Act, 1872.

40. With the exception from March 1977 to January 1980, when there was no predominant majority party in power, the Janata Party then in power (that replaced Mrs Gandhi) consisted of an amalgam of several political parties.

41. In India, a zamindar was the holder of a very large estate or jagir, a landed proprietor. Under the Mughal administration of India, he was a hereditary owner and responsible for the collection of revenue on behalf of the government. When the British conquered large parts of India, they continued the zamindari system.

42. **The Validating Clause (Article 31B) authorised the mere placing of laws (central or state) by Parliament in a newly added schedule (the Ninth Schedule) as above the Constitution and beyond judicial review. It was only in 1981—following the decision of the majority in a bench of thirteen judges—in** Kesavananda Bharati (1973) **that the Supreme Court reinterpreted Article 31B (in the light of that judgement) and held that all laws placed in the Ninth Schedule after 23 April 1973 (date of judgement in *Kesavananda Bharati*) would have to be tested for their validity in thc light of Articles 14, 19, and 31 (in Part-III). It is only after this decision of the Supreme Court of India 'reading-down' Article 31B that this article has now become virtually a 'dead letter'.**

43. In *Shankari Prasad vs. Union of India* (1951), AIR 1951, SC 458.

44. *Sajjan Singh vs. State of Rajasthan*, AIR 1965, SC 845.

45. The Constitution Fourth Amendment Act 1955, inter alia, extended the scope of Article 31A to 'protect' from challenge essential welfare legislation by the centre and states against violation of fundamental rights (under Article 19(1)(f) and Article 31). The Constitution Seventeenth Amendment Act 1964 added 43 laws passed in different states (effectuating land reforms) in the Ninth Schedule, which in terms of Article 31B, prevented such Acts from being challenged in courts for violating any of the fundamental rights including property rights (Article 19(1)(f) and Article 31).

46. *Golaknath vs. State of Punjab*, AIR 1967, SC 1643 (decided by a bench of eleven judges).

47. *Madhav Rao Scindia vs. Union of India*, reported in AIR 1971, SC 530 (bench of eleven judges).

48. *His Holiness Kesavananda Bharati vs. State of Kerala*, AIR 1973 Supreme Court 1461 (7:6) = 1973 Supp. 1 SCR 1 (7:6).

49. AIR 1973 SC 1461 (7:6).

50. By constitutional convention, since 1950, the next seniormost judge in the Supreme Court (after the Chief Justice) is appointed as Chief Justice of India on the retirement of the incumbent Chief Justice.

51. In *Raj Narain vs. Indira Gandhi/Indira Gandhi vs. Raj Narain*, (cross-appeals) the Constitution Bench of five judges consisted of:

    (1) Chief Justice A. N. Ray, who held that the validation of Mrs Gandhi's election in the instant case 'was not applying any law to it and it therefore offended the rule of law'.
    (2) Justice H. R. Khanna who held that clause (4) of Article 329A 'strikes at the basic structure of the Constitution' and it was struck down on the ground that it violated the principle of free and fair elections which was an essential postulate of democracy. Justice Khanna reiterated that 'the power of amendment under Article 368 does not include the power to abrogate the Constitution nor does it include the power to alter the basic structure of the Constitution'.
    (3) Justice K. M. Mathew who held that clause (4) of Article 329A was 'bad'.
    (4) Justice M. H. Beg concurred with Chief Justice Ray holding clause (4) of Article 329A was unconstitutional.
    (5) Justice Y. V. Chandrachud also held that clause (4) of Article 329A was unconstitutional and void.

    Mrs Gandhi's election appeal on merits, however, was decided unanimously in her favour, and the judgement of the Allahabad High Court was set aside. Mrs Gandhi won her appeal, but clause (4) of Article 329A was struck down as unconstitutional.

52. 'Damp squib' is an English phrase that means anything that fails to meet expectations.

53. The bench of thirteen judges included the following who were not there in *Kesavananda*, viz., justices Bhagwati, Krishan Iyer, P. B. Goswami, R. S. Sarkaria, A. C. Gupta, M. Fazl Ali, and P. N. Shinghal.

54. The bench of nine justices consisted of Chief Justice Y. K. Sabharwal and justices Ashok Bhan, A. Pasayat, B. P. Singh, S. H. Kapadia, C. K. Thakker, R. K. Balasubramanyan, Altamas Kabir, and D. K. Jain.

55. Ronald Dworkin: *Law's Empire,* Harvard University Press, Cambridge, Massachusetts, 1986, pages 61-63.

56. Articles 124A, 124B, and 124C had been added in Chapter IV in Part-V of the Constitution w.e.f. 13 April 2015, and by the Constitution 99th Amendment Act, 2014. The proviso to Article 124(2) as originally enacted was omitted (the proviso had said that in the case of appointment of a judge of the Supreme Court (other than the Chief Justice of India, *the Chief Justice of India shall always be consulted).* Likewise in Article 214 and Article 217(1) as originally enacted the requirement that in the case of appointment of a judge of a high court, the Chief Justice of India must always be consulted was also omitted by the NJAC Act and substituted by the requirement of a *recommendation* of the self-same National Judicial Appointment Commission (NJAC) (consisting of six persons—three of them senior-most judges of the Supreme Court of India on the one hand, with the law minister and 'two eminent persons' on the other hand, with a veto power being conferred on the two eminent persons on recommendations for appointment of judges (in the Supreme Court and in the high courts)).

    The final order of the Supreme Court of India in 2016 (5) SCC page 1 (para 1239 on page 801) read:

    > **The system of appointment of Judges of the Supreme Court, and the Chief Justices and Judges of the High Courts; and transfer of Chief Justices and Judge of the High Courts from one High Court to another, as existing prior to the Constitution 99th Amendment Act, 2014 (called 'the Collegium System') is declared to be operative.**

57. *S. P. Gupta vs. Union of India,* 1981 (Supp.) SCC 87 (7J).

58. *Supreme Court Advocates-on-Record Association and Others vs. Union of India,* 1993 (4) SCC 441 (9J).

59. **As stated in a judgement of Justice D. Y. Chandrachud in Jindal Stainless Steel Ltd. vs. State of Haryana & Ors. reported in AIR 2016 SC on page 5853 (when sitting in a bench of nine judges):**

    > **References to benches of nine judges, or at any rate decisions by nine, are a comparative rarity. Despite a prolific tradition of precedent in our judicial institutions, there have been only eight reported decisions by a bench of nine judges since the adoption of the Constitution:**

(i) Ahmedabad St. Xavier's College Society vs. State of Gujarat, AIR 1974 SC 1389.
(ii) Indira Sawhney vs. Union of India, AIR 1993 SC 477.
(iii) Supreme Court Advocates on Record Association vs. Union of India, AIR 1994 SC 268.
(iv) S. R. Bommai vs. Union of India, AIR 1994 SC 1918.
(v) Attorney General of India vs. Amratlal Prajivandas, AIR 1994 (5) SCC 54.
(vi) Mafatlal Industries vs. Union of India, 1997 (5) SCC 536.
(vii) Special Reference No.1 of 1998, AIR 1999 SC 1.
(viii)I. R. Coelho vs. State of TN, AIR 2007 SC 861.

60. Special Reference No.1 of 1998, AIR 1999 SC 1.

61. In the *Third Judges Case,* it was also said that the size of the collegium that was to make the recommendation (as to judges to be appointed) should be increased: 'we think it is desirable that the collegium should consist of the Chief Justice of India and the four senior-most puisne judges of the Supreme Court . . . but if the situation be such that the successor Chief Justice is not one of the four senior-most judges be must invariably be made part of the collegium', AIR 1999 SC 1 on page 16 (paragraphs 14 and 15).

Chapter Seven

Analysis and Comments on Particular Articles

I. **Powers and Privileges of the Parliament, State Legislatures, and Their Members (Articles 105 and 194)**

II. **The Granting of Pardons (Articles 72 and 161)**

III. **The Comptroller and Auditor General of India (Articles 147 to 151)**

IV. **(a). Elections and (b) Election Commission (Articles 324 to 329)**

I. On the Powers and Privileges of Legislatures (Parliament and State Legislatures—Articles 105 and 194)[1]:

Many years ago, visitors to Japan's (then newly built) Supreme Court in Tokyo, were told that the government had made it clear to the judges even before the structure's foundation had been laid, that the court, when constructed, must not be higher than the buildings 'next door'—the Houses of Parliament. That is how the magnificent structure stands today in Tokyo, at precisely the same elevation as its neighbouring building—not an inch taller, not an inch shorter. In India, however, the topic of legislative privileges is not about height, but about power—*which is the more significant under India's Constitution: state legislatures (and Parliament) or the courts?*

The term, 'Parliamentary Privilege', was first invented by the English to exempt its chosen few from the rigours of the ordinary law of the land. Then, with the spread of the British Empire, the colonies desired to share in the 'pomp-and-circumstance' enjoyed by members of England's House of Commons. One of them was the island of Newfoundland (now a part of Canada). The legislators in this new self-governing colony had its own elected assembly and its members claimed that they should have the same privileges as the House of Commons in England, *including the power to adjudicate upon and punish a contempt committed outside the House, and so they decided—a decision that was upheld by the Supreme Court of Newfoundland. But on appeal to the Privy Council, the decision was set aside in the year 1842.*

The great importance of the question raised in this case induced a Bench of the Privy Council, (who heard the first argument), to request that a second argument take place not only before themselves *but before all other members of the judicial committee.* So, in the year 1842, at a second hearing of the case, all eleven of the privy councillors were called in to determine the legitimacy of the claim. The privy councillors presided over by the Lord Chancellor (Lord Lyndhurst) heard extensive arguments and decided (unanimously) as follows:

> Their Lordships are of opinion that the House of Assembly did not possess the power of arrest with a view to adjudication on a complaint of contempt committed *out of its doors*, and consequently that the judgement of the Court below must be reversed.

And the reason was given as follows:

> (*Quote*) We decide according to the principle of the Common Law, that the House of Assembly have not the power contended for. They are a local Legislature, with every power reasonably necessary for the proper exercise of their functions and duties, but they have not what they have

> erroneously supposed themselves to possess—the same exclusive privileges which the ancient Law of England has annexed to the House of Parliament. (*Unquote*)

The Privy Council (all eleven members) therefore held that the House of Assembly of the Island of Newfoundland did not possess the power of arrest with a view to adjudication on a complaint of contempt committed *'out of its doors'*. [2] The italicised words are significant, because they are the origin of the distinction drawn by courts in India between contempt of authority for acts committed *within the House* and acts committed *outside the Houses* of legislature. In the latter case, the House is definitely not the sole judge of its own privileges.

A Trilogy of Cases

There have been three important cases in India that have laid down the contours of the law of privileges:

1. In March 1952, a journalist, Homi Mistry, was arrested in Bombay and taken in custody to Lucknow, to be produced before the speaker of the Uttar Pradesh Legislative Assembly to answer a charge of breach of privilege. He petitioned the Supreme Court of India under Article 32 of the Constitution, alleging a breach of his fundamental right under clause (2) of Article 22, which provides (in the Fundamental Rights Chapter) that no person shall be detained in custody (beyond a period of 24 hours) without the authority of a magistrate. Attorney General Motilal Setalvad (India's first and finest law officer) immediately conceded before a bench of five justices of the court that a constitutional right was infringed, and he could be set at liberty. The Constitution Bench then ordered:

   > In view of the admitted facts, it is perfectly clear that this provision of the Constitution has been contravened and the said Mr Mistry is entitled to his

release. The habeas corpus petition therefore succeeds and we direct that Mr Mistry be released forthwith.[3]

2. Some years later, however (in December 1958), when the prior decision in Mistry's case was relied upon, before another Constitution Bench of five judges, a majority of the justices (4:1) said that the case was not a binding precedent—since it was based on a concession. In what is popularly known as the *Searchlight* case (1959)[4], one Pandit M. S. M. Sharma, editor of an English language newspaper *(Searchlight)* published the entire speech of a member delivered in the U.P. Legislative Assembly *including portions which had been expunged by the speaker.* He was hauled up for a breach of privilege. At that time, the editor's plea was that he was free to repeat what a minister or a member of the Legislative Assembly had said in the House, even though it had been ordered to be expunged. He relied on Article 19(1)(a)—the free speech clause in our Constitution. But four out of five judges of the Supreme Court rejected this plea (Justice Subba Rao dissenting). Chief Justice S. R. Das speaking for the majority, said that Article 194(3) defined the privileges of a House of a state legislature under our Constitution to be such as may 'from time to time be defined by the legislature by law but until so defined', the privileges would be 'those of the House of Commons of the Parliament of the United Kingdom at the commencement of the Constitution', and that this article took precedence over Article 19(1)(a).[5] The majority then went on to say that since both Parliament and state legislative assemblies had powers, privileges, and immunities of the House of Commons, if the petitioner was eventually deprived of his personal liberty as result of proceedings (properly conducted) before the Committee of Privileges, such deprivation would be 'in accordance with procedure established by law', and therefore not a contravention of Article 21 of the Constitution. If

the legislature had the powers and privileges and was entitled to take proceedings for breach thereof—'as we hold it is', the court said 'then it must be left to the House itself to determine whether there has in fact been any breach of its privilege'. On this occasion, 'Parliamentary and Legislative Privileges' was the winner (with a strong note of dissent by a notable future Chief Justice).

3. The third and most important of the great cases is *Keshav Singh's* case (1965)[6] and, at the time, the fate of two judges of a high court depended on its outcome. The facts are interesting. On 14 March 1964, the speaker of the Legislative Assembly of Uttar Pradesh reprimanded one Keshav Singh for having committed contempt of the House and for a breach of its privileges, by distributing within the precincts of the House a pamphlet bearing his signature. The speaker directed that Keshav Singh be committed to prison, because when he was summoned to receive the reprimand, he had written a disrespectful letter to the speaker. A warrant was issued over the signature of the speaker directing that Keshav Singh be detained in the district jail in Lucknow for a period of 7 days. Keshav Singh then applied to the Lucknow Bench of the Allahabad High Court to be released on bail and two judges of that court ordered him to be released on bail. The angry response of the U.P. Legislative Assembly to this order of the court was a resolution (passed unanimously by the U.P. Legislative Assembly) that the two high court judges be committed for contempt! When these judges heard the news broadcast over All India Radio—in those days there was no television—they rushed to Allahabad High Court, and overnight, a writ petition was filed on their behalf. The Chief Justice of the Allahabad High Court constituted (for the first time) a full bench of all 28 judges in the main hall of the high court, one of the largest courtrooms in the country.

The judges solemnly assembled *en banc* (all together) and granted to two of their colleagues interim relief. They issued an order against the assembly's marshal, prohibiting the implementation of the resolution of the U.P. Assembly. The assembly then retracted, but only a little. It passed a clarificatory resolution which virtually said that they did not mean to commit these judges, worthy as they are, of contempt, and if there had been any misunderstanding on that score—the warrants of arrest against them—would be withdrawn, but with notices issued to the two judges to please show cause why they should not be committed for contempt. By then the matter had become too hot to handle at the level of the high court. And the centre moved the Supreme Court of India in a presidential reference under **Article 143** of the Constitution, and a special bench of 7 judges was constituted to determine the important questions raised.

143. Power of President to consult Supreme Court:

1. If at any time it appears to the President that a question of law or fact has arisen, or is likely to arise, which is of such a nature and of such public importance that it is expedient to obtain the opinion of the Supreme Court upon it, he may refer the question to that Court for consideration and the Court may, after such hearing as it thinks fit, report to the President its opinion thereon.
2. The President may, notwithstanding anything in the proviso to article 131, refer a dispute of the kind mentioned in the 3(said proviso) to the Supreme Court for opinion and the Supreme Court shall, after such hearing as it thinks fit, report to the President its opinion thereon.

[During the past 72 years, there have been <u>twelve</u> occasions when the president (i.e., the central government) has moved the Supreme Court of India for its opinion on a question of law (and fact) 'of such public importance that it is expedient to obtain the opinion of the Supreme Court upon it' viz.

1. In *Re: Delhi Laws Act,* 1912 *vs. The Part C States (Laws) Act,* 1950-1951 SCR 747.
2. In *Re: Kerala Education Bill,* 1957—AIR 1958 SC 956.
3. In *Re: Berubari Union*—AIR 1960 SC 845.
4. In *Re: Sea Customs Act,* 1878—AIR 1963 SC 1760.
5. ***In The Matter Of: Under Article 143 (Re: Keshav Singh)—AIR 1965 SC 745.***
6. In *Re: Presidential Elections Act*—AIR 1974 SC 1682.
7. In *Re: Special Courts Bill,* 1978—AIR 1979 S.C. 478.
8. In *Re: Cauvery Water Disputes Tribunal*—AIR 1992 SC 522.
9. In *Dr M. Ismail Faruqui vs. Union of India*—1994 (6) SCC 366.
10. In *Re: Special Reference No.1* of 2002 (Gujarat Assembly Election matter) - 2002 (8) SCC 237 = AIR 2003 SC 87.
11. In *Re: Presidential Reference in the matter of principles and procedure regarding the appointment of Supreme Court and High Court Judges*—AIR 1999 SC 1.
12. In *Re: Special Reference No.1* of 2012—Natural Resources Allocation—2012 (10) SCC 1.]

The opinion of the court in the above matter *(Keshav Singh)* was (pronounced by Chief Justice P. B. Gajendragadkar)—it is one of the most statesman-like decisions ever rendered by the highest court, especially when answering Question 5 in the reference (reproduced below):

Question No. 5:

Whether a Judge of a High Court who entertains or deals with a petition challenging any order or decision of a Legislature imposing any penalty on the petitioner or issuing any process against the petitioner for its contempt or for infringement of its privileges and immunities or who passes any order on such petition commits contempt of the said Legislature and whether the said Legislature is competent to take proceedings against such a Judge in the exercise and enforcement of its powers, privileges, and immunities.

Answer:

(5) In rendering our answer to this question, which is very broadly worded, we ought to preface our answer with the observation that *the answer is confined to cases in relation to contempt alleged to have been committed by a citizen who is not a member of the House outside the four walls of the legislative chamber.* A judge of a High Court who entertains or deals with petitions challenging any order or decision of a Legislature imposing any penalty on the petitioner or issuing any process against the petitioner for its contempt, or for infringement of its privileges and immunities, or who passes any order on such petition, does not commit contempt of the said Legislature; and the said Legislature is not competent to take proceedings against such a Judge in the exercise and enforcement of its powers, privileges and immunities. In this answer, we have deliberately omitted reference to infringement of privileges and immunities of the House which may include privileges and immunities other than those with which we are concerned in the present reference.

After reiterating the view already expressed in the *Searchlight* Case (AIR 1959 SC 395) that where Article 194(3) applied Article 19(1)(a) did not (viz., that the privileges of legislators would trump free speech of citizens), **the court then went on to say (by majority of 6:1) that when Article 194(3) of the Constitution was passed, the framers intended to confer upon the Houses of Parliament and state legislatures, the same jurisdiction with respect to the privileges that the House of Commons enjoyed—*but they definitely did not intend to incorporate the rule that the legislatures were also to be the final judges of those privileges.* The court would have to scrutinise their decision under Article 21 of the Constitution.[7] The general warrants for contempt issued by the British House of Commons could not be subjected to judicial scrutiny, but that was only because that House was also a superior Court of Record. But Parliament and state legislatures in India were not possessed of any such power as was enjoyed—by ancient usage—by the British House of Commons, viz., that of a 'High Court of Parliament'.**

The concluding part of the judgement of Chief Justice Gajendragadkar is reproduced below:

> (*Quote*) In conclusion, we ought to add that throughout our discussion, we have consistently attempted to make it clear that the main point which we are discussing is the right of the House to claim that a general warrant issued by it in respect of its contempt alleged to have been committed by a citizen who is not a Member of the House outside the four walls of the House, is conclusive, for it is on that claim that the House has chosen to take the view that the Judges, the Advocate, and the party have committed contempt by reference to the conduct in the habeas corpus petition pending before the Lucknow Bench of the Allahabad High Court. Since we have held that in the present case, no contempt was committed either by the Judges, or the Advocate, or the party respectively, it follows that it was open to the High Court of Allahabad, and indeed it was its duty, to entertain the petitions filed before it by the two Judges and by the Advocate, and it was within its jurisdiction to

> pass the interim orders prohibiting the further execution of the impugned orders passed by the House.
>
> Before we part with this topic, we would like to refer to one aspect of the question relating to the exercise of power to punish for contempt. So far as the courts are concerned, Judges always keep in mind the warning addressed to them by Lord Atkin in *Andre Paul vs. Attorney-General of Trinidad* (AIR 1936 PC 141). Said Lord Atkin, 'Justice is not a cloistered virtue; she must be allowed to suffer the scrutiny and respectful even though outspoken comments of ordinary men.' We ought never to forget that the power to punish for contempt large as it is, must always be exercised cautiously, wisely and with circumspection. Frequent or indiscriminate use of this power in anger or irritation would not help to sustain the dignity or status of the court, but may sometimes affect it adversely. Wise Judges never forget that the best way to sustain the dignity and status of their office is to deserve respect from the public at large by the quality of their judgements, the fearlessness, fairness, and objectivity of their approach, and by thc restraint, dignity and decorum which they observe in their judicial conduct. We venture to think that what is true of the Judicature is equally true of the Legislatures. (*Unquote*)

The result in the Presidential Reference was that the two judges of the Allahabad High Court were saved from being found guilty of contempt of the U.P. Legislative Assembly, but not poor Keshav Singh, the man who started it all. He was the inconsequential pawn in the great game of chess, between two powerful constitutional authorities. The answer of the Supreme Court to Question No. 5 (quoted above) had sealed his fate. The court having recorded that the answer to Question No. 5 in the reference in relation to contempt was to be read only with respect to matters '*outside the four walls of the legislative chamber*'.

So, when the case went back to the Allahabad High Court, a bench of two judges said that the pamphlet that Keshav Singh wrote and distributed was something that had happened *inside the four walls of the House*, and therefore he must suffer his 7-day sentence. The article of the Constitution that he had relied on (Article 22(2) that he must be produced before a magistrate within 24 hours) was plainly inapplicable since he had already been rightly convicted.

A Fourth Case that Became Infructuous

What might perhaps have been regarded as a resounding verdict—irrevocably and finally—in favour of the freedom of speech and expression, got thwarted in the early 1980s:

An influential Telegu Daily in Andhra Pradesh *(Enadu)* had been campaigning for some time for the abolition of the Upper House (the State Legislative Council) in the state of Andhra Pradesh. In March 1983, it reported (in one of its issues) some of the proceedings in the Legislative Council under a caption that was alleged to be derogatory to members of the Legislative Council. A notice of breach of privilege was issued to its editor and he was summoned. Then (after complying with the principles of Natural Justice), the Privileges Committee found the editor guilty of a breach of privilege, viz., of contempt. And the chairman of the Legislative Council issued a warrant addressed to the commissioner of police of Hyderabad, directing him to bring Mr Ramoji Rao (editor of *Faruqui*) before the House for passing sentence on him. Before complying, the editor moved the Supreme Court of India for relief in a petition under Article 32 of the Constitution. A series of orders were then passed by a Constitution Bench, which consisted of Chief Justice Y. V. Chandrachud, (along with Justices V. D. Tulzapurkar, R. S. Pathak, D. P. Madon, and M. P. Thakkar). After permitting the Editors Guild to intervene in the case, the court granted ex parte (without hearing the other side) an interim stay of the execution of the warrant, and a notice was issued to the chairman and secretary of the Legislative Council to show cause why the contempt proceedings initiated should not be quashed, but these dignitaries refused to accept service of the summons. The matter was reported back to the court and at the request of the petitioner, the court directed that a telegram be sent to the commissioner of police in Hyderabad not to execute the warrant issued by the chairman of the Legislative Council. On that day, the commissioner of police was the most miserable man in Hyderabad. He had a warrant from the chairman of the council to arrest Ramoji Rao and bring him to the House. He had also a direction from a bench of five judges of the Supreme Court, directing him not to execute that warrant. If he obeyed the warrant, he would himself definitely be guilty of contempt, and on the other hand, if he followed the directive of the Supreme Court, he would be equally guilty—of contempt—of the Legislative Council for not complying with the order of its chairman. But the commissioner of police was a resourceful man. He took the warrant of the chairman of the Legislative Council to the residence of Editor Ramoji Rao, and also showed him the direction in the later Supreme Court order. And he gave Ramoji Rao the choice: either to comply with the order of the Council or not to comply with its order because of the directions of the Supreme Court. The editor of *Enadu* did what any sensible man would have done, and the commissioner of police thereupon reported back to the chairman of the Council that Ramoji Rao had chosen not to comply with the warrant issued by the chairman in view of the directions of the Supreme Court of India. By this deft manoeuvre, the commissioner of police kept his job (and Ramoji Rao safeguarded his personal liberty). The next day, the advocate general of the state appeared in the Supreme Court of India, and the matter proceeded to argument for about an hour. After hearing arguments, the Constitution Bench then issued a Rule Nisi (i.e., it admitted the writ petition) and confirmed the order of stay. Written briefs were directed to be filed by all the parties in the writ petition for the final hearing to take place in due course. But then, events overtook the projected final hearing and precluded any authoritative decision.

Pursuant to a law enacted by Parliament under Article 169[8] of the Constitution—based on a resolution previously passed by the Legislative Assembly of the State—the Legislative Council was abolished. Consequently, further proceedings in the Supreme Court of India were rendered infructuous. The dispute did not get resolved only because of extraneous circumstances.

Conclusion

The truth of the matter is that, in the end, the uncodified privileges of Parliament (and of state legislatures) are not so much about Constitutional Law, as about tact and practical wisdom. In November 2003, when feelings ran high and strong words were exchanged between the editor and publishers of the *Hindu* and important officials in the Madras State Legislative Assembly, Prime Minister Atal Bihari Vajpayee—in a typically enigmatic one-liner—advised both parties *'not to cross the Lakshman Rekha'*.[9] Excellent advice, and so pithily put; as Lord Denning always liked to say, (quoting Churchill) *'Short words are best, and old words when short are best of all.'*

II. On the Power of the Governor to Grant Pardons and to Suspend, Remit, or Commute Sentences in Certain Cases (Article 161 in Part-VI;

[*There is a similar provision with regard to the power of the President (Article 72 in Part-V)*
It has been held that the President's power to grant pardon under Article 72 falls squarely in the judicial domain and can be exercised by the Court by way of judicial review—but not on merits: See *Maru Ram vs. Union of India* (1981) 1SCC 107 (5J) and *Kehar Singh vs. Union of India* (1989) 1SCC 204 (5J).

For Presidential pardons in the United States see Article Congressional Research Service https://crsreports.congress.gov dated 14 January 2020 (pages 1-21). See also Brookings commentary on Presidential pardons by Richard Lempert (dated 17 January 2021). https://www.brookings.edu/articles/presidential-pardons-settled-law-unsettled-issues-and-a-downside-for-trump/.]

The constitutional validity of the order of the governor of Bombay under Article 161 of the Constitution suspending the sentence (that had been imposed by a division bench of the high court) on Commander Nanavati, was heard by the Supreme Court of India in the year 1960, by a bench of five judges: AIR 1961 SC 112.

Nanavati was a brave, bright but extremely impetuous officer of the Indian Navy, who shot dead his wife's lover, Prem Ahuja. In view of an impassioned plea by his counsel, Karl Khandalavala, one of the leading criminal lawyers of his time, at the sessions trial)—(which then took place inthe City Civil and Sessions Court in the building adjacent to the High Court) and despite the summing up by the sessions judge—the jury brought in a verdict of not guilty of murder (8:1) (Since then trial by jury was abolished throughout Maharashtra State).

Since the principal sessions judge of the City Civil and Sessions Courts did not agree with the verdict of the jury, the case was referred to the high court under Section 307 of the then Code of Civil Procedure 1898. And the reference was headed by a division bench of two judges of the Bombay High

Court, justices Shelat and Naik. They reached a unanimous conclusion (though for different reasons), holding Commander Nanavati guilty of cold-blooded murder and sentenced him (under Section 302 of the IPC) to imprisonment for life. Y. V. Chandrachud, then government pleader, had successfully argued the reference for the State—a success that was for him the stepping stone to much higher accomplishments.

On the same day, as the sentence was pronounced, the then governor of Bombay, at the instance of the Centre, intervened, and under Article 161 passed an order (in March 1960), suspending the sentence imposed on Nanavati till he had filed his appeal in the Supreme Court. Arguments about the constitutional validity of this order of the governor were heard for several days in the central court by a specially constituted bench of five judges of the Bombay High Court. Since the order of the governor was not shown to be unconstitutional or contrary to law, the bench of five judges upheld the same and directed that the warrant of arrest of Commander Nanavati (which had been returned unfulfilled) should not be reissued, until Nanavati's appeal in the Supreme Court had been disposed of. However, in September 1960, the Supreme Court of India held (in *K.M. Nanavati vs. State of Bombay* (AIR 1961 SC 112)) that the governor's order of suspension of the sentence was invalid and required Commander Nanavati to surrender to a proper jail like all other convicted felons.

The history and genesis of the law of pardon has been elaborated in the 1960 decision of the Supreme Court of India and is reproduced below (para 12):

> (*Quote*) Let us now turn to the law on the subject as it obtains in India since the Code of Criminal Procedure was enacted in 1898. Section 401 of the Code gives power to the executive to suspend the execution of the sentence or remit the whole or any part of the punishment without conditions or upon any conditions which the person sentenced accepts. Section 402 gives power to the executive without the consent of the person sentenced to commute a sentence of death into

> imprisonment for life and also other sentences into sentences less rigorous in nature. In addition, the Governor-General had been delegated the power to exercise the prerogative power vesting in His Majesty. Sub-section (5) of s. 401 also provides that nothing contained in it shall be deemed to interfere with the right of His Majesty, or the Governor-General when such right is delegated to him, to grant pardons, reprieves, respites, or remissions of punishment. This position continued till the Constitution came into force. Two provisions were introduced in the Constitution to cover the former royal prerogative relating to pardon, and they are Arts. 72 and 161. Article 72 deals with the power of the President to grant pardons, reprieves, respites, or remissions of punishment or to suspend, remit, or commute the sentence of any person convicted of any offence. Article 161 gives similar power to the Governor of a State with respect to offences against any law relating to a matter to which the executive power of the State extends. Sections 401 and 402 of the Code have continued with necessary modifications to bring them into line with Arts. 72 and 161. It will be seen, however, that Arts. 72 and 161 not only deal with pardons and reprieves which were within the royal prerogative but have also included what is provided in ss. 401 and 402 of the Code. Besides the general power, there is also provision in ss. 337 and 338 of the Code to tender pardon to an accomplice under certain conditions. (*Unquote*)

Later, in *Kehar Singh vs. Union of India,* (referred to above, reported in AIR 1989 SC 653 (5J)), there was a further elaboration on the law of pardons quoted below:

> (*Quote*) paragraph 10: We are of the view that it is open to the President in the exercise of the power vested in him by Article 72 of the Constitution to scrutinise the evidence on the record of the criminal case and come to a different conclusion from that recorded by the court in regard to the guilt of, and sentence imposed on, the accused In doing so, the President does not amend or modify or supersede the judicial record.

The judicial record remains intact and undisturbed. The President acts in a wholly different lane from that in which the court acted. He acts under a constitutional power, the nature of which is entirely different from the judicial power and cannot be regarded as an extension of it. And this is so, notwithstanding that the practical effect of the Presidential act is to remove the stigma of guilt from the accused or to remit the sentence imposed on him.

***

The legal effect of a pardon is wholly different from a judicial supersession of the original sentence.

It is apparent that the power under Article 72 entitles the President to examine the record of evidence of the criminal case and to determine for himself whether the case is one deserving the grant of the relief falling within that power. The President is entitled to go into the merits of the case notwithstanding that it has been judicially concluded by the consideration given to it by Supreme Court.

(Paragraph 11) The order of the President cannot be subjected to judicial review on its merits except within strict limitations. However, the function of determining whether the act of a constitutional or statutory functionary falls within the constitutional or legislative conferment of power, or is vitiated by self-denial on an erroneous appreciation of the full amplitude of the power is a matter for the court. *The power to pardon belongs exclusively to the President and the Governor under the Constitution. There is also no question involved of asking the reasons for the President's order. The Courts are the constitutional instrumentalities to go into the scope of Article 72 on its merits. The question as to the area of the President's power under Article 72 falls squarely within the judicial domain and can be examined by the court by way of judicial review. (Unquote)*

III. The Comptroller and Auditor General of India (CAG)[10] (Articles 147 to 151): He is the Financial Ombudsman of the Union and of the States

The constitutional authority that supervises all financial matters of the union and the states is the CAG who is appointed by the president, by a warrant, under his (or her) hand and seal, and can only be removed from office in a like manner and on like grounds as a judge of the Supreme Court, i.e., on a motion passed by a two-thirds majority in Parliament for 'proved misbehaviour', not otherwise (Article 148). The CAG is required to submit reports to the president who must place them before each House of Parliament (Article 151). *A large number of questions in Parliament arise because of the reports of the CAG, who, next only to the Supreme Court, exercises a restraining influence on the all-powerful executive under our Constitution.* The fact that the government of the day at the centre, and some of its supporters, are nowadays seen criticising the CAG and his functioning—both in Parliament and outside—points to a dangerous trend, viz., of scant regard for constitutional functionaries and non-observance of constitutional norms.

In an editorial in the *Hindu* (2011)[11], the importance of the institution of the CAG had been (rightly) emphasised:

> (*Quote*) As auditor to a nation whose institutions of oversight are weak and underdeveloped, the Comptroller and Auditor General of India is more than just the keeper of our national accounts. It is, in many ways, a conscience keeper and a watchdog, which may not bite but can bark and warn ordinary citizens that something is amiss in the wider affairs of state. Like the Election Commission and the Supreme Court, the CAG has managed to protect its integrity and independence despite pressure from various arms of the state. If conducted freely and fairly, a robust audit can serve as a catalyst for corrective action. The CAG's report on Bofors in 1989 had major political consequences.

> Its explosive 2010 report on the allocation of 2G spectrum led to the filing of criminal charges against politicians, bureaucrats, and businessmen. Other reports may have been equally useful. The CAG's observations may be politically embarrassing to the government but they clearly contribute to the public good. Democratic India must ensure that the government takes the work of this constitutionally sanctioned institution very seriously and removes the obstacles placed in the path of a more effective and efficient audit process. (*Unquote*)

The officials in the CAG's office were (and are) absolute sticklers for rules—about which there is an amusing story related by John Masters in his autobiography *Bugles and the Tiger* (1956).[12] Way back in the 1940s, a certain Lieutenant Dishington stationed in Multan (in Punjab in British India—now in Pakistan) fell in love with an Anglo-Indian girl. He robbed the battalion chest of its money and eloped with her, by taking the train to Lahore (which was also in British India). His superior, a major, followed him by train and found Dishington outside Falettis Hotel (in Lahore). But the lieutenant with his girl gave him the slip by jumping into a taxi. The major got into another taxi and chased him all around town. Ultimately, Lieutenant Dishington was caught and made to part with the balance of the battalion's money. The major then returned to Multan and claimed reimbursement for train and taxi fare from the office of the comptroller of accounts. The claim was resisted all down the line by fatuous queries from the clerks in the comptroller's office. The first query was, as the major was entitled under FR (Fundamental Rule) 1097 to a charger, why did he not apprehend Dishington by using his horse? The major kept his temper in check and responded by pointing out that he didn't have the time to load his horse onto the train to Lahore, and even if he had, he could not have used his horse in Lahore since Dishington was in a vehicle with an internal combustion engine that ran faster than his horse! Undeterred, another official in the comptroller's office fired a second query: '. . . It is further noted that the alleged culprit, i.e., Lt. Dishington is an adjutant. Adjutants are also entitled to government charger (vide FR 1097). Kindly state why the government charger was not used by Lieutenant Dishington in the alleged flight and oblige.'

When, many years ago, I related this story to one of India's most distinguished CAGs, S. Ranganathan—Rangi, as he was affectionately known to his friends—smiled indulgently and said, 'My dear Nariman, if the babus in the auditor general's office didn't stick to the book, this country would have become bankrupt soon after independence.' He was right. *The CAG had been described by Dr B. R. Ambedkar as the 'most important officer in the Constitution'.*[13] He still is. Those holding the reins of power are always respectful towards the CAG—sometimes a little scared of him—as they rightly should be. His findings have been the subject of 'storms' in Parliament.

IV(a). Elections (Articles 324 to 329)

(1) Part-XV provides that the superitendence, direction and control of elections is to be vested in an Election Commission (Article 324(1). And under Article 324(2) the 'Election Commission' to consist of the Chief Election Commissioner (CEC) and *'such number of other Election Commissioners if any'* *as the President may time to time fix—and the appointment of the Chief Election Commissioner (CEC) and other Election Commissioners shall subject to any law made by Parliament in that behalf be made by the President (i.e., the Central Government).*

The Election Commission is to have:

a. The superintendence, direction, and control of the elections, preparation of the electoral rolls for all elections to Parliament and to the Legislature of every State.

b. The control of elections to the offices of President of India and Vice-President of India.

   [**NOTE:** 'The only dispute ever raised about a presidential election was that of V. V. Giri, president of India from 1969 to 1974. His election was challenged, (unsuccessfully), under the Presidential and Vice-Presidential Elections Rules, 1962, and the judgement of a Constitution Bench of five judges has been reported in *S. K. Singh vs. V. V. Giri* (AIR 1970 SC 2097).']

c. The conduct of all elections to Parliament and to State Legislatures.

d. An advisory role to the President on the question of *disqualification* of any member of Parliament (Article 103(2)); a similar advisory role is to the Governor of a State (Article 191(1)) when a question arises as to whether a member of a House of the Legislature of a State has been subject to any of the disqualifications mentioned in Article 191(1). The President and the

Governor of a State, are respectively required to obtain the opinion of the Election Commission (on the question of disqualification of a member of Parliament or of State Legislature) and to act according to such opinion.

After the insertion of Part-XV in the Constitution of India (Articles 324 to 329), Parliament had enacted:

A. The Representation of People Act 43 of 1950 that provided for:

   1. Allocation of Seats and delimitation of constituencies in the House of the People (Lok Sabha).
   2. Electoral officers.
   3. Electoral rules for Parliamentary (Lok Sabha) constituencies and for constituencies in the Council of State.
   4. Jurisdiction of civil courts being barred.

B. The Representation of People Act of 1951 which provided for:

   1. Qualifications and disqualifications for membership of the House of the People and for membership of the Council of States.
   2. Membership of State Legislatures and their qualifications and disqualifications.
   3. Disqualifications for voting, notifications for general elections, for registration of political parties, and for the general conduct of elections and for the general procedure at elections, and for presentation of election petitions and appeals.

The entire electoral machinery of the union as well as the State's is placed in the hands of a *centralised body*—the Election Commission—which alone is entitled to issue directives to returning officers, polling officers, and others engaged in the preparation and revision of electoral rolls so that no injustice may be done to any citizen of India by any centre, state, or local government.

Clause (5) of Article 324 provides for the security of tenure and it reads:

> (5) Subject to the provisions of any law made by Parliament, the conditions of service and tenure of office of the Election Commissioners and the Regional Commissioners shall be such as the President may by rule determine:
>
> Provided that the Chief Election Commissioner shall not be removed from his office except in like manner and on the like grounds as a Judge of the Supreme Court and the conditions of service of the Chief Election Commissioner shall not be varied to his disadvantage after his appointment:
>
> Provided further that any other Election Commissioner or a Regional Commissioner shall not be removed from office except on the recommendation of the Chief Election Commissioner.

The Election Commission is to be *independent* of executive control inasmuch as members of the Election Commission (and regional commissioners) cannot be removed by the president (i.e. by the central government) except on the recommendation of the chief election commissioner, and the chief election commissioner alone cannot be removed except in the manner provided for in Article 124(4), i.e., by Parliament strictly according to provisions relating to the removal of a judge of the Supreme Court of India.

The object underlying these provisions is not to create a special status for the CEC but to ensure an election free from the control of the political party for the time being in power, without which representative democracy becomes meaningless.[14]

(2) An important question for determination in Part-XV of the Constitution is as to the meaning to be given to Article 329(b) *(Bar to interference by courts in electoral matters).*

The word 'election' has, by long usage, in connection with the process of selection of proper representatives in democratic institutions, acquired both a wide meaning as well as a narrow meaning. In the narrow sense, it is used to mean the final selection of a candidate which may reflect the result of the poll when there is polling, or a particular candidate being returned unopposed when there is no poll. *But in the wider sense, the word is used to connote the entire process culminating in a candidate being declared elected*, and according to the Supreme Court of India, the word 'election' in Article 329(b) has been used in the wider sense, that is to say, to connote the entire procedure that has to be gone through in order to return a candidate to the appropriate legislature. The use of the expression *'conduct of elections'* in Article 324 itself specifically points to the wider meaning, and that meaning can also be read consistently into the other provisions which occur in Part-XV, including Article 329(b)[15].

As to the connotation of the word 'election', the Supreme Court had said in one of the earliest (as well as a leading) case on elections—*N. P. Ponnuswami vs. Returning Officer Namakkal Constituency* (AIR 1952 SC 64 (5J)) the following:

> (*Quote*) Having regard to the important functions which the legislatures have to perform in democratic countries, it has always been recognised to be a matter of first importance that elections should be concluded as early as possible according to time schedule and all controversial matters and all disputes arising out of elections should be postponed till after the elections are over, so that the election proceedings may not be unduly retarded or protracted. (*Unquote*)

In *Ponnuswami* (1952), Justice Fazl Ali delivered the judgement of the Constitution Bench of five judges (they were the very first judges of the Supreme Court of India)—in it he said:

> (*Quote*) This is an appeal from an order of the Madras High Court dismissing the petition of the appellant praying for a writ of certiorari.
>
> The appellant was one of the persons who had filed nomination papers for election to the Madras Legislative Assembly from the Namakkal Constituency in Salem district. On 28 November 1951, the Returning Officer for that constituency took up for scrutiny the nomination papers filed by the various candidates and on the same day he rejected the appellant's nomination paper on certain grounds which need not be set out as they are not material to the point raised in this appeal. The appellant thereupon moved the High Court under article 226 of the Constitution praying for a writ of certiorari to quash the order of the Returning Officer rejecting his nomination paper and to direct the Returning Officer to include his name in the list of valid nominations to be published. The High Court dismissed the appellant's application on the ground that it had no jurisdiction to interfere with the order of the Returning Officer by reason of the provisions of Article 329(b) of the Constitution. The appellant's contention in this appeal is that the view expressed by the High Court is not correct, that the jurisdiction of the High Court is not affected by Article 329(b) of the Constitution and that he was entitled to a writ of certiorari in the circumstances of the case. (*Unquote*)

(The Supreme Court upheld the High Court decision).

And it was held in *Ponnuswami* (AIR 1952 SC 64)—a unanimous decision of a Bench of Six Judges that the word 'election' is used in Article 329(b) in the wide sense of covering the entire process culminating in the election of the candidate and Justice Fazl Ali's judgement eloquently went on as follows:

> (*Quote*) (Paragraph 7): As we have seen, the most important question for determination is the meaning to be given to the word 'election' in Article 329(b). That word has by long usage in connection with the process of selection of proper representatives in democratic institutions, acquired both a wide and a narrow meaning. In the narrow sense, it is used to mean the final selection of a candidate which may embrace the result of the poll when there is polling or a particular candidate being returned unopposed when there is no poll. In the wide sense, the word is used to connote the entire process culminating in a candidate being declared elected. In *Srinivasalu vs. Kuppuswami* (AIR (15) 1928 Mad. 253 at p.255), the learned Judges of the Madras High Court after examining the question, expressed the opinion that the term 'election' may be taken to embrace the whole procedure whereby an 'elected member' is returned, whether or not it be found necessary to take a poll. With this view, my brother, Mahajan J. expressed his agreement in *Sat Narain vs. Hanuman Prasad* AIR (33) 1946 Lah. 85; and I also find myself in agreement with it. *It seems to me that the word 'election' has been used in Part-XV of the Constitution in the wide sense, that is to say, to connote the entire procedure to be gone through to return a candidate to the legislature. The use of the expression 'conduct of elections' in Article 324 specifically points to the wide meaning, and that meaning can also be read consistently into the other provisions which occur in Part-XV including Article 329(b).* That the word 'election' bears this wide meaning whenever we talk of elections in a democratic country, is borne out by the fact that in most of the books on the subject and in several cases dealing with the matter, one of the questions mooted is, when the election begins. The subject is dealt

with quite concisely in Halsbury's Laws of England in the following passage(s) under the heading 'Commencement of the Election':

> Although the first formal step in every election is the issue of the writ, the election is considered for some purposes to begin at an earlier date. It is a question of fact in each case when an election begins in such a way as to make the parties concerned responsible for breaches of election law, the test being whether the contest is 'reasonably imminent'. Neither the issue of the writ nor the publication of the notice of election can be looked to as fixing the date when an election begins from this point of view. Nor, again, does the nomination day afford any criterion. The election will usually begin at least earlier than the issue of the writ. The question of when the election begins must be carefully distinguished from that as to when 'the conduct and management of' an election may be said to begin. Again, the question as to when a particular person commences to be a candidate is a question to be considered in each case. (*Unquote*)

The discussion in this passage makes it clear that the word 'election' can be and has been appropriately used with reference to the entire process which consists of several stages and embraces many steps, some of which may have an important bearing on the result of the process.

(Paragraph 8): The next important question to be considered is what is meant by the words *'no election shall be called in question'*. A reference to any treatise on elections in England will show that an election proceeding in that country is liable to be assailed on very limited grounds, one of them being the improper rejection of a nomination paper. The law with which we are concerned is not materially different, and we find that in section 100 of the Representation of the People Act, 1951, one of the grounds for declaring an election to be void is the improper rejection of a nomination paper.

(Paragraph 9): **The question now arises whether the law of elections in this country contemplates that there should be two attacks on matters connected with election proceedings, one while they are going on by invoking the extraordinary jurisdiction of the High Court under Article 226 of the Constitution (the ordinary jurisdiction of the courts having been expressly excluded), and another after they have been completed by means of an election petition. In my opinion, to affirm such a position would be contrary to the scheme of Part-XV of the Constitution and the Representation of the People Act, which, as I shall point out later, seems to be that any matter which has the effect of vitiating an election should be brought up only at the appropriate stage in an appropriate manner before a special tribunal and should not be brought up at an intermediate stage before any court. It seems to me that under the election law, the only significance which the rejection of a nomination paper has consists in the fact that it can be used as a ground to call the election in question. Article 329(b) was apparently enacted to prescribe the manner in which and the stage at which this ground, and other grounds which may be raised under the law to call the election in question could be urged. I think it follows by necessary implication from the language of this provision that those grounds cannot be urged in any other manner, at any other stage and before any other court. If the grounds on which an election can be called in question could be raised at an earlier stage and errors, if any, are rectified, there will be no meaning in enacting a provision like Article 329(b) and in setting up a special tribunal. Any other meaning ascribed to the words used in the article would lead to anomalies, which the Constitution could not have contemplated, one of them being that conflicting views may be expressed by the High Court at the pre-**

> **polling stage and by the election tribunal, which is to be an independent body, at the stage when the matter is brought up before it.** (*Unquote*)

In *Pampakavi Rayappa Belagali vs. B. D. Jatti* (AIR 1971 SC 1348), it was held (on page 150) that the scheme of Representation of People the Act of 1950 and the amplitude of its provisions show that the entries made in an electoral roll of a constituency can only be challenged in accordance with the machinery provided by the Act and not in any other manner or before any other forum unless, some question of violation of the provisions of the Constitution is involved. And in a still later judgement, in *Mohinder Singh Gill vs. Chief Election Commissioner* (AIR 1978 SC 851 = 1978 (1) SCC 405)—another leading case—Justice Krishna Iyer, speaking for a Constitution Bench of Five Judges, considered at length the scope and meaning of Article 329(b) of the Constitution. Describing that article as the 'Great Wall of China', the learned judge posed the question whether it is so impregnable that it cannot be bypassed even by Article 226 (Power of High Courts to issue certain writs). Observing that 'every step from start to finish of the total process constitutes "election", not merely the conclusion or culmination', the judgement concluded at (AIR 1978 SC 851 at page 862 para 20 = 1978 (1) SCC 405 at page 427 para 26):

> The rainbow of operations, covered by the compendious expression 'election', thus commences from the initial notification and culminates in the declaration of the return of a candidate.

An examination of the scheme of Part-XV of the Constitution and the scheme of the Representative of People Act, 1951 (the law as to the conduct of elections) shows that, before the election machinery can be brought into operation, there are three prerequisites:

1. *First*, that there should be a set of laws and rules making provision with respect to all matters relating to, or in connection with, elections, and it should be decided as to how these laws and rules are to be made (Articles 327/328 deal with this prerequisite).
2. *Second*, that there should be an executive charged with the duty of securing the due conduct of elections (Article 324 deals with this prerequisite).
3. *Third*, that there should be a judicial tribunal to deal with disputes arising out of or in connection with elections (Article 329 deals with this prerequisite)—(originally it used to be a tribunal but for decades now, it is the high court of the state where the election is to be held).

The rest of the Articles in Part-XV, viz., Articles 325 and 326, deal with two matters of principle to which the Constitution framers attached great importance:

1. Prohibition against discrimination in the preparation of, or eligibility for inclusion in, the electoral rolls, on grounds of religion, race, caste, sex, or any of them.
2. Adult suffrage.

The Representation of People Act, 1951 is a self-contained enactment so far as elections are concerned and the writ jurisdiction of the high court under Article 226 of the Constitution is completely barred by The Representation of People Act, 1951 (because of the opening words in Article 329(b) 'notwithstanding anything in this Constitution . . .'), *they exclude the jurisdiction of the high courts to deal with any matter which may arise whilst the election is in progress.*

The law of 'elections' in India does not contemplate that there should be two attacks on matters connected with election proceedings: *one,* while elections are ongoing by invoking the extraordinary jurisdiction of the high court under Article 226 of the Constitution (the ordinary jurisdiction of the courts having been expressly excluded), *and another* after elections are completed by means of an election petition (to be filed under Parliamentary law—the Representation of Peoples Act 1951). Any matter which has the effect of vitiating an election can be brought up only at the appropriate stage in an appropriate manner before the special tribunal (in India currently the special tribunal is the high court in the state). It cannot and should not be brought up at an intermediate stage before any court.

Under the election law, the only significance which the rejection of a nomination paper of a candidate (by the electoral officer) is that it can be used as a ground to call the election in question. Article 329(b) was apparently enacted to prescribe the manner in which and the stage at which this ground, and other grounds which may be raised under the law to call the election in question, could be urged. It follows by necessary implication from the language of this provision that those grounds cannot be urged in any other manner, at any other stage and before any other court. If the grounds on which an election can be called in question could be raised at an earlier stage where errors, if any, get rectified, there would be no meaning in enacting a provision like Article 329(b) and in setting up a special tribunal to deal with disputes concerning elections. Any other meaning ascribed to the words used in the article would lead to anomalies, which the Constitution could never have contemplated.

The underlying principle in Part-XV of the Constitution is where a right or liability is created by statute which gives a special remedy for enforcing it, the remedy provided by that statute can only be availed of. It is fair inference to draw from the provisions of the Representation of the People Act 1951 that the Act provides for only one remedy, that remedy being by an election petition to be presented after the election is over, and there is no remedy provided for at any intermediate stage.

Another problem in all elected democracies is the almost over-powering problem of corruption and in India too, it has reached tidal-wave proportions. The Polish Nobel Laureate Czesław Miłosz[16] expressed the dilemma with poignancy in the following words:

Ill at ease in the tyranny
Ill at ease in the republic
In the one I longed for freedom
In the other (I longed for) the end of corruption.[17]

And courts in India have been conscious of this.

In *Lily Thomas vs. Union of India and other* (2013 (7) SCC 653), it was held by a bench of two judges of India's Supreme Court as follows:

> (*Quote*) Articles 102(1)(e) and 191(1)(e) of the Constitution, have conferred specific powers on Parliament to make law providing disqualifications for membership of either House of Parliament or Legislative Assembly or Legislative Council of the State other than those specified in subclauses (a), (b), (c), and (d) of clause (1) of Articles 102 and 191 of the Constitution. We may note that no power is vested in the State Legislature to make law laying down disqualifications of membership of the Legislative Assembly or Legislative Council of the State and power is vested in Parliament to make law laying down disqualifications also in respect of Members of the Legislative Assembly or Legislative Council of the State. (*Unquote*)

The above-quoted passage was cited again with approval by a bench of five judges in *Public Interest Foundation vs. Union of India* (2019 (3) SCC 224 (5J)).

Conclusion:

In a series of decisions of the Supreme Court of India from 2014 to 2019, the Supreme Court of India has held:

1. That in order to maintain purity of elections and to bring transparency in the process of elections, the Election Commission of India must issue necessary orders, in exercise of its power under Article 324 of the Constitution of India, to call for information on affidavit from every candidate seeking election to the Parliament or a State Legislature as a necessary part of his nomination-paper and furnishing therein information relating to his conviction/acquittal/discharge in any criminal offence in the past, any case pending against him of any offence punishable with imprisonment for two years or more, information regarding assets (movable, immovable, bank balance, etc.) of the candidate as well as of his/her spouse and that of dependants, liability, if any, and the educational qualification of the candidate. See *Resurgence India vs. Election Commission of India,* 2014 (14) SCC 189 at 193 following observations in an earlier decision reported in *People's Union of Civil Liberties vs. Union of India & Anr,* 2003 (4) SCC 399.

2. In a later decision—in *Public Interest Foundation vs. Union of India* (2019 (3) SCC 224)—a Constitution Bench of the Supreme Court of India reiterated directions previously given in various cases and said:

   29.1. The voter has the elementary right to know the full particulars of a candidate who is to represent him in Parliament/Assemblies and such right to get information is universally recognised. Thus, it has been held that the right to know about the candidate is a natural right flowing from the concept of democracy and is an integral part of Article 19(1)(a) of the Constitution.

   29.2. The ultimate purpose of filing of affidavit along with the nomination paper is to effectuate the fundamental right of the citizens under Article

> 19(1)(a) of the Constitution of India. The citizens are supposed to have the necessary information at the time of filing of nomination paper and *for that purpose, the Returning Officer can very well compel a candidate to furnish the relevant information.*
>
> 29.3. Filing of affidavit with blank particulars would render the affidavit nugatory.
>
> 29.4. It is the duty of the Returning Officer to check whether the information required is fully furnished at the time of filing of affidavit with the nomination paper since such information is very vital for giving effect to the 'right to know' of the citizens. If a candidate fails to fill the blanks even after the reminder by the Returning Officer, the nomination paper is fit to be rejected. We do comprehend that the power of Returning Officer to reject the nomination paper must be exercised very sparingly but the bar should not be laid so high that justice itself is prejudiced.
>
> 29.5. When an affidavit is filed with blank particulars item be rejected.
>
> 29.6. The candidate must take the effort to explicitly remark as 'NIL' or 'Not Applicable' or 'Not known' in the columns and not to leave the particulars blank.
>
> 29.7. Filing of affidavit with blanks is simply not permitted.

In *Public Interest Foundation vs. Union of India* (2019 (3) SCC 224 on page 280), the Constitution Bench issued directions regarding elections which were in accord with prior decisions of the court, viz.:

> Each contesting candidate shall fill up the form as provided by the Election Commission and the form must contain all the particulars as required therein.

> It shall state, in bold letters, with regard to the criminal cases pending against the candidate.
>
> If a candidate is contesting an election on the ticket of a particular party, he/she is required to inform the party about the criminal cases pending against him/her.
>
> The political party shall be obligated to put up on its website the aforesaid information pertaining to candidates having criminal antecedents.
>
> The candidate as well as the concerned political party shall issue a declaration in the widely circulated newspapers in the locality about the antecedents of the candidate and also give wide publicity in the electronic media. When we say wide publicity, we mean that the same shall be done at least thrice after filing of the nomination papers.

The court then added:

> (*Quote*) These directions ought to be implemented in true spirit and right earnestness in a bid to strengthen the democratic set-up. There may be certain gaps or lacunae in a law or legislative enactment which can definitely be addressed by the legislature if it is backed by the proper intent, strong resolve, and determined will of right-thinking minds to ameliorate the situation. It must also be borne in mind that the law cannot always be found fault with for the lack of its stringent implementation by the concerned authorities. Therefore, it is the solemn responsibility of all concerned to enforce the law as well as the directions laid down by this Court from time to time in order to infuse the culture of purity in politics and in democracy and foster and nurture an informed citizenry, for ultimately it is the citizenry which decides the fate and course of politics in a nation and thereby ensures that we shall be governed no better than we deserve, and thus, complete information about the criminal antecedents of the candidates forms the

> bedrock of wise decision-making and informed choice by the citizenry. Be it clearly stated that informed choice is the cornerstone to have a pure and strong democracy. (*Unquote*)

(3) When people in developing countries—like India—get fed up with the parliamentary system of democracy, they speak glowingly of the US presidential system. But students of American politics have come up with statistics which show that in U.S. presidential elections since 1788, the American electorate has rejected 'good and superior men' 50 per cent of the time. Not a flattering score for the presidential system. And what of the able men who ran and won? After a careful study of events and personalities over two centuries, Irving Stone's[18] grim conclusion is: '*only by the meanest of margins has democracy been able to prove that it has the discernment to choose the best men available for the most important office in the land.*'

But there are many other things one has to learn from the American electoral system. One of them being the way they operate the checks and balances in the system. They do work and they are real. Another aspect is that people take government and governance seriously. The exit of the 37th President of the United States, Richard Nixon (who served as president from 1969 to 1974), was only possible because of the courage of his appointees who defied him when he attempted to assume dictatorial powers. One of the brave men of the time was Prof. Archibald Cox[19] whom Nixon had fired after Cox had asked Judge John Joseph Sirica[20] to issue a subpoena to the president of the USA to produce the fateful Watergate tapes. Professor Cox's significant comment at the time was: 'It is because the people rose up politically and morally, that the Rule of Law prevailed.'

There is much pathos in a democracy, in fact, a great deal of it, viz., the tragedy of a free people freely participating in electing governments, and then bemoaning their fate in what is often seen as the tragedy of freedom squandered.

IV(b): Election Commission

Under Article 324(1) the superintendence, direction and control of elections has been vested in the Election Commission, and under Article 324(2), the Election Commission is to consist of the Chief Election Commissioner 'and such number of other Election Commissioners, if any, as the President (i.e., the central government) may from time to time fix'. *But it is only the chief election commissioner (under the first Proviso to Clause 5 of Article 324) who cannot be removed from his office 'except in like manner and on like grounds as a judge of the Supreme Court of India', nor can his conditions of service be varied to his disadvantage after his appointment.*

These seemingly odd set of provisions had worked well from 1952 to about 1982 only because—for almost 30 years—the Government of India did not find it necessary to appoint any election commissioners. The entire business of the Election Commission was left to be conducted by the chief election commissioner (CEC) alone and each CEC was a distinguished civil servant who invariably acted, and what is more important, *was also seen to act independently of government.* For example, in early 1982, some prominent members of the Congress Party sought to restrain the Election Commission and its subordinate officers from issuing notifications calling for elections to the West Bengal Legislative Assembly on the ground that the electoral rolls had not been 'duly and properly revised'. Writ petitions were filed in the High Court of Calcutta and interim restraint orders were passed by a learned single judge of the Calcutta High Court, that no notification be issued under Section 15(2) of the Representation of People Act 1951, calling for elections to the West Bengal Legislative Assembly, 'until the rolls were duly revised'.

The then chief election commissioner then moved the Supreme Court on the ground that the election process was being thwarted by 'frivolous and baseless' objections, the electoral rolls (he asserted) had been already updated and properly revised, and the CEC prayed for withdrawal of the writ petition filed in the High Court of Calcutta to the Supreme Court of India, which was granted and the writ petition was finally disposed off by the apex court.[21] It was an important case with vast political implications. The CPI(M) (Communist Party of India (Marxist)) contended that the assembly elections must be called, whilst the Congress Party responded by saying: 'not just yet'. The Union of India (i.e., the central government) was represented before the Constitution Bench in the Supreme Court by all its law officers—the then attorney general of India, the then solicitor general of India, and the then additional solicitor general of India. They all appeared to support the interim order of the High Court of Calcutta. The Election Commission was represented by a counsel of its choice (an assertion of its independent stand) who requested the Supreme Court to vacate the interim order of the Calcutta High Court. The contentions urged by the Election Commission before the Supreme Court were diametrically opposed to those advanced on behalf of the Union of India. The chief election commissioner was then the distinguished civil servant, Mr Shakdher, and this proved to be his finest hour; since the order of the High Court of Calcutta was vacated by the Supreme Court of India.

Election commissioners came to be appointed for the first time only in 1989 and then, with questionable motives. In October 1989, by successive notifications, the number of election commissioners (other than the CEC) was fixed, and two government officials were appointed to fill the posts. Their tenure under the statutory rules then in operation was 5 years but within the first 3 months (in January 1990), the notification of October 1989 fixing the number of election commissioners at two was 'rescinded'! The two election commissioners, though appointed to hold and expected to hold office for 5 years from October 1989, were simply 'dropped' from the Election Commission. They challenged the rescinding notifications before the Supreme Court, but the challenge failed.[22] The Supreme Court (a bench of two Hon'ble Judges) simply held that the two election commissioners, who had been appointed in October 1989, had been appointed without any valid reason. The observations of the court are reproduced below:

> (*Quote*) In the view that we have taken, namely, that there was no need for the posts of the Election Commissioners at the time the appointments were made and that in the absence of a clear definition of their role in the Commission, particularly, vis-a-vis the Chief Election Commissioner, the appointments were an oddity, the abolition of the posts far from striking at the independence of the Commission paved the way for its smooth and effective functioning. In view further of the fact that for reasons stated above, it is not possible to hold that the Election Commissioners have the same powers and the authority as the Chief Election Commissioner, and it may well be that the Chief Election Commissioner has the power to disregard and override the views of the Election Commissioners, the abolition of their posts least infringed on the independence of the Commission. Hence, we are not enamoured of the second contention advanced on behalf of the petitioner, viz., that the abolition of the posts tampered directly or indirectly with the independence of the Commission. (*Unquote*)

Later, in January 1991, the central government decided that the salary, pension, and other conditions of service of the CEC should be equivalent to that of a judge of the Supreme Court of India and of the comptroller and auditor general of India, and that the salary, pension, and conditions of service of an election commissioner should be equivalent to those of a judge of the high court. This decision was translated into law by Parliament enacting the Chief Election Commissioner and other Election Commissioners (Conditions of Service) Act, 1991. But as to how many posts there should be of election commissioners, and when they should be filled, the choice was left to the absolute discretion of the central government. The status of irremovability, during tenure, which had been deliberately conferred on the CEC by the Constitution of India, 1950, (to ensure his independence) was not conferred on the election commissioners—not by the Parliamentary Act of 1991, not even by the later ordinance of 1 October 1993 (which was replaced by Act 4 of 1994). The notification issued under the ordinance only provided for the appointment of two election commissioners w.e.f. 1 October 1993 and also provided that for all decisions in the new multi-member Election Commission, decisions were to be unanimous, and failing unanimity, to be by majority.

The then Chief Election Commissioner, Mr T. N. Seshan, challenged the appointment of these two commissioners as 'unconstitutional'. The allegations made were serious. It was alleged by the CEC in *T. N. Seshan vs. Union of India* (1995 (4) SCC 611 (5J)) that after his appointment on 12 December 1990, he had insisted on strict compliance with the model code of conduct by all political parties and candidates for election and took stern action against infractions thereof regardless of the political party or candidate involved. The ruling party at the centre was irked as a few of the bye-elections of the ruling party leaders/cabinet, ministers were put off because of the government's failure to deploy sufficient staff and police force for the elections and the ruling party lost the elections in Tripura on account of strict action taken by the CEC against erring officials and consequent postponement of elections. *The ruling party made attempts to influence the CEC but could not do so as he did not allow the emissaries of the party to meet him.* The CEC also filed a writ petition in the Supreme Court for enforcing the constitutional right of the Election Commission for staff. The CEC declined to postpone elections for four state assemblies despite requests from the ruling party, including the prime minister, which irritated the ruling party. The ruling party, therefore, with a view to freeze the powers of the CEC and to prevent him from taking any action against violation of the code of conduct chose to amend the law and allegedly misused the power of the president under Article 324(2) of the Constitution by issuing the notification dated 1 October 1993, fixing the number of ECs at two and simultaneously appointing the two ECs.

The Constitution Bench decision of the Supreme Court of India in *T. N. Seshan, Chief Election Commissioner vs. Union of India* (5J) was disappointing. A bench of five judges of the Supreme Court of India first upheld the constitutional validity of the 1991 Act, and then went out of its way to express its concern at the government treating other constitutional dignitaries in the same position as judges of the high court and of the Supreme Court. And the judges of the Supreme Court went out of their way to express their 'concern' in the following words:

> (*Quote*) We mention this because of late we find that even personnel belonging to other fora claim equation with High Court and Supreme Court Judges merely because certain jurisdictions earlier exercised by those Courts are transferred to them not realising the distinction between constitutional and statutory functionaries. We would like to impress on the Government that it should not confer equivalence or interfere with the Warrant of Precedence, if it is likely to affect the position of High Court and Supreme Court Judges, however pressing the demand may be, without first seeking the views of the Chief Justice of India. *We may add that Mr G. Ramaswamy, learned counsel for the CEC, frankly conceded that the CEC could not legitimately claim to be equated with Supreme Court Judges. We do hope that the Government will take note of this and do the needful.* (*Unquote*)

The judges of the Supreme Court rejected the contention of the chief election commissioner (T. N. Seshan) that he was in a superior position to that of the election commissioners and recorded in (paragraph 17 of the judgement) as follows:

> (*Quote*) Under clause (3) of Article 324, in the case of a multi-member Election Commission, the CEC 'shall act'

> as the Chairman of the Commission. As we have pointed out earlier, Article 324 envisages a permanent body to be headed by a permanent incumbent, namely, the CEC. The fact that the CEC is a permanent incumbent cannot confer on him a higher status than the ECs for the simple reason that the latter are not intended to be permanent appointees. Since the Election Commission would have a staff of its own dealing with matters concerning the superintendence, direction, and control of the preparation of electoral rolls, etc., that staff would have to function under the direction and guidance of the CEC and hence it was in the fitness of things for the Constitution-makers to provide that where the Election Commission is a multi-member body, the CEC shall act as its Chairman. That would also ensure continuity and smooth functioning of the Commission. (*Unquote*)

After this judgement, which designedly (and most unfortunately) clipped the wings of the CEC, the question that was asked—not just then but continuously since then—was as to how independent was the Election Commission as a body after the judgement in *T. N. Seshan vs. Union of India?* The answer has been that it is definitely not independent—not because the 1991 law and the notifications were upheld. The court could not have held otherwise since a multi-member commission can only act—if it is to effectively act at all—either unanimously or by majority. *The election commissioners are institutionally not independent, simply because they have no security of tenure.* In *T. N. Seshan,* the court should have enjoined upon government the obligation of maintaining a multi-member Election Commission as a permanent body and, in addition, should have imposed on government as a condition to its upholding the validity of the amending law a further obligation to introduce legislation within a time bound period (by way of Amendment to the 1991 Act) by guaranteeing to the newly-appointed election commissioners (and all subsequent election commissioners) the status of irremovability during their respective tenures.

Whilst declaring that in the decision-making of the multi-member Election Commission, the election commissioner had equal status with the chief election commissioner, the court ought to have ensured:

i. That the number of election Commissioners and their appointment should no longer be left to the sole and unguided discretion of the central government;
ii. That a multi-member Election Commission of three should be mandated by law; and
iii. Above all, that the election commissioners when appointed should have the same assurance of independence during their tenure (then a statutory 6-year term) as was granted to the holder of the office of the chief election commissioner. Only then, could election commissioners claim the right to equal participation in decision-making in the business of the Commission, and *only then could the public be assured that a multi-member Election Commission was institutionally insulated against all governmental influence and pressure.*

I believe that public confidence in the integrity of a three-member Commission can only be maintained if and when it is made a permanent feature beyond the reach of governmental orders and notifications, and when the offices of the election commissioners are institutionally insulated from influence and pressure, and when these officers are seen to be as independent from government control, as has been safeguarded in the case of the office of chief election commissioner. This is why even the latest majority decision of March 2, 2023 of a Constitution Bench of the Supreme Court of India in Anoop Baranwal vs. Union of India (4:1) has not gone far enough. As was argued before the bench in Anoop Baranwal, the functional autonomy of the CEC and the ECs has a direct link with the process by which they are selected.

'In an electoral autocracy, the executive would prevail over the poll-panel in varied ways' (which was the precise complaint of Petitioners Advocate Kaleeswaram Raj before the Supreme Court)[23].

[Please see extract of an article in the *Indian Express* of Friday, March 3, 2023, in footnote No. 23]

Notes and References:

1. Article 105: Powers, privileges, etc., of the Houses of Parliament and of the members and committees thereof.

   2. Subject to the provisions of this Constitution and to the rules and standing orders regulating the procedure of Parliament, there shall be freedom of speech in Parliament.
   3. No member of Parliament shall be liable to any proceedings in any court in respect of anything said or any vote given by him in Parliament or any committee thereof, and no person shall be so liable in respect of the publication by or under the authority of either House of Parliament of any report, paper, votes, or proceedings.
   4. In other respects, the powers, privileges, and immunities of each House of Parliament, and of the members and the committees of each House, shall be such as may from time to time be defined by Parliament by law, and, until so defined, (shall be those of that House and of its members and committees immediately before the coming into force of section 15 of the Constitution (44th Amendment) Act, 1978).
   5. The provisions of clauses (1), (2), and (3) shall apply in relation to persons who by virtue of this Constitution have the right to speak in, and otherwise to take part in the proceedings of, a House of Parliament or any committee thereof as they apply in relation to members of Parliament.

   Article 194: Powers, privileges, etc., of the Houses of Legislatures and of the members and committees thereof.

1. Subject to the provisions of this Constitution and to the rules and standing orders regulating the procedure of the Legislature, there shall be freedom of speech in the Legislature of every State.
2. No member of the Legislature of a State shall be liable to any proceedings in any court in respect of anything said or any vote given by him in the Legislature or any committee thereof, and no person shall be so liable in respect of the publication by or under the authority of a House of such a Legislature of any report, paper, votes or proceedings.
3. In other respects, the powers, privileges, and immunities of a House of the Legislature of a State, and of the members and the committees of a House of such Legislature, shall be such as may from time to time be defined by the Legislature by law, and, until so defined, (shall be those of that House and of its members and committees immediately before the coming into force of section 26 of the Constitution (44th Amendment) Act, 1978).
4. The provisions of clauses (1), (2), and (3) shall apply in relation to persons who by virtue of this Constitution have the right to speak in, and otherwise to take part in the proceedings of, a House of the Legislature of a State or any committee thereof as they apply in relation to members of that Legislature.

2. *Edward Kielley vs. William Carson*—(1842) IV Moore's Privy Council Cases 63 at 92.

3. *Gunupati Keshavram vs. Nafisul Hasan*—a decision handed down on 18 March 1952—reported later in AIR 1954 SC 636 (five judges).

4. *Pandit M. S. M. Sharma vs. Shri Sri Krishna Sinha and Others,* AIR 1959 SC 395.

5. Similar is the wording and effect of Article 105 (Power and privileges of Houses of Parliament).
Justice Subba Rao in his dissent stated as follows:

> 1, therefore, hold that in the year 1950, the House of Commons had no privilege to prevent the publication of correct and faithful reports of its proceedings save those in the case of secret sessions held under exceptional circumstances and had only a limited privilege to prevent mala fide publication of garbled, unfaithful or expunged reports of the proceedings. It follows from my view, namely, that the petitioner's fundamental right under Art. 19(1)(a) is preserved despite the provisions of Article 194(3) of the Constitution, and that the petitioner is entitled to succeed.

6. Special Reference 1 of 1964, under Article 143 of the Constitution reported in AIR 1965 SC 745 (decided by a special bench of seven judges (6:1)).

7. Article 21: Protection of life and personal liberty—No person shall be deprived of his life or personal liberty except according to procedure established by law.

8. Article 160: Abolition or creation of Legislative Councils in States.
    1. Notwithstanding anything in article 168 (Constitution of Legislatures in States), Parliament may by law provide for the abolition of the Legislative Council of a State having such a Council or for the creation of such a Council in a State having no such Council, if the Legislative Assembly of the State passes a resolution to that effect by a majority of the total membership of the Assembly and by a majority of not less than two-thirds of the members of the Assembly present and voting.
    2. Any law referred to in clause (1) shall contain such provisions for the amendment of this Constitution as may be necessary to give effect to the provisions of the law and may also contain such supplemental, incidental, and consequential provisions as Parliament may deem necessary.
    3. No such law as aforesaid shall be deemed to be an amendment of this Constitution for the purposes of Article 368.

9. The Lakshman Rekha: A line, actual or imaginary, the crossing of which may have serious consequences. The figure of speech derives from a story in the Ramayana. During his exile, Lord Ram, his wife, Sita, and his brother, Lakshman, were living in a forest hut. One day, Sita thought she noticed a golden deer (actually a lure, sent by Ram's enemy, King Ravan) and implored her husband to get it for her. Ram left to chase the deer, leaving Lakshman to look after Sita. An urgent call for help was heard from the forest, seemingly in Ram's voice. Before departing, Lakshman encircled the hut with a line on the ground and informed Sita that on no account was she to cross it. Ravan appeared in the guise of a yogi asking for food. Sita could not refuse a holy man's request and she crossed the line and was abducted.

10. Articles 148 to 151: Chapter V in Part-V of the Constitution.

11. Wednesday, 29 June 2011.

12. John Masters: *Bugles and the Tiger*, published Cassell Military Paperbacks (republished by Cassell Military, London, June 2002). John Masters was commissioned into the Gurkha Rifles on the eve

of the Second World War and rose to command one of the Chindit columns fighting behind the lines against the Japanese in Burma. He left the army after the war to pursue a very profitable career as a novelist. Khushwant Singh, a renowned Indian writer, had famously remarked that 'while (Rudyard) Kipling understood India, John Masters understood Indians.' (John Masters, *Pilgrim Son: A Personal Odyssey,* G. B. Putnam and Sons, New York, 1971 edition, page 348.).

13. CAD, Vol. VIII, pages 407-408.
14. CAD, Vol. VIII, page 906.
15. Article 329(b) reads as follows:
    a. ...
    b. no election to either House of Parliament or to the House or either House of the Legislature of a State shall be called in question except by an election petition presented to such authority and in such manner as may be provided for by or under any law made by the appropriate Legislature.
16. Czesław Miłosz (30 June 1911-14 August 2004) was a Polish-American poet, prose writer, translator, and diplomat. He was awarded the 1980 Nobel Prize in literature and is regarded as one of the great poets of the 20th century.
17. Czesław Miłosz's English poem (to Raja Rao - Berkeley, 1969).
18. Irving Stone (14 July 1903-26 August 1989) was an American writer, chiefly known for his biographical novels of noted artists, politicians, and intellectuals. Among the best known are *Lust for Life* (1934) about the life of Vincent van Gogh and *The Agony and the Ecstasy* (1961) about Michelangelo.
19. Archibald Cox Jr. (17 May 1912-29 May 2004) was an American lawyer and law professor who served as US solicitor general under President John F. Kennedy and as a special prosecutor during the Watergate scandal. During his career, he was a pioneering expert on labour law and was also an authority on constitutional law. *The Journal of Legal Studies* has identified Cox as one of the most cited legal scholars of the 20th century.
20. John Joseph Sirica (19 March 1904 – 14 August 1992) was a United States district judge of the United States district court for the District of Columbia, where he became famous for his role in the trials stemming from the Watergate scandal.

21. See *Lakshmi Charan Sen vs. A. K. M. Hassan Uzzaman,* 1984 (4) SCC 689 (bench of five judges, presided over by Chief Justice Y. V. Chandrachud) upholding the stand of the chief election commissioner.

22. See *S. S. Dhanoa vs. Union of India,* judgement of 24 July 1991, reported in 1991 (3) SCC 567 on page 585 (para 28).

23. **Extract of article: 'More Independent Commission' on the editorial page of the *Indian Express* of Friday 3 March 2023:**

> **The immunity granted to the CEC loses its purpose when the selection is vitiated by arbitrariness or favouritism. That apart, for want of security of tenure, the other ECs might be more susceptible to the executive—this was the apprehension placed before the Supreme Court . . .**
>
> **The vacuum in Article 324(2) is essentially a democratic space, which the Constituent Assembly did not want to occupy by way of any prescription whatsoever. This space was left to the future Parliament. The elected Parliament was supposed to legislate on this issue with a greater element of democratic legitimacy. That was a constitutional aspiration rather that a vacuum. It was, however, not fulfilled. As a result, the executive enjoyed the benefit of appointing people as chosen by it as the CEC and ECs. One of the main concerns was that this led to perceptions of bias of the Commission in favour of the ruling party . . .**

Chapter Eight

The Constitution Today and Prospects for the Future

A constitution is no respecter of persons nor of political parties. India's Constitution has not been built around any person or any political figure. But one must not overlook an important fact, viz., that more than half the countries in the world today are governed by constitutions that do not inspire or foster a *spirit of constitutionalism.* They do have written constitutions but how successfully they function depends largely on how persons in power (politicians) work them and how persons in authority (like judges), interpret them.

There is, of course, a felt need for institutional safeguards in every country, not only to protect diversity and to foster unity amongst its people, *but also to preserve the rule of law*. This is an aspect of constitutionalism that can never be ignored. It is only then that the written document becomes a basic document of governance.

But it is important always to keep in mind that a democratic government demands not only a parliamentary majority but also a parliamentary minority. As British historian of the Commonwealth, Ivor Jennings, pointed out way back in 1969:-

> (*Quote*) It is not untrue to say that the most important part of Parliament is the Opposition... 'Attacks upon the Government and upon individual ministers are the functions of the Opposition. The duty of the Opposition

> is to oppose. It adopts Sir Toby's advice: 'So soon as ever thou seest him, draw, and as thou drawest, swear horrible'!! That duty is the major check which the Constitution provides... The minority attacks the Government because it denies the principles of its policy. The Opposition will, almost certainly, be defeated in Parliament because it is a minority. Its appeals are to the electorate. It will, at the next election, ask the people to condemn the Government, and, as a consequence, to give a majority to the Opposition. Because the Government is criticised, it has to meet criticism. Because it must, in course of time, defend itself in the constituencies, it must persuade public opinion to move with it. The Opposition is at once the alternative to the Government and a focus for the discontent of the people. Its function is almost as important as that of the Government. **If there be no Opposition, there is no democracy. 'Her majesty's Opposition' is no idle phrase. Her Majesty needs an Opposition as well as a Government.**[1] (*Unquote*)

All has been adopted in India. In the July 2020 publication of the Parliament of India (Rajya Sabha) ("Role of the Leader of the House, Leader of the Opposition and Whips") it has been stated (quoting Jennings and others):

> (Quote) The task of the Leader of the Opposition is unlike that of the Leader of the House, but it is nevertheless of considerable importance. Opposition is an essential part of democratic Government (*Cabinet Government*, 'Chapter XV—Government and Parliament' (pp. 472 to 510) by Ivor Jennings). What is expected from an opposition is effective criticism (*ibid*). It is therefore, not untrue to say that the most important part of Parliament, is the Opposition. Government governs and opposition criticises (*ibid*). Thus both have functions and rights.
>
> Attacks upon the Government and individual Ministers are the functions of the Opposition. The duty of the

> Opposition is to oppose. The duty is the major check upon corruption and defective administration. It is also the means by which individual injustices are prevented. This duty is hardly less important than that of the Government. The apparent absurdity that the Opposition asks for parliamentary time to be set aside by the Government in order that the Opposition may censure the Government, is not an absurdity at all. It is the recognition by both sides of the House that the Government governs openly and honestly and that it is prepared to meet criticism not by secret police and concentration camps but by rational argument (*ibid*).
>
> The Opposition and Government are carried on alike by agreement. The minority agrees that the majority must govern, and the majority agrees that the minority should criticise. The process of parliamentary government will break down if there was absence of mutual forbearance. The Prime Minister meets the convenience of the Leader of the Opposition and the Leader of the Opposition meets that convenience of the Government (*ibid*). Only by this method, can the system of the parliamentary Government sustain. The Opposition has no right to obstruct, in the sense of making Parliament barren or unproductive (ibid). It would be the clearest proof of the triumph of party spirit over parliamentary spirit if any Government set out to whittle away the rights of the Opposition (*British Parliament, Campion*, 1981, pp.20-21). The uninterrupted respect for the rights of the Opposition which Government shows should be accepted as prima facie evidence of the soundness of its parliamentary faith (*Parliament: A Survey, Campion*, 1952, page 31). (*Unquote*)

The problem in India these past 75 years has been that what has been proudly professed is not practised. Although India boasts of a multi-party system for prolonged periods of time, the system has not worked as it was expected to work. This is because, in these past 75 years, there have been two sets of majoritarian governments at the centre: the majoritarian government consisting of and owing allegiance to the Congress Party from 1952 till, (almost continuously), 1989[2] and a majoritarian government, with the Bhartiya Janata Party in control, between the years 2014 to 2019; and once again, in greater control after the general elections of 2019. And the record of each of these two rival sets of majoritarian governments—*vis-a-vis political parties in opposition* (whether from 1952 to 1989 or from 2014 onwards)—has been dismal—not inspiring at all! In each of these periods, attempts were (and continue to be) made by the government at the centre todiscredit the Opposition, and also to topple or dislodge duly elected state governments that owe allegiance to political parties, different from the majoritarian political party at the centre; this has in turn led WE THE PEOPLE to question whether, in India, majoritarian and super-majoritarian governments are at all able and willing to successfully and effectively work a system of parliamentary democracy on the Westminster model. As observed in Granville Austin's *Working of a Democratic Constitution*[3]:

> (*Quote*) A Constitution however 'living' is inert; it does not 'work' on its own; it is worked by human beings whose conduct it may shape but whose character it cannot improve and whose tasks it cannot perform. (*Unquote*)

In Romila Thapar's latest publication (2023) *The FUTURE in the PAST*, the distinguished historian has written that: "Majoritarianism can easily become – and often does — an authoritative anti-democratic system . . . "

And Neeraja Chowdhury in her most recent book "*How Prime Ministers Decide*" (Aleph – August 2023) poses a striking contrast between the year 1947 and the year 2023:

> (*Quote*) In 1947, India had opted for a Nehru – not a Jinnah – and rejected religion as the basis of a modern nation state. In 2023, it was moving towards becoming a Hindu Rashtra

> —leaving the minorities, no small in number in absolute terms—feeling increasingly insecure and beleaguered in a country that became highly polarised." (*Unquote*)

With this record, what then about the future? Well, the architect of India's Constitution must have the last word.

When India's Constituent Assembly was about to complete its task (of framing a document of governance for free India), the chairman of the drafting committee (Dr B. R. Ambedkar), in the course of his final reply to the debate before the adoption of the Constitution on 25 November 1949—had said (and they are truly memorable words):

> (*Quote*) . . . I shall not enter into the merits of the Constitution. **Because I feel, however good a Constitution may be, it is sure to turn out bad because those who are called to work it, happen to be a bad lot. However bad a Constitution may be, it may turn out to be good if those who are called to work it, happen to be a good lot. The working of a Constitution does not depend wholly upon the nature of the Constitution.** The Constitution can provide only the organs of State such as the Legislature, the Executive, and the Judiciary. The factors on which the working of those organs of the State depend are the people and the political parties they will set up as their instruments to carry out their wishes and their politics.
>
> Who can say how the people of India and their parties will behave? Will they uphold constitutional methods of achieving their purposes or will they prefer revolutionary methods of achieving them? If they adopt the revolutionary methods, however good the Constitution may be, it requires no prophet to say that it will fail. **It is, therefore, futile to pass any judgment upon the Constitution without reference to the part which the people and their parties are likely to play.**[4] (*Unquote*)

Notes and References:

1. Ivor Jennings: *Cabinet Government,* pages 15-16, 472 and 499 published by Cambridge University Press (1969).
2. Except for a brief period between March 1977 to 13 January 1980.
3. Granville Austin, *Working a Democratic Constitution: The Indian Experience,* Oxford University Press, UK, 2000 (page 636).
4. CAD, Book No. 5, Vol. XII, page 975.

   [The Constituent Assembly Debates have been reprinted by the Lok Sabha Secretariat in five books (Book 1 contains Volumes I to VI of the debates, Book 2 contains Volume VII of the debates, Book 3 contains Volumes VIII of the debates, Book 4 contains Volume IX of the debates, and Book 5 contains Volumes X to XII of the debates).]

Acknowledgements

At an advanced age of 94, I have been able (with difficulty) to compose and complete this book. I have much to be thankful for in life, and many persons to be thankful to as well.

First of all, to my wife Bapsi (a pillar of strength of the Nariman family), who passed on in June 2020: for having lived with me, and most lovingly cared for me for sixty long years.

And after Bapsi, to my daughter Anaheeta, who is a professional like her father and her brother—but she is not a lawyer, she is a proficient speech-therapist, who keeps track of me and my home from far away Mumbai, and yet finds time to visit me in Delhi ever so often.

I am also thankful to my brilliant and convivial daughter-in-law, Sanaya, who lives in Delhi with Rohinton (truly, the only genius in the Nariman family). Together, they keep a loving eye over me.

But above all, I am most grateful to my precious granddaughters, Khursheed and Nina (married to Rohan), who together with great-grandchildren, Zarina and Cyrus, keep enlivening me with daily visits.

I must not forget to mention long-serving (and at times, long-suffering) members of my office staff. It is only because of my abysmal ignorance of fast-moving technology that the now longest-serving staff members, Vinod Anand and Narender Kumar, along with Vinod Kumar and Lakhvinder, have assisted me with the typing (and the constant re-typing, cancelling, and correcting page-upon-page) of this book on India's Constitution.

I must also mention my most helpful junior (of vintage year 1986)—now my colleague—Advocate Subhash Sharma, who, since the passing of Bapsi, has been my constant companion and confidante.

I acknowledge with gratitude members of my personal staff—Lalitha, Kaviraj, Haroon, Vijay, Durga, and Jitender—who have loyally served me—many of them for decades—which has helped me keep putting pen-to-paper (the only form of writing that I know).

And, of course, thanks to my publisher Ashok Chopra, who has not only helped publish four of my previous books, *Before Memory Fades* (2010), *State of the Nation* (2013), *God Save the Hon'ble Supreme Court* (2018), and *Harmony amidst Disharmony* (2020)—reprinting them from time to time—but also has actively helped in advising, publishing, and printing this tome (not quite as long as India's Constitution!). Ashok is not just a publisher of other people's books; he is also an accomplished author who has written and published his own works. And last but by no means the least, without the painstaking efforts of the production manager of Hay House Publishers, Rakesh Khattar, editor Aditya Jarial, and Raghav Khattar (designer of the cover), this book would not have been in your hands.

ALSO AVAILABLE!

The Arbitration Series – Volume 1
HARMONY amidst
DISHARMONY
The Indian Framework
Revised & Updated Edition
FALI S.
NARIMAN

The Arbitration Series – Volume 2
HARMONY amidst
DISHARMONY
The International Framework
FALI S.
NARIMAN

GOD SAVE THE HON'BLE
SUPREME
COURT
FALI S. NARIMAN

FALI S.
NARIMAN
THE STATE OF
THE NATION

'The gateways to wisdom and knowledge are always open.'

Louise Hay